Information Structuring in Discourse

Current Research in the Semantics/Pragmatics Interface

Series Editors

Klaus von Heusinger (*University of Cologne*)
Ken Turner (*University of Brighton*)

Editorial Board

Nicholas Asher (*Université Paul Sabatier*)
Johan van der Auwera (*University of Antwerp*)
Betty Birner (*Northern Illinois University*)
Ariel Cohen (*Ben Gurion University*)
Paul Dekker (*University of Amsterdam*)
Regine Eckardt (*University of Constance*)
Markus Egg (*Humbolt University Berlin*)
Donka Farkas (*University of California, Santa Cruz*)
Brendan Gillon (*McGill University*)
Jeroen Groenendijk (*University of Amsterdam*)
Yueguo Gu (*Chinese Academy of Social Sciences*)
Larry Horn (*Yale University*)
Yan Huang (*University of Auckland*)
Manfred Krifka (*Humboldt University Berlin*)
Chungmin Lee (*Seoul National University*)
Claudia Maienborn (*University of Tübingen*)
Alice ter Meulen (*University of Geneva*)
Jaroslav Peregrin (*Czech Academy of Sciences and University of Hradec Králové*)
Allan Ramsay (*University of Manchester*)
Rob van der Sandt (*Radboud University Nijmegen*)
Kjell Johan Sæbø (*University of Oslo*)
Robert Stalnaker (*Massachusetts Institute of Technology*)
Martin Stokhof (*University of Amsterdam*)
Henk Zeevat (*University of Amsterdam*)
Thomas Ede Zimmermann (*University of Frankfurt*)

VOLUME 40

The titles published in this series are listed at *brill.com/crispi*

Information Structuring in Discourse

Edited by

Anke Holler
Katja Suckow
Israel de la Fuente

BRILL

LEIDEN | BOSTON

Library of Congress Cataloging-in-Publication Data

Names: Deutsche Gesellschaft für Sprachwissenschaft. Jahrestagung (39th : 2017 : Saarbrücken, Germany) | Holler, Anke, editor. | Suckow, Katja, editor. | de la Fuente, Israel, editor.
Title: Information structuring in discourse / edited by Anke Holler, Katja Suckow, Israel de la Fuente.
Description: Leiden ; Boston : Brill, 2020. | Series: Current research in the semantics/pragmatics interface, 14727870 ; volume 40 | Papers presented at the workshop, "Information Structuring in Discourse", held in 2017 at the 39th Annual Conference of the German Linguistics Society (DGfS) in Saarbrücken (Germany). | Includes bibliographical references.
Identifiers: LCCN 2020045249 (print) | LCCN 2020045250 (ebook) | ISBN 9789004436718 (hardback) | ISBN 9789004436725 (ebook)
Subjects: LCSH: Discourse analysis–Congresses. | Discourse markers–Congresses. | Grammar, Comparative and general–Semantics–Congresses. | Grammar, Compartaive and general–Syntax–Congresses. | Pragmatics–Congresses.
Classification: LCC P302 .D42253 2017 (print) | LCC P302 (ebook) | DDC 401/.41–dc23
LC record available at https://lccn.loc.gov/2020045249
LC ebook record available at https://lccn.loc.gov/2020045250

Typeface for the Latin, Greek, and Cyrillic scripts: "Brill". See and download: brill.com/brill-typeface.

ISSN 1472-7870
ISBN 978-90-04-43671-8 (hardback)
ISBN 978-90-04-43672-5 (e-book)

Copyright 2021 by Anke Holler, Katja Suckow and Israel de la Fuente. Published by Koninklijke Brill NV, Leiden, The Netherlands.
Koninklijke Brill NV incorporates the imprints Brill, Brill Hes & De Graaf, Brill Nijhoff, Brill Rodopi, Brill Sense, Hotei Publishing, mentis Verlag, Verlag Ferdinand Schöningh and Wilhelm Fink Verlag.
Koninklijke Brill NV reserves the right to protect this publication against unauthorized use. Requests for re-use and/or translations must be addressed to Koninklijke Brill NV via brill.com or copyright.com.

This book is printed on acid-free paper and produced in a sustainable manner.

Contents

List of Figures and Tables VII
Notes on Contributors IX

1 Structuring Information in Discourse: Topics and Methods 1
   Israel de la Fuente, Anke Holler and Katja Suckow

2 Coherence and the Interpretation of Personal and Demonstrative Pronouns in German 24
   Yvonne Portele and Markus Bader

3 Cleft Focus and Antecedent Accessibility: The Emergence of the Anti-focus Effect 56
   Clare Patterson and Claudia Felser

4 Topics and Subjects in German Newspaper Editorials: A Corpus Study 86
   Peter Bourgonje and Manfred Stede

5 Inferable and Partitive Indefinites in Topic Position 112
   Klaus von Heusinger and Umut Özge

6 Projection to the Speaker: Non-restrictive Relatives Meet Coherence Relations 141
   Katja Jasinskaja and Claudia Poschmann

7 Central Adverbial Clauses and the Derivation of Subject-Initial V2 163
   Liliane Haegeman

8 Discourse Conditions on Relative Clauses: A Crosslinguistic and Diachronic Study on the Interaction between Mood, Verb Position and Information Structure 201
   Marco Coniglio and Roland Hinterhölzl

9 What's in an Act? Towards a Functional Discourse Grammar of Platonic Dialogue and a Linguistic Commentary on Plato's *Protagoras* 234
   Cassandra Freiberg

Figures and Tables

Figures

2.1 Percentages of completions referencing the object NP (= the stimulus argument) of context sentence 3 in Experiment 1   35
2.2 Percentages of referents from the context rementioned in sentence initial position in the continuations of Experiment 2   42
2.3 Percentages of referential expressions in either subject or object function used in Experiment 2 for referring to the subj(ect)/experiencer or the obj(ect)/stimulus argument of the last context sentence   44
3.1 Mean first-fixation times per condition in the spillover region, Experiment 1   71
3.2 Mean first-pass times per condition in the spillover region, Experiment 1   71
3.3 Mean first-pass times per condition in the final region, Experiment 1   72
3.4 Mean regression-path times per condition in the spillover region, Experiment 1   74
3.5 Mean regression-path times per condition in the final region, Experiment 1   74
3.6 Mean rereading times per condition in the critical region, Experiment 1   76
3.7 Mean z-scores per condition for Experiment 2   78
4.1 ANNIS3 Graphical User Interface with example query and results   100
5.1 Prince's (1981b, p. 237) taxonomy of assumed familiarity and information status   120
5.2 Exp. 1: Discourse linking (NONE vs. PART vs. INFR vs. BOTH) X Position (TOPIC vs. NONTOPIC): Mean ratings of 29 participants in a web based questionnaire   131
5.3 Exp. 2: Discourse linking (PART vs. BOTH) X Position (TOPIC vs. NONTOPIC): Mean ratings of 96 participants in a web-based questionnaire   133
5.4 Exp. 3: Context (BOTH vs. PART vs. INFR vs. NONE): Mean ratings of 46 participants in a web-based questionnaire   135
8.1 Analysis of V2 relatives   215
8.2 Correlations in OHG and Modern German (respectively)   223
8.3 Correlations based on theoretical accounts   225
8.4 Clausal (In)dependency Marking. Adapted from Gärtner & Eythórsson, 2020   227
9.1 Communicative situations in Platonic dialogue   236
9.2 Communicative situations in the *Protagoras*   242
9.3 FDG-architecture   245
9.4 Basic elements of an exchange and definitory characteristics of a Discourse Act in FDG   250

Tables

2.1	A complete stimulus item for Experiment 1	33
2.2	Percentages of completions congruent with the bias of context sentence 3 in Experiment 1	36
2.3	Example continuations from Experiment 2	41
2.4	Percentages of referents from the context occurring as the only or first referent in the continuations of Experiment 2	42
2.5	Percentages of referential expressions in either subject or object function used in Experiment 2 for referring to the subject/experiencer or the object/stimulus argument of the last context sentence	44
2.6	Application of the Bayesian formula to the data from Experiment 1 and Experiment 2	46
3.1	Mean first-fixation times and first-pass times in milliseconds per condition in the critical, spillover and final regions for Experiment 1	70
3.2	Mean regression-path times in milliseconds per condition in the critical, spillover and final regions for Experiment 1	73
3.3	Mean rereading and total viewing times in milliseconds per condition in the critical, spillover and final regions for Experiment 1	75
4.1	Distribution of thetic and non-thetic spans on different annotation levels	99
4.2	Classification results	104
7.1	V2 transgressions in StD with central adverbial clauses	177
7.2	V2 transgressions in StD with peripheral adverbial clauses	177
8.1	Specificity of the referent and mood in the relative clause	219
8.2	Specificity of the referents of all subjunctive relative clauses in the *Referenzkorpus Altdeutsch*	219
8.3	Specificity of the referent and verb position in the relative clause	221
8.4	Verb position in the relative clause and mood alternation	222
9.1	Discourse structure of Pl. *Prt.* 309a1–b9	284

Notes on Contributors

Markus Bader
Goethe-Universität Frankfurt, Institut für Linguistik

Peter Bourgonje
Universität Potsdam, Department Linguistik

Marco Coniglio
Georg-August-Universität Göttingen, Seminar für Deutsche Philologie

Claudia Felser
Universität Potsdam, Potsdam Research Institute for Multilingualism

Cassandra Freiberg
Humboldt-Universität zu Berlin, Institut für deutsche Sprache und Linguistik

Israel de la Fuente
Université de Lille & CNRS-UMR 8163 "Savoirs, Textes, Langage"

Liliane Haegeman
Universiteit Gent, DiaLing

Klaus von Heusinger
Universität zu Köln, Institut für deutsche Sprache und Literatur I

Roland Hinterhölzl
Università Ca' Foscari Venezia, Dipartimento di Scienze del Linguaggio

Anke Holler
Georg-August-Universität Göttingen, Seminar für Deutsche Philologie

Katja Jasinskaja
Universität zu Köln, Institut für deutsche Sprache und Literatur I

Umut Özge
Middle East Technical University Ankara, Informatics Institute

Clare Patterson
Universität zu Köln, Institut für deutsche Sprache und Literatur I

Yvonne Portele
Goethe-Universität Frankfurt, Institut für Linguistik

Claudia Poschmann
Universität zu Köln, Institut für deutsche Sprache und Literatur I

Manfred Stede
Universität Potsdam, Department Linguistik

Katja Suckow
Georg-August-Universität Göttingen, Seminar für Deutsche Philologie

CHAPTER 1

Structuring Information in Discourse: Topics and Methods

Israel de la Fuente, Anke Holler and Katja Suckow

1 Introduction

It is commonly acknowledged that a text provides more information than a random sequence of sentences as it combines sentence-level information to larger units which are glued together by coherence relations that induce a (hierarchical) discourse structure. A coherent discourse is characterized by the absence of *non sequiturs*. That is why additional information can be conveyed by just juxtaposing two pieces of text, e.g. two sentences or clauses in the simplest case, and every element in the linear flow of information fulfills a given function in discourse structure. It is, hence, a crucial feature of discourse analysis that there is a need to link any new segment to previous ones. Usually, an extra portion of information is provided by coherence relations which either are overtly signaled by a connective or another cue phrase, or remain implicit since an explicit linguistic marker has been omitted. In the latter case, the meaning of the respective coherence relation must be inferred during text comprehension. For instance, the reader's world knowledge can be assumed to readily fill in this information.

Since linguists have begun to explore linguistic units beyond sentence boundaries and to investigate texts as more complex units of linguistic communication, it has been controversially discussed what the appropriate level of analysis of discourse structure ought to be and what the criteria to identify (minimal) discourse units are. Even though the assumption that a piece of discourse is built up from smaller building blocks related to one another in a coherent way is almost universally shared in the literature, there is only weak consensus on what the units of discourse structure are and which method might be most suitable to empirically validate discourse segmentation, cf. Passonneau and Litman (1997), Degand and Simon (2005) among many others. It is obvious that clarifying these issues is no theory-neutral endeavor: a "discourse theory must specify how 'segments' should be identified in light of the questions the theory is set up to answer" as Polanyi, Culy, van den Berg, Thione and Ahn (2004) formulate it. Despite serious differences in individual theories and empirical operationalizations, it seems to be common understanding in the realm of discourse analysis that linguistic structure matters for discourse modeling. More precisely, the extraction and integration of prosodic, syntactic, semantic, and pragmatic information has shown to be at the center of discourse representation and discourse processing. However, its concrete role in discourse segmentation and its contribution to the structuring of information in a coherent discourse is still subject of an ongoing debate.

This collection presents current work on theoretical, diachronic, crosslinguistic, as well as experimental and corpus-based research into the identification, marking and recognition of (elementary) discourse units, and into how discourse coherence can be brought about by information status, coreference resolution, rhetorical relations and other devices of discourse structuring. The aim of this introductory section is to give a brief survey of the state of the art of the broad field of discourse modeling: from a representational as well as a processing perspective, mainly focusing on information structuring in discourse. The term *discourse* is hereby taken as being synonymous with a written discourse or a text which we loosely characterize as a coherent sequence of sentences that provides information on a common topic. As we assume that any text can be split up in elementary discourse units that enter meaningful relationships with one another, understanding a text means to interpret these relationships on semantic and pragmatic grounds and to process the referential, thematic, and intentional structure of the whole text.

After broaching some virulent theoretical issues of discourse modeling in the next section, we will go into a highly relevant empirical domain, i.e. anaphora resolution, to illustrate general research issues with respect to the structuring of information in discourse. Afterwards we will deepen some methodological aspects by presenting empirical methods which are often used to investigate discourse representation and processing, and finally, we will give a brief introduction into all contributions of this volume.

2   Modeling Written Discourse

The general idea that a text can be described as an entity consisting of a set of interrelated, recursively defined discourse units that together provide more information than a mere sequence of sentences, calls for an analysis of text structures that accounts for both, (i) an appropriate identification and representation of all discourse segments involved and (ii) an adequate interpretation of the coherence relations explicitly or implicitly holding between the elementary discourse units.

Starting with Hobbs (1985), a number of frameworks have been developed that target discourse structures. In particular, with the dialogue-oriented algorithmic approach by Grosz and Sidner (1986), the syntactically inspired Linguistic Discourse Model (LDM) by Polanyi (1988) and the more particularly data-driven Rhetorical Structure Theory (RST) by Mann and Thompson (1988) influential discourse models have been proposed that have formulated numerous constraints to restrict the sequencing and attaching of discourse segments at various descriptive levels. In addition, several formal models for discourse generation and interpretation have been evolved. A strong impulse to the field of discourse analysis gave the semantically motivated Segmented Discourse Representation Theory (SDRT) by Asher and Lascarides (2003).

The mentioned frameworks access discourse structures with various research intensions and from different directions. They might emphasize either linguistic or cognitive or computational aspects of discourse interpretation and processing. Apart from these differences in their perspectives on discourse, the models also differ in the data structures which they use as representational device, i.e. trees or graphs, and in the level of analysis of discourse segmentation. For instance, it has been suggested that discourse structure might be defined in terms of communicative intention, attention, topic structure, illocutionary structure, coherence relations, cohesive devices, or others. Related to this, it has been debated whether intonational phrases, syntactic clauses, semantic entities, such as events or propositions, or pragmatic entities, such as speech acts or other communicative units, form appropriate building blocks for recognizing the elementary units of a discourse structure.

In the same way, the inventory of discourse relations that provide local coherence by linking two discourse units has not yet been conclusively defined, which may confirm Grosz and Sidner (1986), who even doubt in principle that the infinite set of possible meanings can be described by a finite set of relations at all. Nevertheless, this attempt has been made many times from several perspectives: from the viewpoint of cognitive modeling, Knott and Sanders (1998) further develop a taxonomic approach by Sanders, Spooren and Noordman (1992) and derive twelve feature-based relations. Kehler (2002) has stipulated three groups with a total of fourteen relations within formal semantics. These comprise resemblance relations (for example, Elaboration, Contrast), causal relations (for example, Explanation, Effect) and contiguity relations (for example, Occasion, Narration), which express spatial or temporal proximity. Much more comprehensive, but also more unrestricted, is the set of relations that RST considers sufficient on the basis of concrete text analyses (although it makes no claim to completeness). The SDRT postulates a set of discourse relations on semantic grounds axiomatically deriving them bottom-up using certain linguistic cues at the text surface. For a comprehensive discussion of the possible inventory of (semantic and pragmatic) discourse relations, please refer to Zeevat (2011).

As a consequence of the continuing interest of grammar theory in discourse phenomena, it has become apparent that the discourse-relational structure has effects for information packaging (Chafe, 1976; Vallduvi & Engdahl, 1996; Krifka, 2007) and contributes to weighting linguistic entities in both complex sentences and texts either by focusing attention on these entities or by placing them in the background. This aspect is closely interwoven with other grammatical means of topic and focus marking, which together create information structure and discourse coherence. The function of the focus-background structure and its visualization through question-answer heuristics was already noticed by Paul (1880) and Weinrich (1964), and was taken up by discourse-semantic and pragmatic theories of question-driven information weighting in discourse, such as the quaestio-approach by von Stutterheim and Klein (1989, 2002) and the formal concept of a question under discussion (QUD) as defined by Roberts (1996); Büring (2003); Beaver and Clark (2008) as well as Simons, Tonhauser, Beaver and Roberts (2010). (For a comprehensive overview of the semantic analysis of questions and their role in structuring discourse see also von Heusinger, Zimmermann, & Onea, 2019, and for original research on the role of questions in understanding text structure and discourse pragmatics see Zimmermann, von Heusinger, & Onea, 2019.) While these approaches tend to be top-down and acting backward-looking in that they model accessibility or connectivity in the already generated (but in part underspecified) discourse tree, other relevant approaches follow a more forward-looking strategy aiming at a step-by-step generation of the discourse tree from the bottom triggered by the actual implicit question, cf. (Kuppevelt, 1995). Related to this view, topicality is considered as the main organizational discourse principle. The central assumption is that every contextually induced (implicit) question that is answered in discourse simultaneously constitutes a topic, which means that the topic is implicitly interrogated and the set of possible answers to this question is identified with the interrogated topic. In addition, Kuppevelt envisages that individual statements—apart from their function of answering a question—are also capable of raising new questions in the respective discourse and thereby establishing a new topic. Thus, they fulfill a cataphoric function. This idea is taken up anew in Onea (2016) with the concept of potential questions formalized in the general framework of Inquisitive Semantics (Groenendijk & Roelofsen, 2009).

The idea of the theme as a central textual object being continuously constituted has been put forward in the early works of Daneš, (1970); he transfers the hitherto more sentence-related theme-rheme structure of the Prague School to the text. Although its definition of local thematic transition patterns in the context of so-called thematic progression is not sufficient in detail, the basic idea pursued has a lot to offer and is ultimately contained in both the topic continuity approach of Givón (1992) and in the centering theory (Grosz, Joshi, & Weinstein, 1995). Unlike Daneš, however, Givón understands thematic progression as mental continuity, which is represented by corresponding discourse speakers and indicated by appropriate linguistic means.

In the next section, we will discuss within the context of experimental findings how the application of online research methods can drive the understanding of the dynamics between syntactic, semantic as well as pragmatic information when establishing discourse coherence. We take anaphora resolution and the factors involved in these processes as a typical application field, and illustrate how discourse segmentation and interpretation may have an impact on resolving anaphoric expressions inter- and intra-sententially.

3   Discourse Structure and Anaphora Resolution

Resolving anaphoric expressions is a task that has made evident the close relationship between linguistic features of utterances and discourse structure. For decades, researchers in the fields of theoretical linguistics, psycholinguistics and computational linguistics have been interested in understanding the factors that guide the processes behind the choice of a particular referring expression over another as well as those factors that influence the selection of a particular antecedent over another for a given anaphoric expression. These processes have been mainly related, on the one hand, to the accessibility, or salience, of potential antecedents in the speaker's mental discourse representation, and, on the other hand, to the inferential establishment of discourse coherence relations during language production and comprehension.

Regarding the account of antecedent salience, the basic idea is simple: the more accessible/salient a discourse entity, the more likely it is that the speaker chooses a less specific form of reference, e.g. a pronoun, to refer back to it; and likewise, the more likely it is that, when confronted with a less specific form of reference, the speaker interprets it as referring to this accessible/salient discourse entity (Prince, 1981; Givón, 1983; Ariel, 1988, 1990; Gundel, Hedberg, & Zacharski, 1993; Grosz et al., 1995). Recurrent factors that have been shown to contribute to antecedent salience are, among others, the syntactic function of the antecedent, with subject antecedents being more accessible than antecedents with other syntactic functions (Crawley, Stevenson, & Kleinman,

1990; Gordon, Grosz, & Gilliom, 1993; Carminati, 2002; Kaiser, 2011); the order of mention of the potential antecedents, with first-mentions being more accessible than subsequent mentions (Gernsbacher, & Hargreaves, 1988); and the information status of the antecedent, with topical entities being more salient than non-topical discourse entities (Arnold, 1998, 1999; Cowles, 2003; Cowles, Walenski, & Kluender, 2007; Frana, 2008; Colonna, Schimke, & Hemforth, 2012; Ellert, 2013). Crucially, however, as example (1) illustrates, the antecedent salience account falls short in explaining all the facts: while *they* can refer to the subject, first-mention, topic antecedent *the city council* in sentence (1a), the same strategy results in a rather odd interpretation in (1b), where the most felicitous interpretation is one where the pronoun refers to *the demonstrators*.

(1) a. The city council denied the demonstrators the permit because they feared violence. [they=the city council]
 b. The city council denied the demonstrators the permit because they advocate violence. [they=the demonstrators]

These facts are explained by the coherence-relations account, which argues that beyond notions like subjecthood or topicality, the mechanisms supporting pronoun production and interpretation are driven predominantly by semantics, world knowledge and inference, in the process of establishing discourse coherence (Hobbs, 1979; Kehler, 2002). Accordingly, in the examples in (1), it is the semantic information encoded in the verbs *fear* and *advocate* that the speaker uses to establish an Explanation relation to 'coherently' relate the two clauses with each other. The interpretation of the ambiguous pronoun *they* as referring to one or the other antecedent would come as the by-product of this reasoning process.

Kehler (2002) proposes a theory of coherence relations to account for pronoun interpretation, which reconciles discrepancies among pure salience-based and coherence-based approaches.[1] His analysis of pronoun interpretation is based on the interaction of two aspects: the linguistic properties of the pronoun itself, and the properties of the process of establishing coherence for three types of relations mentioned above: Resemblance, Explanation, Contiguity. Regarding the first component, Kehler argues, in line with salience-based accounts, that pronouns encode the signal that the level of salience is high, a property that triggers a cue for the hearer to interpret the pronoun against the current discourse representation at the moment at which it is encountered, or

---

[1] In his analysis, he also discusses a third account, the Parallelism account.

soon thereafter. This component would explain cases of garden-path interpretation, where the initial interpretation of a pronoun has to be subsequently revised after further information has been encountered. Regarding the second component, Kehler argues that an analysis of pronoun interpretation must take into consideration the effect that the establishment of coherence has on the operative discourse representation. In particular, he argues that "the process of coherence establishment is capable of redirecting the focus of attention as needed to support the inferencing processing, having the effect of altering the relative salience of discourse entities on a relatively small time scale" and that "the fact that different types of pronoun interpretation preferences arise in different contextual circumstances can be shown to result from the properties of the different mechanisms required to establish the three types of coherence relations" (Kehler, 2002, p. 157).

Miltsakaki (2002) also draws on the notions of salience and coherence and argues that the fact that no single account is capable of accounting for all the cases is mainly due to a failure of these accounts to acknowledge that pronoun resolution within and across sentence boundaries are not subject to the same mechanisms. Based on a series of corpus and experimental studies in English and in Greek, she claims that inter-sentential pronoun resolution is subject to structural factors, namely, topic continuity as proposed by e.g. Centering Theory (preference for salient antecedent), whereas intra-sentential pronoun resolution is subject to syntactic as well as semantic/pragmatic constraints, that is, within the sentence, pronoun resolution is performed locally and is constrained by semantic properties of the predicates (cf. coherence relation account). An important contribution of Miltsakaki's model is the definition of the boundaries of an utterance. Miltsakaki refers to utterances as Centering Update Units (CUU), which she defines as consisting of a matrix clause and all dependent clauses associated with it.

However, the examples in (2)–(4) illustrate more recent experimental findings that seem to go against the predictions of both Kehler's and Miltsakaki's accounts. In particular, the different consequences of clefting within and across sentence boundaries are surprising.

(2) a. John admires Mary because she ...
    b. John admires Mary. She ...

(3) a. Speaking of John, he saw Paul when he was walking on the beach. [he=John]
    b. Speaking of John, he saw Paul. At the time, he was walking on the beach. [he=John]

(4) a. It was John who saw Paul when he was walking on the beach. [he=Paul]
    b. It was John who saw Paul. At the time, he was walking on the beach. [he=John]

Contra the predictions of Miltsakaki's model, it is argued that examples (2) and (3) might be evidence that the strong claim that inter- and intra-sentential pronoun resolution are subject to different mechanisms fails to explain the preferences observed in such cases. In particular, examples (2) and (3) (from Kehler (2002) and Colonna et al. (2012, 2014), respectively) might suggest that the effects of coherence relations (2) and topic-continuity (3) seem to be at work both within- and between-sentence pronoun resolution. Likewise, and contra the predictions of Kehler's account, example (4) indicates that coherence relations alone cannot account for the different interpretation preferences in (4a) and (4b) and that the discourse structure must be taken into account here (as Miltsakaki argues). Intra-sententially focused antecedents are generally dispreferred; they are preferred only inter-sententially.

De la Fuente's (2015) proposal reconciles Miltsakaki's and Kehler's accounts. In line with Miltsakaki, de la Fuente argues that the Discourse Unit (DU) is the optimal domain for the analysis of pronoun interpretation and that differences in inter- vs. intra-DU resolution need to be taken into account. In line with Kehler, de la Fuente points out that pronoun resolution comes as the by-product of coherence establishment processes. However, he argues that these coherence establishment processes will come about differently as function of the discourse structure (inter- vs. intra-DU resolution). Additionally, as opposed to what Miltsakaki claims, de la Fuente suggests that intra- and inter-DU resolution are not subject to different mechanisms, rather it is the relative weight of these mechanisms that varies from context to context. Also, against Miltsakaki's proposal, de la Fuente defends that a purely syntactic-based definition of DU that equates this notion to the sentence fails to account for previous results. Instead, he proposes a 'relational' (rather than purely syntactic) definition of DU based on previous analyses of adverbial clauses (Haegeman, 2003, 2009, 2010; Johnston, 1994), which makes the following predictions regarding DU:

– Non-relational/central clauses (e.g. temporal adverbial clauses) are processed as part of the same DU as the matrix clause.
– Relational/peripheral clauses (e.g. causal adverbial clauses) are processed as a separate DU from the matrix clause.

And the following predictions regarding anaphora resolution:
– Intra-DU: tendency to maintain coherence (e.g. preference to avoid a topic-shift, preference for topic/topic-like entities).

– Inter-DU: tendency to establish coherence (e.g. preferences guided by semantic content of elements such as verbs, connectives, etc.).

De la Fuente (2015) tested these predictions experimentally with a series of sentence interpretation and sentence completion tasks, where he manipulated the interplay between the coherence relation holding between clauses (by means of the connectives *when* and *because*) and the focus-sensitive particles *even* and *only*. Following the sentence onset *Only John called Mary when ...*, there was a general preference for a continuation containing the pronoun *she*, while the sentence onset *Only John called Mary because ...* gave rise to significantly more continuations containing the pronoun *he*. The choice of *Mary* as antecedent in the temporal construction corresponds to a preference for the topical antecedent rather than the focus element within the scope of the particle (*John*); while the choice of *John* as the preferred antecedent in the causal construction seems to be related to the Explanation coherence relation established between clauses. In particular, this choice seems to obey a tendency to explain the exhaustivity of the focused element in relation with the event narrated (i.e. *why John and nobody else called Mary*). In other words, in the causal construction, which represents an inter-DU context, the choice of an antecedent is based on the interplay between the semantics of the connective and that of the focus particle in the process of establishing coherence between both DU. These results are taken as evidence that both salience and coherence affect the choice of an antecedent but their effects seem to vary as a function of the discourse structure, or more precisely the DU configuration.

4 Empirical Methods for Analyzing Discourse Phenomena

We will now give a brief overview about the range of methods, which have been meanwhile developed to reveal the basic building blocks of discourse structure and to analyze discourse coherence. Generally speaking, it depends on the respective research questions which empirical method is typically applied for the investigation of discourse phenomena. While experimental methods are often used for hypothesis testing in the realm of discourse processing, corpus-based methods allow a quantitatively and/or qualitatively analysis of large collections of texts.

Text corpora are especially relevant for research that cannot rely on the performance of living native speakers. While current synchronic research projects regularly exam text corpora, diachronic language research relies most heavily on the collections of texts from a specific time period. Since diachronic research naturally suffers from a lack of native speakers of a language's older stage it is rather impossible to elicit questionnaire and experimental data. Hence, the explanatory power of any discourse analysis on historical texts strongly depends on initiatives that provide deeply annotated corpora comprising complete texts or fragments written in ancient languages. Such grammatically annotated text corpora, like for instance the Referenzkorpus Altdeutsch, offer the opportunity to study linguistic patterns of a specific language at a specific time, e.g. Old High German (Krause & Zeldes, 2016). Under these inevitable circumstances, working on historical stages of a language is not only a tedious task, but also methodologically very valuable for the whole community interested in the rules and regularities of information structuring in discourse, because results achieved on the basis of diachronic texts are most likely to be relevant for synchronic discourse interpretation. As annotated corpora are generally most suitable to study the frequency of specific linguistic expressions and to identify or extract examples of certain linguistic structures, it is no surprise that the inquiry of text corpora is a popular method in the field of discourse analysis and modeling.

While corpora enable the study of specific linguistic patterns in large collections of text, experimental research uses native speakers to test the predictions of a theoretical model in a controlled environment. In discourse structuring research, for example, experimentalists investigate the interplay of linguistic cues and discourse segmentation operators using offline as well as online methods. It is important to note here that the term offline describes data that are observed after a task or process has been completed. These include acceptability judgements, questionnaires or production data from a sentence fragment continuation task. Only after completing a cognitive task such as reading, participants rate the acceptability of the text or expression. The term *online* indicates that data are collected during the processing or comprehension of a text. This will make it possible to break down the comprehension process into different stages by time-locking the observations to assumed cognitive states.

There is a long tradition employing sentence completion tasks to investigate how structural and semantic factors affect discourse processing and structuring. In sentence completion tasks, participants are usually asked to complete a sentence fragment presented to them. There are three versions of completion methods: passage-completion data could either be analyzed (1) in terms of the whole scenario provided by the participants (Holler & Irmen, 2006; Kehler, Kertz, Rohde, & Elman, 2008; Fukumura & van Gompel, 2010; Kaiser, Li, & Holsinger, 2011; Kehler & Rohde, 2013), e.g. "Gary scared/feared Anna after the long discussion ended in a row. This was because ..." (from Fukumura & Van Gompel, 2010, p. 56, free continuation of the fragment and preference for antecedent reference will be analyzed), (2) the form of anaphora used when describing a scenario (Fukumura & van Gompel, 2010; Ellert & Holler, 2011, Holler & Suckow, 2016), e.g. *"Knut scared Lars but ..."* (from Holler & Suckow, 2016, p. 77, continuations had to refer to a highlighted antecedent with a preferred expression, pronoun or full name) or (3) a spoken story-telling paradigm (Arnold, 2001; Zerkle, Rosa & Arnold, 2017) where the passage to be continued is longer and, thus, participants have more time to fully establish discourse relations and make more fully informed predictions.

In comparison, online methods like self-paced reading allow reading time data to be time-locked to cognitive processes. Self-paced reading, is a relatively cost-efficient method to obtain online reading time data. Pressing a key, participants can read a sentence only word-by-word or segment-by-segment without being able to look forward or backward (regressions) in the sentence. It is widely used, which might be in part because it is easy to learn, runs on every platform and is not expensive to set up (Mitchell, 2004). However, because readers cannot make regressions within the sentence, it enforces an unnatural reading behavior. In addition, this method might not be sensitive enough to measure temporary effects.

Eye-tracking, on the other hand, is a more complex method; it requires elaborate training on eye-tracking software and analysis. Despite higher costs, eye-tracking has been found to be more susceptible to effects that occur during the time-course of comprehension. Eye-movements are usually recorded in the visual world paradigm or during reading. In the visual world paradigm, pictures will be presented to participants while they simultaneously listen to pre-recorded linguistic stimuli. Participants' eye-movements on the screen will be observed and are time-locked to the auditory signal. Kaiser, Runner, Sussman and Tanenhaus (2009) used the visual world paradigm in order to investigate the resolution processes of different types of anaphors: pronouns and reflexives. They tested possessorless (*the picture of him/himself* (Kaiser et al., 2009, pp. 2f.)) as well as possessed (*Andrew's picture of him/himself* (Kaiser et al., 2009, pp. 2f.)) picture noun phrase (PNP) stimuli.

It has been argued that while the resolution of possessorless PNP is not governed by structural constraints such as Binding, possessed PNP on the other hand are structurally constrained by binding principles (Pollard & Sag, 1992). Several offline decision and online eye movement experiments suggest that (1) the syntactic structure affects possessorless PNP resolution and (2) structural constraints affect pronouns and reflexives differently. Kaiser et al. (2009) found that pronoun resolution is less governed by structural information than reflexive pronoun resolution (more looks to the reflexives' antecedent without a semantic effect) and that pronoun resolution is stronger affected by semantic information than reflexive information (in interaction with semantic factors there are more looks to the pronoun's antecedent). The eye-movement data showed that these factors influence resolution processes early on and can be long-lasting.

Eye-tracking during reading provides a fine-grained representation in the various early and late reading time measures that can reflect intermediate cognitive processes. Measures like first fixation duration (duration of the first fixation on an interest area IA) and first pass time (sum of fixations from first fixation on IA until fixation on another IA) reflect lexical and initial structural effects while regression path (sum from first fixation on IA until first fixation to the right) and total reading time (sum of all fixations in IA) also reflect regressive eye movements within the sentence. Eye-tracking allows for a more natural reading behavior including skips and regressions within the sentence. One way to illustrate the benefits of eye-tracking over self-paced reading is by comparing these methods when investigating the application of the Principles A, B and C of the Theory of Binding (Chomsky, 1981). Binding principles describe how referential expressions such as pronouns co-refer to their antecedents within a sentence. According to Principle A, a reflexive or reciprocal pronoun can only be integrated with an antecedent in a c-commanding position. Principle B and C, on the other hand, determine that the antecedent cannot be in a c-commanding position when the referring expression is a non-reflexive pronoun (Principle B) or the referring expression is not a pronoun (Principle C) (cf. Chomsky, 1981).

Researchers often compare data from offline questionnaire studies with online reading time data. While various theories can predict observed effects, not all experimental methods are sensitive enough to measure e.g. intermediate effects. A direct comparison of offline and online methods can be crucial to determine what methods are sensitive to what kind of effect. Using eye-tracking during reading, Sturt (2003) investigated online application processes of Binding Principle A and showed that Binding Principles apply very quickly and early in the process. The antecedent of a reflexive pronoun that was not in a c-commanding position (inaccessible antecedent) was not considered in the early reading times. However, later reading times suggest that the gender marking of the inaccessible antecedent affected the reading times: Binding Principle A has been defeated later in the processing time-course. While this was reflected in the eye-tracking data-set, an offline sentence continuation method would not be able to detect short-term or intermediate effects in the time-course.

Referring expressions that are not reflexives cannot be bound to antecedents that are in a c-commanding position (Principle B and C). Patterson, Trompelt and Felser (2014) used offline questionnaire and online eye-tracking reading methods to investigate the binding time-course of pronouns. Neither type of data-sets shows any evidence that participants would even temporarily consider syntactically inaccessible antecedents. Constraints of Binding Principle B were applied early and not violated during later processing. However, Kazanina, Lau, Lieberman, Yoshida and Phillips (2007) and Patterson and Felser (2019) compared self-paced reading with eye-tracking investigating online binding processes of cataphoric reference resolution. Like pronouns, cataphors cannot be bound to items that are in a c-commanding position. Using self-paced reading, Kazanina et al. (2007) as well as Patterson and Felser (2019) did not find anything in the reading times that would suggest that the syntactically illicit antecedent (c-commanding element) was considered during the resolution process. However, Patterson and Felser (2019) comparing these findings with the eye-tracking data (total reading as well as rereading times) actually showed an effect from the item in the c-commanding position. Thus, eye-tracking data could show that Binding Principles of reflexive and non-reflexive referring expressions can be temporarily violated during later resolution processes.

This discrepancy between eye-tracking and self-paced reading might be surprising, however it is actually consistent when looking into the methods themselves. While there is no effect from the illicit antecedent in self-paced reading from both Kazanina et al. (2007) and Patterson and Felser (2019), there is an effect in the eye-tracking data who measure regressions (total reading and rereading times) but in first-pass times in Patterson and Felser (2019). Eye-tracking first pass times are equivalent to self-paced reading times: similar to self-paced reading, first pass reflects the sum of fixations from first entering an interest are until leaving the interest area. Similar to self-paced reading, refixations or regressions are not reflected in this measure. Since effects from the illicit antecedents are argued to occur later when participants reread passages, both self-paced reading and first-pass times could not detect Binding violation effects.

These issues immediately bring us to the topics of the present volume, which shall be introduced in more detail next.

5 Contributions to This Volume

In the second chapter with the title "Coherence and the Interpretation of Personal and Demonstrative Pronouns in German", **Yvonne Portele** and **Markus Bader** present findings of two experimental completion studies investigating how coherence relations affect the interpretation and production of personal and demonstrative pronouns in German. They discuss the collected data with regard to the Bayesian model of pronoun interpretation proposed by Kehler, Kertz, Rohde and Elman (2008), which factors expectations deriving from world knowledge and discourse coherence. According to numerous empirical studies, personal pronouns by default prefer a (sentence-initial and/or topical) subject antecedent, while demonstratives are known to prefer a (sentence-final and/or non-topical) object antecedent. Apart from these structural factors pronoun interpretation is also influenced by semantic factors such as verb semantics and discourse relations. The experiments that the authors report showed the same semantic bias for both types of pronouns from either causal (*nämlich* 'the reason was that') or consequential (*deshalb* 'therefore') discourse markers as there were more object choices with causal than with consequential discourse markers. However, the initial structural bias of the demonstrative pronouns was stronger than for personal pronouns. In addition, the semantic bias had less of an effect on the object choice of demonstrative pronouns than personal pronouns. The authors argue that these results suggest that demonstrative pronouns strongly prefer object antecedents and are less likely to be affected by semantic information than personal pronouns, which confirms that personal and demonstrative pronouns are differentially sensitive to the properties of the preceding context.

Pronoun interpretation preferences in German are also at the center of the third chapter with the title "Cleft Focus and Antecedent Accessibility: The Emergence of the Anti-focus Effect". Starting from the general observation that clefting makes a noun more accessible for pronoun reference, **Clare Patterson** and **Claudia Felser** argue that this effect is critically dependent on discourse units. In an experimental study, they examine how focus affects the accessibility of potential antecedents in cleft constructions by determining the timing of discourse structuring with the focus and anti-focus effect that describes the reduction of accessibility for an antecedent that appears in focus. It is commonly acknowledged that a pronoun is easier to resolve when its antecedent is salient in discourse. The span of this resolution range, however, has received more scrutiny recently. Especially focus effects in online and offline studies appear to call for a more refined model. The authors present an online eye-tracking reading and an offline acceptability experiment contrasting focused clefted sentences and sentences with a focus particle. They found that there are clear focus effects observable, but no anti-focus effects in early reading time measures. However, the acceptability judgements suggest a clear anti-focus effect in the offline data. Discussing the data, the authors argue that discourse structuring and the separation of discourse units appear to occur after the syntactic structuring process. The focus effects were observed early when sentence clauses can be clearly identified; discourse structuring and the identification of the separate discourse units occur later. That would explain why the anti-focus effect, which is necessary to override the initial advantage for the clefted antecedent, was only observed in the offline judgements after the processing of the sentences has been completed. In other words, the anti-focus effect may emerge at a late stage, well after the whole discourse unit has been processed.

The fourth chapter "Topics and Subjects in German Newspaper Editorials: A Corpus Study" turns the perspective to computational issues. **Peter Bourgonje** and **Manfred Stede** offer a corpus-based approach to identify topic information in authentic texts. The authors provide empirical evidence that there is a strong correlation between topichood and grammatical role. By adding another annotation layer with topic information to the Potsdam Commentary Corpus (PCC), comprising 175 German newspaper editorials, they show that aboutness topics coincide with grammatical subjects. Although the association between grammatical subjects and aboutness topics seems to be strong, there are also instances of no subject-topic correspondence. In an additional qualitative study, the authors explore these cases in more depth. They show for different instances of non-correlation that not only grammatical properties like indefiniteness or prominence of the respective subject matter, but also the thematic development in the text. Finally, a classification experiment is reported that tests—using a support-vector machine classifier—whether aboutness topics can be reliably predicted from basic attributes of the referring expressions in a topic span. The authors conclude that the automatic identification of topics yields a better match than a simple model where topics equals the subject of the sentence. Besides the grammatical role the most valuable features were phrase type and anaphoricity.

Semantically, the typical topic is a definite expression. Nevertheless, it is widely accepted that—under certain circumstances—indefinite noun phrases can appear in topic position. In this case, they have to be strong, specific, or discourse linked. On the basis of the results of three acceptability rating studies **Klaus von Heusinger** and **Umut Özge** argue in chapter five titled "Inferable and Partitive Indefinites in Topic Position" that the type of discourse linking itself influences the acceptability. Using Turkish as the target language, due to its clear indication of topichood and indefiniteness, the authors distinguish two types of linking: (i) inferential or conceptual linking, the defining property of inferable indefinites, and (ii) contextual linking, the defining property for partitives. They found that indefinites in topic position are grammatical, even though they are somewhat less acceptable than indefinites in non-topical position. They also found that discourse-linking does contribute to the acceptability of topical indefinites. Indefinites that are not linked, neither by conceptual linking nor by contextual linking, are least acceptable in this position. With respect to the kind of linking, it seems that conceptual linking is significantly better than contextual linking. This reflects the different levels of linking: Conceptual linking—typically encoded in the lexical items—allows for easy inferences, while contextual linking, such as partitives or set-membership relations must be established in the particular context.

The sixth chapter "Projection to the Speaker: Non-restrictive Relatives Meet Coherence Relations" by **Katja Jasinskaja** and **Claudia Poschmann** is the first of three contributions which are concerned with phenomena that cross the syntax-discourse boundary. With regard to non-restrictive relative clauses (NRC) the authors discuss syntactic, semantic as well as pragmatic factors that affect coherence relations. NRCs are understood to not affect the meaning of the main clause. However, the authors present NRCs where it is the case that the scope of their interpretation can reach outside the local domain. Thus, the proposition of NRC can enter the global interpretation of the sentence. This is important in order to find a generalization for the description of projection patterns and, also, the NRC scope on coherence relations. While established models identify the syntactic position of the NRC as the crucial factor of local versus global interpretation, the authors argue that speaker-orientedness is better suited to explain global interpretation observations than discourse-structural subordination. The term *speaker-orientedness* describes a condition by which a speakers' attitude will be expressed using semantic as well as pragmatic linguistic expressions that signal discourse coherence from the position of the NRCs. They claim that it is the opposition between speaker-oriented and non-speaker oriented coherence relation that has direct link to the NRC scope.

The issue of V2 in Germanic is broached in two contributions. The seventh chapter "Central Adverbial Clauses and the Derivation of Subject-Initial V2" comprises **Liliane Haegeman**'s contribution which addresses so-called V2 transgressions. This phenomenon describes V3 patterns that may arise in V2 languages if finite verbs in a second position are preceded by two constituents. In standard Dutch these V2 transgression are unacceptable for native speakers. However, V2 transgressions in which initial central adverbial clauses, i.e. clauses that modify the truth value of the associated clause, combine with non-inverted V2 sentence are acceptable to speakers of West Flemish. Based on a general proposal for the syntax of discourse frame setters, the author accounts for the micro-variation observed and in so doing sheds light on the interface between syntax, semantics and discourse. The presented account uses two core ingredients: A syntax-to-discourse mapping for frame setters is developed, and it is argued that standard Dutch and West Flemish differ with respect to the derivation of subject initial V2 declaratives, which interacts with frame setters at the interface.

German V2 relatives and the mood alternation in Romance is studied by **Marco Coniglio** and **Roland Hinterhölzl** in chapter eight titled "Discourse Conditions on Relative Clauses: A Crosslinguistic and Diachronic Study on the Interaction between Mood, Verb Position and Information Structure". The authors present a cross-linguistic and diachronic study of relative clauses in Old High and Modern German and Italian focusing on two factors: mood alternation and verb placement. Italian shows a distinction between subjunctive and indicative which is related to difference in specificity in the interpretation of the head noun. In comparison, in Modern German the interpretation of the referent of the relative clause is determined through the placement of the verb in relative clauses, while there is no mood distinction between subjunctive and indicative. Crucially, a corpus investigation shows that Old High German makes a similar distinction to that in Italian between indicative and subjunctive relative clauses that is related to the interpretation of the head noun, and, like Modern German, presents also word order alternations. The authors discuss the change from Old High German to Modern German by adopting and expanding Gärtner & Eythórsson's (2020) theory for the Germanic language family whereby older Germanic employs mood to signal clausal (in)dependency, while verb placement responds to prosodic and informational structural factors.

The final contribution with the title "What's in an Act? Towards a Functional Discourse Grammar of Platonic Dialogue and Linguistic Commentary on Plato's *Protagoras*" by **Cassandra Freiberg** also deals with historical data following the orality approach towards Ancient Greek. Working in the framework of Functional Discourse Grammar which conceptualizes so-called discourse acts as the smallest step a language producer takes in order to achieve his communicative goal, the author explores the question of how higher-order discourse structures influence the nature, size and shape of individual Elementary Discourse Units (EDU) in Ancient Greek. Her analysis is based on Platonic dialogue, which presents a special type of complex discourse with a historical influence on Western European thinking. In particular, the author emphasizes the influence of phonological phrasing on discourse segmentation. On the basis of *Protagoras*, one of the earlier Platonic dialogues, the author provides a systematic grammatical analysis of the particular idiom, showing that discourse segmentation in Platonic dialogue will have repercussion on the discourse structure of linguistic features of individual discourse acts.

This volume is a collection of original papers presented at the workshop "Information Structuring in Discourse" held in 2017 at the 39th Annual Conference of the German Linguistics Society (DGfS) in Saarbrücken (Germany). We want to especially thank the series editors for accepting this volume for publication and their continued support during the publication process. We are also grateful to Annika Kaufmann, Evelyn Ovsjannikov and Julia Steinmetz for their attention to detail and editorial support.

All the articles have undergone a double-blind peer-review process with at least two reviews for each paper. We want to take this opportunity to especially thank Andreas Blümel, Ulrike Demske, Stefanie Dipper, Cornelia Ebert, Hans-Martin Gärtner, Melanie Göbel-Hoffmann, Stefan Hinterwimmer, Julie Hunter, Olga Kellert, Anke Lüdeling, Svetlana Petrova, Hagen Pitsch, Frank Savelsberg, Gerhard Schaden, Augustin Speyer, Roger van Gompel, Jacolien van Rij, Jorrig Vogels and Thomas Weskott for their valuable review work.

References

Ariel, Mira. (1988). Referring and accessibility. *Journal of Linguistics, 24*(1), 65–87.
Ariel, Mira. (1990). *Accessing noun phrase antecedents*. London: Routledge.
Arnold, Jennifer E. (1998). *Reference form and discourse patterns*. [Doctoral dissertation, Stanford University].
Arnold, Jennifer E. (1999). *Marking salience: The similarity of topic and focus*. [Unpublished manuscript, University of Pennsylvania].
Arnold, Jennifer E. (2001). The effect of thematic role on pronoun use and frequency of reference continuation. *Discourse Processes, 31*, 137–162.
Asher, Nicholas, & Alex Lascarides. (2003). *Logics of conversation*. Cambridge, UK: Cambridge University Press.
Beaver, David, & Brady Clark. (2008). *Sense and sensitivity. How focus determines meaning*. Oxford: Blackwell.
Büring, Daniel. (2003). On d-trees, beans and b-accents. Linguistics and Philosophy, 26(5), 511–545.
Carminati, Maria Nella. (2002). *The processing of Italian subject pronouns*. [Doctoral dissertation, University of Massachusetts, Amherst].
Chafe, Wallace L. (1976). Givenness, contrastiveness, definiteness, subjects, topics and point of view. In C.N. Li (Ed.), *Subject and topic* (pp. 27–55). New York: Academic Press.
Chomsky, Noam. (1981). *Lectures on Government and Binding*. Dordrecht: Foris.
Colonna, Saveria, Sarah Schimke, & Barbara Hemforth. (2012). Information structure effects on anaphora resolution in German and French: A cross-linguistic study of pronoun resolution. *Linguistics, 50*(5), 991–1013.
Colonna, Saveria, Sarah Schimke, & Barbara Hemforth. (2014). Information structure and pronoun resolution in German and French: Evidence from the visual-world

paradigm. In B. Hemforth, B. Mertins, & C. Fabricius-Hansen (Eds.), *Psycholinguistic approaches to meaning and understanding across languages (studies in theoretical psycholinguistics 44)* (pp. 175–195). Cham: Springer International Publishing.

Cowles, Heidi W. (2003). *Processing information structure: Evidence from comprehension and production*. [Doctoral dissertation, University of California, Santa Cruz].

Cowles, Heidi W., Matthew Walenski, & Robert Kluender. (2007). Linguistic and cognitive prominence in anaphor resolution: Topic, contrastive focus and pronouns. *Topoi, 26*, 3–18.

Crawley, Rosalind A., Rosemary J. Stevenson, & David Kleinman. (1990). The use of heuristic strategies in the interpretation of pronouns. *Journal of Psycholinguistic Research, 19*, 245–264.

Daneš, František. (1970). Zur linguistischen Analyse der Textstruktur. *Folia Linguistica, 4*, 72–78.

De la Fuente, Israel. (2015). *Putting pronoun resolution in context: The role of syntax, semantics, and pragmatics in pronoun interpretation*. [Doctoral dissertation, Université Paris Diderot].

Degand, Liesbeth, & Anne Cathrine Simon. (2005). Minimal discourse units: Can we define them, and why should we? In M. Aurnague, M. Bras, A. Le Draoulec, & L. Vieu (Eds.), *Proceedings of SEM-05. Connectors, discourse framing and discourse structure: from corpus based and experimental analyses to discourse theories* (pp. 65–74). Biarritz, France.

Ellert, Miriam. (2013). Resolving ambiguous pronouns in a second language: A visual-world eye-tracking study with Dutch learners of German. *International Review of Applied Linguistics in Language Teaching, 51*(2), 171–197.

Ellert, Miriam, & Anke Holler. (2011). Semantic and Structural Constraints on the Resolution of Ambiguous Personal Pronouns—A Psycholinguistic Study. In I. Hendrickx, S.L. Devi, A. Branco, & R. Mitkov (Eds.), *Anaphora Processing and Applications: 8th Disourse Anaphora and Anaphor Resolution Colloquium, DAARC 2011, Faro, Portugal, October 6–7, 2011. Revised selected papers* (pp. 157–170). Heidelberg: Springer.

Frana, Ilaria. (2008). The role of discourse prominence in the resolution of referential ambiguities: Evidence from co-reference in Italian. *University of Massachusetts Occasional Papers in Linguistics 37: Semantics and Processing*. Amherst, MA: GLSA.

Fukumura, Kumiko, & Roger P.G. van Gompel. (2010). Choosing anaphoric expressions: Do people take into account likelihood of reference? *Journal of Memory and Language, 62*(1), 52–66.

Gärtner, Hans-Martin, & Thórhallur Eythórsson. (2020). Varieties of Dependent V2 and Verbal Mood: A View from Icelandic. In R. Woods, & S. Wolfe (Eds.), *Rethinking Verb Second* (pp. 208–239). Oxford: Oxford University Press.

Gernsbacher, Morton A., & David J. Hargreaves. (1988). Accessing sentence participants: the advantage of first mention. *Journal of Memory and Language, 27*, 699–717.

Givón, Talmy. (1983). Topic continuity in discourse: An introduction. In T. Givón (Ed.), *Topic continuity in discourse: A quantitative cross-language study* (pp. 1–42). Amsterdam/Philadelphia: John Benjamins.

Givón, Talmy. (1992). The grammar of referential coherence as mental processing instructions. *Linguistics, 30*, 5–55.

Gordon, Peter C., Barbara Grosz, & Laura A. Gilliom. (1993). Pronouns, names, and the centering of attention in discourse. *Cognitive Science, 17*, 311–347.

Groenendijk, Jereon, & Floris Roelofsen. (2009). Inquisitive semantics and pragmatics. In J.M. Larrazabal, & L. Zubeldia (Eds.), *Meaning, content and argument: Proceedings of the ILCLI international workshop on semantics, pragmatics and rhetoric* (pp. 41–72). San Sebastián: Servicio Editorial.

Grosz, Barbara, Aravind Joshi, & Scott Weinstein. (1995). Centering: A framework for modelling the local coherence of discourse. *Computational Linguistics, 21*(2), 203–226.

Grosz, Barbara, & Candace Sidner. (1986). Attention, intention and the structure of discourse. *Computational Linguistics, 12*(3), 175–204.

Gundel, Jeanette K., Nancy Hedberg, & Ron Zacharski. (1993). Cognitive status and the form of referring expressions in discourse. *Language, 69*(2), 274–307.

Haegeman, Liliane. (2003). Conditional clauses: External and internal syntax. *Mind & Language, 18*(4), 317–339.

Haegeman, Liliane. (2009). The movement analysis of temporal adverbial clauses. *English Language & Linguistics, 13*(3), 385–408.

Haegeman, Liliane. (2010). The internal syntax of adverbial clauses. *Lingua, 120*(3), 628–648.

Hobbs, Jerry. (1979). Coherence and coreference. *Cognitive Science, 3*, 67–90.

Hobbs, Jerry. (1985). *On the coherence and structure of discourse* (Tech. Rep. Nos. 85–37). California, USA: University of Southern California.

Holler, Anke, & Lisa Irmen. (2006). What happens beyond the right frontier?—An empirical study. In C. Sidner, J. Harpur, A. Benz, & P. Kühnlein (Eds.), *Proceedings of the workshop on constraints in discourse 2006* (pp. 91–98). Maynooth: National University of Ireland.

Holler, Anke, & Katja Suckow. (2016). How clausal linking affects noun phrase salience in pronoun resolution. In A. Holler, & K. Suckow (Eds.), *Empirical perspectives on anaphora resolution*. Berlin: de Gruyter.

Johnston, Michael. (1994). *The syntax and semantics of adverbial adjuncts*. [Doctoral dissertation, University of California, Santa Cruz].

Kaiser, Elsi. (2011). Focusing on pronouns: Consequences of subjecthood, pronominalisation, and contrastive focus. *Language and Cognitive Processes, 26*, 1625–1666.

Kaiser, Elsi, David Cheng-Huan Li, & Edward Holsinger. (2011). Exploring the lexical and acoustic consequences of referential predictability. In I. Hendrickx, S.L. Devi, A. Branco, & R. Mitkov (Eds.), *Anaphora processing and applications: 8th Disourse Anaphora and Anaphor Resolution Colloquium, DAARC 2011, Faro, Portugal, October 6–7, 2011. Revised selected papers* (pp. 171–183). Heidelberg: Springer.

Kaiser, Elsi, Jeffrey T. Runner, Rachel S. Sussman, & Michael K. Tanenhaus. (2009). Structural and semantic constraints on the resolution of pronouns and reflexives. *Cognition, 112*(1), 55–80.

Kazanina, Nina, Ellen F. Lau, Moti Lieberman, Masaya Yoshida, & Colin Phillips. (2007). The effect of syntactic constraints on the processing of backwards anaphora. *Journal of Memory and Language, 56*(3), 384–409.

Kehler, Andrew. (2002). *Coherence, reference, and the theory of grammar*. Stanford, CA: CSLI Publications.

Kehler, Andrew, & Hannah Rohde. (2013). A probabilistic reconciliation of coherence-driven and centering-driven theories of pronoun interpretation. *Theoretical Linguistics, 39*(1–2), 1–37.

Kehler, Andrew, Laura Kertz, Hannah Rohde, & Jeffrey L. Elman. (2008). Coherence and coreference revisited. *Journal of Semantics, 25*(1), 1–44.

Knott, Alistair, & Ted Sanders. (1998). The classification of coherence relations and their linguistic markers: An exploration of two languages. *Journal of Pragmatics, 30*, 135–175.

Krause, Thomas, & Amir Zeldes. (2016). Annis3. a new architecture for generic corpus query and visualization. *Digital Scholarship in the Humanities, 31*(1), 118–139.

Krifka, Manfred. (2007). Basic notions of information structure. In C. Féry, G. Fanselow, & M. Krifka (Eds.), *The notions of information structure* (pp. 13–55). Potsdam: Universitätsverlag.

Kuppevelt, Jan van. (1995). Discourse structure, topicality and questioning. *Journal of Linguistics, 31*, 109–114.

Mann, William C., & Sandra A. Thompson. (1988). Rhetorical Structure Theory: Towards a functional theory of text organisation. *Text, 8*(3), 243–281.

Miltsakaki, Eleni. (2002). Towards an aposynthesis of topic continuity and intrasentential anaphora. *Computational Linguistics, 28*(3), 319–355.

Mitchell, Don C. (2004). On-line methods in language processing: Introduction and historical review. In M. Carreiras, & C. Clifton (Eds.), *The on-line study of sentence comprehension: Eyetracking, ERPs and beyond* (pp. 15–32). New York: Psychology Press.

Onea, Edgar. (2016). *Potential questions at the semantics-pragmatics interface*. Leiden: Brill.

Passoneau, Rebecca J., & Diane J. Litman. (1997). Discourse segmentation by human and automated means. *Computational Linguistics, 23*, 103–139.

Patterson, Clare, & Claudia Felser. (2019). Delayed application of binding condition C during cataphoric pronoun resolution. *Journal of Psycholinguistic Research, 48*(2), 453–475.

Patterson, Clare, Helena Trompelt, & Claudia Felser. (2014). The online application of binding condition B in native and non-native pronoun resolution. *Frontiers in Psychology*, 5.

Paul, Herrmann. (1880). *Prinzipien der Sprachgeschichte*. Halle: Max Niemeyer.

Polanyi, Livia. (1988). A formal model of the structure of discourse. *Journal of Pragmatics, 12*, 601–638.

Polanyi, Livia, Chris Culy, Martin van den Berg, Gian Lorenzo Thione, & David Ahn. (2004). A rule based approach to discourse parsing. In B. Webber, & D. Byron (Eds.), *Proceedings of the 2004 ACL workshop on discourse annotation* (pp. 25–32). Barcelona, Spain.

Pollard, Carl, & Ivan Sag. (1992). Anaphors in English and the scope of Binding Theory. *Linguistic Inquiry, 23*, 261–303.

Prince, Ellen F. (1981). Toward a taxonomy of given-new information. In P. Cole (Ed.), *Radical pragmatics* (pp. 223–255). New York: Academic Press.

Roberts, Craige. (1996). Information structure: Towards an integrated theory of formal pragmatics. In J. Yoon, & A. Kathol (Eds.), *OSU Working Papers in Linguistics: Papers in Semantics* (Vol. 49, pp. 91–136). Columbus, OH: The Ohio State University.

Rosa, Elise C., & Jennifer E. Arnold. (2017). Predictability affects production: Thematic roles can affect reference form selection. *Journal of Memory and Language, 94*, 43–60.

Sanders, Ted, Wilbert Spooren, & Leo Noordman. (1992). Toward a taxonomy of coherence relations. *Discourse Processes, 24*, 119–147.

Simons, Mandy, Judith Tonhauser, David Beaver, & Craige Roberts. (2010). What projects and why. In N. Li, & D. Lutz (Eds.), *Proceedings of SALT 20* (pp. 309–327). Vancouver, Canada.

Sturt, Patrick. (2003). The time-course of the application of binding constraints in reference resolution. *Journal of Memory and Language, 48*(3), 542–562.

Vallduvi, Enric, & Elisabeth Engdahl. (1996). The linguistic realization of information packaging. *Linguistics, 34*, 459–519.

von Heusinger, Klaus, Malte Zimmermann, & Edgar Onea. (2019). *Questions in discourse* (Vol. 1: Semantics). Leiden: Brill.

von Stutterheim, Christiane, & Wolfgang Klein. (1989). Referential Movement in Descriptive and Narrative Discourse. In R. Dietrich, & C.F. Graumann (Eds.), *Language Processing in Social Context* (pp. 39–76). Amsterdam: Elsevier.

von Stutterheim, Christiane, & Wolfgang Klein. (2002). Quaestio und l-perspectivation. In C.F. Graumann, & W. Kallmeyer (Eds.), *Perspectivity and perspectivation in discourse* (pp. 59–88). Amsterdam/Philadelphia: John Benjamins.

Weinrich, Harald. (1964). *Tempus. Besprochene und erzählte Welt.* Stuttgart: Kohlhammer.

Zeevat, Henk. (2011). Rhetorical relations. In C. Maienborn, K. v. Heusinger, & P. Portner (Eds.), *Semantics: An international handbook of natural language and meaning* (pp. 946–970). Berlin: Walter de Gruyter.

Zimmermann, Malte, Klaus von Heusinger, & Edgar Onea. (2019). *Questions in discourse* (Vol. 2: Pragmatics). Leiden: Brill.

CHAPTER 2

Coherence and the Interpretation of Personal and Demonstrative Pronouns in German

Yvonne Portele and Markus Bader

1   Introduction

In some languages, among them Dutch, Finnish, and German, demonstrative pronouns can be used anaphorically. Anaphoric demonstrative pronouns complement the more common personal pronouns, raising the question of how the two kinds of pronouns differ from each other. An example from German illustrating the basic usage of personal and demonstrative pronouns is given in (1).

(1) a. *Peter$_i$ traf auf der Konferenz   einen ehemaligen Kollegen$_j$.*
       P.   met at   the conference a   former   colleague.
       'Peter met a former colleague at the conference.'

   b. *Er$_i$/Der$_j$ hatte viel   zu erzählen.*
       he/he-DEM had   much to tell.
       'He had much to tell.'

In examples like (1), the preferred antecedent of the personal pronoun (p-pronoun for short) *er* ('he') is the clause-initial subject of the preceding clause. The pronoun *der* (lit. 'the', translated as he-DEM in the following) is one of two commonly used anaphoric demonstrative pronouns in German, the other one being the more formal *dieser* ('this'). Following much of the literature on pronoun use in German, we focus on the anaphoric demonstrative pronoun *der* (d-pronoun for short) in the following; the term 'demonstrative pronoun' will be used for the form *dieser* ('this'). In contrast to the p-pronoun, the d-pronoun preferentially takes the clause-final object NP as antecedent. In addition to structural factors, such as the grammatical function and surface position, pronoun interpretation is influenced by semantic coherence relations. In this article, we investigate how coherence relations affect the interpretation of p- and d-pronouns in German.

1.1 Structural Bias

In (1), syntactic function and linear order are confounded—the subject is the initial NP and the object is the final NP. This confounding can be avoided when in addition to sentences with subject-before-object (SO) order sentences with object-before-subject (OS) order are taken into account. Several experimental investigations comparing the interpretation of p- and d-pronouns following SO and OS context sentences have revealed that p-pronouns show an order-independent subject preference whereas d-pronouns show a preference for the sentence-final NP independently of its syntactic function (cf. Kaiser & Trueswell, 2008 for Finnish; Ellert, 2013, and references there for German). We will use the cover term *structural bias* for all interpretive influences based on the grammatical function, surface position, and information structural status of the antecedent of p- or d-pronouns. Numerous experimental as well as corpus-linguistic investigations of these factors have shown that whereas being the subject, sentence-initial, and/or topic are characteristics of the preferred antecedent of p-pronouns, the opposite holds for d-pronouns, with their preferred antecedent being the object, sentence-final, and/or non-topic (e.g., Fukumura & van Gompel, 2015; Portele & Bader, 2016; see also Patterson & Felser, this volume, for an information structural investigation of focus on pronoun resolution).

1.2 Semantic Bias

For p-pronouns, the often observed subject preference does not hold in general. Since the seminal work of Garvey and Caramazza (1974), it has been known that verb meaning has a strong influence on how referentially ambiguous pronouns are resolved. As an example, consider the sentence pair in (2) (from Garvey, Caramazza & Yates, 1975, p. 228).

(2) a. George telephoned Walter because he wanted sympathy.
b. George criticized Walter because he wanted sympathy.

The pronoun *he* in the embedded *because* clause takes the subject NP of the main clause as preferred antecedent in sentence (2a). In sentence (2b), in contrast, the preferred antecedent is the object NP of the main clause. The sentence pair in (2) illustrates the concept of *implicit causality*. Verbs vary with regard to which argument is considered as responsible for the event described by the verb. For an agentive verb like *telephone*, the cause of the event is typically attributed to the agent argument. For an agentive verb like *to criticize*, which includes an evaluation of the patient argument, it is typically the patient argument which is made responsible for the event described by the verb (see Rudolph & Försterling, 1997, for an overview).

The semantic effect illustrated by the sentence pair in (2) depends not only on verb semantics but also on the presence of the causal connective *because*, as illustrated by the contrast between (3a) and (3b).

(3) a. George flattered Walter because he *was in love*.
     b. George flattered[1] Walter so he *asked for a date*.

Changing the causal connective *because* (3a) to the consequential connective *so* (3b) induces a shift in pronoun resolution (Stevenson, Knott, Oberlander & McDonald, 2000). Whereas the connector *because* biases the interpretation of the ambiguous pronoun toward the agent, the patient is the preferred antecedent in the presence of the connector *so*. Thus, consequences, in contrast to causes, are more likely associated with the patient of the action.

Following Fukumura and Van Gompel (2010), we will use the cover term *semantic bias* for all semantic variables, including verb semantics (e.g., implicit causality) and coherence relations. For personal pronouns, the effect of semantic bias on the interpretation and production of pronouns has been thoroughly investigated (see Holler & Suckow, 2016, for recent evidence on German). For d-pronouns, much less is known in this regard, as discussed in the next section.

1.3   Effects of Semantic Bias on D-pronouns

The first study investigating the effect of coherence relations on the interpretation of d-pronouns that we know of is Kaiser, who had participants continue sentences as in (4) (2011; see also Jasinskaja & Poschmann, this volume, for an investigation of coherence and readings of non-restricted relative clauses).

(4) *Die Schauspielerin hat die Schneiderin gekitzelt und dann hat*
     the actress   has the seamstress tickled   and then has
     sie/die ...
     she/she-DEM
     'The actress tickled the seamstress and then she/she-DEM has ...'

---

[1] We use the verb *to flatter*, because in Au (1986) this was one of the verbs that obviously changed from a bias toward the agent (85%) to a bias toward the patient (83%) depending on the connector. For some agentive verbs like *to hit* that also have been investigated (e.g., Stevenson et al., 1994), a (possible) patient bias caused by the connector *because* (64%) was clearly enhanced in the conditions comprising the connector *so* (80%).

According to Kaiser (2011), *dann* ('then') is ambiguous between a narrative and a consequential interpretation. Using this ambiguity, she analyzed participants' continuations to see whether the pronouns lead comprehenders to expect a certain coherence relation. Kaiser (2011) found that p-pronouns as well as d-pronouns are influenced by coherence relations. When participants used the p-pronoun to refer back to the subject/agent of the sentence (73.45%), the continuation stood in a non-consequence relation to the context most of the time (68.8% non-consequence versus 4.7% consequence; note that *consequence* is referred to as *result* in Kaiser, 2011). Taking up the object/patient with the p-pronoun, on the other hand, leads to more frequent consequence relations (23.4% consequence versus 3.1% non-consequence) between the conjoined sentences. For the d-pronoun, there are more object than subject continuations. All of the object continuations (88.88%) evoke consequence relations and all subject continuations non-consequence relations. Kaiser concludes that though coherence relations do not influence d-pronouns to the same extent as they influence p-pronouns, "d-pronouns nevertheless interact with coherence-related processing by guiding comprehenders' expectations of coherence relations" (Kaiser, 2011, p. 349). In the following, we ask whether the reverse—an influence of coherence relations on the interpretation of d-pronouns—can also be observed.[2]

The effect of verb semantics on the interpretation of d-pronouns has been investigated by Schumacher, Dangl and Uzun (2016) and Schumacher, Roberts and Järvikivi (2017) for German and by Järvikivi, van Gompel and Hyönä (2017) for Finnish. Schumacher et al. (2016) investigated the influence of thematic roles and canonical word order on p- and d-pronouns. The context sentence had either subject-object order, as in (5) and (6), or object-subject order (not shown in the examples below) and contained either agentive verbs (5) or dative object-experiencer verbs (6).

(5) *Der   Feuerwehrmann will   den   Jungen retten,   weil*
    the.NOM fire-fighter   wants the.ACC boy   to-rescue, because
    das Haus   brennt.   Aber er/der   ist zu aufgeregt.
    the house. NOM is-on-fire. But he/he-DEM is too nervous.
    'The fire fighter wants to rescue the boy, because the house is on fire. But he is too nervous.'

---

2 For a similar direction see the experimental study on the structural and semantic influence of German connectives on pronoun resolution reported by Ellert and Holler (2011).

(6) *Der   Terrorist ist dem   Zuschauer aufgefallen, und zwar*
     The.NOM terrorist is the.DAT spectator noticed,   in   fact
     nahe   der Absperrung. Aber er/der   will   eigentlich nur die
     next-to the barrier.   But he/h-DEM wants actually only the
     Feier   sehen.
     ceremony watch.
     'It is the terrorist who the spectator noticed, in fact next to the barrier. But he actually only wants to watch the ceremony.'

Schumacher and colleagues explain their results by concluding that thematic roles are more decisive than grammatical functions for the resolution of ambiguous pronouns. For agentive verbs, the p-pronoun prefers the agent (which is the subject) as its antecedent. The d-pronoun, on the other hand, is resolved toward the patient (which is the object). With object-experiencer verbs that have non-canonical object-before-subject word order, preferences get vague or vanish in some of the conditions. Stated in terms of Dowty (1991), the personal pronoun prefers the proto-agent whereas the d-pronoun prefers the proto-patient. Competing prominence hierarchies might weaken these preferences. Additionally, Schumacher and colleagues showed that the adversative adverbial *aber* ('but') introduces a further cue for pronoun resolution.

In two visual world experiments, Järvikivi et al. (2017) investigated the effect of semantic bias on the interpretation of Finnish p- and d-pronouns. In both experiments, semantic bias was manipulated by including verbs differing with regard to implicit causality (subject- and object-experiencer verbs) within the context sentence, as illustrated in (7a–i) and (7a–ii).

(7) a. Context sentence
    (i) Vladimir Putin pelotti George Bushia Valkoisessa talossa
         'Vladimir Putin (nom-subj) frightened George Bush (ptv-obj) at the White House'
    (ii) Vladimir Putin pelkäsi George Bushia Valkoisessa talossa
         'Vladimir Putin (nom-subj) feared George Bush (ptv-obj) at the White House'
    b.   Target sentence
         Koska *hän/tämä* oli kuluneen viikon aikana antanut useaan otteeseen ymmärtää, ettei maiden Irakin suhteissa olisi näkemyseroja
         'Because *he (p-/d-pronoun)* had during the past week given many times the impression that there would be no differences of opinion concerning the countries' relations with Iraq'

The results of Experiment 2 show that Finnish p- and d-pronouns are both influenced by the implicit causality bias. Both pronouns preferred the stimulus argument as antecedent, which is consistent with implicit causality because the stimulus is the argument causing the experiencer's state. Whereas this is the subject with stimulus-experiencer verbs (7a–i), it is the object with experiencer-stimulus verbs (7a–ii). Differences were found regarding the structural bias. Whereas the p-pronoun showed a first-mention preference, the d-pronoun preferred the second-mentioned antecedent.

1.4 Accounting for Structural and Semantic Bias

The research discussed above as well as many other studies show that pronoun resolution is affected by both semantic and structural bias. A theory of pronoun interpretation that integrates the two kind of biases has been proposed by Kehler, Kertz, Rohde and Elman (2008) (see also Kehler & Rohde, 2013). When presented with an ambiguous pronoun, the listener or reader faces the task of choosing the most likely antecedent of the pronoun out of a set of potential referents given in the prior context. In terms of probability theory, this corresponds to determining for which of the potential referents the conditional probability $p(referent|pronoun)$ is highest. According to Kehler and colleagues, listeners or readers use Bayesian reasoning in order to compute this probability. As shown by the formula in (8), the Bayesian theory of pronoun resolution combines two probabilities in order to compute the probability $p(referent|pronoun)$ for each potential referent of a referentially ambiguous pronoun.

(8) $p(referent|pronoun) = \dfrac{p(pronoun|referent) \times p(referent)}{\sum_{referent \in referents} p(pronoun|referent) p(referent)}$

The probability $p(referent)$ is an estimate of how likely each referent of the preceding context is mentioned again in the next sentence. This probability is heavily dependent on verb semantics and coherence relations. For example, after having processed the sentence fragment *Peter feared Mary because*, Mary is much more likely to be mentioned next than Peter. The reverse is true for the structurally similar example *Peter frightened Mary because*; here, Peter is more likely mentioned next than Mary. The probability $p(pronoun|referent)$ estimates the likelihood that a pronoun is used to refer to a given referent. This probability has been shown to be strongly dependent on structural bias, with the referent's syntactic function playing a particularly important role. For example, a pronoun is very likely used when completing *Peter frightened Mary because* with a reference to the subject *Peter* whereas using a pronoun is much less probable for referring to the object *Mary* when completing *Peter feared*

Mary because. To compute the probability *p(referent|pronoun)*, the resulting probability—*p(referent)* × *p(pronoun|referent)*—is divided by the sum of this probability for all potential referents, causing the probabilities for the individual referents to add up to 1. This way, they can be compared to the proportions observed in interpretation experiments.

1.5 The Current Study

The first aim of this paper is to test whether coherence relations affect the interpretation of p- and d-pronouns in the same way. To this end, we had participants complete short texts as in (9). Since the respective pronoun is included in the fragment, that is, we include a so-called pronoun prompt, the results allow us to determine the preferred interpretation of the anaphoric expressions from the continuation.

(9)   *Der Regisseur war von dem Schauspieler fasziniert.*
       The director was of the actor   fascinated
       'The director was fascinated by the actor.'

   a. Er/Der hat nämlich ... 'This was for the reason that he/he-DEM ...'
   b. Er/Der hat deshalb ... 'This had the consequence that he/he-DEM ...'

The context sentence contains an adjective derived from the psych verb *faszinieren* ('to fascinate'). In this construction, the experiencer argument surfaces as subject NP and the stimulus argument as a prepositional object. Coherence relations are manipulated by including either the inferential discourse marker *nämlich* ('the reason was that') or the consequential discourse marker *deshalb* ('therefore'). Note that the coherence markers follow the pronoun for reasons of uniformity. Whereas the consequential discourse marker can appear clause-initially, the inferential marker cannot.[3] We must leave it as a question for future online studies how sentence interpretation is affected by the late position of the coherence marker relative to the pronoun. For example, the pronoun may first be analyzed assuming a default coherence relation based on the bias associated with the verb of the preceding context sentence. This analysis may be later revised when the discourse marker indicates a different coherence relation.

---

3   Note that *nämlich* can also appear following the first constituent in main clauses, in the so called *Nacherstposition* (e.g., Pasch, Brauße, Breindl & Waßner, 2003; Onea & Volodina, 2009). *Deshalb*, on the other hand, cannot appear between the first constituent and the finite verb.

Given what is known about pronoun use with psych verbs, it is to be expected that the preferred antecedent of the p-pronoun *er* ('he') is the stimulus argument when the continuation sentence stands in a causal relation to the preceding sentence. When context sentence and continuation sentence stand in a consequence relation, however, the experiencer argument is the preferred antecedent. For the d-pronoun, the stimulus argument should be the preferred antecedent according to all accounts discussed above. The stimulus argument is an object, it occurs in final position, it is non-topical, and it is a proto-patient. These are all properties which make the stimulus argument the ideal antecedent of the d-pronoun. The question then is how the coherence relation that is signaled by the discourse marker in the continuation sentence affects the interpretation of the d-pronoun. If Järvikivi et al.'s (2017) finding that verb semantics affects p- and d-pronouns in similar ways generalizes to coherence relations, the preference should be stronger in the case of a causal relation than in the case of a consequence relation. This prediction is tested in Experiment 1.

Kehler et al. (2008) have proposed the Bayesian theory of pronoun resolution based on data from English. This theory is therefore restricted to the interpretation of p-pronouns. The second aim of this paper is to test whether the Bayesian Theory can also account for pronoun resolution in German, which has d-pronouns in addition to p-pronouns. In order to apply the Bayesian formula in (8) to the results of Experiment 1, Experiment 2 obtains estimates of $p(referent)$ and $p(pronoun|referent)$. In this experiment, participants had to complete the same three sentence contexts as Experiment 1, but without a pronoun in the prompt.

The organization of this paper is as follows. Section 2 presents Experiment 1, which tests whether discourse coherence affects the interpretation of d-pronouns in a similar way as it affects the interpretation of p-pronouns. Section 3 presents Experiment 2, which provides the production data necessary to test the Bayesian model of pronoun interpretation proposed by Kehler et al. (2008). Section 4 uses the data yielded by Experiments 1 and 2 in order to test the Bayesian model of pronoun interpretation. The paper concludes with a general discussion in Section 5.

2 Coherence and Pronoun Interpretation: Experiment 1

We conducted Experiment 1 to test whether the interpretation of d-pronouns is affected by coherence relations in the same way as the interpretation of p-pronouns. As already discussed above, Experiment 1 tests short discourses as in (9) (see also Table 2.1). The crucial context sentence always contains a psychological predicate with the experiencer as subject and the stimulus as object. What is varied is the coherence relation between context and continuation—this is either a cause or a consequence relation. The design thus follows Stevenson et al. (2000) and Fukumura and Van Gompel (2010). Given what is known about the interaction of psychological predicates and coherence relations, the hypotheses for the p-pronoun *er* are straightforward. The preferred antecedent for the p-pronoun should be the stimulus given a causal relation whereas the experiencer should be preferred given a consequential relation. This prediction holds despite the structural bias of p-pronouns toward a subject antecedent, which is the experiencer in Experiment 1, because for p-pronouns it is known that semantic bias easily overrides structural bias.

For the d-pronoun *der* ('he'-DEM), expectations are less clear. If the finding of Järvikivi et al. (2017) that verb semantics affects p- and d-pronouns in the same way generalizes to coherence relations, we again expect a preference for the stimulus with a cause relation and for the experiencer with a consequence relation. The structural bias associated with d-pronouns favors an object in clause-final position as antecedent. Structural bias thus favors the stimulus argument throughout. As our review of the pertinent literature has shown, only few studies have investigated the effect of coherence on the interpretation of d-pronouns. In contrast to p-pronouns, it is therefore not known how structural bias and semantic bias are ranked relative to each other. With a causal relation, semantic bias and syntactic bias both favor the stimulus/object as antecedent. With a consequence relation, semantic bias favors the experiencer/subject whereas structural bias favors the stimulus/object. By observing which argument is actually favored, we can estimate the relative weight of structural bias and semantic bias in the case of d-pronouns.

2.1   Method

2.1.1   Participants

Thirty-six students at the Goethe-University Frankfurt participated in Experiment 1 for course credit. All participants were native speakers of German and naive with respect to the purpose of the experiment.

2.1.2   Materials

We constructed 20 experimental items, each consisting of three context sentences followed by a target sentence, as illustrated in Table 2.1. The first context sentence served a scene-setting function by introducing the contextual frame for the following sentences. The second context sentence introduced a male referent by using an indefinite NP. This referent was taken up by a definite

TABLE 2.1   A complete stimulus item for Experiment 1.

Context sentences

[C1]   In unserer Straße wohnen viele junge Familien.
       in our   street   live   many young families

[C2]   Gestern   hatte ein Nachbarsjunge   Geburtstag gefeiert.
       yesterday had   a   neighborhood boy birthday   celebrated

[C3]   Der Junge war aber ganz   schön eifersüchtig auf seinen Bruder.
       the boy   was but totally pretty jealous   of his   brother.
       'Many young families live in our street. Yesterday, a neighborhood boy
       celebrated his birthday. But the boy was quite jealous of his brother.'

Continuation prompt: Er/Der _____ nämlich (*cause*) _____
                       Er/Der _____ deshalb (*consequence*) _____

NP in the third context sentence. The third context sentence also introduced a second male referent, introduced by an indefinite NP or inferable from the context (see Table 2.1: *boy—brother*). The last context sentence always contained a psychological adjective, either a lexical one or one derived from an object-experiencer verb. The referent already introduced in context sentence 2 served as the nominative subject (the experiencer argument) and was the topic of this sentence according to common definitions of sentence topic (Reinhart, 1981; Grosz, Joshi & Weinstein, 1995; Lambrecht, 1996). The referent newly introduced in context sentence 3 acted as sentence-final object (the stimulus argument) and was non-topical. Context sentence 3 was followed by a continuation prompt, which was an incomplete sentence starting with either the p-pronoun *Er* ('he') or the d-pronoun *Der* ('he-DEM') and containing one additional word, either a causal (*nämlich*) or a consequential (*deshalb*) discourse marker. Due to the verb-second nature of German, each sentence fragment contained two blank lines for participants' completions, a first short one for the finite verb in verb-second position and a second long one for the remainder of the sentence.

Crossing the type of pronoun (p- versus d-pronoun) as well as discourse marker (cause versus consequence) in the target sentence resulted in four different versions of each experimental item. The 20 items were distributed across four lists according to a Latin square design. Each list contained exactly one version of each sentence and an equal number of sentences in each condition. 20 filler items that also contained female entities and temporal connectives were added to each experimental list in such a way that experimental items were always separated by one filler item.

2.1.3 Procedure

Participants received a written questionnaire and were asked to read the contexts and complete the target sentences by writing natural-sounding continuations. Participants completed the questionnaires during regular class sessions. Completing a questionnaire took about 20 minutes.

2.1.4 Scoring

Two raters, the first author and a student assistant who was naive regarding our research questions, coded participants' continuations as to whether the pronoun was coreferential with the first or second NP (subject/experiencer or object/stimulus) of the two characters mentioned in context sentence 3. In case of ambiguity or uncertainty as to which of the two NPs was the intended referent of the p- or d-pronoun, the sentence was marked as ambiguous. The agreement rate of the two raters was 91% (between 84% and 98% per experimental condition). Ambiguous as well as non-agreeing continuations were excluded from the following analyses. In total, 617 out of 680 continuations were analyzed.

2.2 *Results*

For all statistical analyses reported in this paper, we used the statistics software R (R Core Team, 2019). The results for Experiment 1 are shown in Figure 2.1. For the p-pronoun *er*, a preference toward the stimulus is observed with a causal relation (80.7%). With a consequence relation, the p-pronoun prefers the experiencer (87.8%). For the d-pronoun *der*, in contrast, the stimulus argument is always the preferred antecedent, but the preference is stronger in the cause condition (98.8%) than in the consequence condition (70.3%).

We analyzed the results by means of logistic mixed-effect modeling using the lme4 package (Bates, Mächler, Bolker & Walker, 2015). The experimental factors and all interactions between them were entered as fixed effects into the model, using effect coding. For the factor COHERENCE, the level 'cause' was coded as 0.5 and the level 'consequence' as -0.5; for the factor PRONOUN TYPE, the coding was 0.5 for the level 'p-pronoun' and -0.5 for the level 'd-pronoun'. In this way, the intercept represents the unweighted grand mean and fixed effects compare factor levels to each other. In addition, we included random effects for items and subjects with maximal random slopes supported by the data,

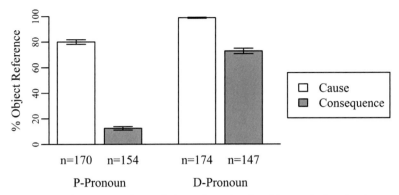

FIGURE 2.1 Percentages of completions referencing the object NP (= the stimulus argument) of context sentence 3 in Experiment 1. Error bars show 95% confidence intervals across participants.

largely following the strategy proposed in Bates et al. (2015). Because we were specifically interested in the influence of semantic bias on the preferred interpretation, we choose congruence with the semantic bias as dependent variable (cf. Stevenson et al., 2000). For continuations in the cause condition, references to the stimulus/the object were coded as congruent, for continuations in the consequence conditions, references to the experiencer/the subject counted as congruent. Table 2.2 shows the results in terms of percentages of congruent continuations as well as the results of the logistic regression model. The model reveals a significant effect of COHERENCE (implemented by the two different discourse markers), no significant effect of PRONOUN TYPE, and a significant interaction between COHERENCE and PRONOUN TYPE. Simple comparisons showed that the effect of COHERENCE on continuations with p-pronouns was not significant (81% vs. 88%, $z = -1.03$, n.s.), whereas it had a significant effect on continuations with d-pronouns (99% vs. 30%, $z = 6.55, p < 001$).

2.3   Discussion

For German p-pronouns, Experiment 1 replicated several findings from the literature. As has been shown for English, their resolution is heavily influenced by semantic bias. Combining the implicit causality bias of a subject-experiencer adjective with the inferential discourse marker *nämlich* ('because'), leads to the resolution of ambiguous pronouns toward the stimulus argument. By changing coherence from cause to consequence, this preference changes. In contexts involving the consequential connective *deshalb* ('so'), the preferred antecedent of the p-pronoun is the experiencer.

For the d-pronoun, a different picture emerges. The d-pronoun showed an interpretive preference toward the stimulus argument under causal as well as

TABLE 2.2 Percentages of completions congruent with the bias of context sentence 3 in Experiment 1. In the coherence condition cause, references to the stimulus/the object are congruent; in the coherence condition consequence, references to the experiencer are congruent.

Cause	Consequence	
p-pronoun	79	88
d-pronoun	99	28

	Estimate	Std. Error	Z-value	$Pr(>|z|)$
Intercept	1.8940	0.2493	7.60	<.001
Coherence	2.5963	0.4859	5.34	0.79
Pronoun Type	0.0664	0.4267	0.16	<.001
Coherence × Pronoun Type	-6.6613	0.8568	-7.77	<.001

consequential coherence. In the condition including the inferential connective *nämlich* ('because'), the preference for the stimulus argument was extremely strong. This preference fulfills not only the semantic, but also the structural bias of the d-pronoun, because the stimulus is the expected referent in terms of implicit causality and it is the sentence-final, discourse-new object. This structural bias is stronger than the semantic bias in the consequence condition, but we nevertheless see a clear influence of the consequential connective, resulting in a substantial number of resolutions toward the experiencer argument.

In line with the findings of Järvikivi et al. (2017), we conclude that p- and d-pronouns are affected by semantic bias—in their case implicit causality, in our case coherence—in the same way. Another prior finding is that the interpretive preference observed for p-pronouns are less robust than those for d-pronouns (e.g., Kaiser, 2011; Schumacher et al., 2016). The results of Experiment 1 are only partially in line with this finding. On the one hand, the strongest preference with about 99% continuations toward the stimulus is found for the d-pronoun in the cause condition. On the other hand, the weakest preference with about 70% continuation toward the stimulus is also found for the d-pronoun, namely with a consequential discourse marker. With 81% and 88%, the two p-pronoun conditions fall in between the limits set by the d-pronoun. A possible explanation for the different strengths of the individual preferences is discussed below.

Our data also show that for the interpretation of p- and d-pronouns, the coherence-induced semantic bias clearly prevails over thematic preferences.

In the cause condition, it is not the experiencer (= proto-agent) that is the preferred antecedent of the p-pronoun, but the causally associated stimulus argument (= the proto-patient). For the d-pronoun on the other hand, the structural bias is too strong to result in a preference shift toward the experiencer, which is the proto-agent.

3   Coherence and Pronoun Production: Experiment 2

The main purpose of Experiment 2 was to collect the production data needed to test whether the Bayesian Theory of Kehler et al. (2008) can account for the interpretive preferences found in Experiment 1. Experiment 2 therefore used the same context sentences as Experiment 1. The only change concerns the continuation prompt. Instead of the pronoun prompt of Experiment 1, which included the pronoun and the discourse marker signaling the coherence relation, Experiment 2 included a no-pronoun prompt, that is, a blank line for participants to write down a continuation. In order to control the coherence relation between context and continuation, each context was followed by a question that asked for the reason or the consequence of the last context sentence. Participants were thus constrained with regard to the coherence relation of their continuation sentence but were otherwise completely free as to how they continued the context.

Experiments of this kind yield two types of results. First, for each referent mentioned in the context, one gets the frequency with which the referent is mentioned again. These frequencies can be used to estimate the term $p(referent)$ in the Bayesian formula in (8). Second, for each referent that is mentioned again, one can compute the frequencies of the alternative anaphoric expressions produced in the continuation sentences. These frequencies serve as estimate for the term $p(pronoun|referent)$ in formula (8).

Prior research that has used the same kind of experimental procedure has found that coherence has a strong effect on how often each referent is mentioned again. Stevenson, Crawley and Kleinman (1994) and Fukumura and Van Gompel (2010) have run experiments that are quite similar to Experiment 2. In Experiment 3 of Stevenson et al. (1994), participants had to complete sentence fragments consisting of a main clause followed either by the causal connector *because* or by the consequential connector *so*. The main clauses instantiated several constructions, among them simple subject-verb-object clauses with either a subject-experiencer verb as in (10a) or an object-experiencer verb as in (10b).

(10) a. Ken admired Geoff, because/so ...
    b. Ken impressed Geoff, because/so ...

When the connector *because* was present, the stimulus argument was mentioned in the completion more often than the experiencer argument, in accordance with prior research on implicit causality. The reverse was found for the connector *so*, which triggered more mentions of the experiencer in the continuation than mentions of the stimulus.

Experiment 2 of Fukumura and Van Gompel (2010) has replicated the findings of Stevenson et al. (1994) for the case of object-experiencer verbs. For sentence fragments as in (11), the majority of continuations following the connector *because* included a reference to the stimulus argument whereas the experiencer argument was referred to in most continuations following the connector *so*.

(11) Gary scared Anna after the long discussion ended in a row, because/so ...

The results of Stevenson et al. (1994) and Fukumura and Van Gompel (2010) show that verb semantics and coherence relations jointly determine which referent is mentioned again. It is controversial, however, whether verb semantics and coherence relations also affect the choice of a referring expression. Stevenson et al. (1994) and Fukumura and Van Gompel (2010) both found that the syntactic function of the referent in the preceding context sentence is the main determinant for the choice of a referring expression. In Stevenson et al.'s (1994) experiment discussed above, p-pronouns were typically used for referring back to an antecedent in subject function, whereas proper names were used for referring to antecedents in object function. In the study of Fukumura and Van Gompel (2010), about 90% of references to the subject antecedent were made using a p-pronoun; for object antecedents, this rate was lower, although with about 80% still on a high level. An additional finding of Fukumura and Van Gompel (2010) is that the rate of pronoun use was higher for the connector *because* than for the connector *so*. However, there was no interaction between syntactic function of the antecedent and the coherence relation. Fukumura and Van Gompel hypothesize that the effect of coherence on the choice of an anaphoric expression is not a semantic effect but a structural effect brought about by syntactic differences between the two connectors *because* versus *so*. While *because* obligatorily introduces an embedded clause, *so* can either introduce a main or an embedded clause.

With regard to the choice of a particular anaphoric expression, an interaction between syntactic function of the antecedent and semantic bias was also absent in Fukumura and Van Gompel's Experiment 1, where semantic bias was investigated by comparing subject- to object-experiencer verbs. Similar results have been reported by Rohde and Kehler (2014) for a different syntactic construction. These authors therefore conclude that semantic bias affects which referent is mentioned next but not how it is referred to. A different position is taken by Arnold (2001) and Rosa and Arnold (2017), who present evidence that the choice of a pronoun also depends on how probable a referent is in terms of semantic bias.

3.1   Method

3.1.1   Participants

Thirty-two students at the Goethe-University Frankfurt participated in Experiment 2 for course credit. All participants were native speakers of German and naive with respect to the purpose of the experiment.

3.1.2   Materials

The material for Experiment 2 was identical to the material of Experiment 1 with the exception of the continuation prompt. In contrast to Experiment 1, the continuation prompt was a blank line in Experiment 2 that was preceded either by the question *Was war der Grund dafür?* ('What was the reason for this?') or by the question *Was war die Folge davon?* ('What was the consequence of this?'). We replaced the discourse markers of Experiment 2 with these questions to establish the relevant coherence relation. Because the prompt did not contain a pronoun, the factor PRONOUN TYPE was no longer included in Experiment 2. Experiment 2 therefore had a one-factorial design with the single factor COHERENCE (levels 'cause' versus 'consequence'). Even though we tried to keep the materials as similar as possible, using a question to indicate the discourse relation creates a difference to the first experiment. The reason for introducing this change was that participants thereby were able to freely produce their continuations, without external constraints like putting a discourse marker at a particular place in the sentence. We cannot rule out that the disruption between context and continuation introduced by the question alters the rate of the different referential expressions compared to other discourse continuations, for example because, due to this disruption, the discourse referents of the context sentence may be less highly activated at the point in time where participants refer back to them. We will return to this issue in the discussion of Experiment 2.

3.1.3 Procedure

Experiment 2 used a sentence production task. Two questionnaires were produced based on the two sentence lists. An instruction included on the first page of the questionnaire told participants to read each context and then to write down a sensible answer to the question that followed each context. The instruction required participants to start a new sentence for the answer but did not impose any constraints with regard to the answer's content. Participants completed the questionnaires either during a regular class session or in the psycholinguistics lab at the University of Frankfurt after they had participated in an unrelated on-line experiment. It took participants about 20 minutes to complete the questionnaire.

3.1.4 Scoring

Because ambiguity was less of a problem in Experiment 2 than in Experiment 1, the results were coded by a student assistant and the resulting coding was then checked by the second author. 15 trials were excluded because no continuation was given ($n = 8$), the continuation was an embedded clause ($n = 1$), or the continuation was referentially ambiguous ($n = 6$). For the remaining 625 completions, we scored which referent of the preceding context was mentioned first and what anaphoric device was used for this purpose. With regard to the choice of a referent, each continuation was scored according to the following four categories: the experiencer was mentioned first, the stimulus was mentioned first, experiencer and stimulus were mentioned together in a single NP, neither experiencer nor stimulus was mentioned. Examples for the four continuation types are shown in Table 2.3. In addition, we coded whether the referent was mentioned as a subject or an object and whether it occurred sentence-initially or not.

For all continuations that contained either the experiencer or the stimulus as first-mentioned referent we scored the linguistic expression used for referring back to the referent according to the following four categories: p-pronoun (*er* 'he'), d-pronoun (*der* 'he-DEM'), demonstrative pronoun (*dieser* 'this'), definite NP (e.g., *der Junge* 'the boy').

3.2 Results

3.2.1 Choice of Referent

Table 2.4 shows how often participants produced the different referent types in their continuations depending on whether the question preceding the continuation prompt asked for the reason or the consequence of the final context sentence. Figure 2.2 provides a graphic summary of the results shown in Table 2.4. Under the labels "experiencer" and "stimulus", Figure 2.2 subsumes those con-

TABLE 2.3 Example continuations from Experiment 2. The context is repeated from Table 2.1.

Context:	In unserer Straße wohnen viele junge Familien. Gestern hatte ein Nachbarsjunge Geburtstag gefeiert. Der Junge war aber ganz schön eifersüchtig auf seinen Bruder. 'Many young families live in our street. Yesterday, a neighborhood boy celebrated his birthday. But the boy was quite jealous of his brother.'
Referent category	*Selected completions given by participants*
Cause:	Was war der Grund dafür? 'What was the reason for this?'
Object/Stimulus	Der war viel beliebter bei den Gästen. 'he-DEM was much more popular with the guests.'
Consequence:	Was war die Folge davon? 'What was the consequence of this?'
Subject/Experiencer	Der Junge hat angefangen zu weinen. 'The boy started to cry.'
Both	Sie haben sich geprügelt. 'They fought each other.'
None	Es kam zum Streit. 'An argument began.'

tinuations that have the crucial NP in sentence-initial position. With a question asking for the reason, the majority of all continuations started with an NP referring to the stimulus argument (74.8%). Continuations starting with an NP referring to the experiencer were also produced, but with a much lower frequency (9.9%). Non-sentence-initial references to the experiencer or the stimulus were overall infrequent, but references to the stimulus again outnumbered references to the experiencer (7.7% vs. 1.3%). In addition, a small number of continuations were produced that contained NPs referring to both the experiencer and the stimulus or that contained no NP referring to one of these arguments.

A rather different referent distribution is observed when a question asking for the consequence preceded the continuation prompt. In this case, NPs occurring sentence-initially and referring back to the experiencer occurred with highest frequency (38.1), followed by NPs occurring sentence-initially and referring back to the stimulus (28.3). References to stimulus or experiencer that did not occur sentence-initially were rare again and also showed a preponderance of references to the experiencer (8.2% versus 2.9%). When comparing cause and consequence continuations, we thus see a switch of the preferred referent as well as a much stronger preference in the cause condition than in

TABLE 2.4   Percentages of referents from the context occurring as the only or first referent in the continuations of Experiment 2.

Position of referent	Referent	Cause	Consequence
Sentence-initial	Subject/Experiencer	9.9	38.1
	Object/Stimulus	74.8	28.3
	Both	1.3	4.6
Not sentence-initial	Subject/Experiencer	1.3	8.1
	Object/Stimulus	7.7	2.9
	Both	0.0	2.3
None	None	3.5	15.6

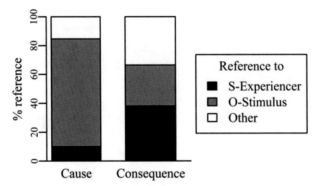

FIGURE 2.2   Percentages of referents from the context rementioned in sentence initial position in the continuations of Experiment 2. The two categories "S-Experiencer" and "O-Stimulus" include only continuations with the referring NP in sentence-initial position.

the consequence condition. Furthermore, there were also somewhat more NPs referring to both the experiencer and the stimulus in the consequence condition, as well as substantially more continuations that referred back to neither of them. Thus, whereas the cause of the psychological state mentioned in the last context sentence was almost exclusively tied to the involved referents, its consequence was less constrained in this regard.

Because relating the production data of Experiment 2 to the interpretation data of Experiment 1 involves only references to the experiencer and the stimulus, we restrict our statistical analysis to the corresponding subset of Experiment 2. A logistic mixed model with references to the experiencer as dependent variable revealed a significant effect of the single factor COHERENCE (estimate = 2.73; std. error = 0.381; z-value = 7.17; $p < .001$), reflecting the finding that there were more references to the experiencer in the consequence than in the cause condition.

3.2.2 Choice of Referential Expression

As shown in Table 2.4, the majority of continuations contained a referential expression in sentence-initial position referring back either to the experiencer argument (the subject) or the stimulus argument (the object) of the preceding sentence. Since these continuations correspond to the continuation prompts provided in Experiment 1, we restrict the following analysis to these cases. Table 2.5 shows the distribution of the different types of referential expressions depending on the argument that was referred to and the question that preceded the continuation prompt. Most of the anaphoric NPs had the syntactic function of subject, with less than 5% object continuations. Because of the rareness of object NPs, we give only total percentages for them in Table 2.5. The four categories of anaphoric expressions shown in this table are accordingly all subject NPs.

The vast majority of continuations contained p-pronouns or definite NPs. For them, Figure 2.3 visualizes the data given in Table 2.5. When referring to the experiencer (the subject) of the preceding sentence, participants most of the time used a p-pronoun. Definite NPs were also used, although much less often. D-pronouns or demonstrative pronouns were never used to refer to the experiencer. For the stimulus (the object), we see the reverse. The majority of references is made using definite NPs whereas p-pronouns occur with low frequency. D-pronouns and demonstrative pronouns are also used to refer to the stimulus, but also with low frequency. In addition to an antecedent effect, Figure 2.3 also reveals a coherence effect. Pronouns of all sorts are used more often in cause continuations than in consequence continuations whereas the reverse is true for definite NPs. This effect of coherence is visible for references to the experiencer and references to the stimulus alike.

Again, using logistic regression modeling, we analyzed the data shown in Table 2.5, Figure 2.3 in three ways. In a first model, the dependent variable was whether the continuation started with a pronoun or not, with COHERENCE and REFERENT as fixed effects. In this model, there were significant main effects of REFERENT (estimate = 4.03; std. error = 0.605; z-value = 6.66; $p < .001$) and COHERENCE (estimate = 1.06; std. error = 0.428; z-value = 2.47; $p < .05$), but the interaction was not significant (estimate = 0.34; std. error = 0.869; z-value = 0.39; n.s.). In a second model, the dependent variable was whether the continuation sentence started with a definite NP or not. This analysis also revealed

TABLE 2.5   Percentages of referential expressions in either subject or object function used in Experiment 2 for referring to the subject/experiencer or the object/stimulus argument of the last context sentence. Raw numbers are given in parentheses.

		Cause		Consequence	
		Subj/Experiencer	Obj/Stimulus	Subj/Experiencer	Obj/Stimulus
Subject	P-pronoun	74.2 (23)	17.5 (41)	64.1 (75)	6.9 (6)
	D-pronoun	0.0 (0)	6.4 (15)	0.0 (0)	4.6 (4)
	Dem. pronoun	0.0 (0)	10.3 (24)	0.0 (0)	0.0 (0)
	Definite NP	19.4 (6)	65.8 (154)	32.5 (38)	85.1 (74)
Object	All Forms	6.5 (2)	0.0 (0)	3.4 (4)	3.4 (3)

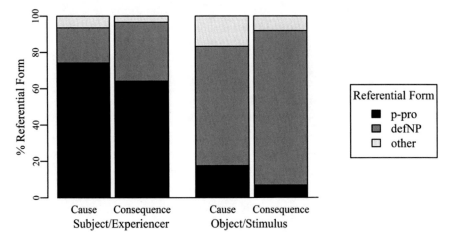

FIGURE 2.3   Percentages of referential expressions in either subject or object function used in Experiment 2 for referring to the subject/experiencer or the object/stimulus argument of the last context sentence.

significant effects of the two main factors (REFERENT: estimate = 3.30; std. error = 0.491; z-value = 6.73; $p < .001$/COHERENCE: estimate = 1.32; std. error = 0.466; z-value = 2.84; $p < .01$) and a non-significant interaction (estimate = 0.89; std. error = 0.798; z-value = 1.12; n.s.).

   D-pronouns and demonstrative pronouns were never produced when referring to the subject/the experiencer of the preceding clause, and even when referring to the object/the stimulus, their frequencies were quite low. Because the experiencer was never referred to with a d-pronoun or a demonstrative, we removed all continuations in the cause condition from the analysis, leaving us with the single factor COHERENCE. In addition, we pooled all occurrences of d-pronouns and demonstrative pronouns into a joint category of demonstrative items. COHERENCE had a significant effect on the production of demonstrative items, which occurred significantly more often in the cause than in the consequence condition (16.7% versus 4.6%; estimate = 2.09; std. error = 0.735; z-value = 2.84; $p < .01$).

3.3 Discussion

The results yielded by Experiment 2 show a high degree of agreement with prior findings from similar experiments in English (Stevenson et al., 2000; Fukumura & Van Gompel, 2010). First, the stimulus argument is preferentially mentioned again when the continuation stands in a causal relation to the preceding context. For continuations connected to the preceding context by a consequential relation, in contrast, it was preferentially the experiencer that was taken up again. Second, for references to the subject/the experiencer, the p-pronoun was the anaphoric device of choice, whereas references to the object/the experiencer were made using definite NPs in the majority of cases. The choice of a particular anaphoric expression was also affected by the coherence relation between the continuation and the context, with more pronouns and less definite NPs in causal continuations in comparison to consequential continuations. We discuss possible implications of this finding in the general discussion. For the d-pronoun, the results of Experiment 2 are in accordance with prior theoretical and experimental studies. The prototypical antecedent of a d-pronoun is a clause-final non-topical object NP. In our experimental stimuli, the stimulus argument had all three properties and the experiencer argument had none. In accordance with this, only the stimulus was referred to using a d-pronoun whereas continuations with a d-pronoun referencing the experiencer were not observed. The same holds for the demonstrative pronoun. Coherence also had an effect on d-pronouns (6.4% versus 4.6%) and demonstrative pronouns (10.3% versus 0%). Given the small numbers in the consequence condition, it is questionable whether the non-occurrence of continuations with demonstrative pronouns in the consequence condition is a real effect. The only other experiment investigating the production of referential forms in German with a no-pronoun prompt that we know of (Experiment 3 of Bader & Portele, 2019) found higher rates of demonstrative pronouns than d-pronouns in all conditions where these pronouns were used at all. In absolute terms, demonstrative pronouns and d-pronouns were also used quite infrequently in this experiment, although the prompt followed the context immediately, that is, without an intervening question. Using a question for determining the coherence relation thus had a minimal effect on the choice of a d-pronoun or demonstrative pro-

TABLE 2.6 Application of the Bayesian formula to the data from Experiment 1 and Experiment 2.

Pronoun type	Coherence	Referent	p(ref)	p(pro|ref)	p(ref) × p(pro|ref)	p(ref|pro) pred.	obs.
P-pronoun	Cause	Subj/Exp	0.099	0.742	0.073	0.359	0.188
		Obj/Stim	0.748	0.175	0.131	0.641	0.812
	Consequence	Subj/Exp	0.381	0.641	0.244	0.926	0.878
		Obj/Stim	0.283	0.069	0.020	0.074	0.122
D-pronoun (Experiment 2)	Cause	Subj/Exp	0.099	0.000	0.000	0.00	0.012
		Obj/Stim	0.748	0.064	0.047	1.00	0.998
	Consequence	Subj/Exp	0.381	0.000	0.000	0.00	0.297
		Obj/Stim	0.283	0.046	0.013	1.00	0.703
D-pronoun (corpus)	Cause	Subj/Exp	0.099	0.01	0.001	0.003	0.012
		Obj/Stim	0.748	0.40	0.299	0.997	0.998
	Consequence	Subj/Exp	0.381	0.01	0.004	0.033	0.297
		Obj/Stim	0.283	0.40	0.113	0.967	0.703

noun at best. While demonstrative pronouns are typically produced more often than d-pronouns in experimental settings as used here, they have not received much attention in the literature on pronoun interpretation (but see Ahrenholz, 2007). Investigating this issue is an important task for future research.

4 A Test of the Bayesian Theory

With the results of Experiments 1 and 2 at hand, we are now in the position to assess the validity of the Bayesian formula proposed in Kehler et al. (2008) for the case of German p- and d-pronouns. This formula, which is repeated in (12), derives interpretation preferences as found in Experiment 1 from production preferences as found in Experiment 2.

(12) $p(\text{referent}|\text{pronoun}) = \dfrac{p(\text{pronoun}|\text{referent}) \times p(\text{referent})}{\sum_{\text{referent} \in \text{referents}} p(\text{pronoun}|\text{referent}) p(\text{referent})}$

The probabilities necessary to compute *p(referent|pronoun)* according to formula (12) are listed in Table 2.6. Let us first consider the predictions for the p-pronoun. The column *p(ref)* shows the probability that the referent given in the column *Referent* is mentioned again in the next sentence. The estimate for this probability comes from Table 2.4 of Experiment 2. The column $p(pro|ref)$ gives the probability that a p-pronoun is used for referring to the selected referent. This probability is estimated from the percentages in Table 2.5 of Experiment 2. Multiplying $p(ref)$ with $p(pro|ref)$ gives the probability that the given referent is mentioned again by using a pronoun. For example, when the continuation sentence stands in a cause relation to the preceding context, the probability that the continuation starts with a pronoun referring back to the experiencer is 0.073 and the probability that the continuation starts with a pronoun referring back to the stimulus is 0.131. These two probabilities do not sum to 1.0 because there are other possibilities to start the continuation, for example with a non-pronominal expression or with an expression referring neither to the experiencer nor the stimulus. However, in an interpretation experiment like Experiment 1, the reader already knows that the continuation sentence starts with a p-pronoun for which only two referents are possible antecedents. In order to reflect this state of affairs, the two probabilities given by multiplying $p(ref)$ with $p(pro|ref)$ must be divided by the denominator in formula (12), which rescales them to sum to one. This finally gives us the conditional probability $p(ref|pro)$ that we need to predict the results of our interpretation experiment.

In sum, the Bayesian theory predicts that the preferred antecedent of the p-pronoun *er* is the stimulus argument (the object) in case of a cause relation but the experiencer argument (the subject) in case of a consequence relation. The preference is predicted to be stronger in the presence of a consequence relation than in the presence of a cause relation. This may seem counterintuitive at first glance because the expectation that the stimulus argument is mentioned again when the continuation sentence contains a causal discourse marker is much stronger than the expectation that the experiencer argument is mentioned again with a consequential discourse marker in the continuation sentence. The predicted preference is nevertheless stronger for the consequence relation than for the causal relation because the probability of using a pronoun is much higher for the referent of a subject NP than for the referent of an object NP. This creates a subject preference which weakens the strong stimulus preference for the cause relation but strengthens the weak experiencer preference for the consequence relation.

In the last column, Table 2.6 shows the proportions of choosing either the stimulus or the experiencer argument as antecedent for the p-pronoun in Experiment 1. A comparison of the probabilities predicted by the Bayesian Theory with the proportions observed in Experiment 1 reveals that the two main predictions are borne out by the data. First and as predicted, the stimulus argument is the preferred antecedent in the cause condition whereas the experiencer argument is preferred in the consequence condition. Second, the preference is stronger in the case of a consequence relation than in the case of a cause relation. In quantitative terms, the fit between model and data is also quite good. It is almost perfect in the consequence conditions. In the cause condition, the predicted preference is somewhat weaker than the observed preference.

We next turn to the predictions for the d-pronoun. The values in the column $p(ref)$ are independent of the referential form and are therefore identical for p- and d-pronoun. The values in the column $p(pro|ref)$ are again taken from Table 2.5 of Experiment 2. Because participants never used a d-pronoun for referring to the experiencer argument (the subject), the Bayesian Theory predicts that a d-pronoun should always be interpreted as referring to the stimulus argument (the object), independently of whether the completion prompt contains a causal or a consequential discourse marker. The varying probabilities associated with $p(ref)$ make no difference in this case. For causal continuations, a comparison of predicted and observed proportions reveals a very close fit. For consequential continuations, in contrast, the fit is not as good. The model captures the finding that the stimulus argument is still the preferred antecedent even with a consequential discourse marker, but it does not capture the finding that the preference is much weaker with a consequential discourse marker than with a causal discourse marker.

As we have just shown, the Bayesian Model fails to predict an effect of coherence on interpreting the d-pronoun because the complete lack of d-pronoun references to the experiencer argument has the consequence that the predicted probabilities $p(ref|pro)$ are totally governed by the term $p(pro|ref)$. Given the low overall frequency of d-pronouns, the zero probability for using a d-pronoun for referring to the experiencer argument may be a sampling artifact. Table 2.6 therefore also contains the predictions of the Bayesian Model when $p(ref|pro)$ is estimated by the corpus frequencies provided in Portele and Bader (2016). In this case, we see an effect of coherence, but it is still a minimal one—the predicted proportion is 1.0 for the causal discourse marker and 0.97 for the consequential discourse marker.

In order to derive a coherence effect of the magnitude seen in Experiment 1, the ratio between the d-pronoun rate for the object and the d-pronoun rate for the subject would have to take on a value of about 3. In written language, d-pronouns are regularly used to refer to the subject, but not often enough to achieve such a ratio (see Portele & Bader, 2016). In spoken language, the situation may be different. In a corpus study comparing a corpus of written newspaper texts to a corpus of spoken language, Bosch, Katz and Umbach (2007) found a rate of d-pronoun use below 7% in the written corpus but a rate of 80% in the spoken corpus. Thus, in the spoken corpus d-pronouns were in fact preferred to p-pronouns. Since Bosch et al. (2007) do not present a detailed analysis of their corpus data, it is not known how often d-pronouns are used for subjects and how often they are used for objects. Furthermore, we also do not know how the probabilities used in the Bayesian formula are computed when spoken and written language lead to different values. For example, do participants have different probabilities $p(pronoun|referent)$ for spoken and written language, or is there only a single probability collapsed across all forms of language use? These are questions that are in need of further research in order to determine whether the Bayesian model of pronoun resolution can account for the interpretive preferences of the d-pronoun as successfully as it can account for the interpretive preferences of the p-pronoun.

5 Conclusions

The experiments presented in this paper extend our knowledge about the interpretation and production of p- and d-pronouns in several ways. Consider first the results for the p-pronoun. In accordance with the literature on implicit causality, Experiment 1 found a preference for the stimulus argument (the syntactic object) when the continuation prompt contained a causal discourse marker. When the continuation contained a consequential discourse marker, the preference reversed and a preference for the experiencer argument (the syntactic subject) showed up. This finding agrees with prior findings showing that semantic bias can override the structural bias of p-pronouns (e.g., Stevenson et al., 2000; Järvikivi et al., 2017).

As to the nature of the semantic bias, our results argue against the hypothesis advanced in Schumacher et al. (2017) that "thematic role is a highly ranked cue during prominence computation of two-antecedent clauses in German". Our results argue instead that interpretive preferences during pronoun resolution result from a more general semantic bias, which derives from a complex interaction of verb semantics and coherence relations. In line with this claim, Experiment 1 did not reveal a general preference for referring back to an antecedent with a particular thematic role. Instead, the discourse marker contained within the continuation prompt was decisive for finding the preferred antecedent of the p-pronoun. We thus conclude that the thematic roles of the potential antecedent NPs are only indirectly involved in finding a referent for a pronoun, namely by contributing to verb meaning and thereby to the overall semantic bias of a sentence. Note that this conclusion gets further support from prior findings concerning the role of implicit causality during pronoun resolution. As already pointed out in the introduction, even agentive verbs differ with regard to which argument is preferred as antecedent by a following pronoun, as illustrated by the sentence pair in (13) (repeated from above). In connection with a causal relation, the preferred antecedent is the agent argument for many agentive verbs, but agentive verbs with an evaluative meaning component show a preference for the patient.

(13) a. George telephoned Walter because he wanted sympathy.
b. George criticized Walter because he wanted sympathy.

Consider next the interpretation of d-pronouns. The results of Experiment 1 confirm Järvikivi et al.'s (2017) finding that semantic bias affects the interpretation of d-pronouns in a similar way as the interpretation of p-pronouns. When semantic bias favored reference to the stimulus argument, as in the case of a causal discourse marker, the stimulus argument was the preferred antecedent for both the p-pronoun and the d-pronoun. When a consequential discourse marker favored reference to the experiencer argument instead, the preference shifted toward the experiencer—resulting in a complete reversal of the preference for the p-pronoun and in a markedly lower preference for the stimulus argument in the case of the d-pronoun. Thus, the effect of semantic bias went in the same direction for both p- and d-pronoun but was substantially stronger for the p-pronoun than for the d-pronoun. This finding makes sense when, as proposed in Kehler et al. (2008), semantic bias competes with structural bias.

A major finding of the production Experiment 2 was that the choice of an anaphoric expression was mainly determined by the antecedent's syntactic function. In the cause condition, participants used a p-pronoun in 74.8% of the time when referring to an antecedent in subject function, whereas p-pronouns were used only in 17.5% of all cases for referring to the object. Thus, p-pronouns were used 4.2 times more often for subject antecedents than for object antecedents in the cause condition.[4] Despite this subject orientation of p-pronouns, the interpretation Experiment 1 found a preference for the object

---

4 Because in our stimuli syntactic functions and thematic roles were confounded, an alternative account of the observed pronominalization rates in terms of thematic roles could be given. However, research in which syntactic functions and thematic roles varied independently (e.g., Fukumura & Van Gompel, 2010; Rohde & Kehler, 2014) has shown that pronoun use depends on syntactic functions, not on thematic roles.

antecedent (the stimulus) in the cause condition. The reason is that the structural bias toward the subject is offset by a semantic bias toward the object in the presence of a cause relation. In this condition, the stimulus was re-mentioned in 74.8% of all cases, the experiencer was re-mentioned in 9.9% of all cases, and the ratio of stimulus to experiencer mentions was 7.6. The semantic bias thus outweighed the structural bias, accounting for the experimentally observed preference for the semantically favored argument.

A further finding of the production experiment was that more p-pronouns were produced in the cause condition than in the coherence conditions, whereas the reverse was true for definite NPs. This finding replicates a similar finding by Fukumura and Van Gompel (2010), but is not compatible with their explanation. As pointed out above, Fukumura and Van Gompel argued that the difference between cause and consequence that they observed with regard to the rate of pronoun use is not a semantic but a syntactic effect. A syntactic explanation is not possible in our case because we did not use different connectors to manipulate coherence but questions that prompted participants to produce a main clause in all cases. There were thus no relevant syntactic differences between the two coherence conditions that could be made responsible for the different rates of pronoun use. An explanation in terms of predictability or bias, for example along the lines of Arnold (2001), is not possible either. Thus, a consequence relation induced a bias toward the experiencer, increasing the proportion of experiencer mentions to 38% and decreasing the proportions of stimulus mentions to 28%. The rate of pronoun use was lower for both, however—for the more predictable experiencer and the less predictable stimulus. In sum, in addition to replicating the effect of coherence on referential choice first observed by Fukumura and Van Gompel (2010), our production experiment supports the hypothesis that we are dealing with a genuine semantic effect. If this hypothesis can be substantiated in later research, it would contradict the claim that referential choice is only affected by structural but not by semantic factors.

Overall, d-pronouns occurred with a rather low frequency, and when they were used at all, then exclusively for referring back to the stimulus argument. This latter finding was not unexpected because the stimulus argument was an object, occurred in clause-final position and was discourse-new/non-topical; that is, all structural properties that are known to increase the likelihood of serving as antecedent of a d-pronoun converged on the stimulus argument. We surmise that the strong structural bias toward the object prevented the semantic bias to cause a complete reversal of the interpretive preference of the d-pronoun. This hypothesis can be tested by investigating sentences in which the two arguments differ less in terms of structural bias. For illustration, consider the short discourse in (14), which is a variation to the discourses investigated in Experiments 1 and 2 (see Table 2.1).

(14) *In unserer Straße wohnen viele junge Familien. Gestern hatte ein*
  in our street live many young families yesterday had a
  Nachbarsjunge Geburtstag gefeiert. Ein Zauberer hat den
  neighborhood-boy birthday celebrated a wizard has the
  Jungen geängstigt.
  boy frightened
  'Many young families live in our street. Yesterday, a neighborhood boy celebrated his birthday. A wizard frightened the boy.'

  a. Er/Der hat nämlich ... 'This was for the reason that he/he-DEM ...'
  b. Er/Der hat deshalb ... 'This had the consequence that he/he-DEM ...'

As in the texts investigated in Experiment 1, the last sentence contains an experiencer argument already introduced in the sentence before and a stimulus argument newly introduced in the final sentence. However, because the last context sentence contains an object-experiencer verb, the topic phrase appears in sentence-final position and the non-topic phrase in sentence-initial position. With regard to the use of a d-pronoun, the stimulus is now favored by being a non-topic whereas the experiencer is favored by being an object in clause-final position. Thus, structural factors are less strongly favoring one of the two arguments as antecedent of a d-pronoun (cf. Portele & Bader, 2016, 2017). For texts as in (14), we therefore expect that coherence leads to a preference reversal in a way similar to the p-pronoun. This prediction was confirmed by Portele & Bader (2018).

In conclusion, our results provide further evidence concerning the relationship between p- and d-pronouns. As has been observed before, p-pronouns and d-pronouns do not stand in a complementary relationship, but are differentially sensitive to the properties of the preceding context (Bosch et al., 2007; Kaiser & Trueswell, 2008). Importantly, this does not hold for all properties of the context alike. In agreement with Järvikivi et al. (2017), we found that the semantic bias affects p- and d-pronouns in similar ways. For the structural bias (e.g., linear position, syntactic function, topichood), in contrast, prior work has shown that the two types of pronouns behave differently. Unlike Järvikivi et al. (2017), we found that the semantic bias caused a preference reversal for the p-pronoun but only a reduction of the strength of the preference for the d-pronoun. This difference may be due to the fact that in our experiment the cause relation induced a stronger semantic bias than a consequence relation.

Alternatively, or in addition, d-pronouns may be associated with a stronger structural bias than p-pronouns. Sorting out the influence of these various factors remains a major task for future research.

References

Ahrenholz, Bernt. (2007). *Verweise mit Demonstrativa im gesprochenen Deutsch: Grammatik, Zweitspracherwerb und Deutsch als Fremdsprache*. Berlin: De Gruyter.

Arnold, Jennifer E. (2001). The effect of thematic roles on pronoun use and frequency of reference continuation. *Discourse Processes, 31*(2), 137–162.

Au, Terry Kit-Fong. (1986). A verb is worth a thousand words: The causes and consequences of interpersonal events implicit in language. *Journal of Memory and Language, 25*(1), 104–122.

Bader, Markus, & Yvonne Portele. (2019). The interpretation of German personal and d-pronouns. *Zeitschrift für Sprachwissenschaft, 38*(2), 155–190.

Bates, Douglas, Martin Mächler, Ben Bolker, & Steve Walker. (2015). Fitting linear mixed-effects models using lme4. *Journal of Statistical Software, 67*(1), 1–48.

Bosch, Peter, Graham Katz, & Carla Umbach. (2007). The non-subject bias of German. In M. Schwarz-Friesel, M. Consten, & M. Knees (Eds.), *Anaphors in Text: Cognitive, Formal and Applied Approaches to Anaphoric Reference* (pp. 145–164). Amsterdam: John Benjamins.

Dowty, David. (1991). Thematic proto-roles and argument selection. *Language, 67*, 547–619.

Ellert, Miriam. (2013). Information structure affects the resolution of the subject pronouns 'er' and 'der' in spoken German discourse. *Discours. Revue de linguistique, psycholinguistique et informatique, 12*(12), 3–24.

Ellert, Miriam, & Anke Holler. (2011). Semantic and Structural Constraints on the Resolution of Ambiguous Personal Pronouns—A Psycholinguistic Study. In I. Hendrickx, S.L. Devi, A. Branco, & R. Mitkov (Eds.), *Anaphora Processing and Applications: 8th Disourse Anaphora and Anaphor Resolution Colloquium, DAARC 2011, Faro, Portugal, October 6–7, 2011. Revised selected papers* (pp. 157–170). Heidelberg: Springer.

Fukumura, Kumikoa, & Roger. P.G. van Gompel. (2010). Choosing anaphoric expressions: Do people take into account likelihood of reference? *Journal of Memory and Language, 62*(1), 52–66.

Fukumura, Kumiko, & Roger. P.G. van Gompel. (2015). Effects of order of mention and grammatical role on anaphor resolution. *Journal of Experimental Psychology: Learning, Memory, and Cognition, 41*(2), 501.

Garvey, Catherine, & Alfonso Caramazza. (1974). Implicit causality in verbs. *Linguistic Inquiry, 5*, 459–464.

Garvey, Catherine, Alfonso Caramazza, & Jack Yates. (1975). Factors influencing assignment of pronoun antecedents. *Cognition*, *3*(3), 227–243.

Grosz, Barbara J., Aravind K. Joshi, & Scott Weinstein. (1995). Centering: A framework for modeling the local coherence of discourse. *Computational Linguistics*, *21*, 203–225.

Holler, Anke, & Katja Suckow. (2016). How clausal linking affects noun phrase salience in pronoun resolution. In A. Holler, & K. Suckow (Eds.), *Empirical Perspectives on Anaphora Resolution* (pp. 61–85). Berlin: De Gruyter.

Järvikivi, Juhani, Roger P.G. van Gompel, & Jukka Hyönä. (2017). The interplay of implicit causality, structural heuristics, and anaphor type in ambiguous pronoun resolution. *Journal of Psycholinguistic Research*, *46*(3), 525–550.

Kaiser, Elsi. (2011). On the relation between coherence relations and anaphoric demonstratives in German. In I. Reich, E. Horch, & D. Pauly (Eds.), *Sinn und Bedeutung 15. Proceedings of the 2010 Annual Conference of the Gesellschaft für Semantik* (pp. 337–352). Saarbrücken: universaar.

Kaiser, Elsi, & John C. Trueswell. (2008). Interpreting pronouns and demonstratives in Finnish: Evidence for a form-specific approach to reference resolution. *Language and Cognitive Processes*, *23*(5), 709–748.

Kehler, Andrew, Laura Kertz, Hannah Rohde, & Jeffrey L. Elman. (2008). Coherence and coreference revisited. *Journal of Semantics*, *25*(1), 1–44.

Kehler, Andrew, & Hannah Rohde. (2013). A probabilistic reconciliation of coherence-driven and centering-driven theories of pronoun interpretation. *Theoretical Linguistics*, *39*(1–2), 1–37.

Lambrecht, Knud. (1996). *Information structure and sentence form: Topic, focus, and the mental representations of discourse referents*. Cambridge: Cambridge University Press.

Onea, Edgar, & Anna Volodina. (2009). Der Schein trügt nämlich. *Linguistische Berichte*, *219*, 291–321.

Pasch, Renate, Ursula Brauße, Eva Breindl, & Ulrich H. Waßner. (2003). *Handbuch der deutschen Konnektoren. Linguistische Grundlagen der Beschreibung und syntaktische Merkmale der deutschen Satzverknüpfer*. Berlin: De Gruyter.

Portele, Yvonne, & Markus Bader. (2016). Accessibility and referential choice: Personal pronouns and d-pronouns in written German. *Discours. Revue de linguistique, psycholinguistique et informatique*, *18*, 1–41.

Portele, Yvonne, & Markus Bader. (2017). Personal pronouns and d-pronouns in German: Connecting comprehension to production. In S. Featherston, R. Hörnig, R. Steinberg, B. Umbreit, & J. Wallis (Eds.), *Proceedings of Linguistic Evidence 2016. Empirical, Theoretical, and Computational Perspectives* (pp. 1–16). Tübingen: University of Tübingen.

Portele, Yvonne, & Markus Bader. (2018). *Semantic bias and topicality in pronoun resolu-*

tion. [Poster], Conference on Architectures and Mechanisms for Language Processing (AMLaP), Humboldt University Berlin, Germany.

R Core Team. (2019). *R: A Language and Environment for Statistical Computing*. R Foundation for Statistical Computing. https://www.R-project.org/

Reinhart, Tanya. (1981). Pragmatics and linguistics: An analysis of sentence topics. *Philosphica, 27*, 53–94.

Rohde, Hannah, & Andrew Kehler. (2014). Grammatical and information-structural influences on pronoun production. *Language, Cognition and Neuroscience, 29*(8), 912–927.

Rosa, Elise C., & Jennifer E. Arnold. (2017). Predictability affects production: Thematic roles can affect reference form selection. *Journal of Memory and Language, 94*, 43–60.

Rudolph, Udo, & Friedrich Försterling. (1997). The psychological causality implicit in verbs: A review. *Psychological Bulletin, 121*(2), 192–218.

Schumacher, Petra B., Manuel Dangl, & Elyesa Uzun. (2016). Thematic role as prominence cue during pronoun resolution in German. In A. Holler, & K. Suckow (Eds.), *Empirical perspectives on anaphora resolution*, 121–147. Berlin: De Gruyter.

Schumacher, Petra B., Leah Roberts, & Juhanni Järvikivi. (2017). Agentivity drives real-time pronoun resolution: Evidence from German *er* and *der*. *Lingua, 185*, 25–41.

Stevenson, Rosemary J., Alistair Knott, Jon Oberlander, & Sharon McDonald. (2000). Interpreting pronouns and connectives: Interactions among focusing, thematic roles and coherence relations. *Language and Cognitive Processes, 15*(3), 225–262.

Stevenson, Rosemary J., Rosalind A. Crawley, & David Kleinman. (1994). Thematic roles, focus and the representation of events. *Language and Cognitive Processes, 9*(4), 519–548.

CHAPTER 3

Cleft Focus and Antecedent Accessibility: The Emergence of the Anti-focus Effect

Clare Patterson and Claudia Felser

1   Introduction

The resolution of personal pronouns such as *she, they* or *her* is a crucial task in discourse interpretation. These pronouns can refer to discourse entities that were mentioned or introduced in the same discourse unit, or they can refer to entities that were mentioned one or more sentences previously. The task of identifying the correct antecedent for a pronoun is a complex one that is influenced by a variety of linguistic and non-linguistic factors. It is generally assumed that personal pronouns refer to entities which are salient in the discourse; we refer to this notion of discourse salience as accessibility.[1]

The importance of the notion of accessibility for pronoun resolution is due to the psycholinguistic mechanisms which support this process. It is commonly assumed, particularly in the psycholinguistics literature, that pronoun resolution is a memory retrieval process that operates over a mental representation of the discourse. On this view, as we read or listen to a text we build up mental representations of entities (such as people, objects and places) and events in the discourse. When a pronoun is encountered, a link must be made between the pronoun and a previously mentioned entity: this involves a retrieval process from memory. Those entities which are highly activated in memory, for instance because they have been mentioned multiple times, will be more easily retrieved than entities with a lower activation. Researchers have tended to equate the easy retrieval of a highly activated entity with higher accessibility for pronoun resolution.

While much research has been devoted to identifying factors that make a particular discourse entity more accessible than others, somewhat less attention has been paid to the span over which these factors operate; indeed, it has often been assumed that they operate in the same manner regardless of

---

[1] The terms *prominence, salience* and *accessibility* have been used somewhat interchangeably in relation to pronoun resolution. A detailed discussion of these terms is beyond the scope of this chapter; see von Heusinger and Schumacher (2019).

whether pronoun resolution takes place within or between sentences or discourse units. More recently there have been efforts to arrive at a more precise understanding of the contribution of various factors based on their linguistic function, how they interact with discourse units, and how this may differ across languages (e.g. Portele & Bader, this volume): in particular, the influence of information-structural factors such as *focus* and *topic* on pronoun resolution has come under new scrutiny in a set of studies that are discussed below. Emerging from these studies is the notion that the discourse unit (e.g. Grosz & Sidner, 1986; Polanyi, 1988; Degand & Simon, 2009), henceforth DU, is the core unit of interest in considering how certain factors affect antecedent accessibility, and that it is important to consider the discourse function of focus and topic in order to understand their contribution to accessibility within and between DUs.

The present study examines how focus affects antecedent accessibility within the DU, providing evidence about how pronoun interpretation preferences emerge during comprehension. We build on and extend previous research by examining how focus contributes to antecedent accessibility over time during processing, tackling an inherent puzzle in the existing literature. In the following section we review previous psycholinguistic work on the role of focus in pronoun resolution, and the subsequent section discusses recent work on how focus affects antecedent accessibility within the DU. The final section of the introduction highlights the puzzle inherent in bringing together these seemingly contradictory findings and sets the context for our own experiments.

1.1 *Focus in Pronoun Resolution*

Focus is an important information-structural notion. The function of focus is said to be presenting new or important information about a topic (Halliday, 1967) although more recently researchers have emphasized its role in indicating the presence of relevant alternatives (Krifka, 2008). There are several ways in which focus is instantiated across languages (see Zimmermann & Onea, 2011, for a review), although in this study we are specifically concerned with clefts and focus-sensitive particles (henceforth, particles), both of which can instantiate focus in German. See (1a–f) for examples in English and German.

(1) a. Sina presented the results.
  b. Sina hat die Ergebnisse vorgestellt.
  c. It was Sina who presented the results.
  d. Es war Sina, die die Ergebnisse vorgestellt hat.
  e. Only Sina presented the results.
  f. Nur Sina hat die Ergebnisse vorgestellt.

Examples (1a,b) are canonically ordered sentences without any syntactic focus device. The same information is presented in (1c,d), but in these examples the proper name *Sina* appears in the focus of an *it*-cleft. *It*-clefts comprise an expletive pronoun, the copula verb *to be*, and the cleft focus (*Sina* in these examples); the clefted constituent is modified by a relative clause. Although the truth conditions of (1a,b) and (1c,d) are the same, the cleft in (1c,d) conveys some additional information. Lambrecht (2001) described this as including (i) a presupposition/background, (ii) a focus, and (iii) an assertion. The presupposition/background is that someone presented the results, the focus is *Sina* and the assertion is that the person in focus (*Sina*) is the person who presented the results (out of a range of alternatives). A similar meaning is conveyed using a particle as in (1e,f). Here, the presupposition/background is the same as in (1c,d), but the assertion depends on the semantics of the individual particle; *only* (*nur* in German) excludes any possible alternatives, making the truth conditions of (1e,f) slightly different from those of (1a,b). Placing the particle in initial position unambiguously associates the particle with the following noun in both German and English.

There is a large body of psycholinguistic work on the effects of focus on memory for linguistic material; this has largely made use of cleft structures in English. The main finding is that there is a memory advantage for information that is presented in focus. While a detailed review is outside the scope of this chapter, much of the literature covers the retrieval of individual words. Singer (1976), for example, demonstrated that focused information is better retained in memory than non-focused information, and Birch & Garnsey (1995) showed that clefted nouns are recognized and named faster and more accurately than non-clefted nouns. The identification of factual errors is higher when the critical information is presented in focus (e.g. Langford & Holmes, 1979; Bredart & Modolo, 1988). The processing mechanism by which the memory advantage arises has also been investigated. Birch and Rayner (1997) demonstrated that readers take longer to read material in cleft phrases such as *There was this ...* and *It was the ...* compared to matched non-clefted counterparts. They proposed that the memory advantage for material in focus may arise from a deeper encoding of focused information, which makes it easier to re-access it later on. These studies are limited in that they have mainly looked at English and have not extensively tested all types of focus.

An advantage for focused information has also been demonstrated in the realm of pronoun resolution. Since pronoun resolution usually involves linking a semantically underspecified (anaphoric) element to earlier linguistic material or prior elements in a discourse structure, something that is recalled more easily or more accurately should have an effect on this process. And indeed, this has been the main finding with respect to pronoun resolution with focused antecedents: Focus has been shown to enhance the availability of an antecedent for coreference construal. Foraker and McElree (2007), using eye-movement monitoring during reading, found that there was a reading-time advantage at the point of the pronoun when the pronoun matched the clefted NP such as *the cheerful waitress* in (2a) below, compared to when the pronoun matched a non-focused NP as in (2b) (examples from Foraker & McElree, 2007, p. 367).

(2) a. It was the cheerful waitress who made the decaffeinated coffee. Reassuringly, she gossiped behind the counter of the diner.
b. What the cheerful waitress made was the decaffeinated coffee. Reassuringly, she gossiped behind the counter of the diner.

Effects of cleft-focusing were restricted to later eye-movement measures, however, leading the authors to conclude that the stronger memory representations of focused compared to non-focused antecedents aid their integration into the emerging discourse model.

Cowles, Walenski and Kluender (2007) tested the effects of topicalization and focusing on pronoun resolution in a cross-modal priming task. They presented auditory stimuli sentences that contained a pronoun and were preceded by context sentences containing both a prominent and a non-prominent potential antecedent. Prominent antecedents were either the discourse topic, the sentence topic or in cleft focus. At the point of hearing the pronoun in the critical sentence, participants saw either the prominent name or the non-prominent name on screen and had to read the name aloud. Naming time was measured as a means for gauging the relative amount of activation for prominent versus non-prominent names. Cowles et al. (2007) found that naming time for prominent antecedents was faster than for non-prominent ones, regardless of whether the prominent antecedent served as the discourse topic, the sentence topic or was in focus. This indicates that the factors of discourse topic, sentence topic and focus all enhance an antecedent's accessibility. The effect for focus was limited to conditions in which the intonation on the focused element had a contrastive pitch accent. It is notable that both topichood and focus gave rise to similar effects on pronoun resolution, despite the fact that their discourse function is very different. Arnold (1999) and Kaiser (2011) also found similar enhancing effects on accessibility when the antecedent was either a topic or in focus. In sum, until recently, it was assumed that focus, along with other information-structural factors such as topichood, made a potential antecedent more accessible for pronoun resolution. The mechanism by which this enhancement comes about may be connected to stronger memory encoding, and correspondingly easier memory retrieval, for these antecedents.

1.2 *Pronoun Resolution within Discourse Units*

An important limitation of the prior research on focus in pronoun resolution was that in all studies, the pronoun appeared in a subsequent DU. This means that potential effects of focus on within-unit pronoun resolution were not examined. While most psycholinguistic approaches to pronoun resolution assume that the influence of any particular factor on antecedent accessibility is the same both within and between DUs, this assumption has been challenged by a recent set of studies (Colonna, Schimke, & Hemforth, 2012, 2015; de la Fuente & Hemforth, 2013; de la Fuente, 2015). The initial study (Colonna et al., 2012) looked at the influence of both topic and focus devices on pronoun resolution within the DU. We concentrate here on the results for focus. Using materials such as the German examples in (3) below in an antecedent selection task, Colonna et al. examined the effect that focus has on within-sentence pronoun resolution in both French and German.

(3) a. *Baseline*
Peter hat Hans geohrfeigt, als er jung war.
'Peter slapped Hans when he was young.'
b. *Focused subject*
Es ist Peter, der Hans geohrfeigt hat, als er jung war.
'It is Peter who slapped Hans when he was young.'
c. *Focused object*
Es ist Peter, den Hans geohrfeigt hat, als er jung war.
'It is Peter who Hans slapped when he was young.'

For German, they found that putting the subject in focus (3b) numerically (albeit not reliably) decreased the likelihood that it would be chosen as an antecedent, compared to the baseline condition (3a). When the object was in focus (3c), the likelihood of choosing it as the antecedent reliably decreased. For French, the findings were similar, with statistically robust differences when the focus conditions were compared to the topic conditions: focus significantly decreased the likelihood of antecedent choices while topichood enhanced the likelihood of antecedent choices. The reduction of accessibility for an antecedent that appears in focus has come to be known as the anti-focus effect. Note that the anti-focus effect stands in stark contrast with prior findings about focus in two important ways: Focus was previously found to increase the accessibility of a referent rather than to reduce it, and prior research mainly found similar effects of topichood and focus on pronoun resolution (such that both increase accessibility). The anti-focus effect observed by Colonna et al. (2012) goes in the opposite direction when compared to the effect of explicit topicalization, however.

While the statistical basis for the anti-focus effect was not very robust in Colonna et al. (2012), subsequent studies have provided further and more reliable evidence for the anti-focus effect. De la Fuente and Hemforth (2013) found a significant anti-focus effect for null pronouns in Spanish for both subject and object clefts, and also a significant effect for object clefts with clitic pronouns. Furthermore, the accessibility of antecedents in cleft focus was significantly lower compared to antecedents that had undergone left-dislocation (topicalization), similar to the findings reported by Colonna et al. (2012). De la Fuente (2015) also found robust anti-focus effects in a series of questionnaire studies in Spanish and English. Both clefts and particles gave rise to the anti-focus effect in these experiments. Finally, Patterson, Esaulova and Felser (2017) found significant anti-focus effects in German and Russian for subject clefts, although the results for particles were not statistically robust. Taken together, results from these studies represent a compelling body of evidence that putting an antecedent in focus decreases the accessibility of that antecedent for subsequent pronoun resolution, when the pronoun appears in the same DU as the antecedent. This contrasts strongly with the enhancement in accessibility that comes from topicalization, and the enhancement in accessibility that arises for focus when the pronoun appears in the subsequent DU.

1.2.1   Why Does Focus Reduce Accessibility?
To understand the anti-focus effect, Colonna et al. (2012) point to the function of focus and highlight the importance of topichood to pronoun resolution. In a cleft sentence such as *It is Peter who slapped Hans when he was young*, the given or presupposed part of the sentence is that somebody slapped Hans, while the focus of the sentence is Peter and the new information is that somebody equals Peter. Having Peter in focus, then, makes Hans part of the given, discourse old information, which increases the topic-like status of Hans (in comparison to the baseline condition (3a), where both Peter and Hans could be assumed to be either discourse-old or discourse-new). Recall that topichood plays an important role in enhancing the accessibility of an antecedent for pronoun resolution. Colonna et al. (2015) point out that the role of focus in presenting new or unexpected information works against the preference for pronouns to refer to more topic-like (discourse-old) antecedents, thus decreasing the accessibility of antecedents that are in focus. Clefting therefore changes the balance

of antecedent choices in comparison to a baseline condition by rendering the non-clefted antecedent more topic-like, and hence preferable.

Colonna et al. (2015) also propose that the difference between the anti-focus effect and the findings in the majority of previous studies, where focus was found to enhance the accessibility of an antecedent when the pronoun appeared in a subsequent DU, lies in the additional function of focus as a signal of an upcoming topic shift. Within the current DU the topic shift has not yet taken place, so the accessibility of the focused antecedent remains low. As a previously focused constituent is a possible topic of the subsequent sentence, and linking to it would help establish discourse coherence, the focused antecedent from the previous DU will become more accessible for a pronoun occurring in the following DU.

1.2.2 Sentence or Discourse Unit?

The crucial distinction between focus reducing accessibility and focus enhancing accessibility seems to hinge on whether the pronoun appears in the same DU as the antecedent, or whether it appears in the following DU. It should be noted that the experimental evidence discussed above cannot distinguish between sentences and DUs as the appropriate domain for pronoun resolution. In studies finding enhanced accessibility, pronouns appeared in a subsequent DU but also in a new sentence, and in studies showing the anti-focus effect, the pronoun was in the same DU but also in the same sentence. De la Fuente (2015) carefully argues for the DU being the appropriate domain over which pronoun resolution should be measured, based on his definition of a discourse unit. Below, we outline the main argumentation in favor of his new DU definition.[2]

Previous literature has not come to a consensus on the definition of a discourse unit. The main proposals relating DUs to pronoun resolution have been to equate the discourse unit either to a sentence or to a clause. However, de la Fuente (2015) argues that these definitions are unsatisfactory because they fail to capture important facts about pronoun resolution (see de la Fuente, 2015, pp. 79–82 for elaboration).

Instead, he proposes a new definition that does not tie the DU to a particular syntactic constituent, but depends instead on semantic criteria. His proposal

---

[2] It was not the main purpose of the current study to test the validity of de la Fuente's (2015) DU definition; to do so, independent evidence coming from other sources than pronoun resolution would have to be sought. However, de la Fuente's proposals form the framework from which we derive our understanding of focus and pronoun resolution, and it is therefore important to outline it here.

is based on Johnston's (1994) analysis of adjuncts, focusing on the difference between temporal and causal adjuncts. Both of these adjuncts are a type of adverbial clause, whose function is to supply additional information about the proposition or event in the matrix clause. Temporal clauses can provide a temporal frame for the proposition in the matrix clause, or they can describe an event with a new reference time that precedes the event in the matrix clause. Causal clauses describe events or contain propositions that are the cause of the event/proposition in the matrix clause. It has been observed that causal and temporal adjuncts differ in their syntactic behavior (for example, causal clauses but not temporal clauses can undergo Embedded Root Transformations) and their pragmatics (causal clauses merely assert content while temporal clauses presuppose content in the matrix clause). Johnston (1994) proposes that such differences between temporal and causal clauses is based on them belonging to distinct semantic classes of adverbial adjuncts, relational and non-relational, based on their interaction with negation and with adverbs of quantification. Causal clauses are classified as relational because they "introduce [higher-order] relations in the semantics which take the semantic contributions of the head and the adjunct clauses as arguments" (Johnston, 1994, p. 149). Temporal clauses, in Johnston's analysis, are non-relational adjuncts because they do not introduce higher-order relations. Instead they restrict an overt or implicit adverb of quantification, for example, in *Jean (always) buys oranges when she goes shopping*, the temporal clause restricts the adverb *always* to particular times (i.e. *when Jean goes shopping*).

De la Fuente (2015) claims that the semantic difference between relational and non-relational adjuncts, which has consequences at both the syntactic and pragmatic levels, also affects the construction of DUs. Non-relational temporal clauses form part of the same DU as the matrix clause, whilst relational causal clauses, which introduce higher-order relations, form a separate DU from the matrix clause.

This new DU definition is supported by pronoun resolution findings. De la Fuente (2015) presents several experiments in which within-sentence pronoun resolution preferences change when the relation between the matrix and subordinate clause changes between relational and non-relational. Importantly for the current study, the new DU definition accounts for the findings on focus: the anti-focus effect is observed when the pronoun appears in the same DU as the antecedent. This was the case for the materials in Colonna et al. (2012), de la Fuente and Hemforth (2013), and Colonna et al. (2015). When the pronoun appears in the subsequent DU, focus enhances accessibility.

The materials in Patterson et al. (2017) and in the current study contain neither temporal nor causal clauses. In the current study, as in Patterson et al.

(2017), we use sentences whose sub-clauses were introduced by the declarative complementizer *dass* ('that'). Under Johnston's (1994) analysis, clausal complements of this type count as non-relational. This means that, under de la Fuente's definition, the complement clause does not constitute a new DU, but both the matrix and complement clause form part of the same DU. Thus, we should find with the current materials that the anti-focus effect comes into play. This was the case in Patterson et al. (2017).

1.3 The Current Study

Thus far, nearly all the evidence for the anti-focus effect comes from offline questionnaires. There are only two studies which have investigated it using processing tasks. Colonna et al. (2015) used the visual-world paradigm to directly compare effects of focus within and between DUs. While they confirmed the anti-focus effect within DUs, their analysis relies on the comparison between single and multiple DUs. Looking at the anti-focus effect only within DUs, the effects were not significant. An earlier study on the effect of focus on children's pronoun resolution (Järvikivi et al., 2014) did not find any significant effects of focus in the adult control group, and a re-analysis of the eye-movement data revealed a fleeting enhancement in accessibility for the antecedent in focus in a late time window.

While processing evidence for the anti-focus effect is minimal, evidence for the enhancement in accessibility of focused antecedents between DUs is very robust, as is the evidence that focus has an enhancing effect on memory. This contrast leaves a puzzle with regard to the processing of focus within the DU. If there is a memory-retrieval advantage for elements in focus, this works against the anti-focus effect, in which focused antecedents are less accessible. Do the retrieval advantage and the anti-focus effect compete within the DU? Or can the two processes be separated in their time-course? The broader question is to what extent memory retrieval and accessibility for pronoun resolution are intertwined. The current study seeks to answer the following question: What is the time-course of accessibility for antecedents in focus within the DU? We report an eye-movement monitoring experiment and a complementary offline judgement experiment which explore this question.

If focusing an antecedent makes it easier to retrieve from memory by boosting its activation in the discourse representation (see Introduction), we might expect antecedents in focus to be easier to link to (compared to non-focused antecedents) when a pronoun is first encountered, as a result of an automatic retrieval advantage. Conversely the anti-focus effect, as discussed above, relies on information-structural cues such as the placement of the current DU within the larger discourse (for instance, deciding whether an entity is discourse old or discourse new), and the computation of discourse instructions associated with focus, such as the expectation of a topic shift. As such, the computation of the anti-focus effect is likely to arise after processing the whole DU. If this line of reasoning is correct, within the DU, the processing of a pronoun may involve an advantage for focused antecedents in early processing measures (enhancement of accessibility from focus) that turns into a disadvantage in later processing measures or in offline measures (computation of the anti-focus effect).

2   Experiment 1

Experiment 1 was an eye-movement-monitoring-during-reading experiment, in which the time course of the accessibility for antecedents in focus was tested.

2.1   *Method*

2.1.1   Materials

24 experimental items were constructed. These were two-sentence mini stories, with a lead-in sentence to set up a context and a critical sentence which contained the focus manipulation, two potential antecedents and one pronoun. We used masculine singular nominative pronouns (*er* 'he') throughout because these forms are morphosyntactically unambiguous. The pronoun always functioned as the subject of a sentence-final complement clause introduced by the complementizer *dass* ('that'). The first NP was always a subject and the second NP always an indirect object.

Each item appeared in six experimental conditions, illustrated in (4) below. Two factors were manipulated: focus type (baseline, cleft, particle) and the pronoun's antecedent (NP1, NP2). The antecedent for the pronoun was manipulated using gender match between the pronoun and the relevant antecedent. In the NP1 conditions, the pronoun matched in gender with the first NP, and in the NP2 conditions with the second NP. The focus status of NP1 was manipulated such that the baseline condition contained no focus device, in the cleft condition NP1 appeared in a syntactic *it*-cleft, and in the particle condition NP1 was put into focus by appearing with a focus particle. There were always four words following the pronoun.

(4) Lead in: Für die folgende Woche war eine Klassenfahrt geplant.
    'A class trip was planned for the following week.'
 a. *Baseline, NP1 reference*
    Herr Müller erklärte der Lehrerin am Freitag, dass er sicherlich nicht mitfahren könne.

'Mr Müller explained to the teacher (fem.) on Friday that he certainly could not come along.'

b. *Baseline, NP2 reference*
Frau Müller erklärte dem Lehrer am Freitag, dass er sicherlich nicht mitfahren könne.
'Mrs Müller explained to the teacher (masc.) on Friday that he certainly could not come along.'

c. *Cleft, NP1 reference*
Es war Herr Müller, der der Lehrerin am Freitag erklärte, dass er sicherlich nicht mitfahren könne.
'It was Mr Müller who explained to the teacher (fem.) on Friday that he certainly could not come along.'

d. *Cleft, NP2 reference*
Es war Frau Müller, die dem Lehrer am Freitag erklärte, dass er sicherlich nicht mitfahren könne.
'It was Mrs Müller who explained to the teacher (masc.) on Friday that he certainly could not come along.'

e. *Particle, NP1 reference*
Ausgerechnet Herr Müller erklärte der Lehrerin am Freitag, dass er sicherlich nicht mitfahren könne.
'Of all people Mr Müller explained to the teacher (fem.) on Friday that he certainly could not come along.'

f. *Particle, NP2 reference*
Ausgerechnet Frau Müller erklärte dem Lehrer am Freitag, dass er sicherlich nicht mitfahren könne.
'Of all people Mrs Müller explained to the teacher (masc.) on Friday that he certainly could not come along.'

The experimental items were mixed with 92 filler items and arranged over six lists in a Latin-square design. There were 18 pseudo-fillers, which resembled the 24 experimental items in syntactic structure, containing the pronoun *sie* ('she/they') to balance out the appearance of masculine pronouns in the experimental materials and to ensure that the pronoun's gender could not be predicted in advance. A further 40 filler items contained pronouns of various types. After 48% of the trials, a yes/no comprehension question appeared. This was to ensure that participants were reading carefully and paying attention to the contents of the sentences. For the experimental items, 42% of the questions probed the referent of the pronouns. Overall in the experiment 13% of trials probed the referent of a pronoun.

2.1.2 Participants

36 native speakers of German (9 male) were tested. Their mean age was 25 years (range 18–40 years). All had normal or corrected-to-normal eyesight. Participants were recruited from the University of Potsdam and from student populations in the Berlin area. All gave their consent to participate and were paid 8 Euros for their participation or given course credit. One participant was removed from the analysis due to excessive track loss.

2.1.3 Procedure

In Experiment 1 the Eyelink 1000, Desktop Mount (SR Research, Canada) was used to display the texts and record the eye-movement data. Experiments 1 and 2 were run in the same experimental session, which took approximately 40–50 minutes. Experiment 1 was always carried out before Experiment 2. After a calibration and five practice trials, participants read the items/fillers silently at their own rate. Between each trial there was a drift correct screen. Participants pressed a button to move to the next item and answered comprehension questions using a PC gamepad. Texts were displayed in Courier New font in black text against a white background. The first line of text always contained the lead-in sentence. The two potential antecedents always appeared on the second line of text and the pronoun on the third line of text.

Experiments 1 and 2 were approved by the ethics committee of the University of Potsdam (application number 37/2011).

2.1.4 Data Preparation

Each experimental trial was checked for drift. Vertical drift correction was carried out manually where necessary. Individual fixations longer than 1000ms were deleted. Fixations shorter than 80ms were merged with a nearby fixation within one degree of visual angle; otherwise fixations shorter than 80ms were deleted. Fixations that fell outside of the interest areas were deleted.

The regions of interest were the critical region, made up of the complementizer *dass* ('that') and the pronoun *er* ('he'), the spillover region (comprising the two words following the critical region), and the final region, which contained the last two words of the sentence (usually a participle and an auxiliary verb). These regions were identical across all conditions within the same item.

Within each trial, regions that were skipped in first-pass reading were removed from the analysis. Skipping rates for the regions of interest were as follows: critical region, 22%; spillover region, 6%; final region, 2%. The high skipping rate in the critical region was likely due to the fact that it appeared at the beginning of the line, leading to some landing inaccuracies.

From the fixation data five eye-tracking measures were calculated: first-fixation time, which is the duration of the first fixation in a given region; first-pass time, which is the sum of durations in a given region before the eye exits to the left or right; regression-path times, which is the sum of durations starting when the eye enters a region and finishing when the eye leaves the region to the right (i.e. to read subsequent material); rereading times, which is the sum of durations in a region after the first-pass time (when no rereading took place, data were counted as missing); and total viewing times, which is the sum of all fixation durations in a given region.

2.1.5   Data Analysis

The reading measures were analyzed in a series of linear mixed-effects models (one per region/measure) using the package lmerTest version 2.0–33 (Kuznetsova et al., 2016) in the R statistical program (R Core Team, 2017). Before submitting them to the model the data were transformed. The transformation was determined with the Box-Cox procedure (Box & Cox, 1964) using recommendations from Osborne (2010). The fixed part of the model contained the sum-coded factors ANTECEDENT (NP1, NP2) and FOCUS TYPE (baseline, cleft, particle) and the (centered) factor trial number, as well as the interactions between these factors. The factor FOCUS TYPE was releveled and the model re-run in order to obtain model estimates for the third level. The random part of the model contained random intercepts for participant and item. The inclusion of by-item and by-participant random slopes for ANTECEDENT and FOCUS TYPE were determined using the function rePCA from the package RePsychLing (Baayen et al., 2015).

The model outputs were interpreted as follows. A main effect of ANTECEDENT (two levels) indicates that the NP1 and NP2 conditions differ, regardless of FOCUS TYPE. The direction of the difference is stated in the results section. For FOCUS TYPE (three levels), the model output gives two estimates and coefficients, which correspond to a difference between one level of the factor and the grand mean; for example, an effect of FOCUS TYPE at the level baseline indicates that the baseline conditions (regardless of ANTECEDENT) differ from the cleft and particle conditions. Interactions between ANTECEDENT and FOCUS TYPE are crucial to our predictions: these interactions are given in the model at each level of the FOCUS TYPE factor, rather than a single overall interaction value (as is standard in ANOVA). An interaction at the level of cleft, for example, indicates that the cleft NP1 condition differs from the cleft NP2 condition. The direction of the effect is reported below.

2.2 Predictions

If the focus devices (clefts and particles) make the NP in focus easier to retrieve from memory, then the NP1 coreference conditions will show less initial processing difficulty than the NP2 coreference conditions in the focus conditions but not in the baseline condition. This should be seen in earlier eye-movement measures such as first-fixation duration and first-pass times at the levels cleft and particle (NP1 < NP2).

Following this initial stage, the rest of the critical sentence is encountered which enables the full generation of pragmatic inferences about the focused antecedents to take place, and which also gives time for information-structural cues to be determined. As such, there should be more difficulty with NP1 coreference in the cleft and particle conditions (NP1 > NP2) in later measures such as regression-path times and rereading times or the cumulative measure (total viewing times), in line with the anti-focus effect shown in previous offline judgement studies.

2.3 Results

All participants scored above 75% on the comprehension question accuracy overall. Mean accuracy was 90% (SD: 5), range 78%–98%. The eye-movement results are presented in three sections: early measures, regression-path times, and late/cumulative measures.

2.3.1 Early Measures

The mean first-fixation times and first-pass times (with standard deviations) per condition in the three regions are shown in Table 3.1 below.

First-fixation times and first-pass times in the critical region show no large differences across conditions.

First-fixation times and first-pass times in the spillover region are shown in Figures 3.1 and 3.2.

In the spillover region the first-fixation times are longest in the baseline conditions ($t = 2.38$, $p = 0.02$), and marginally shortest in the particle conditions ($t = -1.96$, $p = 0.05$). In the cleft conditions there is an advantage for the cleft NP1 condition compared to cleft NP2 ($t = -2.21$, $p = 0.03$). There is a non-significant trend for the first-pass times in the spillover region to be longer in the baseline conditions compared to the other conditions ($t = 1.65$, $p = 0.10$).

In the final region there are no differences in the first-fixation times. First-pass times are shown in Figure 3.3.

In the final region the particle conditions have marginally shorter first-pass times than the cleft and baseline conditions ($t = -1.85$, $p = 0.06$). There is an advantage for the cleft NP1 condition compared to the cleft NP2 condition ($t = -2.02$, $p = 0.04$).

TABLE 3.1 Mean first-fixation times and first-pass times in milliseconds per condition in the critical, spillover and final regions for Experiment 1. Standard deviations are shown in parentheses.

Region of interest	Condition	First-fixation time	First-pass time
Critical	Baseline, NP1	198 (47)	273 (128)
	Baseline, NP2	205 (56)	277 (131)
	Cleft, NP1	202 (60)	282 (128)
	Cleft, NP2	210 (66)	265 (121)
	Particle, NP1	207 (53)	258 (124)
	Particle, NP2	205 (50)	274 (128)
Spillover	Baseline, NP1	220 (71)	387 (234)
	Baseline, NP2	212 (61)	368 (192)
	Cleft, NP1	202 (58)	345 (200)
	Cleft, NP2	213 (67)	356 (186)
	Particle, NP1	209 (66)	351 (192)
	Particle, NP2	199 (50)	345 (170)
Final	Baseline, NP1	240 (82)	599 (375)
	Baseline, NP2	263 (105)	553 (324)
	Cleft, NP1	244 (83)	533 (308)
	Cleft, NP2	247 (84)	589 (348)
	Particle, NP1	251 (82)	537 (321)
	Particle, NP2	246 (76)	512 (289)

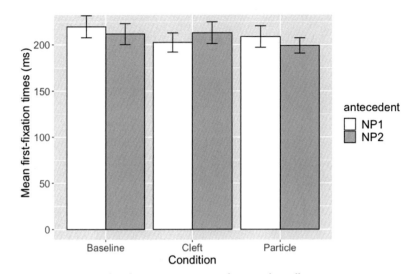

FIGURE 3.1 Mean first-fixation times per condition in the spillover region, Experiment 1. Error bars show 95% confidence intervals, adjusted for within-subject designs as per Morey (2008).

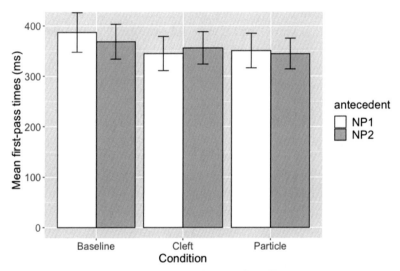

FIGURE 3.2 Mean first-pass times per condition in the spillover region, Experiment 1. Error bars show 95% confidence intervals, adjusted for within-subject designs as per Morey (2008).

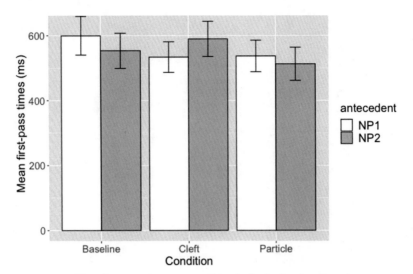

FIGURE 3.3 Mean first-pass times per condition in the final region, Experiment 1. Error bars show 95% confidence intervals, adjusted for within-subject designs as per Morey (2008).

2.3.2 Regression-Path

The mean regression-path times (with standard deviations) per condition in the three regions are shown in Table 3.2 below.

Regression-path times in the critical region show no significant differences. Regression-path times for the spillover region are shown in Figure 3.4 and those for the final region in Figure 3.5.

Regression-path times in the spillover region show an advantage for the cleft NP1 condition compared to the cleft NP2 condition ($t = -2.06$, $p = 0.045$).

In the final region there is a marginal main effect of ANTECEDENT, with lower regression-path times for the NP1 ($t = -1.73$, $p = 0.09$). The main effect is qualified by an interaction with FOCUS TYPE, with an advantage for the NP1 condition in the cleft conditions ($t = -2.13$, $p = 0.03$), and a disadvantage for the NP1 in the baseline conditions ($t = 2.30$, $p = 0.02$).

TABLE 3.2 Mean regression-path times in milliseconds per condition in the critical, spillover and final regions for Experiment 1. Standard deviations are shown in parentheses.

Region of interest	Condition	Regression-path time
Critical	Baseline, NP1	282 (152)
	Baseline, NP2	279 (131)
	Cleft, NP1	289 (161)
	Cleft, NP2	265 (121)
	Particle, NP1	269 (154)
	Particle, NP2	274 (128)
Spillover	Baseline, NP1	469 (271)
	Baseline, NP2	468 (297)
	Cleft, NP1	436 (283)
	Cleft, NP2	509 (401)
	Particle, NP1	475 (394)
	Particle, NP2	444 (371)
Final	Baseline, NP1	1559 (1304)
	Baseline, NP2	1513 (1441)
	Cleft, NP1	1299 (1135)
	Cleft, NP2	1689 (1658)
	Particle, NP1	1473 (1263)
	Particle, NP2	1698 (1402)

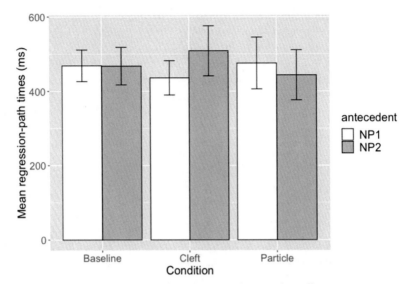

FIGURE 3.4 Mean regression-path times per condition in the spillover region, Experiment 1. Error bars show 95% confidence intervals, adjusted for within-subject designs as per Morey (2008).

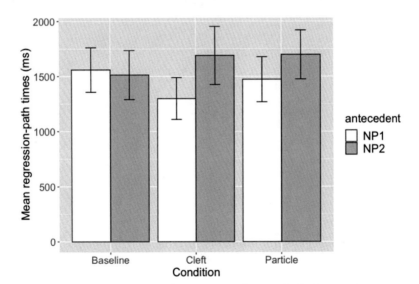

FIGURE 3.5 Mean regression-path times per condition in the final region, Experiment 1. Error bars show 95% confidence intervals, adjusted for within-subject designs as per Morey (2008).

TABLE 3.3 Mean rereading and total viewing times in milliseconds per condition in the critical, spillover and final regions for Experiment 1. Standard deviations are shown in parentheses.

Region of interest	Condition	Rereading time	Total viewing time
Critical	Baseline, NP1	301 (184)	345 (202)
	Baseline, NP2	286 (142)	341 (185)
	Cleft, NP1	275 (84)	339 (193)
	Cleft, NP2	275 (157)	331 (199)
	Particle, NP1	245 (101)	309 (172)
	Particle, NP2	294 (159)	350 (213)
Spillover	Baseline, NP1	437 (319)	542 (336)
	Baseline, NP2	440 (351)	505 (324)
	Cleft, NP1	370 (231)	490 (276)
	Cleft, NP2	448 (290)	537 (324)
	Particle, NP1	389 (253)	482 (264)
	Particle, NP2	364 (241)	474 (272)
Final	Baseline, NP1	451 (287)	697 (414)
	Baseline, NP2	426 (399)	662 (374)
	Cleft, NP1	457 (296)	645 (337)
	Cleft, NP2	432 (264)	688 (385)
	Particle, NP1	425 (268)	647 (376)
	Particle, NP2	484 (351)	640 (365)

2.3.3 Late/Cumulative Measures

The mean rereading and total viewing times (with standard deviations) per condition in the three regions are shown in Table 3.3 above. Rereading times in the critical region are shown in Figure 3.6.

In the critical region rereading times there is a marginal advantage for NP2 compared to NP1 in the cleft conditions ($t = -1.84$, $p = 0.07$), and a significant advantage for NP1 compared to NP2 in the particle conditions ($t = 2.23$, $p = 0.03$).[3] There were no significant effects in the total viewing times. In the spillover region rereading times, there is a marginal effect of FOCUS TYPE, with particle conditions having marginally shorter rereading times than the

---

[3] Note that the direction of the *t*-values for the rereading times in the critical region goes in the opposite direction to previous effects: this is because the data transformation (see Data Analysis section) was a reciprocal (inverse) transformation.

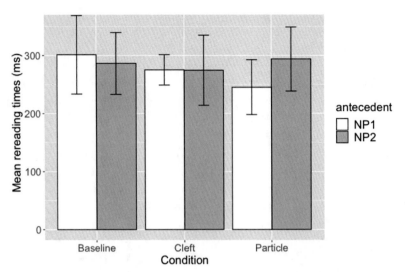

FIGURE 3.6 Mean rereading times per condition in the critical region, Experiment 1. Error bars show 95% confidence intervals, adjusted for within-subject designs as per Morey (2008).

cleft and baseline conditions (t = -1.69, p = 0.09), but no interactions with ANTECEDENT. There were no effects in the total viewing times in this region. There were no significant differences in the rereading times or the total-viewing times in the final region.

2.3.4 Summary

Whilst there were no effects in the earlier measures in the critical region, there was a significant advantage for the cleft NP1 compared to cleft NP2 condition in first-fixation durations and regression-path times at the spillover region. The same pattern was seen for the two cleft conditions in first-pass times at the final sentence region. No corresponding advantages were observed for NPs that were put into focus via the addition of a particle, though. It was only the rereading times in the critical region that showed a different pattern. Here, there was a marginal advantage for the cleft NP2 condition over the cleft NP1 condition. These results are discussed in the general discussion section, following the presentation of Experiment 2.

3 Experiment 2

Experiment 2 was an offline acceptability judgment questionnaire, in which participants' preferences for pronoun resolution involving focus devices were tested.

3.1 Method

3.1.1 Materials

The 24 experimental items were taken from Experiment 1, in all six conditions. These items were mixed with eight fillers (a subset of those appearing in Experiment 1 which were adapted as described below) and distributed over six lists in a Latin-square design. The list distribution was kept the same as in Experiment 1, so that participants were shown exactly the same experimental items that they saw in Experiment 1.

The fillers were adapted such that four of them contained a pronoun and a matching antecedent which was felicitous. Four of the fillers contained a pronoun with no felicitous antecedent. This was to ensure that participants used both ends of the judgment scale over the course of the experiment.

3.1.2 Participants

All the participants from Experiment 1 participated in Experiment 2. The participant who was excluded from the analysis in Experiment 1 was also excluded from Experiment 2.

3.1.3 Procedure

After completion of Experiment 1, participants were given a short break and then carried out Experiment 2. The questionnaires were printed out on paper, which participants filled out by hand. Participants were instructed to evaluate each item on a scale of 1 ('very good') to 7 ('very bad'), based on how the sentence sounded to them. Under each item a numerical scale was shown, with the ends labelled as *sehr gut* ('very good') and *sehr schlecht* ('very bad'). Participants simply had to mark a number on the scale under each item. Participants were not under any time pressure to complete this task.

3.1.4 Data Preparation and Analysis

Scores from 1–7 for each participant and item combination (including fillers) were converted to z-scores, as is generally recommended for judgment data (see Schütze & Sprouse, 2014) to account for participants' variation in the use of the scale. The z-scores were then analyzed in a linear mixed-effects model. The fixed part of the model contained the factors ANTECEDENT (NP1, NP2) and FOCUS TYPE (baseline, cleft, particle) as well as the interaction between them. The random part of the model contained random intercepts for participant and item, and per-item slopes for focus type and antecedent (the maximal model that would converge).

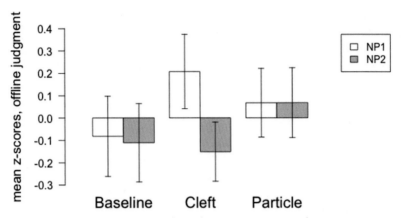

FIGURE 3.7 Mean z-scores per condition for Experiment 2. Note that negative scores, plotted downwards, represent better ratings. Error bars represent +/- 1 standard error.

3.2   Results

The z-scores from Experiment 2 are plotted in Figure 3.7. Note that lower scores, plotted downwards, represent better ratings, since in the original scale 1 was 'very good' and 7 was 'very bad'.

In the baseline and cleft conditions, NP2 coreference is rated as better than NP1 coreference. The particle conditions do not show this difference. Statistically, there was an effect of FOCUS TYPE, with cleft conditions overall being rated as worse than the baseline conditions (t = 2.54, p = 0.01). There was also an interaction with ANTECEDENT for the cleft conditions (t = -2.18, p = 0.03), with the NP2 cleft condition rated significantly better than the NP1 cleft condition. The interaction with ANTECEDENT was not significant for the baseline or particle conditions. These results are discussed below.

4   General Discussion

The results of Experiment 1 showed a processing advantage for sentences containing pronouns that were linked to clefted compared to non-clefted antecedents. This advantage was seen during participants' initial reading of the post-pronoun regions as well as in their regression-path times. Evidence of a reversal of the above pattern was seen only participants' rereading times in the pronoun region, where the cleft NP2 condition elicited marginally shorter reading times than the cleft NP1 condition, but this effect did not reach full significance. No comparable advantages or disadvantages were found for antecedents that were focused using a particle.

The results from Experiment 2 show a different pattern. Here participants rated the cleft sentences as worse than the baseline sentences overall, and in particular they rated cleft sentences in which the pronoun referred to NP1 as worse than sentences in which the pronoun referred to NP2. In the baseline and particle conditions there was no effect of ANTECEDENT. This finding is in line with the predictions of the anti-focus effect (Colonna et al., 2012), as well as aligning with previous offline results for cleft sentences in native speakers of German (Patterson et al., 2017) and with offline results from English and Spanish (de la Fuente & Hemforth, 2013).

How can the differences between the results from our two experiments be explained? The observed online/offline differences indicate that the anti-focus effect emerges during later processing stages. In Experiment 1 the pattern we saw in early reading-time measures fits with the prediction of a retrieval advantage for an antecedent in focus. As discussed in the introduction, many studies have shown that there is a retrieval advantage for material in focus, and this advantage has been attributed to a stronger encoding of this new/unexpected material in memory (Birch & Rayner, 1997; see also Hofmeister, 2011, for a similar retrieval advantage for syntactically complex material, which takes longer to encode). We expected to see such an advantage in fairly early measures such as first-fixation times and first-pass reading times, and indeed this prediction was confirmed in Experiment 1.

The demonstration of a retrieval advantage for material in focus (in the cleft conditions) is important for understanding the processing mechanisms behind the anti-focus effect. Previously, the anti-focus effect has been demonstrated in offline measures such as antecedent choice and acceptability judgement tasks. While this gives us information about the final outcome of the pronoun resolution process and/or participants' evaluation of how felicitous a particular pronoun–antecedent relationship is, it does not reveal the processing involved to reach this point. The results from Experiment 1 show that the opposite effect appears during early processing stages. The initial advantage we saw for antecedents in focus when the pronoun was first encountered, despite the fact that the pronoun and the antecedent appeared in the same discourse unit, demonstrates clearly that the anti-focus effect does not emerge early in processing, and indeed has to overcome a bias in the opposite direction.

What was not predicted was that the retrieval advantage for material in focus would remain visible in slightly later measures, i.e. in the regression-path times. This measure includes the time readers spend revisiting earlier material before moving on to the next region, and normally indicates the early stages of integration. However, while reading measures offer an insight into how processes unfold over time, it is often found that an effect is 'smeared' over several measures or regions (Vasishth, von der Malsburg, & Engelmann, 2013), since there are differences between participants and items in precisely where an effect emerges. And while different measures can broadly be associated with earlier and later processes, the link between particular eye-movement measures and linguistic processes is not yet fully understood. We take the retrieval advantage for clefted antecedents in the regression-path times as confirmation of the effect found in the earlier measures.

An anti-focus effect was observed during participants' rereading of the critical region, but this effect was (i) marginal and (ii) rather fleeting in that it was not visible in any other eye-movement measures or sentence regions. However, the same stimulus materials did show a robust anti-focus effect for clefts in Experiment 2, in line with previous findings.

We further predicted that clefts and particles would have similar effects in Experiment 1, but this prediction was not borne out. This was also the case for Experiment 2, where the cleft conditions showed the anti-focus effect whereas there was no difference for the particle conditions. Particles have not been so extensively tested as clefts in previous work, and where they have been tested, results are not always robust (e.g. Patterson et al., 2017). Also, the semantics of individual particles needs to be taken into account (see the argument in Patterson et al., 2017, p. 20). Note that clefting, but not the mere addition of a prenominal particle, results in a marked or non-canonical global sentence structure. This may lead to constituents in cleft focus being more salient, or more strongly encoded in memory, compared to non-clefted NPs preceded by a particle, which may also make them stronger predictors of an upcoming topic shift.

The strong anti-focus effect seen in Experiment 2 for clefts confirms and extends previous evidence for anti-focus effects within the discourse unit. It also provides further evidence for the role of clause linking for determining discourse units. Clause-linking with the complementizer *dass* ('that'), which we used in the current study as well as in Patterson et al. (2017), does not seem to start a new discourse unit. This is in line with de la Fuente's (2015) analysis and extends evidence beyond temporal connectors of the kind that were mainly used in previous studies. The results from Experiment 1 further extend previous findings by showing that even within the discourse unit, the likelihood of a focused antecedent being considered varies over time.

Why might anti-focus effects emerge only relatively late during comprehension, though? One possibility is that the anti-focus effect is only detectable when participants are asked to engage in explicit reasoning. Recall that there was a clear task difference between Experiment 1 and Experiment 2. In Experiment 1, participants were asked to read sentences for comprehension, and are not asked to provide any judgement or evaluation. This is in contrast with Experiment 2, where participants' task was to evaluate the stimulus sentences explicitly using scalar judgements, even though participants were not asked to concentrate on the pronoun resolution in particular. If the anti-focus effect is indeed restricted to tasks that involve explicit reasoning, either through offline tasks or through the presentation of ambiguous pronouns and simultaneous presentation of pictures (Colonna et al., 2015), which may well encourage participants to consciously engage in the process of pronoun resolution, this would imply that the factor(s) giving rise to the anti-focus effect do not affect normal unconscious processing.

Another possibility is that DUs are not computed until relatively late during comprehension, following the syntactic analysis carried out during first-pass parsing. Incoming strings of words are assigned a phrase-structural representation during incremental processing, with clauses having long been known to be major processing units (e.g. Fodor & Bever, 1965; Fodor, Bever, & Garrett, 1974). Clauses are more basic processing units than DUs: Identifying DUs presupposes the computation of a sentence's clausal structure, but identifying clausal units does not presuppose the computation of DUs. For the processing system to decide whether or not two or more clauses form a DU, more information must accumulate and be integrated at a higher level of processing than is necessary for the identification of clausal units. So if at the point at which a pronoun is first encountered, clause boundaries have been identified whilst DUs have not yet been determined, then a clefted antecedent and a pronoun may be part of different processing units even though they form part of the same DU. At this relatively early stage of real-time comprehension, no anti-focus effect would be expected to be found as its emergence is contingent on the identification of DUs. There may be a general accessibility advantage for clefted antecedents that appear in a previous clause regardless of whether the clauses involved are separated by a sentence boundary. This would explain why the results from our Experiment 1 align with those from previous online experiments where antecedent-pronoun relationships held across sentence boundaries (e.g. Cowles et al., 2007; Foraker & McElree, 2007). Offline tasks, on the other hand, grant participants sufficient time for computing DUs and re-evaluating antecedent salience during second-pass parsing or later comprehension stages in the light of global sentence and discourse-level information.

One important point that our study demonstrates is that it is not always possible to equate easier processing with greater antecedent salience or accessibility, even though this is often an underlying assumption in many real-time pronoun resolution studies. On the one hand, when the pronoun was encountered, the antecedent in focus was retrieved, based on its greater activation in the discourse representation. However, this easily-retrieved entity was not the one that was ultimately preferred as the antecedent for the pronoun. The subsequent consideration of information-structural cues led to the anti-focus effect seen in Experiment 2, making the alternate entity preferred. These two processes (initial retrieval and later integration with the discourse) appear to contribute to the process of pronoun resolution at different points in time or under different conditions. Our results suggest that the likelihood of an antecedent being considered is determined by the interaction over time between early automatic memory search routines and higher-level pragmatic processing which takes into account global information-structural cues. This is reminiscent of two-stage pronoun processing models, which involve an initial bonding stage and a later resolution stage (Garrod & Sanford, 1990; Garrod & Terras, 2000; Rigalleau et al., 2004). Our results suggest that not only does pronoun resolution involve the integration of different types of cues, but that these may unfold at different points in time. Furthermore, the ultimate antecedent for a pronoun may not always be the one that is initially easier to retrieve.

Acknowledgements

This research has been supported by the Deutsche Forschungsgemeinschaft (DFG, German Research Foundation) through grant no. FE 1138/1–1 awarded to CF, by an Alexander-von-Humboldt Professorship to Harald Clahsen (Potsdam Research Institute for Multilingualism), and by the Deutsche Forschungsgemeinschaft (DFG, German Research Foundation), Project-ID 281511265, SFB 1252 "Prominence in Language" in the project C07 "Forward and backward functions of discourse anaphora" at the University of Cologne. Our thanks go to Janna Drummer, Cecilia Puebla, Judith Schlenter, Thea Villinger and Özlem Yetim for their help in preparing materials, running participants and pre-processing the data.

References

Arnold, Jennifer E. (1999). *Marking salience: The similarity of topic and focus.* [Unpublished manuscript, University of Pennsylvania].
Baayen, Harald, David Bates, Reinhold Kliegl, & Shravan Vasishth. (2015). RePsychLing: Data sets from psychology and linguistics experiments. *R Package Version 0.0.4.*
Birch, Stacy L., & Susan M. Garnsey. (1995). The effect of focus on memory for words in sentences. *Journal of Memory and Language, 34*, 232–267.

Birch, Stacy L., & Keith Rayner. (1997). Linguistic focus affects eye movements during reading. *Memory and Cognition, 25,* 653–660.

Box, George E., & David R. Cox. (1964). An analysis of transformations. *Journal of the Royal Statistical Society. Series B (Methodological)*, 211–252.

Bredart, Serge, & Karin Modolo. (1988). Moses strikes again: Focalization effect on a semantic illusion. *Acta Psychologica, 67,* 135–144.

Colonna, Saveria, Sarah Schimke, & Barbara Hemforth. (2012). Information structure effects on anaphora resolution in German and French: A crosslinguistic study of pronoun resolution. *Linguistics, 50,* 991–1013.

Colonna, Saveria, Sarah Schimke, & Barbara Hemforth. (2015). Different effects of focus in intra- and inter-sentential pronoun resolution in German. *Language, Cognition and Neuroscience, 30,* 1306–1325.

Cowles, Heidi W., Matthew Walenski, & Robert Kluender. (2007). Linguistic and cognitive prominence in anaphor resolution: Topic, contrastive focus and pronouns. *Topoi, 26,* 3–18.

de la Fuente, Israel. (2015). *Putting pronoun resolution in context: The role of syntax, semantics, and pragmatics in pronoun interpretation* [Doctoral dissertation, Université Sorbonne-Paris Cité & Université Paris Diderot].

de la Fuente, Israel, & Barbara Hemforth. (2013). Effects of clefting and left-dislocation on subject and object pronoun resolution in Spanish. In J. Cabrelli Amaro, G. Lord, A. de Prada Perez, & J. Elana Aaron (Eds.), *Selected proceedings of the 16th Hispanic Linguistics Symposium* (pp. 27–45). Somerville, MA: Cascadilla Proceedings Project.

Degand, Liesbeth, & Anne-Catherine Simon. (2009). On identifying basic discourse units in speech: Theoretical and empirical issues. *Discours: revue de linguistique, psycholinguistique et informatique, 4.*

Fodor, Jerry A., & Thomas G. Bever. (1965). The psychological reality of linguistic segments. *Journal of Verbal Learning and Verbal Behavior, 4,* 414–420.

Fodor, Jerry A., Thomas G. Bever, & Merrill F. Garrett. (1974). *The psychology of language. An introduction to psycholinguistics and generative grammar.* New York: McGraw-Hill.

Foraker, Stephanie, & Brian McElree. (2007). The role of prominence in pronoun resolution: Active versus passive representations. *Journal of Memory and Language, 56,* 357–383.

Garrod, Simon, & Anthony J. Sanford. (1990). Referential processes in reading: Focusing on roles and individuals. In *Comprehension processes in reading* (pp. 465–485). New Jersey: Lawrence Erlbaum Associates, Inc.

Garrod, Simon, & Melody Terras. (2000). The contribution of lexical and situational knowledge to resolving discourse roles: Bonding and resolution. *Journal of Memory and Language, 42*(4), 526–544.

Grosz, Barbara J., & C.L. Snider. (1986). Attention, intentions, and the structure of discourse. *Computational Linguistics, 12*, 175–204.

Halliday, Michael. (1967). Notes on transitivity and theme in English. Part II. *Journal of Linguistics, 3*, 199–244.

von Heusinger, Klaus, & Petra B. Schumacher. (2019). Discourse prominence: definition and application. *Journal of Pragmatics, 154*, 117–127.

Hofmeister, Philip (2011). Representational complexity and memory retrieval in language comprehension. *Language and Cognitive Processes, 26*, 376–405.

Järvikivi, Juhanni, Pirita Pyykkönen-Klauck, Sarah Schimke, Saveria Colonna, & Barbara Hemforth. (2014). Information structure cues for 4-year-olds and adults: Tracking eye movements to visually presented anaphoric referents. *Language, Cognition and Neuroscience, 29*, 877–892.

Johnston, Michael. (1994). *The syntax and semantics of adverbial adjuncts* [Doctoral dissertation, University of California].

Kaiser, Elsi. (2011). Focusing on pronouns: Consequences of subjecthood, pronominalisation, and contrastive focus. *Language and Cognitive Processes, 26*, 1625–1666.

Krifka, Manfred. (2008). Basic notions of information structure. *Acta Linguistica Hungarica, 55*(3–4), 243–276.

Kuznetsova, Alexandra, Per B. Brockhoff, & Rune H.B. Christensen. (2017). lmerTest Package: Tests in Linear Mixed Effects Models. *Journal of Statistical Software, 82*, 1–26.

Lambrecht, Knut (2001). A framework for the analysis of cleft constructions. *Linguistics, 39*, 463–516.

Langford, John, & Virginia M. Holmes. (1979). Syntactic presupposition in sentence comprehension. *Cognition, 7*, 363–383.

Osborne, Jason W. (2010). Improving your data transformations: applying the Box-Cox transformation. *Practical Assessment, Research and Evaluation, 15*(12).

Patterson, Clare, Yulia Esaulova, & Claudia Felser. (2017). The impact of focus on pronoun resolution in native and non-native sentence comprehension. *Second Language Research, 33*, 403–429.

Polanyi, Livia. (1988). A formal model of the structure of discourse. *Journal of Pragmatics, 12*, 601–638.

R Core Team. (2017). *R: A Language and Environment for Statistical Computing.* R Foundation for Statistical Computing. https://www.R-project.org/

Rigalleau, Francois, David Caplan, & Vanessa Baudiffier. (2004). New arguments in favour of an automatic gender pronominal process. *The Quarterly Journal of Experimental Psychology Section A, 57*(5), 893–933.

Schütze, Carson T., & Jon Sprouse. (2014). Judgment data. In R.J. Podevsa, & D. Sharma (Eds.), *Research methods in linguistics* (pp. 27–50). Cambridge: Cambridge University Press.

Singer, Murray. (1976). Thematic structure and the integration of linguistic information. *Journal of Verbal Learning and Verbal Behavior, 15*, 549–558.

Vasishth, Shravan, Titus von der Malsburg, & Felix Engelmann. (2013). What eye movements can tell us about sentence comprehension. *Wiley Interdisciplinary Reviews: Cognitive Science, 4*, 125–134.

Zimmermann, Malte, & Edgar Onea. (2011). Focus marking and focus interpretation. *Lingua, 121*, 1651–1670.

CHAPTER 4

Topics and Subjects in German Newspaper Editorials: A Corpus Study

Peter Bourgonje and Manfred Stede

1   Introduction

Attempts to reliably identify sentence topics in authentic language have shown that this task is notoriously difficult for human annotators and leads to relatively low agreement among their decisions (Cook & Bildhauer, 2013; Lüdeling, Ritz, Stede & Zeldes, 2016). One reason is the well-known observation that annotation tasks in the realms of semantics and especially pragmatics "by nature" involve more subjective judgment than those on other linguistic levels. Another reason, however, lies in the status of the notion of *topic* itself: While it has received considerable attention in theoretical linguistics, this work has almost always centered on fabricated examples that serve to neatly illustrate the relevant phenomenon. But proposals for operationalizing *topic* in the shape of precise guidelines that can be applied to authentic language (be it spoken or written) have so far been rare. (We provide an overview in Section 6 below.)

In our previous work, we presented an annotation study (Stede & Mamprin, 2016) where the annotator agreement shows some improvement over the state of the art. Using the guidelines of that study, we have now annotated the Potsdam Commentary Corpus (PCC; Stede, 2016a), a collection of 176 German newspaper editorials, with aboutness topics in the sense of, *inter alia*, Jacobs (2001).[1] Since the corpus is also annotated with other layers of information, and available within the search engine ANNIS3, it is possible to look into correlations between phenomena on different layers that have been independently annotated.

For our purposes here, we are interested in two questions:
1.   To what extent do aboutness topics coincide with subjects, which are widely assumed to frequently correlate with topics in many languages? What are the reasons for instances of non-correlation?

---

1   For a discussion of aboutness and an alternative notion of topic, see von Heusinger and Özge, this volume.

2. To what extent is it possible to predict aboutness topics from "lower-level" features of the noun phrases, such as definiteness, position in the sentence, or position in the coreference chain?

Our perspective is an empirical and "pre-theoretical" one in the sense that we attend to authentic text and use annotation guidelines that do not make reference to specific linguistic constraints (with the exception that topics are restricted to nominal referring expressions, as explained in subsection 2.1). An overarching assumption, however, is that information structure needs to be described on different layers, none of which can be derived from the others. With Molnár (1993) and others, we assume that the dichotomies of topic/comment, focus/background, and theme/rheme play different roles in constituting the information packaging (Chafe, 1976) of a sentence, cannot be reduced to one another, and interact in often quite complicated ways. With this starting point, the availability of annotated data—in a suitable database—is particularly important, because it allows for assessing annotation decisions in the light of other layers of information, comparing (and possibly reconsidering), and thus anchoring theoretical proposals in a non-trivial set of examples.

A crucial factor for handling authentic text is the role of segmentation: Which minimal units (sentences, clauses, fragments) are to receive an aboutness topic, such that—for instance—its correspondence with subjects can be studied? In our approach, we follow Matic, van Gijn and van Valin (2014) in distinguishing between d-subordination (one complex proposition with the matrix clause) and ad-subordination (two distinct propositions). For the annotation of topic in the designated minimal units, we then follow proposals from the literature that try to operationalize the intuitive notion of aboutness in the first place by means of various paraphrase tests, avoiding any references to specific syntactic or other linguistic features.

For the rest of the chapter, we proceed as follows: In Section 2, we explain the notion of aboutness topic we started from and how we operationalized it for our annotation project. Section 3 gives information about the nature of the corpus and the annotation processes. It also describes the linguistic database we are using to process multi-layer annotations (ANNIS3, Krause & Zeldes, 2016). Then, Section 4 addresses our research question (1) and gives an analysis of the topic-subject correlation, as studied with the help of ANNIS3. Section 5 turns to question (2) and presents an experiment to perform an automatic classification of topics in the corpus, based on a set of pre-defined features. Finally, in Section 6 we set our work against the backdrop of related research and then conclude in Section 7.

2 Operationalizing 'Aboutness Topic'

With the term 'operationalizing' we here refer to the step of transferring a theoretical concept to the realm of reliable application by trained human annotators on the basis of written guidelines. These have to be flexible and clear at the same time, so that authentic utterances or text can be marked up with sufficient agreement by different annotators.

2.1 *Aboutness*

Our starting point is the relatively uncontroversial idea of a topic/comment dichotomy, where the topic is the phrase in a clause that the rest of the clause, i.e., the comment, is making a statement about. Beyond this first characterization, different strands of research propose somewhat different definitions, and to a good extent this is due to the choice of language(s) being studied, since languages can use different means of encoding or marking topic. (For an overview of the historical development of the notion of topic, see Krifka & Musan, 2012.) The work of Gundel (1988, p. 210) explicitly separated the study of language-specific topic realization from a "universal" and hence pragmatic definition of topic/comment:

- *Topic Definition*:
  An entity, E, is the topic of a sentence, S, iff in using S the speaker intends to increase the addressee's knowledge about, request information about, or otherwise get the addressee to act with respect to E.
- *Comment Definition*:
  A predication, P, is the comment of a sentence, S, iff, in using S the speaker intends P to be addressed relative to the topic of S.

Sometimes, topic is used interchangeably with theme, which the systemic-functional tradition (e.g., Halliday, 1994) sees as "the starting point of the clause". While this conflation has its merits in the theory,[2] we do not subscribe to the view that theme/topic is to be defined as being sentence-initial. Instead, our aim is to exploit the notion of aboutness in a theory-neutral way as far as possible and to ask annotators to make a judgment that is not driven by positional or syntactic considerations, even though we will formulate certain tendencies for attributes of topics, as part of our annotation guidelines, to be explained below. First, however, for illustration we quote a classical example from Reinhart (1981):

---

[2] Systemic-functional grammar distinguishes between different kinds of topic, which operate on different levels of the grammatical description (called 'metafunctions'). Accordingly, a sentence may have multiple topics, of which only one is in sentence-initial position.

(1) a. [Aristotle Onassis]$_{topic}$ married Jacqueline Kennedy.
b. [Jacqueline Kennedy]$_{topic}$ married Aristotle Onassis.

While (a) and (b) may well describe the very same event, they do so from different perspectives, which results in different assignments of aboutness topic. Reinhart took the step to relate aboutness to the notion of common ground, the knowledge shared by speaker and addressee, which is incrementally updated while the discourse progresses. Within this representation, the topic is conceived as the "address" under which the information provided by the comment is being recorded.

A useful analysis along these lines was provided by Jacobs (2001), who largely followed the conceptions of topic by Strawson (1964) and Reinhart (1981), and proposed three underlying features of topics:

1. *Informational separation*:
   In the linguistic form, the topic is being presented as separate from the remaining material in the clause;
2. *Predication*:
   The remaining material can be construed as a semantic predicate that is applied to (the referent of) the topic;
3. *Addressation*:
   The information given in the remaining material is stored under the 'address' of the topic.

For operationalizing such concepts in the form of annotation guidelines for authentic text, (3) corresponds quite closely to the notion of aboutness that, as pointed out above, is often stated as the main feature of topics, and (1) can be seen as an additional criterion for identifying topics. (2) characterizes the relationship between topic and comment, but is less amenable to an annotation process aiming at potentially-complex sentences, because it seems quite difficult to have annotators first mentally construct semantic representations of the material before making annotation decisions.

Similar to Cook and Bildhauer (2013), we therefore decided to make 'aboutness' the central feature of topic, to explain it in the first place with the help of Jacobs' criterion (3), and to use (1) and (2) as additional guidelines for the annotators. One commitment that follows from our overall annotation project[3] but

---

3 In the multi-layer Potsdam Commentary Corpus, our early syntactic annotation had identified phrases, and referring expression annotation had marked the subset of those nominal phrases that can properly refer. Then, for topic annotation, only these phrases are made available for annotators to mark as aboutness topics.

is also compatible with most of the literature, is to restrict aboutness topics to nominal referring expressions (i.e., a potentially complex noun phrase, prepositional phrase or a pronoun). Then, we provide three linguistic tests, which have also been used in related work, to be employed as heuristics for judging whether a phrase X should be identified as topic of the surrounding unit (often: clause; but see the next subsection) S:

- "What about X" question:
  If the unit S can be read as an answer to this question, then constituent X is a good candidate for the topic. For example (1a) above, the question is *What about Aristotle Onassis?*
- "Concerning X" paraphrase:
  If the unit S can be paraphrased as "Concerning X, S'", with S' being S with X replaced by a pronoun, then X is a good candidate for the topic of S. Applied to (1a): *Concerning Aristotle Onassis, he married Jacqueline Kennedy.*
- Left-dislocation:
  If the unit S can be paraphrased with X being in left-dislocated position, then X is a good candidate for the topic. (This test often works better for German than it does for English.) Applied to (1a): *Aristotle Onassis, he married Jacqueline Kennedy.*

Notice that the 'concerning'-test and the left-dislocation test reflect Jacobs' criterion (1): It should be possible to present the topic separate from the remaining material (the 'comment'). In principle, the criteria and tests are independent, but "prototypical" aboutness topics will fulfill all three. In authentic text, however, the situation can be complicated, and thus the task will be to find the candidate that *best* fulfills them. For illustration, here is the translation of a short excerpt from one of our corpus texts; we mark the aboutness topics with an 'ab' subscript:

(2) (Context: Author describes current escalations of the war in Afghanistan, 2003)
   a. Now there are political concerns that [the war against the Taliban]$_{ab}$ might develop into a full-fledged civil war.
   b. Should [the Northern Alliance]$_{ab}$ start acting like the ruler of Afghanistan, nothing would be gained.

The first test works well for both (2a) and (2b):
- What about the war against the Taliban?
  There are political concerns that it might develop into a full-fledged civil war.
- What about the Northern Alliance?
  Should it start acting like the ruler of Afghanistan, nothing would be gained.

On the other hand, the left-dislocation test produces less natural discourse (as indicated by the '?') when the topic candidate is embedded in the sentence, as in (2a):
- ? The war against the Taliban, there are concerns that it might develop into a full-fledged civil war.

Similarly, applying the first test on an alternative candidate yields somewhat less acceptable results:
- ? Concerning a full-fledged civil war, there are political concerns that the war against the Taliban might develop into one.
- ? What about Afghanistan?
  Should the Northern Alliance start acting like its ruler, nothing would be gained.

Often, topics are associated with the information status of given, and sometimes, conversely the comment is taken to be new information. Gundel (1988) discussed different facets of this relationship, rejected the notion that comments have to be new, but stated a condition for topics that they be familiar in the sense that speaker and hearer have previous knowledge of them. Similarly, sometimes a correlation of topics with definiteness is being assumed, *inter alia* for the reason that in English, certain dislocated syntactic positions require NPs to be definite. In our guidelines, we do not mention definiteness as a condition for topics, because it would mix a formal feature into an otherwise pragmatic characterization. As for familiarity, we regard this term as a little too strong: We see no problem for a phrase like *the biggest mountain in Argentina* to be a topic, and annotators might be confused by the criterion whether they are already "familiar" with it. Instead, we posit that a topic be identifiable, i.e., a reader should not have any problem in finding the appropriate discourse referent in the common ground, or constructing it on the basis of prior world knowledge.

In summary, our operationalization of aboutness topic avoids referring to linguistic notions such as subject, definiteness, specificity, or to syntactic position; instead, aboutness is to be judged merely on the grounds of a rather abstract characterization in combination with paraphrase tests. This decision allows for investigating the mentioned linguistic phenomena and their correlations later on in the annotated data.

2.2 *Sentences, Clauses, and Other Units*

A crucial clarification needed for annotation guidelines concerns the segmentation of text into those units wherein topics are to be identified. For simple sentences such as example (1) above this is a trivial matter. But consider another sentence from our corpus:

(3) Und auf der im Winter vereisten Brücke in Altfriesack hat das Straßenbauamt Kyritz gar den Gehweg beseitigt und durch eine Leitplanke ersetzt (ähnlich wie das Autobahnamt in Tarnow)—obwohl die Altfriesacker Brücke innerorts liegt und obwohl es schon eines erheblichen Maßes an fahrerischem Unvermögen bedarf, um hier bei Tempo 50 von der Straße abzukommen und durchs Geländer in den Rhin zu stürzen.
'And on the bridge in Altfriesack, which is icy in winter, the Kyritz roads office even removed the sidewalk and replaced it with a crash barrier (similar to the highway office in Tarnow)—even though the bridge is within the city limits and even though a considerable amount of driving incapacity is needed in order to get off the road at a speed of 50 and to fall through the railing into the Rhin.'

The example demonstrates that for annotation purposes, we need rules prescribing where to break a complex sentence into smaller units, i.e., which type of clause is to constitute what we here call a 'topic span'. The linguistics literature does not offer much insight on this question, or, as Matic et al. (2014) put it, it is an "understudied phenomenon". An assumption generally made is that material in subordinate clauses is presupposed (and therefore not a topic span) whereas that in main clauses is asserted; however, as Erteschik-Shir (2007) has shown, this is often too much of a simplification. Matic et al., in their analysis of information structure (IS) in complex sentences, follow earlier research in Role and Reference Grammar in distinguishing two types of subordination and corresponding kinds of clauses—a line that we also follow in our annotation guidelines:

– *d-subordination* (daughter subordination) is a predicate-argument relationship that forms one complex proposition, and hence a single topic span:

(4) [Mary thought that Sally would arrive late.]

– *ad-subordination* links an adjunct to the superordinate clause, which corresponds to two separate propositions:

(5) [Mary was sad][because Sally arrived late.]

Further, Matic et al. distinguish between a clause-internal information structure (in particular, a topic/focus dichotomy) and an external IS that describes the informational contribution made by the subordinate clause to the host clause. Our annotation scheme is generally compatible with that proposal;

as we will elaborate in Section 3, we regard main clauses, main clause fragments, adverbial subordinate clauses and so-called weiterführende Nebensätze ("topic-shifting clauses") as topic spans.

Example (3) demonstrates that rules are needed not only for subordination but also for coordination. In brief, when full sentences are being coordinated, each constitutes a separate topic span; but when the subject (and possibly more material) is elided in the second clause, we join them into a single topic span. Applying this to example (3) leads to the following segmentation:

(3') [Und auf der im Winter vereisten Brücke in Altfriesack hat das Straßenbauamt Kyritz gar den Gehweg beseitigt und durch eine Leitplanke ersetzt (ähnlich wie das Autobahnamt in Tarnow)] [—obwohl die Altfriesacker Brücke innerorts liegt] [und obwohl es schon eines erheblichen Maßes an fahrerischem Unvermögen bedarf, um hier bei Tempo 50 von der Straße abzukommen] [und durchs Geländer in den Rhin zu stürzen.]

A second problem besides complex sentences is posed by fragments, i.e., incomplete sentences that qua punctuation seem to play the role of sentences. Such units can either introduce the following sentence or provide add-on information to the previous one. Annotators are therefore asked to identify initializing and final fragments, as in this excerpt from our corpus:

(6) [Zum Beweis:]$_{\text{frag-init}}$ [Die damalige Aufsichtsratschefin Margit Spielmann wird am Samstag von der SPD nominiert.] [Na dann viel Glück.]$_{\text{frag-final}}$
'As proof: The former chairperson of the board, Margit Spielmann, will be nominated by the SPD on Saturday. Then good luck.'

Thus for each such fragment, annotators have to decide whether it prepares the reader for the subsequent segment, or adds information to the previous one. From a pragmatic viewpoint, the two fragments in example (6) also play different roles, as the second one, despite its syntactic incompleteness, constitutes a distinct speech act by which the author evaluates the information presented in the previous sentence. For topic annotation, however, neither type of fragment constitutes a topic span.

2.3 Other Kinds of Topics
In addition to the aboutness topic, our guidelines use two further variants of topics, which are sometimes discussed in the literature.

- *Frame-setting topics* (see, e.g., Krifka & Musan, 2012) provide a (temporal, local, conceptual) context for the predication and thereby restrict its validity. They typically co-occur with aboutness topics in the clause. We mark them with a subscript 'fs'.

    (7) [Historisch gesehen]$_{fs}$, haben [die Stuarts]$_{ab}$ einen legitimeren Anspruch auf die englische Krone.[4]
    'Historically speaking, the Stuarts have a more legitimate claim to the English crown.'

- *Contrastive topics* (see, e.g., Roberts, 1996) are relatively rare: The text first mentions some general term, and subsequent spans of discourse then address more specific variants (often by hyponymy). We use the subscript co>n for contrastive topics, where n is an index attached to the preceding general phrase.

    (8) Berlin uses different kinds of [buildings]$_1$ for hosting refugees. [Sports halls]$_{co>1}$ have been temporarily converted and equipped with beds; [empty warehouses]$_{co>1}$ have been cleaned up and stocked with the necessary equipment.

The three categories are not mutually exclusive: A topic span can be assigned both an aboutness topic and a frame-setting topic. Also, a contrastive topic may simultaneously serve as aboutness or frame-setting topic. However, the same phrase cannot at the same time be a frame-setting and an aboutness topic.

2.4   Theticity

The final phenomenon to be mentioned here is that of topic-less clauses (or, in our terminology: spans). The so-called thetic sentences are sometimes characterized by the phrase "all-new", thus alluding to the stipulation that topics ought to have the information status given (cf. our discussion of familiarity/identifiability above). Typically, thetic spans start a text or a new part of a text, often a paragraph. Metaphorically speaking they place all their referents on an "empty stage". A test is to check whether the sentence more naturally answers the question "What's new?" rather than a "What about X?" question. In this way, annotators need to decide for any span whether it is either thetic or should have an aboutness topic. Following Sasse (1987), we further distinguish two types of

---

[4] Source: http://www.spiegel.de/spiegel/print/d-28957473.html (Access: 30-09-2015).

theticity: The main function of an entity-central thetic sentence is to introduce a new entity into the discourse, which often then serves as the aboutness topic of the next sentence. The following example could be the beginning of a news story:

(9) [Detectives investigating phone hacking at News International have arrested a 31-year-old woman.]$_{\text{thetic-entity}}$ [[The woman]$_{\text{ab}}$ is believed to be ...]

In contrast, an event-central sentence does not primarily introduce a specific entity but presents an entire situation. An example from our corpus:

(10) [Kein Kind weiß heute noch, was Pocken sind.]$_{\text{thetic-event}}$
'Nowadays no child has an idea what pox are.'

3 Corpus, Annotation and Database

3.1 *Potsdam Commentary Corpus*

The Potsdam Commentary Corpus or PCC (Stede & Neumann, 2014; Stede, 2016a) is a collection of 176 newspaper commentaries from a regional German newspaper. It was deliberately collected as an "unbalanced" single-genre corpus, so that research questions on subjectivity and argumentation can be addressed. The texts consist of 10–12 sentences (on average, around 190 words) and deal with local, regional, national, and international topics in the early 00s. Being a local newspaper, the language is not overly complicated, yet one occasionally finds somewhat involved sentence structure, as illustrated above with example (1).

The PCC in its original version has been annotated with sentential syntax, nominal coreference, and rhetorical structure in terms of Rhetorical Structure Theory or RST (Mann & Thompson, 1988). Later, a layer of discourse connectives and their arguments in the spirit of the Penn Discourse Treebank (Prasad et al., 2008) has been added. All these annotations and the primary data have been made publicly available,[5] and all annotation guidelines are published online in (Stede, 2016b). This volume also contains the guidelines for annotating aboutness topic, which is the most recently added layer. It is available from our website in version 2.1 of the corpus.

---

5 http://angcl.ling.uni-potsdam.de/resources/pcc.html.

The various layers have been annotated largely independently (i.e., directly on the source text), the exceptions being that (i) a layer of nominal referring expressions is the basis for both coreference and topic annotation, and (ii) a layer of discourse segments is the basis for rhetorical structure as well as for topic spans, as explained in the next section. We discuss our annotation guidelines, which "spell out" the design decisions that we motivated above in Section 2.

3.2 Annotation Process for Aboutness Topic

All annotation layers in the PCC rely on a notion of minimal unit. For referring expressions, this is defined by the NPs and PPs marked up as part of syntactic structure,[6] while for the other layers it is based on clause-like units. For making "clause-like" precise, we follow a two-step procedure:

A task-independent segmentation into elementary discourse units identifies sentence and clause boundaries, and labels every clause with a type. For this step, we used the inventory proposed by Bußmann (2002) with small modifications, now distinguishing nine types of subordinate clauses, plus an 'unknown' category for cases where the annotator is unsure. Also, full main (and coordinate) clauses receive a corresponding label, as do main clause fragments where some material has been elided. This has been illustrated above with example (2).

The second stage of the segmentation process is geared towards the specific task. From the general segment types identified in step one, a subset is chosen that defines the independent units for the target layer, in our case the topic spans. All the units of other types are being added to their embedding units. In this way, for example, non-restrictive relative clauses can be either treated as independent units for a layer of discourse annotation, or they can be kept as part of their host clauses for an argumentation analysis. As mentioned in Section 2, for topic spans, we consider units of type sentence, incomplete sentence, adverbial subordinate clause, and *weiterführende* (topic-changing) subordinate clause.

Following the segmentation of the text, all potential topic spans are being considered in an incremental manner. Annotators are instructed to make their decisions in the light of the previous context, but without reading ahead. (Notice this is not merely a technical matter; it means that annotators should not check whether some entity will be referred to again later in the text.) The

---

6 For various reasons, our guidelines for referring expressions prescribe that prepositions are part of the markable, and hence both NPs and PPs will be candidates for the later stage of topic annotation.

annotation tool we use is EXMARaLDA.[7] It was built primarily for labelling spoken language and accordingly does not provide a 'full text' view, but a horizontal stream of tokens, to which annotations can be added on different layers. The annotator in charge of topics receives the text with pre-marked referring expressions (from the respective PCC layer) and with potential topic spans, and considers them one after the other. For each span, they decide whether the unit is either thetic or should contain one or more topics.

Regarding aboutness topics, the guidelines allow for marking more than one candidate. This is not a theoretical claim, but merely a decision made for the operationalization procedure. In principle, when annotators are in doubt as to the most likely topic, they can either be forced to select one, or allowed to choose several; we opted for the latter, so that the difficult cases can later on be studied. However, annotators are required to provide a ranking of the candidates. While the guidelines do not state any upper limit, in practice, the annotation never yielded more than two candidates for aboutness topic within a span.

Our guideline document is available online[8] and its central aspects align with the theoretical considerations explained in Section 2. The actual annotation procedure is specified as follows, asking the annotator to go through the steps for each potential topic span (TS):

1. Is there a fragment unit adjacent to the TS? If so, check whether for topic assignment it should be integrated with the TS.
2. Is the TS thetic, i.e., an "all new" statement? If yes, mark it as such, and stop. Otherwise, proceed with 3.
3. Apply the aboutness test to all candidate referring expressions in the TS. If there is one such candidate, mark it, and proceed with 5. If there is no candidate, reconsider step 2. If there are multiple candidates, proceed with 4.
4. Decide on a ranking of the candidates and mark them as ab1, ab2, and so forth. Proceed with 5.
5. Check whether any frame-setting topic should be marked. Then proceed with 6.
6. Check whether there is any configuration of contrastive topics involving this TS, and if so, mark the expressions as such.

Due to cases of disagreement caused by various types of embedded clauses in an early stage of the annotation process, the segmentation task was split off

---

7 http://exmaralda.org/en/.
8 https://publishup.uni-potsdam.de/frontdoor/index/index/docId/8276.

and done prior to topic labeling. This contributed to the efficiency of the overall annotation process. It might be the case, though, that our criteria for selecting possible topic spans will need to be refined; this is a question we leave to future work.

The other central source of complication in this annotation project is theticity and the corresponding "all-new" question. A notorious problem is in judging whether a particular discourse referent, which has not been mentioned in the text before, is to be taken as "hearer-old" (Prince, 1992) qua world knowledge and thus makes a good candidate for an aboutness topic. This issue arises in many reference-related annotation projects, and we do not have a good solution; our guidelines merely appeal to the annotator's intuition for deciding whether some entity should be "generally known" or not.

Finally, we noticed that when a unit has multiple topic candidates, their relative "weight" can play a role for annotators. Referring expressions like possessive pronouns or pronominal adverbs (e.g., German *damit* 'with that') have additional functions besides reference, and seem "lighter" than full NPs or personal pronouns. As explained earlier, in our guidelines we strive to not give structural criteria for choosing topics. Another factor that plays a role here is that we ask annotators to consider the previous context when judging a segment, but not to look forward; thus, the "persistence" of a discourse referent in the subsequent text should not affect the decision on topicality. While we are generally happy with this rule, it seems to contribute to the difficulty of judging those "light" referring expressions.

When the guidelines had been finalized, we conducted an inter-annotator agreement study on 10 PCC texts, which had been segmented beforehand, so that the annotation focused just on the topic assignment decisions. For theticity, the agreement was $\varkappa = 0.6$, and for aboutness topic $\varkappa = 0.71$, using Cohen's Kappa in both cases. For details, see Stede and Mamprin (2016); we will briefly compare these figures to those of the related work in Section 6.

The resulting annotation layer for the PCC resulted in 2,899 topic spans across four levels of embedding. Spans on level 0 are main clauses or complete sentences (plus adjacent fragments, if any); those on levels 1 to 3 are recursively embedded. The number of spans on level 0 does not include those on levels 1–3, and so on. Table 4.1 also shows the distribution of thetic and non-thetic spans on the various levels. Within the non-thetic spans, there are 1,749 topics, 1,417 of which are aboutness topics. 175 of these have a secondary candidate annotated in the same TS.

TABLE 4.1   Distribution of thetic and non-thetic spans on different annotation levels

Level of embedding	Total spans	Thetic	Non-thetic
0	2,213 (76%)	988 (79%)	1,255 (76%)
1	621 (21%)	234 (19%)	387 (23%)
2	58 (2%)	28 (2%)	30 (2%)
3	7 (<1%)	1 (<1%)	6 (<1%)
Total	2,899	1,251	1,648

3.3   Syntax: Subjects

We combined the information of the minimal units that were annotated on topic-level with information from the coreference and syntax annotation layers of the PCC. This includes several attributes for referring expressions (phrase type, information on anaphoricity, referentiality, ambiguity, and reference on text level versus in (in)direct speech (see Stede, 2016b, pp. 53–63)), which we will utilize later in Section 5 when studying the correlation between those features and aboutness topics. Also, for relating topics to subjects in Section 4, the annotations of grammatical role are important, which distinguishes subject, direct object, indirect object and other (PPs and embedded elements). The syntactic information in PCC is annotated according to the TIGER scheme (Brants et al., 2004), which provides constituent trees with grammatical role labels.

3.4   The Database: From EXMARaLDA to ANNIS

The tool we use for merging annotations from several different layers is ANNIS3[9] (Krause & Zeldes, 2016). ANNIS3 comes with several importer modules for popular annotation formats (such as GATE, CONLL, MMAX2, EXMARaLDA, etc.) and is easily extendable by importing modules for new annotation formats. The different annotation representations are merged on the basis of a common identifier (the token, requiring identical tokenization for all annotation formats) and exported to the ANNIS3-internal format. This format can be loaded in a GUI that comes with a query engine. Text spans can be visualized for manual inspection of the different annotation layers mapped on top of each other, with different visualization paradigms being available for different

---

9   http://corpus-tools.org/annis/.

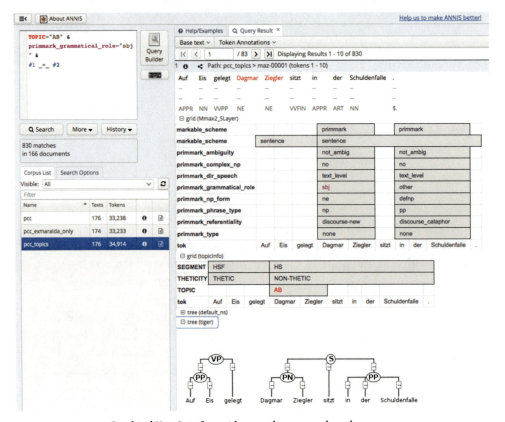

FIGURE 4.1 ANNIS3 Graphical User Interface with example query and results

types of annotation (underlining in full-text view; stacked layers in grid view; constituent syntax trees; dependency syntax graphs; rhetorical structure trees). Also, automated queries can be executed to count the frequencies of certain feature combinations, either within a layer or across different layers. A sample view of the ANNIS3 GUI is shown in Figure 4.1, where one instance of the results for a query for aboutness topics that also have the grammatical role of subject can be investigated on different annotation layers.

4   Correlation of Topic and Subject

Generally, the association between grammatical subjects and aboutness topics is assumed to be strong. Chafe (1976) went so far as to in fact use the attribute of "aboutness" for characterizing subjects; he was skeptical toward the need for a "topic" category for languages that are regarded as subject-prominent (e.g., English) rather than topic-prominent (e.g., Chinese). Therefore, given our parallel annotations, we now take a closer look at the mismatches we find.

Our base set is the 1,417 aboutness-topics or AB-topics in the corpus; for the present purpose, we ignore the secondary annotations of alternative candidates (175) and just regard them as non-topics. 1,184 AB-topics have a grammatical role annotation, and the remaining 233 are merely overlapping with a unit having such a role; this includes many cases (86) of topics being embedded in longer subjects (just a part of a complex NP). Since we are now interested in determining the reasons for AB-topics being *not* subjects, we focus here on the 347 topics that correspond exactly to a unit with a grammatical role annotation, and where this role is not subject. These 347 amount to 24% of all AB-topics.

Investigating their grammatical role, we find that 97 are direct objects, 51 are indirect objects, and 193 are annotated as "other"—mostly prepositional objects, but also phrases that are part of the subject (genitives or PP supplements). To determine why these topics did not "make it" to subject position, we randomly chose 30 instances from the three groups, i.e. 90 in total, and manually checked the type of the subject in the respective span.

The biggest group (28 instances = 31%) are "impersonal" subjects that either are not referring (*man* 'one/they', as in *Man hat Bosse aus der Stadt gejagt* 'They kicked Bosse out of the city') or do not serve as recurring discourse entities (*die Politiker der Stadt* 'the politicians of the city'). Next, we find subjects that are expletive pronouns (*Es gibt zu* ⟨ab-topic⟩ *keine Alternative* 'There is no alternative to ⟨ab-topic⟩'), which account for 27% of all cases. In 11%, the subject is an event or a demonstrative pronoun referring to an event, and hence cannot serve as ab-topic according to our guidelines. 10% of all instances are parts of subjects (*die Hälfte [der Abfälle]* 'half of [the waste]'; *der Weg [mit dem gelben Sack]* 'the walk [with the yellow bag]'),[10] and 2% are part of an idiomatic expression.

This leaves 16 instances (18%) that cannot be explained on purely structural or syntactic grounds—and hence are the "interesting" cases. These can be further broken down as follows:
- The subject is not impersonal but a non-specific, indefinite entity:
  Nun bestätigt eine Studie [den Entertainer] ('Now a study supports [the entertainer]')

---

10   Note that these cases can still be part of the set under investigation here if their grammatical role annotation did not align with the information structure annotation.

- The subject is a discourse-new yet hearer-old entity, because it is prominent qua world knowledge, or linked to the previous discourse via a bridging relation:
  Nun hat die künftige Schulkonferenz Zeit, [den Standort] zu wählen ('Now the future school conference has time to choose [the location]')
- The whole text is somewhat topic-less, describes what "people do" in a particular situation and thus deals mostly with nonspecific entities.
- The text in fact talks about two specific entities at the same time, thereby creating some ambiguity for topic annotation (and in some of these cases the annotator marked this ambiguity with a secondary-topic).
- The sentence realizes a prototypical topic switch—it starts with the old topic as oblique phrase and finishes with the upcoming new discourse topic, the subject.
  [Mit dem Krieg] beschäftigte sich am Sonnabend auch die Kreissynode der Evangelischen Kirche ('[With the war] dealt on Saturday also the local synod of the protestant church')

So, the analysis of our 90 samples of non-subject topics showed that in 82% of the cases, the author chose a grammatical construction that made it impossible for the subject to function as AB-topic. Conversely, in 18% of the cases, we find a regular referring NP that could in principle be the AB-topic of the span. In the subclassification above, we do not provide absolute or relative frequencies, as the overall number is relatively small to begin with. Nonetheless, these are the phenomena where there is no straightforward subject-topic correspondence for reasons of the thematic development in the text, and which in future work invite further scrutiny and generalization.

5 Experiment: Predicting Topics

In this section, we shift the perspective of the discussion to that of an automatic identification of topics. Specifically, we consider whether it is possible to reliably predict AB-topics from basic attributes of the referring expressions, and to what extent this prediction is stronger than a rule of thumb that would simply say "subject equals topic". For this to be meaningful, we restrict the experiment to the non-thetic spans in the corpus (because in thetic spans, there is no extra information in the fact that the subject is not a topic); for a practical application working on raw text, we therefore will also need a thetic/nonthetic span classifier, which for now is left to future work.

We cast the task as a classification problem, which means to map a vector of features to a class prediction. To prepare the data, we extract all referring expressions from non-thetic segments and collect all features from the coreference layer (see Section 3.3) and add some additional features (length of the chain of mentions that this expression is part of; position in that chain; and position in the sentence). The target class label for every data instance is either *true* (AB-topic) or *false* (not AB-topic).

The AB-topic can be embedded in longer syntactic units (the topic being part of a complex NP, for example) and match only partially (in terms of token spans). An example of this is the sentence *Der Auftakt, den die Grundschüler gestern gaben, ist gelungen* ('The prelude, which the pupils gave yesterday, has been successful'), where *die Grundschüler* ('the pupils') is annotated as AB-topic, whereas the full referring expression for which we have a grammatical role (i.e., subject) annotation is *Der Auftakt, den die Grundschüler gestern gaben* ('The prelude, which the pupils gave yesterday').—An example the other way around is *Aus dem Börsengang wurde nichts, auch Artemedia selbst scheint nun am Ende* ('Nothing came of the IPO, and also Artemedia itself now seems to face its end'), where the AB-topic is *auch Artemedia* ('also Artemedia'), whereas the referring expression with grammatical role information here covers the pronoun *Artemedia* only.

Because the conditions for such cases, where the syntactic information relates to larger (or smaller) spans than topic information, are not systematically known for our data set, we here restrict ourselves to only those cases where the topic information and syntactic information relate to the exactly matching token span. This results in 3,544 data instances (referring expressions in non-thetic topic spans), of which 1,171[11] are AB-topics and 2,373 are not. 834 of these 1,171 topics have the grammatical role of subject (71%). Considering the strong correlation between grammatical role and topic annotation, we compare our classifier to a baseline that simply assigns the label *true* to all referring expressions that have the grammatical role of subject. Using a support-vector machine classifier (SVM henceforth) (Pedregosa et al., 2011), we obtain the numbers shown in Table 4.2. All numbers reported are the result of micro-averaging over 10-fold cross-validation using a 90–10 division of training and test data (due to the relatively small amount of data for such classification tasks, we refrain from setting aside a development set).

The baseline appears difficult to beat, and we improve only by just over 2 points. To gain insight into which features contribute the most to the predicted

---

11 Note that because of the restriction to exactly matching token spans, this number is smaller than the 1.417 reported in Section 4.

TABLE 4.2 Classification results

	Baseline	SVM classifier
Precision	65.70	65.07
Recall	71.18	76.69
F1-score	68.33	70.40

label, we extracted the coefficients from the classifier.[12] The three features (of 13 in total) that proved most valuable were phrase type (NP, PP or other), whether the expression was anaphoric or not, and grammatical role (subject, direct object, indirect object or other).[13] While the grammatical role feature relates to the subject-topic resemblance, the phrase type might here be specific to our data: For NPs, the picture is relatively balanced, with 1,056 NPs being topic and 1,406 NPs not being a topic, but there are only 115 PP topics, compared to 966 non-topic PPs. As for the anaphoricity feature, the anaphoric expressions were relatively balanced (721 topics vs. 690 non-topics), but the non-anaphoric expressions were mostly non-topic (1,562 vs. 418).

The three least important features for the classifier were ambiguity, position in the sentence, and position in the coreference chain. The feature indicating position in the sentence was included to test whether topics are more often sentence-initial than not, but it does not seem to be a very reliable indicator for the classifier. The coreference chain features were included to test whether topics are more often than not part of a coreference chain (and if so, whether they would appear chain-initial). Recall, however, that the human annotators were instructed not to read ahead, and hence would not know, at time of annotating, whether this particular expression is part of a longer chain of mentions or not.

For all three least important features, the true/false labels were distributed relatively evenly over the different values. Another thing that sets these features

---

[12] Note that this is only possible for a SVM with linear kernel, whereas the results in Table 2 are using a polynomial kernel, because this performed better.
[13] The other ten features being complex NP (yes/no), NP form (definite/indefinite NP or other), referentiality (discourse-new, discourse-cataphor, referring or other), ambiguity of antecedent assignment (yes/no), anaphor type (nominal or other), embedded speech (is the NP part of direct or indirect speech), length of span (in tokens), length of and position in coreference chain (in tokens) and position in sentence (in tokens).

apart from the rest is the relatively large number of different feature values. The ambiguity feature has 7 different possible values and the length and position features have even more.[14]

Because information on feature importance cannot directly be extracted from the best performing classifier (SVM with polynomial kernel), we ran ablation tests leaving out the three most informative features for the linear kernel scenario. This showed a slightly different image, with the grammatical role feature leading to the largest drop in performance when left out (precision, recall and F1-score of 61.27, 68.00 and 64.45, respectively), followed by phrase type (63.96, 74.55 and 68.85) and the anaphoricity feature (64.25, 75.47 and 69.41). To establish performance in a scenario where only syntactic information (as opposed to additional coreference information, which we use above) is available, we trained a classifier using only syntactic features (phrase type, NP form, whether the NP is complex or not, grammatical role, length of the span and position in the sentence). This resulted in a precision, recall and F1-score of 63.10, 72.35 and 67.41, respectively, indicating that in this scenario the baseline approach is the better option.

As mentioned above, in our classification experiments we limit the data to the exactly matching token spans. This means that for some data instances (complex NPs, for example), the label is inaccurate (no topic spanning exactly this token span was annotated), while the span could be encompassing a topic. This may result in certain feature values to appear in combination with an incorrect label, confusing the classifier. We leave to future work the task of looking into the specific conditions under which this happens, in order to understand the implications of this on classification.

6   Related Work

Among the subfields of information structure, research in computational linguistics has given the most attention to the notion of information status, as it is closely related to coreference, which in turn is an important subtask of many applications involving text understanding. (For larger overviews of computational linguistics approaches to information structure, see Kruijff-Korbayová & Steedman, 2003; Stede, 2012.) Focus has to a good extent been studied for

---

14   In principle these are, of course, continuous. To decrease variation, we grouped them (1, 2–5, 6–10, etc.) and got better results with this setup, but variation still is larger than for most other features.

spoken language, where it has applications in dialogue systems; for written language, we mention the work by De Kuthy, Ziai and Meurers (2016) on detecting focus as part of evaluating reading comprehension with learners of German.

Concerning topics in written language, the largest annotation effort is found in the Prague Dependency Treebank 2.01, a multi-layer corpus of Czech text, which has also been extended to Arabic and English. The PDT was developed in accordance with the theory of the Prague School of functional and structural linguistics (Sgall, Hajičová, Panevová, 1986). As Czech is a free-word-order language, information structure plays a prominent role in the approach, and the central notion for our purposes here is the topic-focus articulation (TFA). Topics have been annotated on top of the syntactic dependency structures, which means that they can easily be queried and analyzed in their syntactic context, bearing in mind that their selection was constrained by the syntactic considerations (which is in contrast to our own project). In particular, Buráňová, Hajičová and Sgall (2000) proposed explicit rules for identifying topic and focus on dependency trees.

One of the first corpus-based studies of IS in German was done by Ritz, Dipper and Götze (2008), who had information status, focus and topic annotated in a variety of genres. Topic was assigned within sentences, with the rule that for complex sentences, first the matrix clause was to be handled and then every finite clause, with the exception of restrictive relative clauses, which did not receive a topic. The markables were various types of NPs, which the guidelines (Götze et al., 2007) differentiated in terms of their syntactic and semantic properties. For deciding on a topic candidate X, annotators were to use diagnostics very similar to those we used here. (Our current work is based on the experiences gained in the experiments by Ritz et al.) Among the differences is a set of rules for specific indefinites, generics, and adverbially quantified sentences that contain singular indefinites. On texts from the Potsdam Commentary Corpus, the annotator agreement for topic was $\varkappa = 0.44$. For other genres, the results were better: elicited question/answer pairs—$\varkappa = 0.75$; oral dialogues—$\varkappa = 0.51$. More recently, Cook and Bildhauer (2013) used a revised version of the Götze et al. guidelines and conducted a new study on newspaper texts. Four annotators labeled 56 sentences and achieved a Fleiss-$\varkappa$ of 0.447 on topic assignment— essentially the same value as that of the Ritz et al. study. For deciding whether a sentence had a topic or was topic-less (thetic; see Section 4.2.), the agreement was only $\varkappa = 0.225$. Cook and Bildhauer provided a very informative error analysis of problematic cases. Notice that our experiments conducted on the PCC and using the guidelines described here, yielded a higher agreement of two-rater $\varkappa = 0.6$ for theticity and 0.71 for topic assignment, as stated above in section 3.2. While these kappa values cannot be directly compared to those of

Cook and Bildhauer (differences in number of annotators, amount of training received, etc.), we take our results as an indication that the problem of reliably annotating topic is not insurmountable.

None of the studies quoted above conducted experiments on automatic topic classification, though, as no dataset of significant size has been available at the time.

The correlation between topic and subject was empirically investigated by Taboada and Wiesemann (2010). Once again, results cannot be directly compared—these authors work with English and Spanish casual conversations, and they define topic as identical to the 'backward-looking center' of Centering Theory (Grosz, Joshi & Weinstein, 1995). Still, we mention here their finding that the topic was realized as subject in 80% of the English and 73% of the Spanish utterances.

7 Summary and Conclusion

The work reported in this paper builds on the results of Stede and Mamprin (2016), who found that using new annotation guidelines, aboutness topics can be annotated in German newspaper editorials more reliably than previous research had found. We then proceeded to add topic annotation to all 176 texts of the Potsdam Commentary Corpus, merged this new layer of information with the ones already present in the corpus (sentence syntax, coreference, rhetorical text structure) and made it all available in the ANNIS3 linguistic database, which allows for querying the corpus for combinations of information from the different layers.

One important aspect of the topic annotation is to decide on the types of clauses that are subject to topic assignment, and we explained how we made this decision. In total, the corpus has 2,213 sentence-size spans (some include initiating or final fragmentary sentences), and 686 embedded spans. Of all these spans these, 1,648 are non-thetic, and they have 1,417 AB-topics. Finally, of these 1,417, 1,184 have a grammatical role annotation, i.e. the units annotated for syntax and for referring expressions match.

Taking the 1,148 aboutness topics as the base set for our correlation study with subject, we found that 347 (24%) of the topics are not realized as grammatical subject. To look into the reasons, we randomly selected 90 instances (30 cases each of the topic being direct object or indirect object or another element). For the vast majority (82%), we found that certain grammatical constructions, often involving expletive *es* ('it') or impersonal *man* ('one') prevent a full NP from becoming subject, and hence the topic has to have a different role. For the remaining 18%, the subject in fact expressed a different discourse referent, so the thematic text structure is in a sense unusual, and we gave some reasons that we observed.

We then performed a classification experiment that considers the referring expressions in a topic span and tries to predict which one is the aboutness topic. (A priori we worked only with non-thetic spans, so a topic should be there.) On the basis of the syntactic annotation in the PCC, a simple baseline rule saying "Subject is Topic" yields an F1-score of 68.33 (65.7% of these predictions are correct, and 71.18% of all topics are detected by the rule). We built a support-vector machine classifier that employs additional features about the referring expressions—syntactic attributes of the NP, position in coreference chains—and achieved a somewhat better F1 score of 70.4.

The result indicates that the subject baseline is indeed strong, but still it helps to take other information into account, in particular, as we found, the feature whether the referring expression is anaphoric or not. Notice that all these results are determined on manually-annotated "gold" labels. In a computational application setting, where an automatic parser has to determine syntactic attributes, subjects, and coreference information, the performance will be lower.

The availability of the multi-layer corpus now invites further investigations. We plan to look into the interplay of the coreference chains and the topics, as part of studying the thematic development patterns in the text. One aspect can be testing the predictions that would be made by Centering Theory, similar to the study on English and Spanish conversations by Taboada and Wiesemann (2010), mentioned in Section 6. Our data then also allows for revisiting results of Strube and Hahn (1996), who had postulated that for German, Centering Theory needs to be adapted to the effect that rather than grammatical role, a topic feature is more important for explaining a felicitous thematic text structure.

Acknowledgments

We are grateful for the constructive suggestions made by the two reviewers of an earlier version of this paper. Also, we acknowledge financial support from the Deutsche Forschungsgemeinschaft (DFG, Project-ID: 323949969).

References

Brants, Sabine, Stefanie Dipper, Peter Eisenberg, Silvia Hansen, Esther König, Wolfgang Lezius, Christian Rohrer, George Smith, & Hans Uszkoreit. (2004). TIGER: Linguistic Interpretation of a German Corpus. *Journal of Language and Computation, 2,* 597–620.

Buráňová, Eva, Eva Hajičová, & Petr Sgall. (2000). Tagging of very large corpora: Topic-focus articulation. In *Proceedings of the 18th International Conference on Computational Linguistics (COLING)* (pp. 138–144). Santa Fe, NM, United States.

Bußmann, Hadumod. (2002). *Lexikon der Sprachwissenschaft.* Stuttgart: Kroner.

Chafe, Wallace. (1976). Givenness, contrastiveness, definiteness, subjects, topics and point of view. In C.N. Li (Ed.), *Subject and Topic* (pp. 27–55). New York: Academic Press.

Cook, Philippa, & Felix Bildhauer. (2013). Annotating information structure. The case of "topic". *Dialogue and Discourse, 4*(2), 118–141.

De Kuthy, Kordula, Ramon Ziai, & Detmar Meurers. (2016). Focus Annotation of Task-based Data: A Comparison of Expert and Crowd-Sourced Annotation in a Reading Comprehension Corpus. In *Proceedings of the 14th Language Resource and Evaluation Conference (LREC)* (pp. 3928–3934). Portorož, Slovenia.

Erteschik-Shir, Nomi. (2007). *Information structure: The syntax-discourse interface.* Oxford: Oxford University Press.

Götze, Michael, Cornelia Endriss, Stefan Hinterwimmer, Ines Fiedler, Svetlana Petrova, Anne Schwarz, Stavros Skopeteas, Ruben Stoel, & Thomas Weskott. (2007). Information structure. In M. Götze, S. Dipper, & S. Skopeteas (Eds.), *Information structure in cross-linguistic corpora: Annotation guidelines for morphology, syntax, semantics, and information structure, ISIS Working papers of the SFB 632* (Vol. 7, pp. 145–187). Potsdam: University of Potsdam.

Grosz, Barbara, Aravind Joshi, & Scott Weinstein. (1995). Centering: A framework for modelling the local coherence of discourse. *Computational Linguistics, 21*(2), 203–226.

Gundel, Jeanette. (1988). Universals of topic-comment structure. In M. Hammond, E.A. Moravcsik, & J. Wirth (Eds.), *Studies in syntactic typology* (pp. 209–239). Amsterdam/Philadelphia: John Benjamins.

Halliday, Michael A.K. (1994). *Introduction to Functional Grammar* (2nd ed.). London: Edward Arnold.

Jacobs, Joachim. (2001). The dimensions of Topic–Comment. *Linguistics, 39*(4), 641–681.

Krause, Thomas, & Amir Zeldes. (2016). ANNIS3: A new architecture for generic corpus query and visualization. *Digital Scholarship in the Humanities, 31*(1), 118–139.

Krifka, Manfred, & Renate Musan. (2012). Information structure: Overview and linguistic issues. In M. Krifka, & R. Musan (Eds.), *The Expression of Information Structure* (pp. 1–44). Berlin: De Gruyter Mouton.

Kruijff-Korbayová, Ivana, & Mark Steedman. (2003). Discourse and information structure. *Journal of Logic, Language and Information: Special Issue on Discourse and Information Structure, 12*(3), 249–259.

Lüdeling, Anke, Julia Ritz, Manfred Stede, & Amir Zeldes. (2016). Corpus Linguistics and Information Structure Research. In C. Féry, & S. Ishihara (Eds.), *The Oxford University Press Handbook of Information Structure*. Oxford: Oxford University Press.

Matic, Dejan, Rik van Gijn, & Robert van Valin. (2014). Information structure and reference tracking in complex sentences: An overview. In R. van Gijn, J. Hammond, D. Matic, S. van Putten, & A.V. Galucio (Eds.), *Information structure and reference tracking in complex sentences* (pp. 1–42). Amsterdam/Philadelphia: John Benjamins.

Molnár, Valeria. (1993). Zur Pragmatik und Grammatik des TOPIK-Begriffes. In M. Reis (Ed.), *Wortstellung und Informationsstruktur* (pp. 155–202). Tübingen: Niemeyer.

Pedregosa, Fabian, Gael Varoquaux, Alexandre Gramfort, Vincent Michel, Bertrand Thirion, Olivier Grisel, Mathieu Blondel, Peter Preffenhofer, Ron Weiss, Vincent Dubourg, Jake Vanderplas, Alexandre Passos, David Cournapeau, Matthieu Brucher, Matthieu Perrot, & Edouard Duchesnay. (2011). Scikit-learn: Machine learning in Python. *Journals of Machine Learning Research, 12*, 2825–2830.

Prasad, Rashmi, Nikhil Dinesh, Alan Lee, Eleni Miltsakaki, Livio Robaldo, Aravind Joshi, & Bonnie Webber. (2008). The Penn Discourse Treebank 2.0. In *Proceedings of the 6th Language Resource and Evaluation Conference (LREC)* (pp. 2961–2968). Marrakech, Morocco.

Prince, Ellen F. (1992). The ZPG letter: Subjects, definiteness, and information status. In W. Mann, & S. Thompson (Eds.), *Discourse description: Diverse linguistic analyses of a fund-raising text* (pp. 223–255). Amsterdam/Philadelphia: John Benjamins.

Reinhart, Tanja. (1981). Pragmatics and linguistics. An analysis of sentence topics. *Philosophica, 27*, 53–94.

Ritz, Julie, Stefanie Dipper, & Michael Götze. (2008). Annotation of information structure: An evaluation across different types of texts. In *Proceedings of the 6th International Conference on Language Resources and Evaluation (LREC)*, (pp. 2137–2142). Marrakech, Morocco.

Roberts, Craige. (1996). Information structure in discourse: Towards an integrated formal theory of pragmatics. In J. Yoon, & A. Kathol (Eds.), *OSU Working Papers in Linguistics: Papers in Semantics* (Vol. 49, pp. 91–136). Columbus, OH: The Ohio State University.

Sasse, Hans-Jürgen. (1987). The thetic/categorical distinction revisited. *Linguistics, 25*(3), 511–580.

Sgall, Petr, Eva Hajičová, & Jamila Panevová. (1986). *The Meaning of the Sentence in Its Semantic and Pragmatic Aspects*. Prague: Academia and Dordrecht: Reidel.

Stede, Manfred. (2012). Computation and modeling of information structure. In M. Krifka, & R. Musan (Eds.), *The Expression of Information Structure*. Berlin: De Gruyter Mouton.

Stede, Manfred. (2016a). Das Potsdamer Kommentarkorpus. In H. Lenk (Ed.), *Persuasionsstile in Europa II. Kommentartexte in den Medienlandschaften europäischer Länder*. Hildesheim: Olms.

Stede, Manfred (Ed.). (2016b). *Handbuch Textannotation—Das Potsdamer Kommentarkorpus 2.0*. Potsdam: Universitätsverlag Potsdam. https://publishup.uni-potsdam.de/frontdoor/index/index/docId/8276

Stede, Manfred, & Arne Neumann. (2014). Potsdam Commentary Corpus 2.0: Annotation for discourse research. In *Proceedings of the 12th Language Resource and Evaluation Conference (LREC)* (pp. 925–929). Reykjavik, Iceland.

Stede, Manfred, & Sara Mamprin. (2016). Information structure in the Potsdam Commentary Corpus: Topics. In *Proceedings of the 14th Language Resource and Evaluation Conference (LREC)* (pp. 1718–1723). Portorož, Slovenia.

Strawson, Peter F. (1964). Identifying reference and truth-values. *Theoria, 30*, 96–118.

Strube, Michael, & Udo Hahn. (1996). Functional centering. In *Proceedings of the 34th Annual Meeting of the Association for Computational Linguistics* (pp. 270–277). Santa Cruz, CA, United States.

Taboada, Maite, & Loreley Wiesemann. (2010). Subjects and topics in conversation. *Journal of Pragmatics, 42*, 1816–1828.

CHAPTER 5

Inferable and Partitive Indefinites in Topic Position

Klaus von Heusinger and Umut Özge

1 Introduction

Topic-comment structure is an information structural partition of the sentence into an argument (the topic) the sentence is about and the material that is predicated about this argument (Reinhart, 1981). The notion of topic is also used to describe that a sentence adds information about an already established or familiar discourse item (Kuno, 1972). Thus, a definite and familiar expression is best suited to fill in the topic position. Therefore, definite expressions such as personal pronouns, proper names, or definite noun phrases as in (1) are perfect candidates for topics (Prince, 1981c, p. 251). Quantifiers, on the other side, can generally not be used as topics, as they do not introduce a referential expression, as illustrated in (2), including existentially quantified indefinite noun phrases in (2c).

(1) a. You I didn't think would leave.
    b. Mary I told that I wasn't chosen.
    c. The window, it's still open. (Gundel, 1988)

(2) a. *Every boy, Mary likes.
    b. *No horse, Bill observes.
    c. *A window, it's still open. (Gundel, 1988)

Indefinite noun phrases express an existential entailment and may introduce a new and unfamiliar discourse referent. In their purely existential function, they are typically banned from the topic position in a sentence. However, referential indefinites can be topical, such as the specific indefinite in (3a) or the generic in (3b).

(3) a. When she was five years old, *a child of my acquaintance* announced a theory that she was inhabited by rabbits. (Reinhart, 1981, p. 66)
    b. *A barber*, he has to talk about everything—baseball, football, basketball, anything that comes along. Religion and politics, most barbers stay away from. Very few barbers that don't know about sports. (Prince, 1981c, p. 254)

We also find non-specific indefinites in topic position if certain conditions hold. Indefinites that are anchored to an explicit referential expression ("containing inferable"; Prince, 1981b), as in (4a) (from Gundel, 1985, p. 88), indefinites that are inferentially linked to the previous discourse, as in (4b), or part of an already introduced set, as in (4c).

(4) a. *A daughter of a friend of mine*, she got her BA in two years.
   b. Brains you're born with. *A great body* you have to work at. (Brooke Shields, in health club commercial) (Ward & Prince, 1991, p. 170)
   c. Then I make a schedule of what's to be done during the day. I try to assign as many tasks as possible to my staff, so I can reduce my work. I need two or three additional people. *A couple who are not pulling their weight* I'm in the process of replacing. This is very painful. (Prince, 1981c, p. 252)

In this paper, we focus on (weakly) familiar or discourse-linked indefinites in topic position and distinguish two types: (i) partitive, i.e. contextually linked indefinites that establish a membership relation to an already introduced set, and (ii) inferable or conceptually linked indefinites. We define a partitive indefinite as an indefinite that selects one element from a set that was explicitly introduced into the discourse. In (5), the anchor expression *a smoking crowd* introduces a set of referents so that the indefinite *a student* refers to one of those referents. In (6), the anchor expression *cinema* introduces a concept that allows for inferring further concepts such as the concept of a director. Thus the indefinite *a director* is linked to its anchor expression *cinema* by an inference relation at the level of concepts (or at the level of lexical meaning). (Examples 5 and 6 are the English translations of Turkish examples from experiment 1 presented below.)

(5) In the opening event of a shopping mall, **a smoking crowd** blocking the entrance caused a tense situation. The manager of the mall went out and started to talk to the crowd. After some discussion, the manager terribly punched **a student**.

(6) In the cabinet meeting, there appeared a consensus on the importance of **cinema** in promoting the country. In this regard, the culture minister started a supporting **program** for **cinema**. As the first action of the program, the minister awarded **a director** generously.

We assume that there is a clear difference between these two kinds of discourse linking. The partitive indefinite has to establish a membership relation in that particular context between the anchor expression and the indefinite. So the (weak) familiarity of the indefinite is established via contextual (and encyclopedic) information. On the other hand, inferable indefinites are (weakly) familiar according to a lexical relation such as a cinema creating a frame with a director. We further argue that the discourse linking is established on two different levels: the partitive relation between (sets of) individuals and the inferable relation between concepts. We hypothesize that an inferable relation is easier to establish, as it is lexically given, and therefore we predict that weak familiar indefinites based on lexical relations are better topics than partitive indefinites.

We thus suggest the following three hypotheses:
H1: Indefinites in non-topic position are more felicitous than in topic position;
H2: Indefinites in topic position are felicitous if discourse linked;
H3: Inferable indefinites are better suited for a topic position than partitive indefinites.

In order to test these hypotheses, we conducted a series of acceptability judgment studies on differently linked indefinites in topic and non-topic positions. The results provide evidence that discourse linking is realized at two different levels, a conceptual level and a contextual level, which interact closely. In section 2, we present a brief overview of the conditions that license indefinites in topic position and discuss the difference between partitive indefinites and inferable indefinites. In section 3, we discuss topical indefinites in Turkish, in particular the partitive and inferable type. In section 4, we discuss the design and results of the first pilot experiment with the contrast between topical and non-topical position and four different contextual conditions. In section 5, we present the results of an experiment that focuses on the contrast between topical vs. non-topical position and two contextual conditions (partitive vs. both). Finally, in section 6 we present the results of an experiment that compares the four contextual conditions (partitive, inferable, both and none). Section 7 provides a general discussion.

2 Indefinite Topics

2.1 *Topics*

The information structural division of the sentence into the topic-comment structure establishes a structure—independent of syntactic structure—that mirrors the "flow of information" in a more adequate way. Hockett (1958, p. 201) has provided the classic characterization of topic:

> The most general characteristic of predicative constructions is suggested by the terms 'topic' and 'comment' for their ICs [= immediate constituents, KvH & UÖ]: the speaker announces a topic and then says something about it.

The classic tests for topic are questions like *what about X* (Gundel, 1985), *say about X that S* (Reinhart, 1981), *as for X* or *speaking of X* (see for a comparison Roberts, 2019, p. 388). Topics can be explicitly marked in syntax, typically by left dislocation as in English or German. In the following we illustrate this with German left dislocation that requires a coreferential resumptive pronoun in the non-topical part (see Frey, 2004):[1]

(7) What about Maria? As for Maria …
    Maria, die   ist eine sehr talentierte Sängerin.
    Maria, RP-FEM.NOM.SG is a   very talented   singer
    'Maria is a very talented singer.'

In (7), the topic *Maria* is what the sentence is about. This view of topic is generally known as "aboutness topic" and it is assumed to be referential. The literature generally assumes an argument-predicate interpretation of the topic-comment partition (see for a critical evaluation of this proposal von Heusinger, 1999, ch. 3). Therefore, it is assumed that the topic must be a referential expression, such as personal pronouns, proper names or definite noun phrases, as in (8). Quantifiers are not licensed in topic position, as in (9). Note that indefinite noun phrases 'out of context' are generally not good in topic position.

(8) a. You I didn't think would leave.
    b. Mary I told that I wasn't chosen.
    c. The window, it's still open. (Gundel, 1988)

---

[1] A reviewer correctly noted that the conditions of left dislocation are different in German and English (and most probably in other languages as well).

(9) a. *Every boy, Mary likes.
 b. *No horse, Bill observes.
 c. *A window, it's still open. (Gundel, 1988)

At the same time, one can take the topic as the discourse item the sentence will provide more information on (Kuno, 1972). In this view, the topic must be familiar, as the hearer must be able to identify the referent the comment is about. In other words, the topical element *X* is associated with an explicit or implicit question of the type *What about X?* Thus, the topic is discourse-established, while the comment gives new information with respect to the topic. The typical definite expressions, as in (8), are both, referential and familiar. However, theories differ with respect to which of these two features is central for the nature of being a topic. So we can distinguish two main families of topicality (see Frey, 2004, p. 2):

(10) (i) A topic is an expression whose referent the sentence is about (...). The concept topic is a category of pragmatic aboutness (aboutness concept of topic).
 (ii) Topics are those expressions whose referents have been already introduced into the discourse or are for other reasons already familiar to the discourse participants (familiarity concept of topic).

Reinhart (1981), Frey (2004), Endriss (2009), and Ebert and Hinterwimmer (2009) assume that aboutness, i.e. referentiality is the central characteristic for topicality, while Kuno (1972), Gundel (1985), Prince (1981c), and Ward and Prince (1991) assume that familiarity is the central notion.

2.2 Indefinites in Topic Positions

Indefinite noun phrases in argument position typically express an existential entailment and introduce a new and unfamiliar discourse referent. In this existential function they cannot be used as topics, as illustrated by (9c). However, indefinites can also be used referentially, i.e. as specific or generic noun phrases (as already noted by Reinhart, 1981).

Geist (2011, p. 157) provides some examples of specific indefinites in topic position. In (11a) the indefinite pronoun *ein gewisser* ('a particular') provides speaker intentions to refer to one particular referent. In (11b) the relative clause determines the reference; (11c) is an example of what Prince (1981b, p. 236) calls "brand new anchored", in this case by the indexical expression *mine*. In (11d) the indefinite stands for a particular individual, introduced by a proper name. Endriss (2009) discusses "quantificational topics" as in (11e):

(11) a. *Ein gewisser Kollege, (der) ist gestern wieder zu spät*
a particular colleague RP is yesterday again too late
gekommen.
come
'A certain colleague, he arrived too late again yesterday.'

b. *Ein Fenster, [das ich gestern gestrichen habe] (das) ist*
a window which I yesterday painted have RP is
immer noch offen.
still open
'A window which I painted yesterday, it is still open.'

c. *Ein Freund [von mir], (der) kommt.*
A friend of mine RP will-come
'A friend of mine, he will come.'

d. *Einen Lehrling, (den) will die Firma einstellen, nämlich*
a trainee RP wants the company hire namely
Peter P.
Peter P.
'The company wants to hire a certain trainee, namely Peter P.'

e. *Einen Politiker, den kennt jeder.*
some politician RP knows everybody.
'One politician everybody knows.'

While the aboutness theory assumes that indefinites can be used as topics if they are more referential than regular existential indefinites, the familiarity theory rather assumes that indefinites that are (weakly) familiar are good candidates for topic position. This goes back to Prince (1981c) and Gundel (1985), who emphasize the familiarity aspect of topics and assume that there are different degrees of familiarity. Ward and Prince (1991) argue in the same direction and claim that topics are not necessarily definite; they can be indefinite as long as the referent is (inferentially) related to the previous discourse. They illustrate this with indefinites that are not specific, but related to some anchor expression in the previous context, as in (12):

(12) a. Brains you're born with. *A great body* you have to work at. (Brooke Shields, in health club commercial) (Ward & Prince, 1991, p. 170)
b. Then I make a schedule of what's to be done during the day. I try to

assign as many tasks as possible to my staff, so I can reduce my work. I need two or three additional people. *A couple who are not pulling their weight* I'm in the process of replacing. This is very painful. (Prince, 1981c, p. 252)

Prince (1981c, p. 253) assumes that indefinites that stand "in a salient set-relation to something already in the discourse" are licensed, but not in a more general inference relation. She illustrates this with the infelicitous use of *the bell* as topic in (13b).

(13) a. I went to his house and I rang the bell.
     b. #I went to his house and *the bell* I rang

Prince (1981c, p. 253) therefore postulates condition (14), which only allows membership relations, as in (12b), but not other inferential relations, as in (12a).

(14) Condition for topicalization
     The NP in TOP must represent either an entity that is already evoked in the discourse or else one that is in a salient set-relation to something already in the discourse.

Ward and Prince (1985, p. 173) provide the more flexible discourse condition (15) on indefinites in topic position. Their "partially ordered set relation" is an abstract description of lexical relations such as 'IS-PART-OF', 'IS-A-SUBTYPE-OF' or 'IS-A-MEMBER-OF':

(15) Discourse Condition on Preposing
     The entity represented by the preposed constituent must be related, via a salient partially ordered set relation, to one or more entities already evoked in the discourse model

In the following we focus on the familiarity conditions on indefinites in topic position and we assume, against Prince (1981c), that not only partitive indefinites are licensed, but also inferable indefinites in topic position. It is along this line that we direct our inquiry. We assume that an indefinite has two main parts—the description and the referent, both of which can be discourse-linked, as observed by Enç (1991). Among the various types, we focus on two relations: (i) partitivity (contextual relations) primarily involves the referent; and (ii) conceptual relations (inferability, bridging) is a relation between the description and the context.[2] See Brocher and von Heusinger (2018) for processing effects of these two relations of descriptive noun phrases. In the following, we discuss two kinds of familiar or discourse-linked indefinites, partitive indefinites and inferable indefinites.

2.3 Partitive Indefinites

Partitive indefinites are indefinites that select a discourse referent out of a set of already established ones. Research on partitive constructions focuses on explicit partitives, i.e. on constructions of the type *NP1 of NP2* such that the whole construction is indefinite while the superset NP2 must be definite as in (16a). NP1 is the subset and NP2 is the superset. Often NP1 consists only of the determiner as in (16b) or of further modifiers, but without the head noun, as in (16c). (Hoeksema, 1996; de Hoop, 2003; Ionin, Matushansky & Ruys, 2006; Koptjevskaja-Tamm, 2006; Falco & Zamparelli, 2019).

(16) a. two girls of the children
 b. two of these eight girls
 c. two intelligent (ones) of these eight students

In the following, we focus on implicit partitives, i.e. on partitives that have their superset introduced in the previous discourse, rather than as a constituent of the noun phrase itself. In these cases, the superset can be introduced by an indefinite expression; what is important is that the set must be introduced in order to interpret the indefinite. English, like many other languages, does not morphologically flag a partitive indefinite, while Turkish does (see section 3.2).[3]

(17) a. Many children entered the room. Two girls went to the window.
 b. Eight girls entered the room. Two (of them) went to the window.
 c. Many protesters entered the hall. Two students approached the stage.

---

[2] See Enç (1991, p. 21) for a distinction between different types of linking of indefinites: (i) relational specifics vs. partitive indefinites.

[3] English nouns or pronouns are not marked for d-linking, but question words are (Pesetsky, 1987). The indefinite *an American* could be part of the set introduced by *some men* or not, but the question word *which* can only relate to the introduced set, while the question word *who* refers to other than established referents.
 (i) a. Some men entered the room. Mary talked to an American.
     b. Some men entered the room. Which (ones) did Mary talk to?
     c. Some men entered the room. Who did Mary talk to?

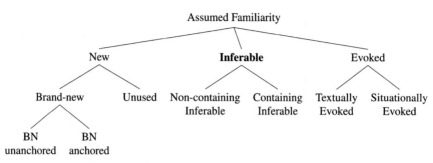

FIGURE 5.1 Prince's (1981b, p. 237) taxonomy of assumed familiarity and information status

In the following, we define the partitive relation as a membership relation. The referent introduced by the partitive indefinite must be part of a set already established. The focus is on the membership relation and not on additional lexical relations between the descriptive content of the superset (anchor) expression and the subset expression. While in (17a) *girls* shows a lexical relation to *children* (hyponymy), there is no such lexical relation between *two* and *girls* in (17b) or between *students* and *protesters* in (17c). We assume that the membership relation can be supported by lexical relations, as in (17a), but also by the context, as in (17c), and we are interested in the effects of this contextually induced partitivity.

2.4   Inferable Indefinites

The more common link to the previous discourse is an inference, which is most often prompted by inferences, typically induced by lexical relations or frames. We call this type of indefinites 'inferable indefinites', going back to Prince (1981b, 1992) who introduces the concept of inferables as an additional information status between new and given (evoked) (see Figure 5.1).[4]

Prince (1992, p. 305, ex. 17) illustrates inferable definite and indefinite noun phrases by example (18) below. They are partly hearer-old since the relation between a team and a captain is known, and partly hearer-new, as the particular captain is not known (and therefore discourse-new). Much research has been conducted on inferable definites (bridged definites, associate anaphoric definites, etc., see below for references), but very little on inferable indefinites. The difference between the bridged definite *the captain* in (18b) and the inferable indefinite *a defender* in (18c) is uniqueness, but both are related to the

---

[4] We diverge from Prince's (1981b, 1992) spelling, namely "inferrable". As far as we can judge, "inferable" is a more standard spelling in present-day English. The term 'inferred indefinites' is also used with the same meaning.

context via their descriptive material: The concept *team* is the anchor for both, *captain* and *defender*.

(18) a. The **team** was handsomely rewarded after the tournament.
b. The **captain** received half a million Euros.
c. A **defender** received half a million Euros.

There are various types of inference relations between the anchor and the inferable expression, which are best studied for definite expressions under the heading of 'bridging' or 'associative anaphora' (Clark, 1977; Clark & Marshall, 1981; Asher & Lascarides, 1998). We will restrict the type of inference to frame-induced inferred referents, as in (19). We assume that the anchor expression, here *cancer*, induces a frame with certain slots including a slot for an oncologist.

(19) The Ecological Life Initiative announced at the arranged press conference that the factors causing the increase in **cancer** cases will be investigated. After the conference the initiative commissioned **an oncologist** in the area.

We have defined the partitive relation exclusively via the membership relation induced by the contextual information, and the inference relation induced by the lexical semantics of the anchor and inferable expressions. While we do find these two types of discourse-linked indefinites in isolation, more often we find both relations together, as in (20).

(20) There was a large **group of guests** at the reception at the Chinese **embassy**. Towards the middle of the address, the **ambassador** gave a speech to the **guests**. Towards the end of the speech, the ambassador called **a diplomat** to the podium.

The anchor *group of guests* establishes a set and the anchors *embassy* and *ambassador* introduce a frame in which we expect diplomats, which are taken out of the set introduced by the *guests*.

Summarizing, there are various parameters that license indefinite expressions in topic position. We focus on two types of discourse linking: implicit partitivity, defined above as membership relation established in the particular context, and inferability as a lexically-induced, typically frame-induced relation, at the level of conceptual information. While most often these two levels of discourse linking work together to establish a weakly familiar indefinite, we are interested in the mechanism of each of these levels—in particular, we predict that contextual discourse linking is less successful than conceptual linking. Contextual or partitive linking must be established using information from the linguistic and situational context. Conceptual linking, i.e. using lexical relations or other lexically induced inferences is based in our linguistic knowledge and does not need additional information. Therefore, we assume that inferable indefinites are better topics than partitive indefinites (against Prince, 1981c, Condition for topicalization—see (14)). In order to test this hypothesis, we turn now to our object language, namely Turkish.

3 Topical Indefinites in Turkish

3.1 *Topic Position in Turkish*
Turkish is basically an SOV language with case marking, rich verbal inflection and flexible word-order, without a definite article, but with the indefinite article *bir* ('a') (Kornfilt, 1997; Göksel & Kerslake, 2005). There is a wide consensus that the primary function of word-order variation is the realization of information structure (Erkü, 1983; Erguvanlı, 1984; Işsever, 2003). In spite of some small differences in the definitions of information structural categories, it is generally held that the initial segments of a sentence are reserved for possibly cascaded topical constituents (Işsever, 2003, p. 1028) and the preverbal constituent is the focus. Background material that is neither topical nor focal (*tail* in the terminology of Vallduvi, 1990—see Işsever, 2003, p. 1027) can either stand between these regions, or it can be post-verbal (Erguvanlı, 1984; Kornfilt, 1997; Işsever, 2003). Within this setting, word-order variation becomes a means to realize a particular informational requirement by setting the positions of constituents in congruence with their informational status. In a standard question contextualization for aboutness topics adapted to Turkish, where clausal scrambling is the method to obtain the right information structure, (21a) is an appropriate answer to the question *What did Ali do?*, while (22b) is appropriate for the question *What happened to the apple*? The contexts (or answers) are strictly non-interchangeable.

(21) What about Ali? What did Ali do?
    a. *Ali elma-yı   yedi.*
       Ali apple-ACC ate
       'Ali ate the APPLE.'

b. #Elma-yı   Ali   yedi.
apple-ACC Ali ate
'ALI ate the apple.'

(22) What about the apple? Who ate it?
a. #Ali elma-yı   yedi.
Ali apple-ACC ate
'Ali ate the APPLE.'

b. Elma-yı   Ali yedi.
apple-ACC Ali ate
'ALI ate the apple.'

There are, however, some restrictions for the topic position, first observed by Erguvanlı (1984): While definite noun phrases are licensed for the topic position as in (23a), indefinites, like the one in (23b), are not felicitous in topic position in the absence of contextual support (Erguvanlı, 1984, pp. 13, 15). Partitive (or "specific" in Enç's, 1991 terms) indefinites, on the other hand, are licensed in topic position. The indefinite *bir misafir* ('a guest') in (23c) is related to the set of 15 people and can therefore act as topic (Erkü, 1983, p. 128).

(23) a. *Lamba adam-ın   oda-sın-da   yan-ıyor.*
lamp man-GEN room-POSS-LOC burn-PROG
'The lamp is burning in the man's room.'

b. **Bir lamba adam-ın   oda-sın-da   yan-ıyor.*
a lamp man-GEN room-POSS-LOC burn-PROG

c. (*Dün   gece onbeş kişi   vardı   ya*)
yesterday night 15 people there-PST PART
bir misafir sigara-sın-ı   yanık   unut-muş.
a guest cigarette-POSS-ACC burning forget-PERF
'(There were fifteen people last night you know).
A guest left his/her cigarette burning.'

Işsever (2003, p. 1041) summarizes two families of assumptions with respect to the conditions for a topic as in (24), which correspond to the aboutness-concept and the familiarity-concept in (10), respectively:

(24) sentence-topic position in Turkish
a. Only definites or 'overtly' specific and/or [+animate] indefinite DPs are allowed (Erguvanlı, 1984).
b. Only definite DPs/NPs or indefinite DPs that belong to a definite set, i.e. partitives, are allowed (Erkü, 1983; Kılıçaslan, 1994; Aksan, 1995).

It is interesting to note that Erguvanlı (1984) focuses on the referential property of topics, while the other family of approaches reduces d-linking to partitivity. Neither type of approach brings the conceptual aspect of the linking together with its referential aspect. It is therefore an open and worthwhile research question whether and under which conditions inferable indefinites in Turkish are licensed in topic position.[5]

3.2 Partitive and Inferable Indefinites in Turkish

In the present paper, we are interested in basically two types of linking to the previous discourse: implicit partitivity (contextually induced) and inferability (conceptually induced). As briefly mentioned above, Turkish utilizes an explicit marking of partitivity. Enç (1991) discusses partitivity in Turkish and argues that it is the underlying structure for specificity, and thus for Differential Object Marking in Turkish. In (25), the case-marked *iki kızı* ('two girls') refers to two of the children mentioned in the first sentence, while the unmarked *iki kız* ('two girls') refers to some other set of two girls.

(25) a. *Oda-m-a   birkaç çocuk gir-di.*
       room-1SG-DAT several child enter-PAST
       'Several children entered my room.' (Enç, 1991, ex. 16)

   b. *İki kız-ı   tanı-yor-du-m.*
       two girl-ACC know-PROG-PAST-1SG
       'I knew two girls.' (Enç, 1991, ex. 17)

---

[5] A reviewer raises the question whether the first position in the Turkish sentence is indeed a topic position or just a position with particular familiarity conditions. The reviewer asks whether one can use quantifiers in that position—if so the position would not qualify as topical, since the topic position cross-linguistically bans quantifiers. In the context (19), repeated as (i), we can use a quantifier 'more than three', but only if it is interpreted partitively, in the sense of "picking from an established set of oncologists".

(i) The Ecological Life Initiative announced at the arranged press conference that the factors causing the increase in **cancer** cases will be investigated.
Ücten fazla onkoloğu inisiyatif bölgede görevlendirdi.
'More than three oncologists the initiative in the area commissioned.'

c. İki kız tanı-yor-du-m.
two girl know-PROG-PAST-1SG
'I knew two girls.' (Enç, 1991, ex. 18)

Enç takes partitivity as a type of d(iscourse)-linking and specific indefinites are understood as contextually restricted and presupposed indefinites (see also Portner & Yashubita, 2001). However, Farkas (1994) and later von Heusinger and Kornfilt (2005) have shown that specificity is orthogonal to partitivity. Moreover, the correlation between case marking and partitivity in Turkish does not hold as closely as Enç (1991) assumes (Kelepir, 2001; Özge, 2011; von Heusinger & Kornfilt, 2017). In any case, the correlation between case marking and partitivity, at least for a restricted type of constructions, cannot be overlooked (see also Özge, Özge & von Heusinger, 2016 on the discourse function of 'strong' indefinites). The significance of this fact vis-à-vis our current purposes is as follows.

As mentioned above, most research on topical indefinites in Turkish has focused on partitive indefinites, partly because since Enç (1991) partitivity is taken as the basic function of case-marked direct objects (but see von Heusinger & Kornfilt, 2005, for a different view). In the present study, we assume that, apart from morpho-syntactically indicated partitivity of the Enç (1991) variety, there are further dimensions to discourse linking that are hypothesized to be relevant to licensing indefinite aboutness topics. These are contextually signaled implicit partitivity and conceptually supported inferability. As we investigate implicit partitivity in its discourse dimension, we need to be wary of any potential explicit indicators of partitivity. Von Heusinger and Kornfilt (2005) make the following crucial observation: The discourse linking function of the accusative marker is valid only when the indefinite is at the canonical immediately pre-verbal position; at other positions the marker is correlated with the licensing of scrambling (see also Gračanin-Yüksek & Işsever, 2011). In the experiments presented below, we avoided any immediately preverbal accusative-marked indefinites on the basis of this observation, in order to ensure that any partitivity effect is a result of contextual inference, rather than an outcome of direct morphosyntactic signaling. We now present these categories.

The general setup of our experiments is providing a context and presenting a sentence with an indefinite either in a topic or a non-topic position. By manipulating the context in certain ways, we manipulate the type of linking between the indefinite and the context. We observe the effect of the linking type on the acceptability of topical versus non-topical target sentences. As we can see in (26), in a context where the anchor expression *cancer* activates a frame with *oncologist*, the context (26a) can be continued with (26b/c) with the indefinite *bir onkoloğu* in topic position (26b) and non-topic position (26c). It is crucial to note that in the non-topic condition the accusative-marked indefinite is not at the immediately pre-verbal position, due to the intervening locative *bölgede* ('in the area'). Therefore, whatever linking relation is detected in both conditions is triggered by the context and/or conceptual background.

(26) a. Başkent yakınlarındaki bir köyde **kanser** vakalarındaki ani artış dikkatleri çekti. Ekolojik Yaşam İnisiyatifi düzenlediği basın toplantısında **kanser** artışının sebebinin araştırılacağını belirtti.
In a village near the capital the sudden increase in **cancer** cases attracted attention. The Ecological Life Initiative announced at the arranged press conference that the factors causing the increase in **cancer** cases will be investigated.
b. Toplantının ardından, **bir onkoloğu** inisiyatif bölgede görevlendirdi.
After the conference, the initiative commissioned **an oncologist** in the area.
c. Toplantının ardından, inisiyatif **bir onkoloğu** bölgede görevlendirdi.
After the conference, the initiative commissioned **an oncologist** in the area.

Before we move on to our experiments, we would like to take stock of what we have seen so far. We are particularly interested in conditions under which indefinite noun phrases can serve as aboutness topics. We assume that the conceptual type of relation (inferability) provides a better licensing environment than the contextual link, since the former is part of the lexical knowledge, while the latter must be computed in processing the particular context. Therefore, we are comparing cases of (i) discourse linking with both types of relations, (ii) with only one type of relation, and (iii) with no relation at all. Our hypotheses regarding the felicity of indefinites in topic position are:
H1: Indefinites in non-topic position are more felicitous than in topic position.
H2: Indefinites in topic position are felicitous if discourse-linked.
It is also known that indefinites can be licensed as topics provided that they are linked to the previous discourse. One option here is explicit partitives. We focus on linking that is not morpho-syntactically signaled, distinguishing between two basic types of such linking. One is implicit partitivity, where a set membership relation is induced by the context; we call such items partitive indefinites throughout, intending them to be understood to be implicit partitives.

The other type is inferable linking, where a linking relation is induced by conceptual knowledge; we call such items inferable indefinites. We formulate the following hypothesis:

H3: Inferable indefinites are better suited for a topic position than partitive indefinites.

In order to test these hypotheses, we conducted three grammaticality judgment studies: Experiment 1 is a broad pilot on topic vs. non-topical position and different linking conditions. Experiment 2 is a more focused study on topic vs. non-topical position and only two linking conditions, while Experiment 3 focuses on all four linking conditions for topical indefinites.

4 Experiment 1: Position (2) x Discourse Linking (2×2)

We conducted a pilot grammaticality judgment questionnaire in order to test (i) whether indefinites in non-topical positions are better rated than indefinites in topic position (H1), and (ii) what are the effects of the two discourse linking relations (H2; H3): the partitive relation in terms of set-membership induced by the particular context and inferability induced by the lexical semantics of the anchor expression. Thus, we employed a design with two syntactic positions, as in (27), and four types of discourse linking, as in (28). We placed the direct object in the non-topical position, as in (27a), and in topic position as in (27b). In all critical sentences we used a ditransitive verb, so that the element at the immediately pre-verbal position is a dative-marked noun phrase and never an accusative-marked indefinite.

(27) a. Büyükelçi **bir diplomatı** podyuma çağırdı.   NONTOPIC
     b. **Bir diplomatı** büyükelçi podyuma çağırdı.   TOPIC
     'The ambassador called **a diplomat** to the podium.'

The four types of discourse linking can be divided into two parameters: contextual linking, i.e. partitivity, and conceptual linking, i.e. inferability. We assume that partitivity is contextually induced—therefore we provide the feature [+context]—while inferability is conceptually induced, marked by the feature [+concept]. These two features can be combined and yield four combinations: NONE, i.e. there is no conceptual or contextual relation between (potential) anchor and indefinite. PART describes the case of contextual relation, but no conceptual relation; INFR covers cases of conceptual relatedness, while BOTH describes cases where conceptual and contextual information come together either from one anchor expression or two anchor expressions.

(28) Types of discourse linking of indefinite noun phrases
    a. NONE ([-concept] [-context])   ... *governor ... An expert ...*   (29)
    b. PART ([-concept] [+context])   ... *protesting group ... A student ...* (30)
    c. INFR ([+concept] [-context])   ... *cancer ... An oncologist ...*   (31)
    d. BOTH ([+concept] [+context]) ... *ambassador, guests ... A diplomat ...*
                                                                                          (32)

In this pilot we provided a context with three sentences (S1–S3), partly with more than one occurrence of the anchor expression in order to create a more natural sounding context. The fourth and final sentence (S4) alternated between the indefinite in non-topical position (SOV) and the indefinite in topic or first position (OSV). (29) represents an example with no relation to the discourse (NONE) and the NONTOPIC condition. Such examples are difficult to construct as participants are likely to try to accommodate some kind of coherence to the previous text. We tried, however, not to provide explicit anchor expressions that would pre-activate the noun *an expert* in the critical sentence.

(29) NONE
    S1 Hafta boyunca devam eden sağanak yağış şehir merkezi ve ilçelerde büyük hasara yol açtı.   The rainstorm caused major damage in the city and districts.
    S2 Vali bölge halkının şikayetleriyle ilgilenmek amacıyla bir girişim başlattı.   To handle the complaints of the residents the governor launched an initiative.
    S3 Girişimin ilk adımı olarak,   As the first step of the initiative,
    S4 Vali **bir uzmanı** bölgeye davet etti.   The governor invited **an expert** to the region.

(30) illustrates the general structure of a context with the discourse relation PARTitivity. The anchor expressions *a smoking crowd* and *the crowd* introduce a set such that the indefinite *a student* in the critical sentence selects a referent out of the set of referents introduced by the anchor expressions. In the PART condition there is no conceptual relation between the anchor and the indefinite—there is no lexical relation between a crowd and a student.

(30) PART
    S1 Bir AVM'nin açılışında sigara içen bir **kalabalığın** girişi kapatması gerginliğe sebep oldu. — The other day, there was **a smoking crowd** almost blocking the entrance to the shopping mall we went.

    S2 AVM müdürü dışarı çıkarak **kalabalıkla** konuşmaya başladı. — The manager of the mall went out and started to talk to **the crowd.**

    S3 Kısa bir tartışmanın ardından, — After some discussion,

    S4 Müdür **bir öğrenciyi** sertçe azarladı. — The manager harshly scolded **a student.**

The INFR condition is illustrated by (31), where the anchor expression *cancer* triggers a frame with the slot of *an oncologist*, thus the concept of the indefinite is pre-activated. In this condition there is no previously introduced set as in the PART condition.

(31) INFR
    S1 Başkent yakınlarındaki bir köyde **kanser** vakalarındaki ani artış dikkatleri çekti. — In a village near the capital the sudden increase in **cancer** cases attracted attention.

    S2 Ekolojik Yaşam İnisiyatifi düzenlediği basın toplantısında **kanser** artışının sebebinin araştırılacağını belirtti. — The Ecological Life Initiative announced at the arranged press conference that the factors causing the increase in **cancer** cases will be investigated.

    S3 Toplantının ardından, — After the conference,

    S4 İnisiyatif **bir onkoloğu** bölgede görevlendirdi. — The initiative commissioned **an oncologist** in the area.

Finally, we examined the condition BOTH with both discourse relations, a partitive and an inferential relation. We think that this condition seems to be the most natural context for indefinites in topic position—on the one hand the text introduces a set out of which the indefinite can select a referent and on the other hand the descriptive noun in the indefinite is already per-activated by an appropriate frame. Here *group of guests* introduces the set, and *embassy* the frame that pre-activates *diplomat*.

(32) BOTH
S1 Çin **büyükelçiliğindeki** resepsiyonda geniş **bir davetli kitlesi** vardı.
There was **a large group of guests** at the reception at the **Chinese embassy**
S2 Davetin ortalarına doğru **büyükelçi davetlilere** hitaben bir konuşma yaptı.
Towards the middle of the invitation **the ambassador** gave a speech to the **guests**.
S3 Konuşmanın sonuna doğru,
Towards the end of the speech,
S4 Büyükelçi **bir diplomatı** podyuma çağırdı.
The ambassador called **a diplomat** to the podium.

According to our hypotheses H1-H3, we predict that (i) non-topical indefinites are more acceptable than topical ones; (ii) the NONE condition is worse than any other linking condition in the topic condition, but there should be no difference in the non-topic condition; and (iii) that INFR indefinites are better than PART indefinites.

4.1 *Design*

We supplied 4 critical items for each condition (16 in total) and 16 filler items.[6] Note that we had lexically different test items such that we needed only one list. However, the comparison between the items was difficult as they contained different contextual and lexical material. The study was conducted as a web-based questionnaire. 29 participants rated the examples on a 10-point scale with regards to how natural they found the target sentence as a continuation of the three sentence discourse given above.

4.2 *Observations*

The results of this pilot experiment are presented in Figure 5.2. We can observe that indefinites in non-topical position (mean value: 7,36, standard deviation: 2,42) are better rated than indefinites in topical position (mean value: 6,2; sd: 2,16). Thus, we see that indefinite direct objects in the neutral position (NON-TOPIC) are clearly better-rated but we can also observe that indefinites in topic position are judged as grammatical. The second observation is that we do not see clear contrasts between the conditions of the discourse relations. Upon inspection we see that the NONE condition of topical indefinites is worse than

---

6 Please do not hesitate to contact the authors for a comprehensive list of all items, which can also be found at http://lfcs.ii.metu.edu.tr/var/Appendix-inferable-and-partitive-indefinites.pdf.

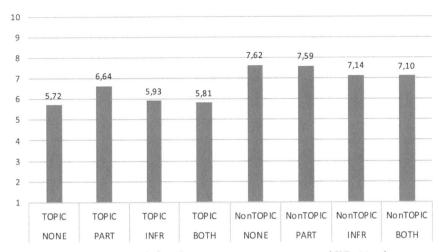

FIGURE 5.2   Exp. 1: Discourse linking (NONE vs. PART vs. INFR vs. BOTH) X Position (TOPIC vs. NONTOPIC): Mean ratings of 29 participants in a web based questionnaire

the other linking conditions, but the difference to the condition BOTH in minimal. Statistical analysis shows that the contrast between non-topical and topical is significant, but the others are not.[7]

4.3   Discussion

The results confirm H1 that direct object indefinites are better-rated in non-topic position than in topic position. But they also show that indefinites in topic position are grammatically acceptable. The results were inconclusive with respect to H2 and H3, namely the question of whether the discourse linking conditions contribute to a better rating of topical indefinites, and the issue of whether the conceptual discourse linking (inferability) provides a better or easier link than partitivity, i.e. the contextual linking. So this pilot provided us with a first step to answering our hypothesis. But it was not detailed enough to support either H2 or H3. We therefore designed another experiment.

---

[7] Statistical analyses were conducted in R version 1.0.136 using the lme4 package (Bates, Mächler, Bolker & Walker, 2015) to perform linear mixed-effect models (LMEM) with the score as outcome variable. As fixed effects, we entered discourse linking (NONE vs. PART vs. INFR vs. BOTH) and syntactic position (TOPIC vs. NONTOPIC) into the model. As random effects, we had intercepts for subjects and items. The discourse linking BOTH and the syntactic position NONTOPIC were mapped onto the intercept. Overall mean ratings are shown in Figure 5.2. The results show a significant main effect for position TOPIC vs. NONTOPIC $b = -1.29$, $SE = 0.35$, $t = -3.66$. There is no significant interaction of discourse linking and syntactic position.

5 Experiment 2: Position (2) x Discourse Linking (2)

In Experiment 2, we wanted to compare two discourse linking conditions with the two informational structural positions. In particular, we wanted to test H3, i.e. whether we can detect a difference between the different discourse linking condition. We chose PART and BOTH, since BOTH is easier to control than INFR. Thus, we had a 2×2 design NONTOPIC vs. TOPIC with PART vs. BOTH. We expected that indefinites in the NONTOPIC position would be better rated than in the TOPIC position and that indefinites in the BOTH conditions would be better rated than in the PART condition.

5.1 *Design*

We created 12 test items with the indefinite direct object in non-topical and in topical position. We then created two different context sentences for the two conditions PART and BOTH, respectively, see (33):

(33) Test items for experiment 2

PART	BOTH
Ödül töreni için **jüri üyeleri** sahnenin yanında toplanmışlardı.	**Rektörlük** seçimleri için **akademisyenler** konferans salonunda toplanmışlardı.
'For the award ceremony, **the members of the jury** were gathered near the stage.'	'For the **presidential** elections, **the academicians** were gathered in the conference room.'

    NONTOPIC Fatma form doldurmak için masaya **bir profesörü** cağırdı (SOV)
                    'Fatma called **a professor** to the table in order to fill out a form.'

    TOPIC   **Bir profesörü** Fatma form doldurmak için masaya cağırdı (OSV)
                    'Fatma called **a professor** to the table in order to fill out a form.'

We composed four balanced lists with one condition for each sentence, having included 12 fillers with some pragmatically inappropriate sentences and some grammatical ones as controls. 99 participants were asked to judge the appropriateness of the continuation sentence on a scale from 1 to 7 (bad–good). 3 participants were excluded, because they took 2 standard deviation above the mean duration for the questionnaire.

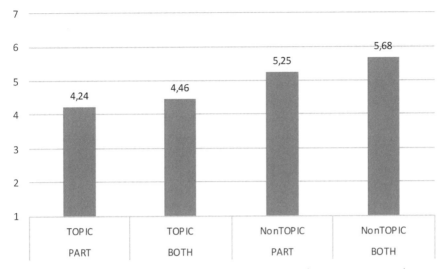

FIGURE 5.3 Exp. 2: Discourse linking (PART vs. BOTH) X Position (TOPIC vs. NONTOPIC): Mean ratings of 96 participants in a web-based questionnaire

5.2   Results and Discussion

The results clearly show that both parameters are significant:[8] Indefinites in non-topical position are clearly better rated than in topic position (confirming H1), but licensing indefinites in topic position by a partitive relation and an inferential relation (BOTH) is better than only by a partitive relation (PART), somewhat confirming H2. Both parameters are independent and therefore "add up".[9] Against the first experiment, experiment 2 provides significant evidence that a partitive relation is accepted to a different degree than one that is partitive and inferential. As we had yet to test H3, i.e. that the inferential relation is stronger than the partitive, we designed experiment 3.

---

8   Statistical analyses were conducted in R version 1.0.136 using the lme4 package (Bates et al., 2015) to perform linear mixed-effect models (LMEM) with the score as outcome variable. As fixed effects, we entered Discourse linking and Position into the model. As random effects, we had intercepts for subjects and items. The results show a significant main effect for Context $b = 0.33$, SE $= 0.15$, $t = 2.20$ and for Position $b = 1.12$, SE $= 0.15$, $t = 7.28$. There is no significant interaction of Context and Position.

9   An anonymous reviewer correctly suggested that this result could also be explained by the assumption that both parameters contribute to a higher coherence in general. We think, however, that the inspection of the results of experiment 1 suggested—contrary to the results of experiment 2—that the type of discourse linking has a different effect for topical indefinite than for non-topical indefinites.

6 Experiment 3: Discourse Linking (NONE vs. PART vs. INFR vs. BOTH)

In order to test H3, i.e. that the inferential (or conceptual) relation is a stronger licenser for the topic position than the partitive relation, we conducted another experiment in which we compared all four discourse linking conditions in the topic condition, see (34). We created four different contexts expressing the four types of discourse linking. And we tested then the same second sentence in these four conditions:

(34) Sample test item for Expt 3
BOTH Rektörlük seçimleri için akademisyenler konferans salonunda toplanmışlardı. 'For the university **presidential** elections **the academicians** were gathered in the conference hall.'
PART Yönetim Kurulu seçimleri için dernek **üyeleri** spor salonunda toplanmışlardı 'For the directory board elections **the members** (of the foundation) were gathered in the sports hall.'
INFR **Konferans** salonunda havalandırma çalışmıyordu. 'Air conditioning was not working in the **conference** hall.'
NONE Büyük spor salonu oldukça havasızdı. 'The grand sports hall was practically suffocating.'

Bir profesörü Fatma kahve içmek için dışarı çıkardı.
'Fatma took **a professor** out to have coffee.'

6.1 Design

We created 12 test items with the indefinite direct object in topical position and four different context sentences for the four discourse linking conditions. In contrast to experiment 1, we used the same critical sentence for each type of context, thereby providing a more reliable experimental setup. We composed four balanced lists with one condition for each sentence, along with 12 filler items involving different case markings and arranged in a spectrum of acceptability by manipulating coherence. We conducted a web-based questionnaire with 52 participants. They were asked to judge the appropriateness of the continuation sentence on a scale from 1 to 7 (bad–good). 2 participants were excluded, because they took 2 standard deviation above the mean duration for the questionnaire; 4 participants who had given the same response to all items were also excluded.

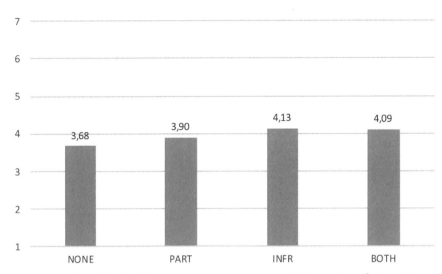

FIGURE 5.4 Exp. 3: Context (BOTH vs. PART vs. INFR vs. NONE): Mean ratings of 46 participants in a web-based questionnaire

6.2 Results and Discussion

Participants rated inferable topical indefinites (INFR) significantly better than non-linked topical indefinites (NONE). When it comes to the BOTH context, where the indefinite is both contextually and conceptually linked, indefinites in the condition BOTH were marginally significantly better-rated than non-linked indefinites. Solely partitive indefinites (PART) ranked quite close to non-linked indefinites. The results provide some support to our hypothesis H3 as the INFR condition is significant better than the NONE condition, while this is not the case for the PART condition. It is interesting to note that PART does not contribute to a better acceptability of indefinites in topic position.[10]

---

10 Statistical analyses were conducted in R (version 3.4.3) using the lme4 package (Bates et al., 2015). We fitted a linear mixed effects model and predicted ratings by the participants as a function of discourse linking (NONE or INFR or PART or BOTH). That is, ratings were included in the model as dependent measure and context as predictor with four levels. We also included random intercepts as well as a random slope for context for both participants and items. Results show that inferable topical indefinites were rated as significantly more acceptable than their non-linked counterparts, $b = 0.46$, $SE = 0.20$, $t = 2.67$. There was also a statistical, albeit non-significant trend indicating that when the referent was both contextually and conceptually linked, ratings improved compared to the non-linked condition, $b = 0.41$, $SE = 0.23$, $t = 1.77$.

7 General Discussion and Conclusions

Indefinites introduce new discourse items and are therefore not very felicitous in topic position, which requires referential and/or familiar referents. We have focused in this study on the familiarity aspect of topics (Kuno, 1972; Prince, 1981c; Gundel, 1985, 1988; Ward & Prince, 1991). Weakly familiar indefinites are possible in topic position. There is, however, a controversy about the source of this weak familiarity. Prince (1981c) assumes that the membership relation of partitive indefinites (see also Enç, 1991) is the crucial source for topicalized indefinites (in English). In our study we focused on two types of discourse relatedness or linking: (i) implicit partitivity, a contextually induced set membership relation; and (ii) inferability, a conceptually/lexically induced linking relation. We were interested in whether there are different degrees of linking to previous discourse, so that the particular level has a bearing on the felicity of an indefinite noun phrase in topic position. We formulated the following hypotheses:

H1: Indefinites in non-topic position are more felicitous than in topic position.
H2: Indefinites in topic position are felicitous if discourse linked.
H3: Inferable indefinites are better suited for a topic position than partitive indefinites.

We used Turkish as a case domain. Our choice of Turkish was motivated by its clear surface indication of topicality manifested in word order variation, making it suitable for testing in a text-based questionnaire setup. To test our hypothesis, we conducted three acceptability judgment studies in the form of web-based questionnaires. We manipulated the context to construct the four linking types: (i) partitive (PART), (ii) inferable (INFR), (iii) both partitive and inferable (BOTH), and (iv) no linking (NONE). Through word order variation we manipulated the topic status of the target indefinite between TOPIC and NONTOPIC.

In a pilot experiment (Exp. 1), where context types were crossed with position, we obtained significant evidence that non-topical indefinites are better-rated than topical ones, and linking does indeed improve the felicity of topical indefinites (H1 and H2). Inspection suggested some contrasts between the types of linking for topical indefinites: the NONE condition was worse than the other conditions PART, INFR and BOTH. This contrast did not prove significant. We conducted a second study (Exp. 2), where we focused on PART versus BOTH, still manipulating topicality. Our aim was to test H2, namely whether different linking types show differences in acceptability. The second experiment, again, showed that, overall, indefinites are less acceptable in topic position compared to non-topic position. We also observed that when the INFR and PART types come together (i.e. BOTH), the acceptability is higher in comparison to having just INFR. This suggests that linking to previous discourse might come in different levels, one operating in the referential domain (partitive) and the other in the conceptual domain (inferability).

To reach a better account of the contributions of different types of linking, we conducted a third study (Exp. 3), supplying all four possible combinations of linking types, including the no-linking condition, as we did in Experiment 1. The two differences from that experiment were that the experiment was more tightly controlled by having the same target sentence for all types of linking, and that we employed only the topical condition, in order to simplify the setup. Through this experiment we were able to confirm our hypothesis H3, namely that inferable indefinites are better rated than partitive indefinites. The reason we were expecting this was that inferability derives from a lexical relation while partitivity involves an inferential mechanism that goes beyond lexical knowledge. One confusing aspect of our findings at this point was that the BOTH condition was not the best-rated context type. This is contrary to our expectation formulated as hypothesis H3.

These experiments have contributed to our understanding of the linking of weak familiar indefinite topics to previous discourse. The studies also show that familiarity is a crucial parameter for identifying topics, as most of our examples involved non-specific indefinites. However, the nature of topics and in particular of indefinite topics is still an open research issue.

Acknowledgements

Earlier versions of this paper were presented at the workshop "Information Structuring in Discourse", at the 39th Annual Conference of the German Linguistic Society (DGfS 2017), Saarbrücken (Germany); at the Linguistics seminar at Syracuse University, in October 2017, and at the workshop "Information structure at the interfaces" at the 51st Annual Meeting of the Societas Linguistica Europaea (SLE), in Tallinn in August 2018. We would like to thank the audiences for critical questions and comments, the editors of this volume Anke Holler, Katja Suckow, and Israel de la Fuente for their support and helpful comments, the two anonymous reviewers for their very constructive suggestion and comments, and Elyesa Seidel for her support with the statistics. The first author acknowledges the financial support by the Deutsche Forschungsgemeinschaft (DFG, German Research Foundation), Project-ID 281511265, SFB "Prominence in Language" in the project C04 "Conceptual and referential activation in discourse" at the University of Cologne, Department of German Language and Literature I, Linguistics.

References

Aksan, Yeşim. (1995). *Functional Universals and some Aspects of Sentence Topic in Turkish* [Doctoral dissertation, Hacettepe University].

Asher, Nicholas, & Alex Lascarides. (1998). Bridging. *Journal of Semantics*, 15(1), 83–113.

Bates, Douglas, Martin Mächler, Ben Bolker, & Steven Walker. (2015). Fitting linear mixed-effects models using lme4. *Journal of Statistical Software*, 67(1), 1–48.

Birner, Betty J. (2006). Inferential relations and noncanonical word order. In B.J. Birner, & G. Ward (Eds.), *Drawing the boundaries of meaning, Neo-Gricean studies in pragmatics and semantics in honor of Laurence R. Horn* (pp. 31–51). Amsterdam: John Benjamins.

Brocher, Andreas, & Klaus von Heusinger. (2018). A dual-process activation model: Processing definiteness and information status. *Glossa: A Journal of General Linguistics*, 3(1), 108, 1–34.

Clark, Herbert H. (1977). Bridging. In P.N. Johnson-Laird, & P.C. Wason (Eds.), *Thinking: Readings in cognitive science* (pp. 169–174). Cambridge: Cambridge University Press.

Clark, Herbert H., & Catherine R. Marshall. (1981). Definite reference and mutual knowledge. In A.K. Joshi, B.L. Webber, & I.A. Sag (Eds.), *Elements of discourse understanding* (pp. 10–63). Cambridge: Cambridge University Press.

Ebert, Cornelia, & Stefan Hinterwimmer. (2009). The interpretation of topical indefinites as direct and indirect aboutness topics. In M. Zimmermann, & C. Féry (Eds.), *Information Structure: Theoretical, Typological, and Experimental Perspectives* (pp. 89–113). Oxford: Oxford University Press.

Enç, Mürvet. (1991). The semantics of specificity. *Linguistic Inquiry*, 22, 1–25.

Endriss, Cornelia. (2009). *Quantificational topics. A scopal treatment of exceptional wide scope phenomena*. Berlin: Springer.

Erguvanlı, Eser Emine. (1984). *The function of word order in Turkish grammar*. Berkeley, CA: University of California Press.

Erkü, Feride. (1983). *Discourse pragmatics and word order in Turkish* [Doctoral dissertation, University of Minnesota].

Falco, Michelangelo, & Roberto Zamparelli. (2019). Partitives and Partitivity. *Glossa: A Journal of General Linguistics*, 4(1) 111, 1–49.

Farkas, Donka. (1994). Specificity and scope. In L. Nash & G. Tsoulas (Eds.), *Actes du Premier Colloque Langues & Grammaire*, 1, 119–137.

Frey, Werner. (2004). A medial topic position for German. *Linguistische Berichte*, 198, 153–190.

Geist, Ljudmila. (2011). *Indefiniteness and Specificity: Lexical Marking and Information-Structural Conditions* [Habilitation thesis, University of Stuttgart].

Göksel, Aslı, & Celia Kerslake. (2005). *Turkish: A comprehensive grammar*. London: Routledge.

Gračanin-Yüksek, Martina, & Selçuk İşsever. (2011). Movement of bare objects in Turkish. *Dilbilim Araştırmaları*, 22(1), 33–49.
Gundel, Jeanette. (1985). 'Shared knowledge' and topicality. *Journal of Pragmatics*, 9(1), 83–197.
Gundel, Jeanette. (1988). Universals of topic-comment structure. In M. Hammond, E. Moravcsik, & J.R. Wirth (Eds.), *Studies in syntactic typology* (pp. 209–239). Amsterdam: John Benjamins.
von Heusinger, Klaus. (1999). *Intonation and information structure. The representation of focus in phonology and semantics*. Konstanz: Universität Konstanz.
von Heusinger, Klaus. (2002). Specificity and definiteness in sentence and discourse structure. *Journal of Semantics*, 19(3), 245–274.
von Heusinger, Klaus, & Jaklin Kornfilt. (2005). The case of the direct object in Turkish: Semantics, syntax and morphology. *Turkic Languages*, 9, 3–44.
von Heusinger, Klaus, & Jaklin Kornfilt. (2017). Partitivity and case marking in Turkish and related languages. *Glossa: A Journal of General Linguistics*, 2(1), 1–40.
Hockett, Charles. F. (1958). *A course in modern linguistics*. New York: The Macmillan Company.
Hoeksema, Jacob. (1996). Introduction. In J. Hoeksema (Ed.), *Partitives: Studies on the syntax and semantics of partitive and related constructions* (pp. 1–24). Berlin: De Gruyter.
de Hoop, Helen. (2003). Partitivity. In L. Cheng, & R. Sybesma (Eds.), *The second Glot international state-of-article book. The latest in linguistics. Studies in Generative Grammar* (Vol. 61, pp. 179–212). Berlin: De Gruyter Mouton.
İşsever, Selçuk. (2003). Information structure in Turkish: The word order-prosody interface. *Lingua*, 113(11), 1025–1053.
Ionin, Tania, Ora Matushansky, & Eddy G. Ruys. (2006). Parts of speech: Toward a unified semantics for partitives. In C. Davis, A.R. Deal, & Y. Zabbal (Eds.), *Proceedings of NELS* (Vol. 36(1), pp. 357–370). Amherst, MA: University of Massachusetts, GLSA.
Kelepir, Meltem. (2001). *Topics in Turkish syntax: Clausal structure and scope* [Doctoral dissertation, Massachusetts Institute of Technology].
Kılıçaslan, Yılmaz. (1994). *Information Packaging in Turkish* [Doctoral dissertation, University of Edinburgh].
Koptjevskaja-Tamm, Maria. (2006). Partitives. In K. Brown (Ed.), *Encyclopedia of languages and linguistics* (2nd ed., pp. 216–221). Amsterdam: Elsevier.
Kornfilt, Jaklin. (1997). *Turkish*. London: Routledge.
Kuno, Susumu. (1972). Functional sentence perspective: a case study from Japanese and English. *Linguistic Inquiry*, 3(3), 269–320.
Özge, Umut. (2011). Turkish indefinites and accusative marking. In A. Simpson (Ed.), *Proceedings of the 7th Workshop on Altaic Formal Linguistics (WAFL 7)* (pp. 253–267). Cambridge, MA: MIT Working Papers in Linguistics.

Özge, Umut, Duygu Özge, & Klaus von Heusinger. (2016). Strong indefinites in Turkish, referential persistence, and salience structure. In A. Holler, & K. Suckow (Eds.), *Empirical perspectives on anaphora resolution* (pp. 169–191). Berlin: De Gruyter.

Pesetsky, David. (1987). Wh-in-situ: Movement and Unselective Binding. In E.J. Reuland, & A.G.B. ter Meulen (Eds.), *The Representation of (In)definiteness* (pp. 98–129). Cambridge, MA: MIT Press.

Portner, Paul, & Katsuhiko Yabushita. (2001). Specific indefinites and the information structure theory of topics. *Journal of Semantics, 18*, 217–297.

Prince, Ellen F. (1981a). On the inferencing of indefinite-*this* NPs. In B. Webber, A.K. Joshi, & I. Sag (Eds.), *Elements of Discourse Understanding* (pp. 231–250). Cambridge: Cambridge University Press.

Prince, Ellen F. (1981b). Toward a taxonomy of given-new information. In P. Cole (Ed.), *Radical pragmatics* (pp. 223–255). New York: Academic Press.

Prince, Ellen F. (1981c). Topicalization, focus-movement, and Yiddish-movement: A pragmatic differentiation. In *Proceedings of the Seventh Annual Meeting of the Berkeley Linguistics Society* (pp. 249–264) Berkley, CA.

Prince, Ellen F. (1992). The ZPG letter: Subjects, definiteness, and information-status. In W.C. Mann, & S.A. Thompson (Eds.), *Discourse Description: Diverse Linguistic Analyses of a Fund-Raising Text* (pp. 295–325). Amsterdam: John Benjamins.

Reinhart, Tanya. (1981). Pragmatics and linguistics: An analysis of sentence topics. *Philosophica, 27*, 53–94.

Roberts, Craige. (2019). Topics. In P. Portner, C. Maienborn, & K. von Heusinger (Eds.), *Semantics—Sentence and Information Structure* (pp. 381–412). Berlin: De Gruyter Mouton. Reprint from: K. von Heusinger, C. Maienborn, & P. Portner (Ed.). (2011). *Semantics* (Vol. 2, pp. 1908–1934). Berlin: De Gruyter Mouton.

Vallduví, Enric. (1990). *The informational component* [Doctoral dissertation, University of Pennsylvania].

Ward, Gregory L., & Ellen F. Prince. (1991). On the topicalization of indefinite NPs. *Journal of Pragmatics, 16*, 167–177.

CHAPTER 6

Projection to the Speaker: Non-restrictive Relatives Meet Coherence Relations

Katja Jasinskaja and Claudia Poschmann

1   Introduction

Non-restrictive relative clauses (NRCs) belong to a range of phenomena at the interface between syntax and discourse. On the one hand, they are syntactically embedded clauses. On the other hand, they do not contribute to the meaning of the main clause, but are interpreted like independent sentences, outside the scope of all operators in the embedding sentence (Chierchia & McConnell-Ginet, 1990; Potts, 2005; Simons, Tonhauser, Beaver & Roberts, 2011; Koev, 2013).[1] For example, the NRC *who hates me* in (1) is embedded in a conditional clause. Nevertheless, the sentence entails that the dean hates the speaker. That means that the proposition expressed by the NRC enters the semantic representation in the global context, outside the scope of the conditional, i.e. the NRC is interpreted *globally*. If the NRC were interpreted *locally* at its position inside the conditional, the sentence should be paraphrasable as 'if Peter called the dean and if the dean hates me, ...' However, this reading is not available in (1).

(1)   If Peter called the dean,
      who hates me,   [→ The dean hates me.]
      I would be in trouble.   (adapted from Schlenker, 2013, p. 7)

This wide-scope behavior of NRCs has received a number of theoretical accounts. Syntactic accounts (e.g. McCawley, 1982) argue that NRCs are attached high in the syntactic tree (at CP-level or discourse level), i.e. occur outside the scope of operators like *if* in (1) not only semantically, but also

---

1   Among the topics addressed in this volume, other phenomena that cross the syntax/discourse boundary include German V2 relatives and the mood alternation in Romance studied by Coniglio and Hinterhölzl (this volume), as well as V2 transgressions caused by adverbial clauses (Haegeman, this volume).

syntactically. Another group of accounts assumes that NRCs are syntactically embedded, but that their content is not interpreted in its embedded position but projected to the global context, either because it constitutes a separate dimension of semantic meaning (e.g. not-at-issue content in Potts, 2005), or because it has a different pragmatic status, being pragmatically not-at-issue (Simons et al., 2011), evoking an immediate Common Ground update (Ander-Bois, Brasoveanu & Henderson, 2011), or having its own illocutionary force (Koev, 2013). All these accounts predict that NRCs invariably receive global interpretation, i.e. contribute a proposition outside the scope of all semantic operators in the sentence.

However, Schlenker (2013) points out a number of puzzling examples from English and French, in which the NRC appears to receive a local interpretation. For example, the NRC in (2) does not necessarily commit the speaker to the assumption that the dean already called the chair.

(2) If Peter called the dean,
 who then called the chair, [↛ The dean called the chair.]
 I would be in trouble. (adapted from Schlenker, 2013, p. 7)

However, the conditions that license such local readings are poorly understood. The main goal of this paper is to find the generalization that best describes the projection pattern of NRCs, and to move towards a better theoretical understanding of this phenomenon. We will start in section 2 by giving a brief overview over the contrasts reported by Schlenker (2013) and recapitulating related experimental results of Poschmann (2018), which both point towards a dependency of NRC scope on coherence relations. In section 3, we will review some ideas on what could stand behind these observations, and argue that the availability of local readings cannot be reduced to the syntactic differences between appositive and continuative relative clauses described by Holler (2005, 2008) or to anaphoric trapping in the sense of van der Sandt (1992). On the basis of the observations accumulated up to that point, most notably, the apparent tendency of NRCs to be interpreted locally if they are connected to their host clause by a coordinating coherence relation like *Narration* or *Contrast* (in contrast to subordinating relations in the sense of Asher & Vieu, 2005), section 4 will finally motivate a change of perspective upon the problem: Instead of taking projection from NRCs as the normal case and explaining local readings, we will take local interpretation as the default, and try to explain projection within the observed limits. In section 5 we will argue ultimately that NRCs project only if they are speaker-oriented, and that they are speaker-oriented only if the speaker's atti-

2 Local Readings

2.1 *Local Readings Are Local Readings*

We agree with Schlenker (2013) that examples such as (2) provide a strong argument for the assumption that NRCs can be both syntactically and semantically embedded. His argument is twofold. Firstly, he shows that NRCs can have truly local, not only modally subordinated readings. The NRC in (3) does not tell us that the dean called the chair (global reading), it does not even have the reading that in any case in which Peter called the dean, the dean would call the chair (modal subordination reading), it really seems to have the reading that the speaker would be in trouble on two conditions: if Peter called the dean and if the dean called the chair (local reading), which is comparable to the reading of a local conjunction.

(3) If Peter called the dean, **who then called the chair**, I would be in deep trouble.
    a. ↛ The dean called the chair. (global)
    b. ↛ If Peter called the dean, the dean would call the chair. (modal subordination)
    c. → If Peter called the dean and (if) the dean called the chair, ... (local)

Second, he argues that NRCs in this respect differ structurally from the corresponding parenthetical or matrix-clause paraphrases. Note that the sentence receives no local interpretation and the past tense is no longer bound by the conditional if the NRC is replaced by a parenthetical (4a) or a postposed matrix clause (4b).

(4)   a. ??If Peter called the dean (**he then called the chair**), I would be in deep trouble.
    b. If Peter called the dean, I would be in deep trouble. ??**He then called the chair.** (adapted from Schlenker, 2013, p. 7)

This indicates that the NRC in (3) is indeed interpreted locally. In other words, contrary to standard assumptions (Chierchia & McConnell-Ginet, 1990; Potts, 2005; Simons et al., 2011; Koev, 2013), the projection pattern of NRCs seems to be flexible.

2.2 Local Readings Are Not Always Available

As Schlenker (2013) concedes, local readings are not always readily available. The acceptability of the NRC in (1) degrades considerably if we force the NRC under the scope of the conditional by setting the NRC's verb in the past tense as in (5b).

(5) a. If Peter called the dean, **who then called the chair**, I would be in deep trouble.
b. ??If Peter called the dean, **who hated me**, I would be in deep trouble.

(adapted from Schlenker, 2013, p. 7)

But why should a local reading be available with (5a) and not with (5b)? (5a) and (5b) differ at least in (i) the predicate type of the NRC (state/event) and (ii) the presence/absence of the anaphoric expression *then*. In addition, Schlenker (2013) remarks that (iii) the NRCs in (5a) and (5b) establish different coherence relations to their host clause. While in (5a) the event described in the NRC follows in time the event described in the antecedent of the *if*-clause and the NRC, hence, establishes a *Narration* relation with its host clause, the NRC in (5a) seems to provide an *Explanation* for the proposition asserted in the rest of the sentence that the speaker would be in trouble if Peter called the dean.

Note that *Narration*, according to Asher and Vieu (2005), is a coordinating coherence relation while *Explanation* is a subordinating one.[2] Informally, in coordinating relations (*Contrast, Parallel, Narration*) the discourse units are on a par and the discourse progresses in a normal left-to-right fashion, whereas subordinating relations (*Elaboration, Explanation*) lead to hierarchical structures and discourse embedding, and do not "push the discourse forward". As Asher and Vieu (2005) highlight, this distinction is crucial for explaining how the dis-

---

2 According to this classification coordinating coherence relations include *Narration* (temporal sequentiality), *Result* (forward causal relation), *Parallel* (similar states of affairs), and *Contrast* (opposite states of affairs, argument-counterargument relation, denial of expectation). Subordinating relations include *Elaboration* (subordinate segment gives more detail), *Explanation* (subordinate segment presents the cause of the event or the reason to believe the statement) and *Background* (subordinate segment describes the background state of the event).

course progresses and how anaphoric relations are resolved. Therefore, it seems like a sensible hypothesis that the contrast in (5) is due to a contrast between coordinating vs. subordinating coherence relations expressed by the NRC.

In three experiments on German, Poschmann (2018) tested the availability of local readings depending on several factors such as the sentence type (NRC/parenthesis/*and*-conjunction/postposed matrix clause), the NRC's predicate type (event/state) and the coherence relation between the NRC and its host-clause (subordinating/coordinating). In her experiments, each item consisted of a short context story and a target sentence and the participants had to judge whether the target was appropriate as part of a summary of the information given by the story. The stories were constructed such that the wide-scope reading and a modal subordination reading of the target sentences were explicitly ruled out. For example, the target sentences in (6) were presented in a context in which Gerd got bitten by a poisonous snake and only can be saved if he reaches Dr. Meier and Dr. Meier gives him the right antidote. The context made clear that we do not know, whether Gerd can be saved even if he reaches Dr. Meier, since it is unclear whether Dr. Meier has got the right antidote available. Thus, if the participants only got a wide-scope or modally subordinated reading, according to which Gerd is saved as soon as he reaches Dr. Meier (because in this case Dr. Meier will for sure inject him the right antidote), they were expected to reject the target as part of a summary of the context. Only if the participants interpreted the NRC as contributing conjunctively to the antecedent of the *if*-clause (such as the conjunction in (6b)), were they expected to accept the target sentence as a summary of the context-story. Experiment 1 contrasted NRCs (6a) with embedded conjoined clauses (6b), and matrix clause parentheticals (6c). Experiment 2 contrasted NRCs (6a) with postposed matrix clauses (*Der verabreicht ihm das passende Gegengift.*/'He gives him the right antidote.'), which followed the entire complex sentence containing the NRC.

(6) Wenn Gerd rechtzeitig Dr. Meier erreicht, (…)
'If Gerd reaches Dr. Meier in time, (…)'
   a. **der ihm das passende Gegengift verabreicht,**
      'who gives him the right antidote, (…)' (NRC)
   b. **und der ihm das passende Gegengift verabreicht, (…).**
      'and he gives him the right antidote, (…)' (conjunction)
   c. **(der verabreicht ihm das passende Gegengift), (…).**
      '(he gives him the right antidote), (…)' (parenthesis)
      '… kann Gerd gerettet werden.'
      'can Gerd be saved.'

In experiments 1 and 2, the items were constructed so that they did not contain discourse markers or anaphors which could force a particular reading. However, the most salient discourse relations for the event type were *Narration/Result* (coordinating) and for the state type *Explanation/Background* (subordinating). In *Narration/Result*, the occurrence of the event in the NRC was dependent on the event in the matrix clause, which might favor an embedded interpretation. Therefore, experiment 3 only tested NRCs in which either a *Contrast* or a *Narration* interpretation (both coordinating) was forced, by inserting either *dann* ('then') or *wider Erwarten* ('against expectations'):

(7) a. (...), der ihm **(dann/wider Erwarten)** (NRC event)
    das passende Gegengift verabreicht, (...)
    'who (then/against expectation) gives him the right antidote'
  b. (...), der **(dann/wider Erwarten)** (NRC state)
    über das passende Gegengift verfügt, (...)
    'who (then/against expectation) has got the right antidote'

In addition, Poschmann (2018) manipulated the predicate type (event vs. state) of the target sentences in all the three experiments:

(8) a. (...), der ihm das passende Gegengift **verabreicht**, (...)
    'who gives him the right antidote' (NRC event)
  b. (...), der über das passende Gegengift **verfügt**, (...)
    'who has got the right antidote' (NRC state)

The results of all three experiments clearly show that NRCs indeed can be interpreted as embedded but that the availability of embedded readings is dependent on factors such as the predicate type of the NRC and the absence or presence of discourse marker. In the first two experiments, the participants accepted the NRCs with event predicates in around 50% of all cases, less often than the corresponding conjunctions (around 90%), but significantly more often than the matrix clause parenthesis (20%) or postposed matrix clauses (10%). NRCs with state predicates, by contrast, rated nearly as low (25%) as the corresponding matrix clause parenthesis. In experiment 3, however, where a coordinating discourse relation was forced, either by introducing a temporal connective *dann* ('then') (*Narration*) or a contrastive *wider Erwarten* ('against expectations') (*Contrast*), the acceptance rate increased dramatically (up to 85%) even for NRCs with state predicate type. These results suggest that NRCs are indeed flexible in scope. Since both aspect (event vs. state) and connectives serve as cues to coherence relations, the fact that NRC interpretation was found to depend on both parameters suggests that the coherence relation is, in fact, the primary factor that affects the projection pattern of NRCs.

3 Possible (Non-)explanations

Why should the type of coherence relations, holding between the NRC and its host clause, affect the scope of the NRC? Before we try to give an answer to this question, we will investigate two alternative explanations for the reported contrasts in this section. Neither gives a satisfactory account for the observed projection data.

3.1 Appositives vs. Continuatives

The observations by Schlenker (2013) and Poschmann (2018) are particularly interesting for German. For independent reasons like differences in position effects and intonation contours, Holler (2005, 2008) argues that there are two structurally distinct types of non-restrictive relative clauses in German, so-called *appositive* and *continuative* relative clauses, which differ in their predicate type, position, coherence relation as well as in their syntactic attachment point (DP- vs. CP-level). At first sight, the restrictions on local readings observed by Schlenker (2013) and Poschmann (2018) fit quite nicely the characteristics described in Holler (2005, 2008) for continuative relative clauses. Continuative relative clauses establish a coordinating relation (in the sense of Asher and Vieu (2005), such as *Narration, Result, Contrast*) with their host clause and typically relate two events. Typically, the event described in the host clause precedes the event in the continuative relative in time. In contrast, appositive relative clauses express a subordinating discourse relation and are rather flexible in their predicate type as well as in the temporal order described. According to Holler (2005, 2008), the NRCs in (5a) an (8a) are continuatives and the NRCs in (5b) and (8b) appositives. The first idea that comes to mind is that the effects we observe reflect the structural differences between continuative and appositive relative clauses, which only allow continuatives to have local readings.

We have two reasons to doubt this explanation. First, Poschmann (2018) reports that state predicates disfavor but do not exclude local readings. As soon as a coordinating relation is forced, local readings improve with event as well as with state predicate type. However, according to Holler (2005, 2008) state predicates should block continuative readings. Second, the structural analysis suggested by Holler (2005, 2008) does not really account for the reported contrasts. Holler (2005, 2008) assumes that appositives are attached at DP-level, while continuatives are attached high in the syntactic tree (CP-level/discourse level). But this predicts that only appositives (if anything) can get local readings, while continuatives should necessarily be interpreted globally. However, we observe just the reverse pattern.

3.2 *Trapping*

Another hypothesis, suggested e.g. by Martin (2016), is that the contrasts reported by Schlenker (2013) could be due to trapping the anaphors occurring in the NRC in the scope of the conditional. Most of Schlenker's examples of locally interpreted NRCs include anaphoric expressions such as *then* referring back to the proposition or event described by the host clause. Martin (2016) suggests that the contrast between (5a) and (5b) is due to the need to bind the anaphoric *then* in (5a), which only finds an appropriate antecedent (the event of Max calling the dean) in the scope of the conditional—a solution parallel to van der Sandt's (1992) trapping for anaphors and presuppositions. Compare examples (9a) and (9b) of van der Sandt (1992, p. 332): In (9a) the presupposition that John has a wife, triggered by the possessive *his*, can neither be bound by nor accommodated in the global context, since this would make the sentence incongruent (#*John has a wife and if he has a wife ...*). The antecedent of the conditional, however, provides a suitable antecedent for the presupposition and therefore can bind it locally. Similarly, the personal pronoun *she* in (9b) is bound by *a wife*, which blocks a specific interpretation of the personal pronoun.

(9) a. If John has a wife, his wife will be happy.
    b. If John has a wife, she will be happy.   (van der Sandt, 1992, p. 332)

Could the local readings of NRCs be reduced to anaphoric trapping? In this case we would predict that: (a) NRCs project if there is no anaphor to trap; and (b) if there is an anaphor to trap, i.e. if the sentence has a coherent interpretation only if the anaphor is resolved to an antecedent in the conditional, then a local reading should be available. Both predictions, however, are wrong.

Concerning (a), Poschmann's experiments (2018) show that inserting a temporal *dann* ('then') may improve the availability of local readings, especially in the case of NRCs of state predicate type, but local readings are available even in the absence of such temporal anaphoric expressions.

(10) a. Wenn Gerd Dr. Meier erreicht, der ihm (dann) das passende Gegengift verabreicht, kann Gerd gerettet werden.
    'If Gerd Dr. Meier reaches, who (then) gives him the right antidote, Gerd can be saved.'

b. #³ Wenn Gerd Dr. Meier erreicht, der (dann) über das passende Gegengift verfügt, kann Gerd gerettet werden.
'If Gerd Dr. Meier reaches, who (than) has got the right antidote available, Gerd can be saved.'

As an anonymous reviewer correctly observes, the examples in (10) contain an anaphoric link between the NRC and the host clause even if the temporal *dann* ('then') is omitted, since the relative pronoun *der* ('who') refers back to *Dr. Meier*, the antecedent of the NRC. However, since *Dr. Meier* is a proper name, which by itself is interpreted globally (independently of the conditional sentence in which it occurs), it cannot force the NRC inside the scope of the conditional. Instead, one might expect it to piggy-back the NRC in the sense of Venhuizen, Bos, Hendriks and Brouwer (2014) and force it to project to the global level. That this is not happening shows once more that anaphoric trapping is too weak to account for the scopal behavior of NRCs.[4]

This argument could perhaps be countered by Zeevat's (2016) recent extension of trapping from anaphoric identity to causal relations. He suggests the following generalization: "If the presupposition is inferred to be caused by or identical with a referent that is given by a non-entailed clause in the sentence, it does not project" (Zeevat, 2016, p. 16). In (11), for example, the factive verb *stopped* triggers the presupposition that Mary used to eat snails. Although this presupposition is not entailed by the antecedent of the *if*-clause, it does not project, but is interpreted locally. Zeevat (2016, p. 16) argues that in this case the presupposition is bound inside the conditional by the inference that being French causes, i.e. increases the probability of a person eating snails.

(11) If Mary is French, she has stopped eating snails.
[↛ Mary used to eat snails.]

Applying this reasoning to (10), Gerd reaching Dr. Meier increases the probability of Dr. Meier giving Gerd the antidote. That is, the NRC has a causal antecedent in the *if*-clause, and should not project. Likewise, the dean in Schlenker's example (3) probably only calls the chair, if he has been called by Peter. In both cases the "NRC is presented as being a consequence of the content of the antecedent of the *if*-clause" (Schlenker, 2013, p. 42). In contrast, whether

---

4 The same holds for Schlenker's (2013) original examples in (2), where the antecedent of the NRC is a definite noun phrase, which again is interpreted globally, while the NRC itself is interpreted locally. This clearly shows that the scope of NRCs is independent of the scope of its antecedent.

or not Dr. Meier has got the antidote available in (10b) does not depend on Gerd reaching him, and whether or not the dean hates the speaker does not depend on Peter calling the dean (5b). In both cases, the NRC need not be bound by the conditional, and therefore projects. In other words, it seems that Zeevat's causal version of trapping can explain Schlenker's examples and Poschmann's experimental results, on the assumption that propositions contributed by NRCs are treated in the same way as presuppositions.

However, it turns out that local readings are available even without any causal or standard identity-based anaphoric relation of the NRC to the conditional antecedent. For instance, the coherence relation in (12) can be understood as *Parallel*, which implies no causal or even temporal relation between the clauses it connects. Nevertheless, the NRC is interpreted locally in the scope of *if*:

(12) If Mary stands in front of Peter, who (first/then/also) moves a little closer to Max, everyone will fit into the picture.

This means that trapping, no matter if in van der Sandt's classical version or Zeevat's causal version, is too weak and does not predict local readings of NRCs in some cases, like (12), where they are obviously present.

On the other hand, trapping is also too strong. Prediction (b), that the NRC should be interpreted locally if it contains an anaphor that can only be resolved to an antecedent in a non-entailed context, is falsified by example (13). The pronoun *him* in the NRC can be bound by the indefinite *someone* in the *if*-clause. The resulting interpretation makes sense and can be felicitously expressed by a conjunction under *if*, cf. (13b). Nevertheless, this reading is not available for the NRC in (13a).

(13) If someone$_1$ wears this jacket,
    a. #which is too big for him$_1$,
    b.   and it is too big for him$_1$,
    he will look silly.

In other words, trapping goes a long way in explaining Schlenker's and Poschmann's examples, but ultimately breaks down in the face of new counterexamples.

4 Taking Stock and Changing Tack

We saw in the previous section that neither a structural approach of Holler (2005, 2008), nor an approach based on local binding, parallel to the trapping of presuppositions, predicts the observed (non-)projection pattern of NRCs. We have also seen examples supporting the hypothesis formulated by Poschmann (2018), that an NRC is interpreted locally if its relation to the host clause is coordinating: *Narration* in (5a) and *Parallel* in (12). Local readings of NRCs that express other kinds of coordinating coherence relations—*Contrast* and *Result*—are exemplified in (14) and (15), respectively.

(14) If Sue stays married to Max, who **nevertheless** continues his affair with Jim, they will regret it in the end.

(15) Wenn Eva Max kritisiert, der sich **deshalb** ärgert, dann ist die Stimmung im Eimer.
'If Eva criticizes Max who for that reason gets annoyed, then the party mood is ruined.'

In sum, the mapping of projection to discourse-structural subordination and local interpretation to discourse-structural coordination appears to be the best approximation of the observed pattern so far. The problem with this generalization is that it is rather mysterious. Why would coordination/subordination have anything to do with projection?

We believe that the relationship between these two dimensions is indirect and can be described by the following generalizations:

(16) a. NRCs project whenever they are *speaker-oriented*.
b. NRCs tend to express subordinating coherence relations.
c. NRCs that express subordinating coherence relations tend to be speaker-oriented.

In the rest of this paper we concentrate on the generalization (16a). The notion of speaker-orientedness, which it refers to, was originally applied to adverbials like *unfortunately* and *frankly* in *Unfortunately/Frankly, Ed fled*. (Potts, 2005, pp. 14–16), since they characterize the speaker's attitude towards the content of the clause they modify: The speaker deems it unfortunate that Ed fled; the speaker frankly utters the sentence *Ed fled*. In this paper we carry over the notion of speaker-orientedness from the adverbials to clauses they modify, and more generally, to clauses that express propositions towards which the speaker holds an attitude and that attitude is communicated somehow—by a speaker-oriented adverbial or some other conventional or pragmatic means. To test for speaker-orientedness one can follow up the sentence with an explicit denial of the attitude towards the proposition expressed by the clause in question, which will result in an infelicitous continuation if the clause is speaker-oriented (Potts, 2005, p. 117). For instance, (17) shows that the relative clause is speaker-oriented, whereas the complement clause *Chuck ... should be locked up* is not.

(17) Sheila believes that Chuck, who is a confirmed psychopath, should be locked up.
   a. #But I don't believe he is a psychopath.
   b. But I don't believe he should be locked up.

The speaker's attitude may be that of belief, desire, intention, etc. or any combination thereof (although belief is the one we will have to deal with most in connection with projection from NRCs).[5] This requires the presence of an appropriate attitude operator in the semantic representation, which must either be linguistically realized, or convincingly motivated, if implicit. Then the generalization in (16a) can be formulated more precisely as in (18):

(18) If the proposition p expressed by the NRC is in the semantic scope of an operator O that encodes the speaker's attitude to p, then $O(p)$ projects.

Notice that this implies a change of perspective upon the problem. The dominant view so far has been that NRCs *always* project *because* they are speaker-oriented as a matter of linguistic convention, or by definition of the type of semantic content they convey (conventional implicature in Potts, 2005). So it would seem that the challenge is to explain the exceptions presented by Schlenker (2013). We take a different tack. We assume that non-restrictive rel-

---

5 To a limited extent, the role of the speaker can be played not only by the actual speaker of the utterance, but also by the subject of a speech or attitude verb, as in indirect speech or attitude reports, or by a perspectival center in free indirect discourse (Harris & Potts, 2009). For instance, in (i) the negative attitude towards the content of the NRC can be attributed to Mary, in which case the NRC can be interpreted in the scope of Mary's belief. However, it is not that the NRC is simply interpreted locally. It projects past the conditional, but just until it encounters a context with a "pseudospeaker" that can be the holder of the attitude expressed by the speech act adverbial.
   (i) Mary believes that if Peter called the Dean, who **unfortunately** hates her, she would be in trouble. But I don't think this is so unfortunate.

atives are just like other subordinate clauses in that they are generally interpreted in their syntactic position.[6] On this approach, local readings do not require any special explanation. The challenge is to explain why NRCs project, and our central claim is that they project *if* they are speaker-oriented.

The generalizations (16b) and (16c) in turn address the question why NRCs project *most of the time*. For reasons of space we cannot discuss this issue in detail here. In Jasinskaja and Poschmann (2018), we summarize the results of corpus studies that suggest that there is a statistical tendency for an alignment between hierarchical structures in syntax and in discourse. That is, syntactically subordinate clauses, and NRCs in particular, tend to realize subordinating coherence relations, cf. (16b). On the other hand, unlike other kinds of subordinate clauses, relative clauses do not normally encode a semantic relation between the propositions expressed by the main and the relative clause. While adverbial clauses are projected by expressions like *when, because, although*, etc. that explicitly encode such a relation (temporal, causal, concessive, etc.), which then enters compositional semantics in the usual way, relative clauses establish a connection to the main clause via a shared participant of the described situations (e.g. the Dean in (1)), the relation between the situations or propositions themselves remains to be pragmatically inferred. The general pragmatic principles that apply in that case are the same as those at work in the inference of coherence relations between independent sentences. But those principles, as we argue in Jasinskaja & Poschmann (2018), mostly lead to the inference of what we call speaker-oriented coherence relations. Altogether, this results in the tendency of NRCs to be speaker-oriented (16c).

Having said that, we now come back to (16a) and the role of the speaker's attitude in the projection behavior of NRCs.

5 Speaker-Orientedness

In this section we argue that NRCs are not speaker-oriented by definition or due to some general conventional rule, but only under a number of well-defined conditions: (a) if some linguistic expressions present in the sentence indepen-

---

[6] We follow Poschmann (2018) in assuming that NRCs are normally attached at their host DP (Heim & Kratzer, 1998), but in extraposed position can be attached at higher sentential nodes—e.g. at IP-level. This ensures, for instance, that the NRC in Schlenker's example (i) can take intermediate scope—under if, but above the quantifier every and negation.
  (i) If each of the faculty had mentioned the fact that he didn't like the Chair, who had gotten fired as a result, we would now feel terrible.   (Schlenker, 2013, p. 17)

dently signal the speaker's attitude; or (b) if the speaker's attitude towards the proposition expressed by the NRC results from the position of the NRC in the discourse structure. Condition (a) might appear obvious. Nevertheless, it is useful to look at the case of explicitly marked attitudes first, in order to better understand the cases of type (b). We also show that speaker orientation is *a priori* independent of discourse-structural coordination/subordination, i.e. that there are speaker-oriented NRCs that realize a coordinating relation, and they project, and that there are non-speaker-oriented NRCs that realize a subordinating relation, and they are interpreted locally.

5.1 *Speaker-Oriented Adverbials*

The speaker's attitude towards a proposition can be expressed by speaker-oriented adverbials (Ernst, 2009). The clearest case is that of speech act adverbials and discourse particles such as the English *frankly* and *by the way*, or the German *ehrlich gesagt/offengestanden* ('frankly speaking') and *übrigens* ('by the way'). These expressions mark the proposition they modify as something the speaker says, e.g. *frankly p* ≈ 'the speaker says frankly that p', *by the way p* ≈ 'the speaker says p although it is not related to the current discourse topic'. Therefore, the speaker must be committed to p to the same extent as to anything he or she says. Note that sentence (3), repeated in (19), is infelicitous if such speaker-oriented adverbials are inserted. The local reading forced by *then* and the forward-shifted past tense is simply incompatible with the global interpretation as an independent speech act.[7]

(19) If tomorrow Peter called the Dean, who then (*frankly/*by the way/ ...) called the Chair, I would be in deep trouble.

Epistemic/evidential and evaluative adverbials can also force projection, but what is projected is not necessarily the proposition they modify (p), but the attitude O described by the adverbial towards that proposition: $O(p)$. Whether the speaker is also committed to p depends on the nature of O. For instance,

---

7 The compatibility with speech act adverbials is often used as a test whether or not a relative is non-restrictive. Therefore, some people doubt that the examples such as (3) or (19) are indeed non-restrictives (Koev, 2013; Martin, 2016). This seems quite odd, considering the fact that the relative in these examples is attached to definite heads or proper names, which ensures a non-restrictive interpretation. In view of examples like (19), we should rather ask ourselves what these tests are disambiguating restrictive and non-restrictive readings or local and global ones.

the relative clause in (20) without the adverbials can be interpreted in the scope of *if*, as a further condition on turning Sue's room into a living room ([A∧B]→C). Inserting the evidential *allegedly* or the evaluative *unfortunately* makes this interpretation impossible. The proposition *alleged*(B) or *unfortunate*(B), respectively, is projected: *alleged/unfortunate*(B)∧[A→C]. However, *alleged* is a non-factive predicate, which, moreover, explicitly marks the speaker's non-commitment to B, whereas *unfortunate* is factive, leading to the effect that the speaker is committed both to the proposition that Bill moved to the former kitchen and to the evaluation of this fact as unfortunate: B ∧ *unfortunate*(B) ∧ [A → C].

(20) If Sue moved to Bill's room,   A
     who (*allegedly/unfortunately*) moved to the former kitchen,   B
     then Sue's room could become the new living room.   C

In (20), the coherence relation between *A* and *B* is *Parallel*, the clauses describe who moved or would move where—similar events with varying participants (cf. the definition of *Parallel* by Kehler, 2002). As was already mentioned, *Parallel* is a coordinating relation, nevertheless the NRC is interpreted globally if an appropriate speaker-oriented adverbial is present. Contrary to the hypothesis in Poschmann (2018), this suggests that projection is the effect of the adverbial rather than the type of coherence relation in this case.

5.2 *Speaker-Oriented Discourse Connectives*

Adverbials like *allegedly* and *unfortunately* take one propositional semantic argument. Discourse connectives take two propositional arguments, and some of them are also speaker-oriented, i.e. indicate that the speaker holds an attitude towards one or both of those propositions. The subjectivity dimension in discourse connectives is best studied in the domain of causal markers (Sweetser, 1990; Sanders & Sweetser, 2009). The difference between speaker-oriented and non-speaker-oriented causal markers can be illustrated by the German *deshalb* ('that's why') vs. *also* ('so'). The contrast between A *deshalb* B and A *also* B is roughly as between the paraphrases 'A, and for that reason B' and 'A, and for that reason I believe B', respectively.

(21) a. Eva hat Max kritisiert. **Deshalb** ärgert er sich.
       'Eva criticized Max. That's why he is annoyed.'
   b. Eva hat Max kritisiert. **Also** ärgert er sich.
       'Eva criticized Max. So he is annoyed.'

This difference maps to a contrast in projection behaviour. As expected, *deshalb* favors local interpretation. In (22), *deshalb* makes sure that the NRC is interpreted inside the conditional: The mood will be ruined if two things happen— Eva criticizing Max and Max getting annoyed, where the first causes the second. In contrast, *also* makes the NRC project, but the causal antecedent of the speaker's belief that Max is annoyed is not accessible in the global context,[8] therefore (22) is less felicitous with *also*. However, *also* is fine in (23), where the causal antecedent for *also* is found in the previous sentence *The meeting lasted 6 hours*.

(22) Wenn Eva Max kritisiert, der sich **deshalb**/**??also** ärgert, dann ist die Stimmung im Eimer.
 'If Eva criticizes Max, who [Ger. *deshalb/also*] gets annoyed, then the party mood is ruined'

(23) Die Sitzung hat 6 Stunden gedauert! Wenn wir Peter, der **also** ziemlich müde gewesen sein muss, gefragt hätten, ob er auf ein Bier mitkommt, hätte er bestimmt abgesagt.
 'The meeting lasted 6 hours! If we had asked Peter, who [Ger. *also*] must have been quite tired, to come along for a beer, he would have refused.'

Notice again, that the NRC is attached to the context by a coordinating coherence relation, and nevertheless projects, like in example (20) above. Both *deshalb* and *also* express a *Result* relation, however, *deshalb* encodes a causal relation at the event level, whereas *also* encodes a causal relation between epistemic states of the speaker, which makes the NRC speaker-oriented.

5.3 *Speaker-Oriented Coherence Relations*

The contrast between speaker-oriented and non-speaker-oriented discourse connectives extends to coherence relations more generally (Sanders, 1997). That is, the understood relationship between two clauses may or may not involve or be based on the speaker's attitude to the content of one or both of the clauses, no matter if that attitude is signaled by an appropriate linguistic

---

8 Some speakers interpret the relative clause as a consequence of the potential situation of Eva criticizing Max, but not as part of the condition for ruining the mood. The sentence can then be paraphrased as: 'If Eva criticizes Max, then he will be annoyed (I conclude) and the mood will be ruined'. This requires projection followed by modal subordination in the consequent of the conditional, similar to a potential modally subordinated reading of (3b).

expression (e.g. a speaker-oriented connective), or remains implicit. In the latter case, figuring out what kind of relationship the speaker must have had in mind is a matter of pragmatic inference.

What we refer to here as speaker orientation corresponds closely to a well-established parameter in most of the existing taxonomies of coherence relations. Sanders, Spooren and Noordman (1992) call this parameter the source of coherence and distinguish between semantic and pragmatic relations. "A relation is semantic if the discourse segments are related because of their propositional content. In this case the writer refers to the locutionary meaning of the segments. The coherence exists because the world that is described is perceived as coherent." (Sanders et al., 1992, p. 7.) For instance, a causal relation between the events in (21a) is in this sense a manifestation of coherence in the real world, and the connective *deshalb* expresses a semantic coherence relation. In contrast, "a relation is pragmatic if the discourse segments are related because of the illocutionary meaning of one or both of the segments. In pragmatic relations the coherence relation concerns the speech act status of the segments. The coherence exists because of the writer's goal-oriented communicative acts." (Sanders et al., 1992, p. 8.) In this sense, the coherence relation expressed by *also* in (21b) is a causal relation between two assertions. A similar distinction between ideational and pragmatic relations is made by Redeker (1990). Mann & Thompson (1988) in turn distinguish subject matter vs. presentational relations: "Subject matter relations are those whose intended effect is that the reader *recognizes* the relation in question; presentational relations are those whose intended effect is to *increase some inclination* in the reader, such as the desire to act or the degree of positive regard for, belief in, or acceptance of the nucleus." (Mann & Thompson, 1988, p. 257.) This is not the same distinction as Sanders et al.'s source of coherence but overlaps substantially with it.

In this paper, we assume a somewhat weaker notion of speaker orientation than both Sanders et al.'s pragmatic source of coherence and Mann and Thompson's presentational category. Whenever the coherence relation implies that the speaker holds an attitude to one or both of the discourse segments the relation is speaker-oriented. We do not commit to the assumption that this must necessarily result from the segment having its own illocutionary force, which is a condition that follows from Sanders et al.'s definition of pragmatic relations. However, if it does have an illocutionary force, then the speaker necessarily holds an attitude towards its propositional content, e.g. belief in the case of an assertion. Similarly, it is not necessary for a speaker-oriented coherence relation that one segment is intended to affect the hearer's attitude towards the other, as is the case for Mann and Thompson's presentational relations. However, if a relation is presentational, then it is also speaker-oriented, because the speaker expresses the desire that the hearer holds a particular attitude towards the content of one segment, and presents the other segment with the goal to affect that attitude, which implies that it has an illocutionary force. Therefore, the speaker holds an attitude towards both segments, so the relation is speaker-oriented.

Our main claim is that in the cases where the coherence relation by which an NRC is connected to its context is not explicitly marked, and there are no other linguistic cues that force projection (such as speaker-oriented adverbials), its projection behavior will depend on the inferred coherence relation. If a speaker-oriented relation is inferred, the proposition expressed by the NRC is attributed to the speaker and therefore projects. For instance, this is the case in examples (1) and (10b), repeated below as (24) and (25), as well as in (26), a variant of (13), where the unspecific indefinite *someone* is replaced by a definite *Peter*. In all the three cases, the conditional as a whole is more plausible with than without the NRC. That is, the conditional probability of 'if A then C' given B is higher than the unconditional probability of 'if A then C', which is a case for a speaker-oriented *Explanation** relation (or *Evidence* Asher & Lascarides, 2003, p. 162), where the subordinate segment gives the reason to believe the superordinate one: *Explanation** ('if A then C', B).[9]

(24) If Peter called the Dean,   A
      who hates me,   B
      I would be in trouble.   C

(25) Wenn Gerd Dr. Meier erreicht,   A
      der über das passende Gegengift verfügt,   B
      kann Gerd gerettet werden.   C
      'If Gerd reaches Dr. Meier, who has the right antidote, Gerd can be saved.'

(26) If Peter wears this jacket,   A
      which is too big for him,   B
      he will look silly.   C

---

9 While it is usually assumed that the coordination/subordination feature classifies coherence relations, that is, for instance, *Explanation* is always subordinating, and *Contrast* is always coordinating, the speaker orientation feature "crosscuts" coherence relation, so we get a speaker-oriented and a non-speaker-oriented version of the same relation. We adopt the *-notation (e.g. *Explanation**) used in Segmented Discourse Representation Theory (SDRT, Asher & Lascarides, 2003) for a narrower category of metatalk relations to indicate that a speaker-oriented version of the relation is meant.

In all these cases the coherence relation unpacks to something like: The speaker asserts B to make 'if A then C' more plausible to the hearer. This entails in the first place that the speaker asserts B, that is, the speaker is committed to B as to anything she asserts.

If a non-speaker-oriented relation is inferred between the NRC and its host clause, such as *Parallel* in (12) or *Narration* in (10a), repeated below, the NRC is interpreted locally.

(27) If Mary stands in front of Peter,
      who moves a little closer to Max,   *Parallel*
      everyone will fit into the picture.

(28) Wenn Gerd Dr. Meier erreicht,
      der ihm das passende Gegengift verabreicht,   *Narration*
      kann Gerd gerettet werden.
      'If Gerd reaches Dr. Meier, who gives him the right antidote,
      Gerd can be saved.'

There is not much to say about these cases. Nothing special forces a global interpretation here, no speaker-oriented adverbial or connective, no speaker-oriented coherence relation, so the NRCs are interpreted in their syntactic position as any other subordinate clause.

Finally, the following example shows that an NRC connected to its host clause by a subordinating but non-speaker-oriented coherence relation is also interpreted locally. The *Elaboration* in (29) is an instance of such a relation. Strictly speaking, this is an instance of *Entity-Elaboration (E-Elaboration)*. "Normal" *Elaboration* holds between two descriptions of the same eventuality. *E-Elaboration* gives a more detailed description of an entity mentioned in the first sentence. In (29), the NRC provides details on the content of Bill's email, mentioned in the conditional clause.

(29) If you get an email from Bill, who writes that he got a new job, don't trust it.

Obviously, the sentence does not imply that Bill does or will write that he got a new job in any case, or if the addressee gets his email. The NRC contributes a further condition in the scope of *if*. This shows once again that local vs. global interpretation of NRCs depends primarily on speaker orientation, rather than on discourse-structural subordination.

6 Conclusion and Outlook

In this paper we set out to investigate the conditions under which non-restrictive relative clauses can have local readings. We have found additional evidence for Schlenker's (2013) and Poschmann's (2018) view that a major factor determining whether an NRC is interpreted locally or globally is the coherence relation by which it is attached to its host clause or broader context. Furthermore, we have shown that some ideas circulating in the community and in the literature towards a theoretical explanation of this phenomenon do not prove fruitful in the face of new observations that we have presented. In particular, although Holler's (2005) syntactic account of continuative vs. appositive relative clauses at first glance seems to be sensitive to just the right feature of coherence relations—discourse-structural coordination vs. subordination—for embedded NRCs it predicts a pattern exactly opposite to the observed one. Similarly, an attempt to treat local readings of NRCs by analogy with the trapping of presuppositions along the lines of van der Sandt (1992) and Zeevat (2016) both generates unwanted local readings in some cases, and fails to predict attested ones in other cases.

Although we believe that the actual pattern is approximated rather well by Poschmann's (2018) generalization that NRCs attached to their host clauses by coordinating coherence relations tend to be interpreted locally, and otherwise globally, we have argued that this relationship must be indirect. Crucially, it is not coordination/subordination, but rather Sanders et al.'s (1992) source of coherence—the opposition between speaker-oriented and non-speaker-oriented coherence relations—that has a direct link to NRC scope. In particular, if an NRC is connected to its host clause by a non-speaker-oriented coherence relation it can be interpreted locally (even if the relation is subordinating), and if the NRC is speaker-oriented it is interpreted globally (even if its relation to the host clause is coordinating).

One of the most radical conclusions of our study is perhaps that NRCs must be interpreted locally by default, just like other kinds of subordinate clauses. In order for an NRC to be interpreted globally, speaker-orientedness must be either explicitly indicated by an adverbial or connective, or it must follow from a speaker-oriented coherence relation. The idea is that in all these cases an appropriate attitude operator anchored to the speaker takes scope over the proposition contributed by the NRC.

However, this approach still leaves open the most crucial question. Why are NRCs interpreted globally, i.e. as speaker-oriented, most of the time? Why does it take so much effort—setting up the context right and introducing explicit markers—to make the local, i.e. continuative/non-speaker-oriented interpretation accessible? For reasons of space we could not pay due attention to this question. Some more detailed discussion of this issue can be found in Jasinskaja and Poschmann (2018), although it largely remains a task for future research.

Acknowledgements

The research reported in this paper was funded by the German Research Foundation (DFG) as part of the SFB 1252 "Prominence in Language", Project-ID 281511265 in the project C06 "Prominence in subordinating rhetorical relations" at the University of Cologne. We also thank the audience of the Workshop on "At-issueness, scope and coherence" (ASC, July 9–10, University of Cologne) and the anonymous reviewers for their insightful comments on previous versions of this paper.

References

AnderBois, Scott, Adrian Brasoveanu, & Robert Henderson. (2011). Crossing the appositive/at-issue meaning boundary In N. Li, & D. Lutz (Eds.), *Proceedings of SALT 20* (pp. 328–346). Vancouver, Canada.

Asher, Nicolas, & Alex Lascarides. (2003). *Logics of Conversation. Studies in Natural Language Processing*. Cambridge: Cambridge University Press.

Asher, Nicolas, & Laure Vieu. (2005). Subordinating and coordinating discourse relations. *Lingua, 115*, 591–610.

Chierchia, Gennaro, & Sally McConnell-Ginet. (1990). *Meaning and grammar*. Cambridge, MA: MIT Press.

Ernst, Thomas. (2009). Speaker-oriented adverbs. *Natural Language & Linguistic Theory, 27*(3), 497–544.

Harris, James A., & Christopher Potts. (2009). Perspective-shifting with appositives and expressives. *Linguistics and Philosophy, 32*(6), 523–552.

Heim, Irene, & Angelika Kratzer. (1998). *Semantics in Generative Grammar*. Oxford: Blackwell.

Holler, Anke. (2005). *Weiterführende Relativsätze. Empirische und theoretische Aspekte*. Berlin: Akademie Verlag.

Holler, Anke. (2008). A discourse-relational approach to continuation. In A. Benz, & P. Kühnlein (Eds.), *Constraints in Discourse* (pp. 249–265). Amsterdam/Philadelphia: John Benjamins.

Jasinskaja, Katja, & Claudia Poschmann. (2018). Attachment in Syntax and Discourse: Towards an explanation for the flexible scope of non-restrictive relative clauses.

In S. Maspong, B. Stefánsdóttir, K. Blake, & F. Davis (Eds.), *Proceedings of SALT 28* (pp. 433–453). Cambridge, MA, United States.

Kehler, Andrew. (2002). *Coherence, Reference, and the Theory of Grammar*. Stanford: CSLI Publications.

Koev, Todor K. (2013). *Apposition and the structure of discourse* [Doctoral dissertation, Rutgers University, New Brunswick].

Mann, William C., & Sandra Thompson. (1988). Rhetorical Structure Theory: Toward a functional theory of text organization. *Text*, *8*(3), 243–281.

Martin, Scott. (2016). Supplemental update. *Semantics and Pragmatics*, *9*(5), 1–61.

McCawley, James D. (1982). Parentheticals and discontinuous constituent structure. *Linguistic Inquiry*, *13*, 91–106.

Poschmann, Claudia. (2018). Embedding non-restrictive relative clauses. In U. Sauerland, & S. Solt (Eds.), *Sinn und Bedeutung 22* (Vol. 2 of ZASPiL 61, pp. 235–252). Berlin: Leibniz-ZAS.

Potts, Christopher. (2005). *The Logic of Conventional Implicatures*. Oxford: Oxford University Press.

Redeker, Gisela. (1990). Ideational and pragmatic markers of discourse structure. *Journal of Pragmatics*, *14*(3), 367–381.

Sanders, Ted. (1997). Semantic and pragmatic sources of coherence: On the categorization of coherence relations in context. *Discourse Processes*, *24*, 119–147.

Sanders, Ted, & Eve Sweetser. (Eds.). (2009). *Causal categories in discourse and cognition*. Berlin: De Gruyter Mouton.

Sanders, Ted, Wilbert Spooren, & Leo Noordman. (1992). Toward a taxonomy of coherence relations. *Discourse Processes*, *15*(1), 1–35.

Schlenker, Philippe. (2013). *Supplements without bidimensionalism* [Unpublished manuscript, Institut Jean-Nicod and New York University].

Simons, Mikael, Judith Tonhauser, David Beaver, & Craige Roberts. (2011). What projects and why. In N. Li, & D. Lutz (Eds.), *Proceedings of SALT 20* (pp. 309–327). Vancouver, Canada.

Sweetser, Eve. (1990). *From Etymology to Pragmatics: Metaphorical and Cultural Aspects of Semantic Structure*. Cambridge: Cambridge University Press.

van der Sandt, Rob A. (1992). Presupposition projection as anaphora resolution. *Journal of Semantics*, *9*(4), 333–377.

Venhuizen, Noortje J., Johan Bos, Petra Hendriks, & Harm Brouwer. (2014). How and why conventional implicatures project. In T. Snider, S. D'Antonio, & M. Weigand (Eds.), *Proceedings of SALT 24* (pp. 63–83). New York, NY, United States.

Zeevat, Hendrik. (2016). Local satisfaction explained away. In M. Moroney, C.-R. Little, J. Collard, & D. Burgdorf (Eds.) *Proceedings of SALT 26* (pp. 264–283). Austin, TX, United States.

CHAPTER 7

Central Adverbial Clauses and the Derivation of Subject-Initial V2

Liliane Haegeman

1   Introduction and Background

This chapter explores aspects of the syntax of what have been referred to as V2 transgressions (Catasso, 2015), i.e. patterns in V2 languages in which the finite verb is linearly preceded by two constituents rather than by the expected one constituent. The focus is on those cases in which the initial constituent in the V2 transgression is an adverbial clause. The data are drawn from Dutch and from the West Flemish dialect; it is expected that the core observations carry over to German (see a.o. Reis, 1997; d'Avis, 2004, for German).

In the literature, it has been proposed that where V2 languages seem to allow for V2 transgressions, the resulting V3 patterns can be brought in line with the V2 generalization on the assumption that the initial constituent which effectively leads to the V3 order is 'main clause external' (Broekhuis & Corver, 2016, pp. 1679–1733), 'extra cyclic' (Zwart, 2005) or 'extra sentential' (Astruc-Aguilera, 2005). By this reasoning, the combination of the main clause external constituent and the V2 root clause would be one that is in the domain of discourse syntax and should, at first sight, not be sensitive to the internal narrow syntax properties of its components. Being main clause external, the initial constituent in a V3 pattern would be predicted to be unable to participate closely with the internal syntax and semantics of the associated V2 clause which it precedes and combines with and hence, in a V3 pattern with an adverbial clause as the first constituent, this adverbial clause would be expected to be of the non-integrated type (see below for more details). Conversely, all things being equal, it is expected that adverbial clauses that have to be semantically integrated with their associated clause would not be able to constitute the initial, i.e. main clause external, constituent in a V3 configuration. For instance, being in a main clause external position, a temporal/conditional adverbial clause which is in the extra sentential position would not be able to value the temporal/modal coordinates of the associated matrix domain.

At first sight these predictions may seem correct. In Standard Dutch (1a), a V3 pattern results from the combination of a temporal adverbial clause with a fully-fledged V2 root clause. This entails that the adverbial clause must be occupying a main clause external position. The example is ungrammatical. In (1b), the initial adverbial clause is a relevance conditional, which has the hallmarks of being less integrated with the associated domain (see Section 1.1) and this clause is unproblematic in the same configuration:[1]

(1) a. *[_Adj-XP_ Als mijn tekst morgen klaar is,] [_CP_ [ik] zal je hem
 if my text tomorrow ready is, I will you him
 opsturen.]
 send
 'If my text is ready tomorrow, I will send it to you.'[2]

 b. [_Adj-XP_ Als je honger hebt,] [_CP_ er ligt nog wat brood in die
 if you hungry are, there lies still some bread in that
 kast.]
 cupboard
 'If you are hungry, there is bread in that cupboard.'

However, the prediction above is not always confirmed. First, the degradation of a V3 pattern with an initial temporal adverbial clause like that illustrated in (1a) is not general: it is restricted to the V3 combination of this type of adverbial clause with a subject-initial V2 clause with information structurally undistinguished subject. Data such as (13) in Section 2.3.1. show that non subject-initial V2 clauses can in fact combine with a temporal adverbial clause leading to acceptable V3 patterns. In addition, while (1a) is unacceptable in Standard Dutch, its counterpart in West Flemish, which is a *bona fide* V2 language, is grammatical.

---

1 The same contrast obtains for German, as shown by (i).
 (i) *[Wenn es regnet,] [ich] gehe spazieren.
 [when it rains,] [I] go walk
 'If it rains, I'll go for a walk.' See d'Avis (2004).
2 The conjunction *als* ('if') often corresponds either to *if* or to *when*, i.e. with a conditional or future temporal reading. When both readings were available I have opted for the conditional reading, to maximize similarity with cases such as relevance conditionals in which only the conditional reading is available. However, where the two readings are available the judgements do not differ if the conditional reading is replaced by a temporal reading.

Based on the cartographic analysis for main clause external constituents developed in Greco and Haegeman (2016) and Haegeman and Greco (2018), the present chapter will account for the restrictions on V3 patterns with a temporal/conditional adverbial clause in first position. Among other things, the data discussed here will provide new empirical support for an asymmetric analysis of V2.

Before dealing with the V2 transgressions I will first provide an overview of a typology of adverbial clauses based on English data, which I will then use in the subsequent discussion of Dutch.

1.1 A Typology of Adverbial Clauses: Central vs. Peripheral

There is by and large a consensus in the literature that what are commonly called 'adverbial clauses' include a wide range of relatively disparate types of modifying clauses which are distinguished—among other things—by the degree of syntactic and semantic integration into the matrix clause. The difference between adverbial clauses is aptly illustrated by examples like (2), in which two *if*-clauses appear in initial position.

(2) a. If you fail the entrance exam, you will have a chance to retake it.
    b. If you are hungry, I left some biscuits in the cupboard.

In (2a) the *if*-clause is closely integrated with the associated clause: it encodes a condition for the realization of the main clause event. In (2b), the *if*-clause is a relevance conditional (Haegeman, 1991, 2009), sometimes referred to as *biscuit conditional* in the literature (Austin, 1956), which encodes a felicity condition for the following utterance. In (2b) the conditional clause is not closely integrated with the associated clause: the condition 'if you are hungry' does not impact on the truth conditions of the associated clause, which is true independently of whether the interlocutor is hungry. In earlier work (Haegeman, 1991, 2009) I have labelled the 'integrated' adverbial clauses 'central' adverbial clauses, and will use this term here (but see Frey & Haegeman, forthcoming, for a nuanced view). Because of the lesser syntactic and semantic integration of the *if*-clause in (2b), I introduced the label 'peripheral adverbial clause' to refer to the type of adverbial clauses whose function is that of modifying the illocution and structuring the discourse.

Haegeman (1991, 2008) proposes to treat peripheral adverbial clauses as 'orphans', i.e. constituents that are not syntactically integrated with the clause they modify. However, note that even a relevance conditional such as that in (2b) remains to some extent integrated with the clause that it associates with. Support for this comes from the observation that when the associated clause is introduced by a coordinating conjunction, this conjunction must precede the *if*-clause, as shown in (3a), and bears on the combination of the *if*-clause and the clause it modifies. The conjunction cannot simply be associated only with the modified main clause (3b). (See d'Avis, 2004, p. 147 for this argument.)

(3) a. And, [if you're hungry,] there are biscuits in the cupboard.
    b. *[If you're hungry,] ... and there are biscuits in the cupboard.

That adverbial clauses may be more or less integrated with the clause they modify is well known from the literature and the variation in the degree of integration has received attention. In terms of Huddleston's (1984, p. 379) terminology, for instance, peripheral adverbial clauses, while subordinated to the clause they are associated with, are not 'embedded'. Importantly for our purposes, Huddleston does assume that the degree of integration be represented syntactically (Huddleston, 1984, p. 379). There is a considerable literature on the typology of adverbial clauses which I will not review here. For more discussion see, among other, the following: van der Auwera (1986), Haspelmath and König (1998), König and van der Auwera (1988), Reis (1997), d'Avis (2004), Reis and Wöllstein (2010).

In the next sections I briefly show that central and peripheral adverbial clauses pattern differently both in terms of their external syntax and in terms of their internal syntax. I will not go into these points in much detail but refer to the literature cited and for my own take on the data, which I will be adopting here, I refer to my own published work (Haegeman, 1991, 2002, 2003, 2004, 2006, 2009 and 2012).

1.2 *External Syntax of Adverbial Clauses*

Haegeman (2012) proposes that central adverbial clauses be merged at a TP-internal level of the clause, while peripheral adverbial clauses be merged outside the CP layer. Peripheral adverbial clauses are thus in what could be labelled a main clause external position (Broekhuis & Corver, 2016, pp. 1679–1733).

(4) a.

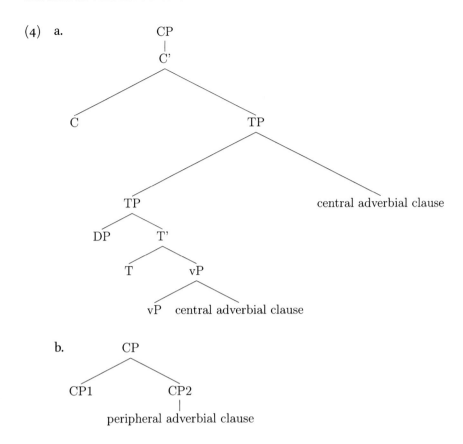

b.

The proposal is that central adverbial clauses are fully syntactically (and hence semantically) integrated in the clause they modify, and that peripheral adverbial clauses are integrated to a lesser degree. Evidence for the lower level of integration has been provided in the literature. For instance, central adverbial clauses can be shown to be within the scope of matrix operators, while peripheral adverbial clauses remain outside the scope of the same operators. For instance, (5) shows that central adverbial clauses (5a) can, and peripheral adverbial clauses (5b) cannot be clefted (Haegeman, 2006, 2012).

(5) a. It is only if you fail the entrance exam that you will have a chance to do a retake.
   b. *It is only if you are hungry that I left some biscuits in the cupboard.

Similarly, the central conditional clause in (2a) can be used in reply to a *wh* question, while this is not possible for the relevance conditional in (2b):

(6) a. A: When will I have a chance to do a retake?
   B: If you fail the entrance exam.
   b. A: When did you leave biscuits in the cupboard?
   B: If you are hungry.

For additional evidence see Haegeman (1991, 2002, 2003, 2004, 2006, 2009, 2012).

1.3 Organization of the Chapter

In the present chapter, I explore the implications of the hypotheses concerning the degree of syntactic integration of adverbial clauses as outlined above for the syntax of verb second clauses.

The chapter is organized as follows. Section 2 shows that, contrary to expectation, even in Standard Dutch, central adverbial clauses, which should by hypothesis be structurally integrated, do occur as the initial 'main clause external' constituents in a subset of V3 configurations and it will be argued that the availability of these configurations depends on the presence or absence of inversion in the root clause as well as on the information structural nature of the subject of the root clause. Section 3 addresses the analysis of 'unintegrated' main clause external constituents in a V3 configuration. Section 4 returns to the 'problematic' data uncovered in Section 2, i.e. central adverbial clauses which occupy what looks like the 'unintegrated' main clause external position in a V3 configuration. Section 5 analyses the patterns in terms of the syntactic analysis of the V2 configuration, proposing an asymmetric analysis for V2 in Dutch and arguing that there is micro variation among varieties of Dutch. Section 6 is a summary of the chapter.

2 Initial Adverbial Clauses and V2: The Case of Dutch

2.1 Verb Second

Dutch is a V2 language: in root declaratives, the finite verb is preceded by just one constituent. In (7a), the initial constituent is a direct object; in (7b), it is the verbal part of the predicate; in (7c), it is an adjectival predicate. For each example, having two constituents to the left of the finite verb leads to ungrammaticality, as shown in the primed examples. In all cases, the definite subject nominal will immediately follow the finite verb.

CENTRAL ADVERBIAL CLAUSES

(7) a. *Dienen oto ee Valère gisteren voor zen dochter gekocht.*
    that car has Valère yesterday for his daughter bought

a'. **Dienen oto Valère ee gisteren voor zen dochter gekocht.*
    that car Valère has yesterday for his daughter bought

b. *Gekocht ee Valère dienen oto voor zen dochter niet.*
   bought has Valère that car for his daughter not

b'. **Gekocht Valère ee dienen oto voor zen dochter niet.*
    bought Valère has that car for his daughter not

c. *Styf diere is den wyn tegenwoordig niet.*
   very expensive is the wine nowadays not

c'. **Styf diere den wyn is tegenwoordig niet.*
    very expensive the wine is nowadays not

In terms of the structural representation of the V2 clause I will provisionally adopt the format in (8), with the finite verb moving to C and the initial constituent moving to SpecCP. I assume that the CP level is the level at which illocutionary force is encoded. Some revisions will be discussed in Section 5.

(8)
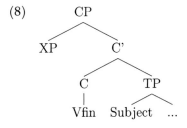

2.2 Peripheral Adverbial Clauses in V2 Transgressions in Dutch

Peripheral adverbial clauses do not impact on the truth conditions of the associated proposition but instead provide discourse-related specifications concerning, for instance, felicity conditions of the speech act they associate with or processing restrictions on the associated matrix clause. Some examples are given in (9) with an initial conditional clause. The event or state of affairs encoded in the matrix CP is not conditional on the realization of the state of affairs encoded in the peripheral conditional clause (labelled Adj-XP): the main speech act (assertion, question) in the V2 root clause remains valid regardless of Adj-XP. I assume that peripheral adverbial clauses combine with a root CP, i.e. a root V2 clause:[3]

(9) a. [$_{Adj\text{-}XP}$ Als je honger hebt,] [$_{CP}$ in die kast ligt er nog
       if you hungry are,   in that cupboard lies there still
wat brood.]
some bread
'If you are hungry, there is some bread in that cupboard.'

b. [$_{Adj\text{-}XP}$ Als het je interesseert,] [$_{CP}$ in PARIJS zal er ook een
       if it you interests,   in Paris will there also a
vacature zijn.]
vacancy be
'If you are interested, in Paris there is also a vacancy.'

c. [$_{Adj\text{-}XP}$ Als je abstract toch klaar is,] [$_{CP}$ waarom heb je het
       if your abstract PART ready is,   why have you it
nog niet opgestuurd?]
PART not sent
'If—as you say—your abstract is ready, why haven't you sent it already?'

d. [$_{Adj\text{-}XP}$ Als je honger hebt,] [$_{CP}$ er ligt nog wat brood in die
       if you hunger have,   there lies still some bread in that
kast.]
cupboard
'If you are hungry, there is bread in that cupboard.'

The presence of the initial peripheral adverbial clauses in (9) leads to a V3 order. These patterns remain compatible with the general assumptions on the derivation of V2: the peripheral adverbial clauses in (9) are non-integrated, they are 'main clause external constituents' in the sense of Broekhuis and Corver (2016), and hence they do not 'count' for V2. CP encodes speech act properties, and the peripheral adverbial clause is added 'onto' that, i.e. it does not itself encode the speech act of the matrix clause. (10) is a schematic representation:

---

[3] Anticipating the discussion in Section 5, the West Flemish analogues for the examples discussed in this section show the same patterns as their Standard Dutch counterparts.

CENTRAL ADVERBIAL CLAUSES   171

(10)

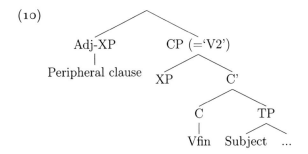

As already pointed out: peripheral adverbial clauses are not totally independent from the associated clause. As was the case for the English relevance conditional (2b), Dutch peripheral adverbial clauses follow the coordinating conjunction (11a–d) and cannot precede it (11e–f):

(11) a. *maar/en als je honger hebt, in die kast ligt er nog*
       but/and if you hungry are, in that cupboard lies there still
       wat brood.
       some bread
       'but/and if you are hungry, there is some bread in that cupboard.'

   b. *maar/en als het je interesseert, in PARIJS zal er ook een*
      but/and if it you interests, in Paris will there also a
      vacature zijn.
      vacancy be
      'but/and if you are interested, in Paris there is also a vacancy.'

   c. *maar/en als je abstract toch klaar is, waarom heb je het*
      but/and if your abstract PART ready is, why have you it
      nog niet opgestuurd?
      PART not sent
      'but/and if—as you say—your abstract is ready, why haven't you sent it already?'

   d. *maar/en als je honger hebt, er ligt nog wat brood in die*
      but/and if you hunger have, there lies still some bread in that
      kast.
      cupboard
      'but/and if you are hungry, there is bread in that cupboard.'

e. *Als je   honger hebt, maar/en in die   kast   ligt er   nog
   if   you hunger have, but/and in that cupboard lies there still
   wat   brood.
   some bread

f. *?Als het je   interesseert, maar/en in PARIJS zal er   ook een
   if   it you interests   but/and in Paris will there also a
   vacature zijn.
   vacancy be

g. *?Als je   abstract toch   klaar is, maar/en waarom heb je
   if   your abstract PART ready is, but/and why   have you
   het nog   niet opgestuurd?
   it PART not sent

h. *Als je   honger hebt, maar/en er   ligt nog wat   brood in
   if   you hunger have, but/and there lies still some bread in
   die kast.
   that cupboard

In contrast with peripheral adverbial clauses, central adverbial clauses modify the truth conditions of the associated clause. This implies that central adverbial clauses must be integrated in the main clause and the prediction would be that central adverbial clauses cannot constitute a 'main clause external' constituent. Dutch (1a), repeated as (12a), is correctly predicted to be ungrammatical, because the initial conditional clause is 'central', it encodes a condition on the realization of the main proposition and should thus be semantically and syntactically integrated. The grammatical variant is (12b).

(12) a. *[_{Adj-XP} Als mijn tekst morgen   klaar is,] [_{CP} [ik] [zal] je   hem
              if   my text tomorrow ready is,   I   will you him
   opsturen.]
   send
   'If my text is ready tomorrow, I will send it to you.'

   b. [_{CP} [Als mijn tekst morgen   klaar is,] [_{C} zal] [_{TP} ik je   hem
            if   my text tomorrow ready is,   will   I you him
   opsturen.]]
   send
   'If my text is ready tomorrow, I will send it to you.'

A straightforward account for the ungrammaticality of (1/12a) might seem to be that it violates the V2 condition: the finite verb *zal* ('will') is preceded by two constituents, the subject *ik* ('I') and the adverbial clause *als mijn tekst morgen klaar is* ('if my text is ready tomorrow'). However, it is far from clear that this is the way to approach this example, and this for at least two reasons. (i) As shown in Section 5, the West Flemish (from now on WF) equivalent of (12a) is acceptable, while WF is also a *bona fide* V2 language. (ii) The second obstacle to a V2 account for (12a) is that Standard Dutch does allow for V2 transgressions in which the initial constituent in the V3 pattern is a central adverbial clause which modifies the temporal values of the associated TP, these will be discussed in the next section. If such transgressions are possible, then the unacceptability of (12a) is by no means accounted for simply in terms of the V2 restriction.

2.3 Central Adverbial Clauses in V2 Transgressions in Dutch

2.3.1 Non Subject-Initial V2

In linear terms, the examples in (13) instantiate V3 patterns but in contrast with the examples in (9) and relevant for the discussion here, the initial adverbial clause is central: it modifies the temporal/modal coordinates of the matrix clause. Nevertheless, these examples are acceptable.

(13) a. [_Adj-XP_ Als ik klaar ben met de handout,] [_CP_ [aan wie] moet ik
             if   I   ready am with the handout,   to whom should I
hem tonen?]
him show
'If my handout is ready, to whom should I show it?'

b. [_Adj-XP_ Als er morgen een probleem is,] [_CP_ [MIJ] moet je
          if there tomorrow a problem is,   ME must you
niet bellen.]
not call
'If there is a problem tomorrow, don't call ME.'

While the V3 patterns in (13) are accepted by most speakers of Standard Dutch (from now on abbreviated as StD),[4] example (12a) above, which seems to instantiate the same pattern, is not grammatical.

---

4 Judgements, based on an informal questionnaire, were obtained from ten speakers, seven originating from the Netherlands and three from Belgium.

For a subset of StD speakers, the V2 transgressions in (13) are degraded; these speakers systematically require the insertion of an appropriate resumptive adverbial—*dan* ('then')—in the matrix clause, as shown in (14):[5]

(14) a. [*Adj-XP* Als ik klaar ben met de handout,] [*CP* [aan wie] moet ik
           if I ready am with the handout   to whom must I
     hem dan tonen?]
     him then show
     'If my handout is read, to whom should I show it?'

   b. [*Adj-XP* Als er morgen een probleem is,] [*CP* [MIJ] moet je
          if there tomorrow a problem is   me must you
     %dan niet bellen.]
      then not call
     'If there is a problem tomorrow, then don't call me.'

An important proviso here is the following: even for StD speakers who only accept the version with *dan* ('then') in (14), inserting a resumptive adverbial (*dan* 'then' or *toen* 'then') in (1)/(12a) does not remove the degradation, as shown in (15a). In the acceptable alternative to (15a), the resumptive adverbial *dan* would have to occupy the initial position in the adverbial resumptive V3 pattern, as shown in (15b).

(15) a. *[Als mijn tekst morgen klaar is,] [ik] zal je hem **dan**
        if my text tomorrow ready is I will you him then
     opsturen.
     send
     'If my text is ready tomorrow, I will send it to you.'

   b. [Als mijn tekst morgen klaar is,] **dan** zal ik je hem
        if my text tomorrow ready is then will I you him
     opsturen.
     send
     'If my text is ready tomorrow, I will send it to you.'

The generalization that emerges from the data presented here is that the acceptability of a central adverbial clause as the initial constituent in a V3 pat-

---

5 Boogaert (2007, p. 14) signals that with respect to conditionals, there is variation in the presence of resumptive *dan* ('then') between Northern Dutch and Belgian Dutch. The nature of the variation requires further study.

tern depends on the specific instantiation of the V2 pattern in the CP which it precedes and combines with:

(i) a V2 transgression consisting of a central adverbial clause combined with a subject-initial V2 root clause (Mikkelsen, 2015) is unacceptable, as shown in (1a)/(12a)/(15a);

(ii) a V2 transgression consisting of a central adverbial clause combined with a non subject-initial V2 root clause is acceptable (13) (with the proviso of *dan*-insertion for a subset of speakers).

2.3.2   Subject-Initial V2

The descriptive generalization sketched in the conclusion of the preceding section is not quite adequate in that not all combinations of central adverbial clauses and subject-initial V2 clauses lead to unacceptable V3 patterns: the acceptability of such V3 patterns also depends on the nature of the subject. As shown by (16), the V3 combination of a central adverbial clause with a subject-initial V2 root clause whose subject is informationally distinguished (in the sense of Mikkelsen, 2015) is acceptable. In (16a), the central adverbial clause precedes a subject-initial V2 clause with a focused subject PIET, and this example is accepted by my StD informants. Similarly, the subject in (16b) is a *wh*-subject and the V3 configuration is accepted.

(16) a. [Als er   morgen   een probleem is,] [PIET] zal ons niet
         if there tomorrow a   problem is   Piet   will us not
         helpen.
         help
         'If there is a problem tomorrow, Piet won't help us.'

     b. [Als er   morgen   een probleem is,] [wie] zal ons helpen?[6]
         if there tomorrow a   problem is   who   will us help
         'If there is a problem tomorrow, who will help us?'

---

6   Thanks to Fred Weerman for bringing these data to my attention.
    Observe that in (16b) (and in (17b)) Flemish speakers prefer *er* ('there') insertion. For Dutch speakers, (i) and (ii) are degraded.
    (i) %Als er   morgen   een probleem is, wie zal er ons helpen?
         if there tomorrow a   problem is, who will er us help
         'If there is a problem tomorrow, who will help us?'
    (ii) %Als er   morgen   een probleem is, wie zal er ons dan helpen?
         if there tomorrow a   problem is, who will er us then help
         'If there is a problem tomorrow, who will help us?'
    For completeness' sake, it should be pointed out that *er*-insertion was also preferred by Flem-

Informants who found (13) degraded without the resumptive adverbial *dan*, also found (16a) degraded; for those speakers, insertion of *dan* ('then') again rendered the example acceptable (17a). All StD informants accepted (16b). In an informal survey with native speakers, speakers who found (16a) degraded noted only a slight degradation (a score 6/7) for (16b), and expressed a slight preference for (17b) with resumptive *dan* (a score of 7/7).

(17) a. [*Als er   morgen   een probleem is,* [**PIET**] *zal ons dan niet*
         if there tomorrow a   problem is   Piet   will us then not
         helpen.
         help
         'If there is a problem tomorrow, PIET won't help us.'

   b. [*Als er   morgen   een probleem is,*] [*wie*] *zal ons dan*
         if there tomorrow a   problem is   who   will us then
         helpen?
         help
         'If there is a problem tomorrow, who will help us?'

2.3.3   V2 Transgressions in Standard Dutch

On the basis of the data discussed in Section 2.3.2, I revise the descriptive generalizations as follows:

(i) a V2 transgression consisting of a central adverbial clause combined with a subject-initial V2 root clause in which the subject is information structurally undistinguished (Mikkelsen, 2015) is unacceptable;

(ii) a V2 transgression consisting of a central adverbial clause combined with a non subject-initial V2 root clause is acceptable (with the proviso of *dan*-insertion for a subset of speaker);

(iii) a V2 transgression consisting of a central adverbial clause combined with a subject-initial V2 root clause in which the subject is information structurally distinguished (Mikkelsen, 2015) is acceptable.

The descriptive generalizations are summarized in Table 7.1: the relevant pattern is summarized in the first column, the StD judgement is given in the second column, the third column provides a reference to the relevant text-example.

Observe that the nature of the V2 pattern or the nature of the subject do not affect the status of the V2 transgressions with peripheral adverbial clauses, as summarized in Table 7.2.

---

ish speakers who do not accept V3 patterns with subject-initial adverbial clauses. The distribution of *er*-insertion requires further study.

TABLE 7.1   V2 transgressions in StD with central adverbial clauses

V2 transgression	StD	Example number
Adj-XP undistinguished Subj Vfin	*	(12a)
Adj-XP distinguished Subj Vfin	✓	(16)–(17)
Adj-XP non-Subj[+WH] Vfin	✓	(13)–(14)

TABLE 7.2   V2 transgressions in StD with peripheral adverbial clauses

V2 transgression	StD	Example number
Adj-XP Subj Vfin	✓	(9d)
Adj-XP *wh*-phrase Vfin	✓	(9c)
Adj-XP non-Subj Vfin	✓	(9a,b)

From this survey, the following question emerges: if V2 transgressions are acceptable with central adverbial clauses in (13) and (16), why are they not acceptable in (12a)? Put differently: If, despite its status as main clause external, the initial central adverbial clause in (13) and in (16) can modify the temporal/modal values of the associated V2 clause in what looks like a V3 pattern, why can it not do so in (12a)?

2.4   *Irrelevance Conditionals (d'Avis, 2004)*

Observe that while combining a conditional clause which modifies the modal coordinates of the associated subject-initial matrix clause leads to unacceptability in (12a), repeated in (18a), in the same context, what might appear to be a closely similar irrelevance conditional (in the sense of d'Avis, 2004) does not lead to a degradation, as shown by the acceptability of (18b). This observation was made in d'Avis (2004):

(18) a. *[Als mijn tekst morgen   klaar is,] [ik] zal je   hem
         if   my   text tomorrow ready is   I   will you him
       opsturen.   (= 12a)
       send
       'If my text is ready tomorrow, I will send it to you.'

b. [*Of mijn tekst morgen klaar is of niet,*] [*ik*] *zal je hem*
if my text tomorrow ready is or not I will you him
opsturen.
send
'Whether my text is ready or not tomorrow, I will send it to you.'

Irrelevance conditionals differ from central conditional clauses in that "the truth of a set of propositions that can be derived from the I[rrelevance] C[onditional] is irrelevant for the truth of the proposition of the M[atrix] C[lause]." (d'Avis, 2004, p. 142)

2.5 Research Questions

The survey of the data provided above leads to several questions:
(i) Why can central adverbial clauses appear as the main clause external constituent in V3 patterns at all?
(ii) Why can central adverbial clauses appear as the main clause external constituent in V3 patterns in only a subset of V2 transgressions?
(iii) Why and how does the difference between subject-initial and non subject-initial V2 clauses bear on the acceptability of V2 transgressions with a central adverbial clause?
(iv) Why and how does the information structural status of the subject bear on V2 transgressions with central adverbial clauses?

To address these issues, I first summarize a proposal elaborated in Greco and Haegeman (2016) and in Haegeman and Greco (2018) for the syntax and interpretation of main clause external constituents.

3 Peripheral Adverbial Clauses as Main Clause External Constituents

There is a consensus that the initial peripheral adjunct in the licit examples in (9) does not violate the V2 constraint, because it is 'outside' the syntax. There are numerous proposals in the literature for representing this 'external' status: (19a–d) offers just some examples. Auer (1996) refers to a 'Vor-vorfeld' (prefrontfield) in contrast to the Vorfeld (front field) (19a); Skårup (1975) uses the label 'extraposition' (19b); in Broekhuis and Corver's (2016, pp. 1679–1733) simplified representation (19c), the external constituents are simply represented as outside the main clause. (19d) is based on my own work (cf. (4)).

(19) a. [Vor-Vorfeld [Vorfeld ... V_{fin}]]

(Auer, 1996)

b. [Extraposition] [Preverbal zone[7] [[VERBAL ZONE]   Postverbal
                                                       zone]]
                                                  (Skårup 1975, p. 179)[8]
c. [[MAIN CLAUSE   ]]
                              (Broekhuis & Corver, 2016, pp. 1679–1733)
d. [CP Peripheral adjunct [CP ... [TP   ]]]
                                                  (Haegeman, 2004, 2006, 2012)

In what follows I outline the approach developed in Haegeman and Greco (2018), which explores an insight due to Auer (1996) which brings to the fore the framing function of the Vor-Vorfeld. Haegeman and Greco (2018) propose that the combination of the main clause external constituent with CP leads to a novel projection, their 'FrameP'.

(19) e.

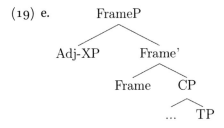

The following are the main ingredients of the proposal:

(i) The projection FrameP results from the merger of the main clause external adjunct (Adj-XP) and a constituent labelled ForceP in Haegeman and Greco (2018). Haegeman and Greco (2018) borrow the label ForceP from the cartographic tradition (Rizzi, 1997): ForceP is the constituent layer that encodes illocutionary force. For our purposes, it can be taken to correspond to the root V2 clause. For ease of exposition, Haegeman and Greco's (2018) label ForceP is replaced by the label CP in (19e); throughout the reader should bear in mind that in (19e) CP encodes illocutionary force and is crucially distinct from the 'propositional' TP layer.

(ii) For the interpretation of the FrameP configuration, Greco and Haegeman (2016) and Haegeman and Greco (2018) propose that the initial adjunct XP-Adj in SpecFrameP introduces an entity (or a set of entities) in the

---

7 The preverbal zone is also called 'fondement', i.e. 'foundation'.
8 The slot labelled 'Extraposition' is a position "outside the clause proper 'hors de la proposition', p. 179) but nonetheless attached to the following clause (p. 416)" (Donaldson, 2012, p. 1028).

discourse which will serve as the context with respect to which the proposition expressed by the associated V2 clause is interpreted as relevant.

(iii) For Haegeman and Greco (2018), the merger of the main clause external constituent (here Adj-XP) with CP is a discourse structuring ('framing') operation. It creates a discourse entity, FrameP. The specifier of FrameP is not syntactically integrated with the associated clause.

Haegeman and Greco's FrameP in (19e) corresponds to several proposals in the literature, including, among others, Banfield's (1982) E-node, Cinque's (2008) HP (also adopted in Giorgi, 2014; Frascarelli, 2016), Koster's (2000) :P ('colonP'), de Vries' (2009) ParP (also adopted in Griffiths & De Vries (2013)). In this respect, their (19e) differs from those who take the relevant V3 transgression to be a further extension of the "Rizzian" left periphery (cf. Holmberg, 2015).

The two constituents of FrameP (19e) will be construed relatively independently: in this case, the denotation of Adj-XP does not impact on the truth conditions of the V2 root clause, CP. For instance, in (20a) the peripheral conditional clause modifies the speech act, which is presented as relevant 'if the hearer must know'; the conditional clause must be construed as relevant with respect to the root clause speech act (CP1), and it cannot be construed as a condition on the embedded speech act reported under the verb of saying (CP2). The choice of the subject pronouns in the conditional clause reflects this: in (20a) the conditional clause targets the addressee of the root speech act, 'you'. The intended addressee of the conditional clause in (20c) would be that of the embedded speech act, 'I', but this is infelicitous. (20b) represents the acceptable reading; (20d) schematizes what would be the illicit reading.

(20) a. [$_{FrameP}$ [Als je het moet weten,] [$_{CP1}$ [ze] zei [$_{CP2}$ da-ze het
     if you it must know   she said   that-she it
niet kon betalen.]]]
not could pay
'If you must know, she told me she couldn't pay for it.'

b. [$_{FrameP}$ Adj-XP [$_{Frame}$] [$_{CP1}$ ... [$_{CP2}$ ...]]]

c. *[$_{FrameP}$ [Als ik het moet weten,] [$_{CP1}$ [ze] zei me [$_{CP2}$ da-ze
      if I it must know   she told me   that-she
het niet kon betalen.]]]
it not could pay

d. *[$_{FrameP}$ Adj-XP [$_{Frame}$] [$_{CP1}$ ... [$_{CP2}$ ...]]]

Put differently, not being syntactically integrated with CP, the initial main clause external speech act modifier in SpecFrameP cannot be construed CP-internally at the level of the embedded domain. To capture this restriction, Haegeman and Greco (2018) postulate a strict locality condition on the interpretation of FrameP. While initially formulated on the basis of the interpretation of peripheral adverbial clauses in the specifier of FrameP, they then postulate that the locality condition be generalized and that its scope also includes central adverbial clauses in FrameP.[9]

4 Central Adverbial Clauses as Main Clause External Constituents

4.1 Inverted V2 and the Derivation of Temporal Readings

Interpretively, a central adverbial clause functions as a restrictor for the evaluation conditions of the proposition expressed in the main clause.[10] A priori, one would not expect a central adverbial clause to be able to be merged as a main clause external constituent in SpecFrameP. By Haegeman and Greco's generalized locality condition on the interpretation of FrameP (cf. (20b)), a central adverbial clause in SpecFrameP can only provide a value for a temporal or modal variable in the matrix clause provided it has a strictly local relation with the temporal or modal value encoded in the main clause. Following widespread assumptions (a.o. Reichenbach, 1947; Cinque, 1999; Demirdache & Uribe-Etxebarria, 2004; Sigurdsson, 2016, etc.), temporal and modal values of

---

9 The absence of low construal is documented in more detail in Greco and Haegeman (2016) and Haegeman and Greco (2018).

   The construct FrameP being, by hypothesis, 'outside the narrow syntax', one might conceive of the generalized strict locality requirement governing its interpretation as constraining the building of discourse relations. Concomitant with this position, one might speculate that the syntactic relations such as Probe and Agree cannot apply at the discourse level, i.e. outside of the syntax, and that this is what ultimately precludes low construal. Thanks to Luigi Rizzi (p.c.) for bringing this point up.

   On the nature of his discourse projection HP, Cinque (2008) writes:
   "In the spirit of Williams (1977), we must also assume that the 'Discourse Grammar' head H, as is the general rule for sentences in a discourse, blocks every 'Sentence Grammar' relation between its specifier and complement (internal Merge, Agree, Binding, etc.), despite the asymmetric c-command relation existing between the two under the extension of the LCA to Discourse Grammar" (Cinque, 2008, p. 199).

10 I assume that in the resumptive strategies with *dan* ('then')/*toen* ('then'), the demonstrative adverbs *dan* ('then')/*toen* ('then') function as resumptive elements of the adjunct clause (Comrie, 1986; Iatridou, 1994; Bhatt & Pancheva, 2006). A full analysis of the role of *dan*, though relevant, would take me too far.

the proposition are encoded on specialized TP-internal temporal/modal functional projections, e.g. RefT (reference time) and EvT (evaluation time). (21) is a schematic representation: Observe crucially that, as it stands, these values are NOT encoded at the CP level.

(21)

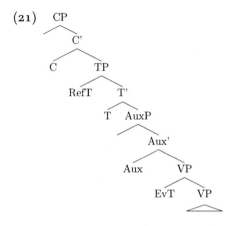

Consider now the interpretation of (22a), which is acceptable and in which the initial main clause external constituent is a central conditional. (22b) is an initial take on the representation of the interpretation of (22a), using the format in (20): the interpretation represented by (22b) is that the constituent in the specifier of FrameP, Adj-XP, should bind a TP-internal temporal or modal variable. I represent the intended reading by co-subscripting the temporal adjunct and the locus that encodes the Reference Time.

(22) a. [Als ik klaar ben met de handout,] [$_{CP}$ [aan wie] moet ik hem
      if I ready am with the handout,   to whom should I him
tonen?]
show
'If my handout is ready, to whom should I show it?'

b. *[$_{FrameP}$ Adj-XP [$_{Frame}$] [$_{CP}$ [$_{C}$] [$_{TP}$ Ref-T [T] ... [$_{VP}$ Ev-T [$_{VP}$ ...]]]]]

However, representation (22b) actually violates the locality condition postulated above because the temporal coordinates, Reference time (Ref-T) and Event time (Ev-T) in (21), are TP-internal and these layers do not have the strictly local relation to SpecFrameP that Haegeman and Greco (2018) postulate as a condition on its interpretation, hence the *: the temporal coordinates are inaccessible for construal with Adj-XP. In the absence of the required local relation with the TP-internal temporal coordinates, the clause-external central adverbial clause will not be able to value the temporal relation of the main clause. However, (22a) is acceptable with the initial temporal adjunct successfully interpreted as a modifier of the main clause's temporal values. This means that there must be a way to derive the appropriate reading which is compatible with Haegeman and Greco's locality condition on the interpretation of the constituents in FrameP. The question arises then how this can be attained.

The proposal elaborated in Haegeman and Greco (2018) to account for the fact that (22a) is acceptable with the appropriate reading for the adverbial clause is that representation (22b) must be 'reconfigured' and that it must in fact be supplanted by a representation that does achieve the required locality relation. Put differently: there must be a representation in which the temporal features of TP are transmitted to C and can thus attain a local configuration with the constituent in FrameP. A natural proposal that comes to mind here is to explore the fact that (22a) is a case of an inverted V2 pattern in which the matrix finite verb *moet* ('must') has inverted with the subject *ik* ('I'), and to propose that the required local configuration arises as the by-product of the movement of the finite verb to the C-domain. In other words, (22a) is represented not as (22b) but as (22c): head-movement of the finite verb *moet* ('must') creates a head chain, C-T, and the chain 'indirectly' establishes a local connection between the constituent in SpecFrame and the temporal coordinate of the clause.

(22) c. [$_{FrameP}$ [als ik klaar ben met de handout] [$_{Frame}$]
[$_{CP}$ [aan wie] [$_C$ moet$_i$] [$_{TP}$ ik ... [$_{Ti}$ t$_{moet}$] [$_{VP}$ ... t$_{aan\ wie}$]]]]

As must be clear, the same reasoning will also apply to (23a), in which the fronting of the direct object has led to subject-verb inversion. In (23b), the initial central adverbial attains a local relation with the temporal value of the finite verb in C.

(23) a. [$_{Adj-XP}$ *Als er morgen een probleem is,*] [$_{CP}$ [*MIJ*] *moet je*
       if there tomorrow a problem is, me must you
   niet bellen.]
   not call
   'If there is a problem tomorrow, don't call me.'

   b. [$_{FrameP}$ [als er morgen een probleem is] [$_{Frame}$]
              [[$_{CP}$ [MIJ] [$_C$ moet] [$_{TP}$ je ... [$_{Ti}$ t$_{moet}$] [$_{VP}$ ... t$_{mij}$]]]]

Recall from the discussion in Section 2.3 that while central adverbial clauses are interpretable as first constituents in a V3 configuration with non subject-initial V2 clauses, the situation in subject-initial patterns is more complex. I turn to them in the next section.

4.2   Central Adverbial Clauses and Subject-Initial V2

There is an asymmetry in the compatibility of non subject-initial V2 clauses and subject-initial V2 clauses with V3 configurations with initial central adverbial clauses, as shown in Section 2. In the present section I address this asymmetry, which I will derive from the difference in the syntactic derivation of subject-initial V2 clauses and non subject-initial V2 clauses. First, I briefly discuss the derivation of subject-initial V2 clauses and then I consider it in relation to the interpretation of the initial constituent located in the specifier of FrameP.

4.2.1   Subject-Initial V2

Given that in a V3 configuration with an initial central adverbial clause, subject-initial V2 clauses and non subject-initial V2 clauses pattern differently, it would appear that the so-called asymmetric approach to the derivation of verb second initiated by Travis (1984) and later adopted by, a.o., Zwart (1997a,b), and Mikkelsen (2015) is the more promising one. In this approach, inverted V2 patterns and non-inverted, i.e. subject-initial, V2 patterns have a different derivation, with the verb remaining in a lower position in the latter case.

Empirical support for the hypothesis that the verb remains lower in subject-initial V2 than in non subject-initial V2 comes from double agreement patterns in the East Netherlandic variety of Dutch (Zwart, 1997, p. 140). (24) shows the agreement patterns for the first person plural. The dialect has two forms of agreement: *-e* and *-t*. As can be seen in (24a), complementizer agreement is realized as *-e*, the sentence-final finite verb in this example has the ending *-t*. In (24b), the verb occupies second position in a subject-initial V2 pattern; its agreement is realized as *t*, i.e. the same form as in (24a). In (24c), the finite verb has inverted with the subject and is marked by *-e*, i.e. it shows the form of agreement displayed by the complementizer in (24a).

(24) a. *datt-e wy speul-t/*e.*
       that-e we play-t/*e
       'that we are playing'

   b. *Wy speul-t/*e.*
       we play-t/*e
       'We are playing.'

c. *Woar speul-e/*t wy?*
   where play-e?*t we
   'Where do we play?' (Zwart, 1997, p. 140. (49) is his (73))

I focus on the core features of the asymmetric analysis here, and leave details of specific implementation as well as a cartographic revision of the proposal (Haegeman & Greco, 2018) aside: the main idea is that inverted V2 patterns are derived by movement of the finite verb to the CP layer, as represented in (25a), while in the non-inverted subject-initial pattern, the subject remains in its canonical position (Spec,TP) and the finite verb occupies a TP-internal head, say T (25b). In terms of the derivations in (25), the generalization is then that when the verb remains in a TP-internal position, it is associated with the *-t* ending, when it has moved to C, it displays the *-e* ending.

(25) a.
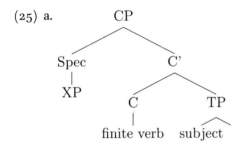

b.
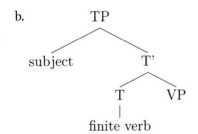

Two preliminary comments are to be made at this point. First, to rule out V2 transgressions with central adverbial clauses and subject-initial V2, one might propose that Frame selects CP and hence that (25b) simply cannot constitute the complement of Frame. However, this account would incorrectly rule out the acceptable combination of a peripheral adverbial clause with a subject-initial V2 clause. These patterns are acceptable, as illustrated in (9d).

Representation (25b) also raises some independent issues. Observe that subject-initial V2 clauses are declaratives and function as assertions. If illocutionary force is encoded at the CP level, a subject-initial V2 clause represented as in (25b) would in fact lack the encoding of illocutionary force. This suggests that (25b) is not fully adequate with respect to the representations adopted here.

Potentially there is also a theory internal objection to adopting (25b) as the representation of subject-initial V2 clauses, at least with respect to certain assumptions. Under the recent reinterpretation of the relation between the functional heads C and T (Chomsky, 2008), it is proposed that the Agree (φ-) and Tense features associated with the inflectional system are not an inherent property of T; rather, they belong to the 'phase' head C and are lowered onto the T layer. If the formal features of finite T are taken to originate in C, then in the absence of the C projection, in (25b), T will lack relevant features.

The proposal adopted here is that while in subject-initial V2 clauses the finite verb does not move to C, and (25b) as such represents the TP layer of subject-initial V2 root clauses, it must be enhanced with a CP layer encoding illocutionary force dominating the TP layer hosting the subject-initial V2 configuration as in (25c).[11,12]

(25) c.

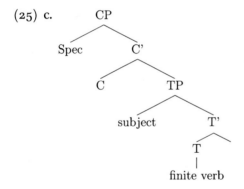

---

11 As it stands (25c) makes subject-initial V2 similar to a regular subject-initial root clause in English or in French.

    The asymmetric analysis can (and should) be recast in a cartographic approach according to which, for instances, non-inverted V2 is derived by V-movement to Fin and inverted V2 implicates a higher projection. See Greco and Haegeman (2016), who follow Poletto (2013), Biberauer and Roberts (2014), and Wolfe (2016).

    In a cartographic approach, asymmetric V2 may be derived by the finite verb moving either to Fin (subject-initial V2 patterns) or to Force (inverted V2 patterns). This means that in asymmetric languages too the verb would always leave TP. I don't go into this issue here and refer the reader to Greco and Haegeman (2016) and Haegeman and Greco (2018) and the papers cited. Purely for expository reasons, I use the simpler representation here.

12 In contrast to the asymmetric approach to V2, Schwartz and Vikner (1996), and Craenenbroeck and Haegeman (2007) argue that in subject-initial V2, the verb also moves to C, i.e. that representation (25a) captures all V2 sentences. In a cartographic approach, the asymmetric approach can be reconciled with the proposal that the verb always leaves

4.2.2 V2 Transgressions and Subject-Initial V2

If we assume that the representation of StD subject-initial V2 clauses is as in (25c), (26b) below will correspond to the crucial parts of the representation of the unacceptable (26a). In this representation, in the absence of V to C movement, the local configuration required for the interpretation of FrameP is not attained. By hypothesis, the central adverbial clause in SpecFrameP does not have access to the TP-internal temporal and modal coordinates.[13] As a result, the temporal adjunct in SpecFrameP cannot be interpreted as a temporal modifier of the event encoded TP-internally, as informally indicated by co-subscripting in (26b).

(26) a. *[Als mijn tekst morgen klaar is,] ik zal je hem
　　　　if my tekst tomorrow ready is I will you him
　　　　opsturen.　　　　　　　　　　　　　　　　　　(= 12a)
　　　　send

　　b. *[$_{FrameP}$ Adj-XP$_i$ [$_{Frame}$] [$_{CP}$ [$_C$] [$_{TP}$ ik [$_T$ zal +Ref-T$_i$] ...]]]

Recall that not all subject-initial V2 root clauses are incompatible with the V3 pattern with an initial central adverbial clause. As mentioned, such patterns are acceptable if the subject is information structurally distinguished, for instance in the form of having contrastive focus (27a) or being a *wh*-phrase (27b):

(27) a. [Als er morgen een probleem is,] [*PIET*] zal ons niet helpen.
　　　　if there tomorrow a problem is PIET will us not help
　　　　'If there is a problem tomorrow, PIET won't help us.'

　　b. [Als er morgen een probleem is,] [*wie*] gaat (er) ons
　　　　if there tomorrow a problem is who goes (there) us
　　　　helpen?
　　　　help
　　　　'If there's a problem tomorrow, who will help us?'

Following Mikkelsen (2015, pp. 597, 628–629), I assume that in a subject-initial V2 pattern, an information structurally undistinguished subject remains TP-

---

　　　the TP domain in V2 root clauses. See note 11 and Greco and Haegeman (2016) and Haegeman and Greco (2018).
13　Various implementations to formalize the locality condition are conceivable. The locality condition can, for instance, be rephrased in terms of phases and phase boundaries.

internally and the finite verb does not move to C, as outlined above, while an information structurally distinguished subject moves to a position in the left periphery triggering verb movement to C. Support for V-movement to C with *wh*-subjects comes from the fact that for Flemish speakers *wh*-subjects require *er*-insertion. If expletive *er* occupies the canonical subject position, then from (28) we conclude that the finite verb *heeft* ('has'), which occurs in a position to the left of the canonical subject position, must have moved to C. I do not pursue this point here.

(28) *Wie heeft er dat boek gelezen?*
who has there that book read
'Who has read that book?'

4.3   Initial Adverbial Clauses in V2 Transgressions
4.3.1   Speech Act Modifiers

The analysis straightforwardly predicts that conditionals acting as speech act modifiers, like those in (29), will be compatible with a subject-initial V2 clause in a V3 combination.[14] Like relevance conditionals, these initial adjuncts do not establish a temporal value for the proposition expressed in the main clause; rather, they modify the temporality of CP i.e. the speech act. Thus, in contrast with unacceptable V3 patterns in which the central adverbial clauses cannot be related to the TP-internal matrix temporal and modal values, central adverbial clauses which modify the speech act in (29) are directly construed with CP.

(29) a. *Als ik eerlijk mag zijn, dat was gisteren ook al zo.*
if I honest may be that was yesterday also already like that
'To be honest, it was already like that yesterday.'

b. *Als het je interesseert, ik heb gisteren Peter ontmoet*
if it you interests I have yesterday Peter met
'If you are interested, I met Peter yesterday.'

4.3.2   Irrelevance Conditionals and Concessive Free Relatives

Recall that while in a V3 configuration, central adverbial clauses are not compatible with subject-initial V2 (30a), irrelevance conditionals are compatible with subject-initial V2: (18b) is repeated as (30b):

---

14   For some discussion see also Haegeman (2012, pp. 181f.).

(30) a. *[_Adj-XP Als mijn tekst morgen klaar is,] **ik zal je hem**
           if   my   text tomorrow ready is, I will you him
   opsturen.   (= 12a)
   send
   'If my text is ready tomorrow, I will send it to you.'

   b. [_Adj-XP Of mijn tekst morgen klaar is of niet,] **ik zal je hem**
           if   my   text tomorrow ready is or not   I will you him
   opsturen.   (= 18b)
   send
   'Whether my text is ready or not tomorrow, I will send it to you.'

In (30a), the truth value of the main assertion (CP) is conditional on Adj-XP: Adj-XP provides a value for a temporal/modal variable in the matrix CP and to do so it needs to be in a strictly local relation with the TP-internal variable. In the absence of V to C movement, this local relation is not available. In (30b), on the other hand, the truth value of the main assertion in the V2 clause is not conditional on Adj-XP: the assertion in the V2 clause remains valid regardless of Adj-XP. This means that the looser relation between SpecFrameP and the V2 main proposition is sufficient: the adjunct clause does not need to provide a value for a TP-internal temporal or modal variable in the matrix clause. As a result, V to C movement is not required to derive the interpretation.

Along the same lines, concessive adverbial free relatives also are fully compatible with subject-initial V2 root declaratives with an information structurally undistinguished subject, as shown by (31a), which contrasts with the unacceptable (31b), in which a central adverbial clause combines with a subject-initial V2 root declarative with information structurally undistinguished subject:

(31) a. [Hoe hard je ook werkt,] [je] haalt   het toch niet
        how hard you PART work   you succeed it PART not
   'However had you work, you won't succeed.'

   b. *[Als je   hard werkt,] je haalt   het wel.
        if you hard work   you succeed it well
   'If you work hard, you'll manage.'

As was the case with speech act modifiers in (29) and with irrelevance conditionals in (30b), the truth conditions of the matrix clause in (31a) are independent of those in the concessive free relative so that the initial constituent does not need to be related to the TP-internal temporal or modal coordinates.

5 V2 Transgressions and Micro Variation: West Flemish

5.1 *The Data*

5.1.1 V2 Transgressions with Subject-Initial V2 Root Clauses

(32a) and (32b), in which a central adverbial clause combines with a subject-initial V2 clause, are accepted by some (West) Flemish (WF) speakers. The pattern is attested in WF and has been documented and discussed in the descriptive literature (see Vercouillie, 1885; Debrabandere, 1976; Vanacker, 1977; Devos & Vandekerckhove, 2005; Saelens, 2014; Lybaert, De Clerck, Saelens & Decuypere, 2019).[15] The StD analogues are unacceptable, as shown by (12a), repeated in (32c).

(32) a. *Oa menen tekst morgen gereed is, 'k zan em ipstieren.*
　　　 if　 my　 text　 tomorrow ready　is　I　will him send
　　　'If my text is ready tomorrow, I'll send it.'

　　 b. *Oa-n-k tegen em klapen, je (en) zeg tjie niets.*
　　　 if-1SG-I against him talk　 he PART says he nothing
　　　'If I talk to him, he doesn't answer.'

Cf. c. **Als mijn tekst morgen klaar is, ik zal je hem opsturen.*　　　(= 12a)
　　　 if　my　 text　 tomorrow ready is, I　will you him send
　　　'If my text is ready tomorrow, I will send it to you.'

In WF, the non-inverted pattern always alternates with regular V2,[16] as shown in (33):

15　As can be observed, most examples cited here have a pronominal subject in the V2 clause, but this is not obligatory as shown by the attested (34d) and the constructed (35c). Saelens (2014) shows that non-inverted V3 is compatible with nominal and with pronominal subjects. For the 1960 corpus they consulted, Saelens (2014) and Lybaert et al. (2019) show that the DP vs. pronoun contrast is not statistically significant. We refer to their work for details.

16　The opposite does not hold, cf. Section 5.3 and Greco and Haegeman (2018) and Haegeman and Greco (2018).

CENTRAL ADVERBIAL CLAUSES   191

(33) a. *Oa menen tekst morgen gereed is, zan-k em ipstieren.*
      if   my   text   tomorrow ready is will-I him send
      'If my text is ready tomorrow, I'll send it.'

    b. *Oa-n-k tegen em klapen, (en) zegt je niets.*
      if-1SG-I against him talk   PART says he nothing
      'If I talk to him he doesn't answer.'

5.1.2   WF Non-inverted V3 as a Framing Device

The non-inverted V3 pattern is typically used in oral narrative contexts. Contemporary attestations are provided in (34).

(34) a. *Om wieder een feestje geven by ons thus, m'en altijd over.*
      if-1PL we   a   party give at our house we-have always
      leftover
      'If we give a party at our place, we always have leftovers.' (Dominique Persoone (°Bruges), TV-chef, *Njam*, Jun. 15th, 2016)

    b. *Als je tegen dienen gast klapt, je merkt dat gewoon.*
      if you against that   guy talk   you notice that simply
      'If you talk to that guy, you simply notice.' (overheard on the train, Nov. 19th, 2016, male speaker, 25–30)

    c. *Je moet overal opnieuw erbeginnen.*
      he has   everywhere again   start afresh
      'He has to start from zero every time.'
      Ot'n   in China komt, je kent der geen bal van.
      if-3SG-he in China come, he knows there no   ball of
      'If he goes to China, he doesn't have a clue.' (overheard in waiting room hospital, AZ St Jan, Dec. 12th, 2016, male speaker 50–60)

    d. *En ame em zien ankommen, zegt ze Pierre vult dat ton in*
      and if-1PL-we him see arrive,   says she, Pierre fills that then in
      PART
      'And if we see him [the ticket collector] arrive, she says, Pierre fills out the rail card.' (overheard on the train, Jun. 3rd, 2018, female speaker, 40–50)

Non-inverted V3 patterns create an effect of heightened 'immediacy': the pattern puts speaker/hearer *in medias res* and tends to be used in contexts with high speaker involvement. Haegeman and Greco (2018) assume that the initial constituent in such non-inverted V3 patterns occupies the specifier of FrameP. In narrative contexts (35a), its role is to move the narrative forward by providing a new frame to which the main proposition is related. It can also be used to characterize a subject by a range of properties and the V3 patterns with subject-initial V2 is used to go through each of them (35b). The use of the V3 pattern may also create an effect of heightened suspense and the use of a V3 pattern with non-inverted V2 root clause may contribute to creating an effect of surprise (35c).

(35) a. *Die reuke kwaam to in myn us.*
that smell came to in my house
'The smell reached my house.'
Mo oan-k gisteren ipstoengen, t-was gedoan.
but when-I yesterday up stood, it-was finished
'But when I got up yesterday, it was gone.'

b. *Dat is toch een roare:*
that is PART a strange (one)
'She's a strange person:'
Oa-j eur vroagt, ze komt niet.
if-you her invite, she comes not
'If you invite her, she doesn't come.'
Oa-j eur nie vroagt, z'is dul.
if-you her not invite, she-is angry
'If you don't invite her, she gets angry.'

c. *Oa-me tuskwamen, de voordeure stond open en de lucht was an.*
when-we home came the front door stood open and the light was on
'When we came home, the front door was open and the light was on.'

5.2 *Non-inverted V3: Micro Variation in the Derivation of Subject-Initial V2*

In the initial debate concerning the derivation of subject-initial V2, the literature tacitly converged on the hypothesis that V2 languages presented a unified picture, i.e. that if the asymmetric derivation was shown to suit one language, it was generalized to apply across all V2 patterns and V2 languages. Observe, though, that the nature of the argumentation deployed at the time already suggested that a unified view need not be optimal, in that the evidence for one derivation or the other originated with different varieties of V2 languages. Zwart's (1997a,b) empirical support of the asymmetric view of Dutch as in (25) mainly invokes evidence from Dutch dialects (see (24)); in contrast, in support of the alternative symmetric view, Craenenbroeck and Haegeman (2007) mainly invoke Flemish data. One piece of evidence concerns the distribution of the Flemish particle *tet*. In WF, for instance, the particle *tet* occupies a left most position in the TP domain (Haegeman, 1986; Greco, Haegeman & Phan, 2017). This is illustrated in (36): in (36a) *tet* follows the complementizer *dat* ('that') and precedes *Valère*, the subject of the finite clause; in (36b) it follows the preposition *met* ('with') which introduces a non-finite clause with an overt subject, here *Valère*.

(36) a. *Kpeinzen dat tet Valère da   nie goa willen doen.*
       I.think   that *tet* Valère that not go   want do
       'I think that Valère won't want to do that.'

   b. *me   tet Valère da   nie te zeggen*
      with *tet* Valère that not to say
      'Valère not having said that'

As can be seen in (37), in root clauses *tet* invariably follows the finite verb, both in non subject-initial V2 (37a) and in subject-initial V2 (37b). Craenenbroeck and Haegeman (1997) construe this as evidence that in (37a), as well as in (37b), the finite verb has exited the TP area.

(37) a. *Morgen   goa tet Valère da   niet willen doen.*
       tomorrow goes *tet* Valère that not want do
       'Valère won't want to do that tomorrow.'

   b. *Valère goa tet da   morgen   nie willen doen.*
      Valère goes *tet* that tomorrow not want do

Postma (2011) raises the hypothesis that subject-initial V2 is not unified across the Germanic languages and his proposal, though with a different implementation, is taken up in Haegeman and Greco (2018). These authors propose that there is micro variation in the derivation of subject-initial V2 across varieties of

Dutch. For StD, it is proposed that the finite verb does not move to C (38a); for WF they propose that the finite verb does move to C (38b).

(38) a. StD: [$_{CP}$ [$_C$]   [$_{TP}$ Subject [Vfin] ...]]
     b. WF: [$_{CP}$ Subject [$_C$Vfin] [$_{TP}$ t$_{Subject}$ ... t$_{Vfin}$ ...]]

The immediate prediction of this differentiation in the derivation of subject-initial V2 is that a StD V3 configuration in which a central adverbial clause combines with a subject-initial root clause is unacceptable (38c), but that the same pattern will be acceptable in WF, where by virtue of V-movement to C, the initial adverbial clause attains access to the temporal and modal values encoded in the verbal domain (38d):

(38) c. *StD: [$_{FrameP}$ Adj-XP [$_{CP}$ [$_C$]   [$_{TP}$ ik   [zal] ...]]]
     d. ✓WF: [$_{FrameP}$ Adj-XP [$_{CP}$ ik [$_C$ zan] [$_{TP}$ t$_{ik}$ ... t$_{zan}$ ...]]]

As also demonstrated in Haegeman and Greco (2018), an initial adjunct in a regular V2 root clause can be reconstructed to a clause-internal position. In contrast, the initial adverbial constituent in the non-inverted V3 pattern cannot be so reconstructed. I provide one set of data to illustrate this point. In a regular V2 pattern, the initial central adverbial clause can be interpreted as modifying either the matrix event time (i.e. in (39a), 'the claim was made when it was ready') or the event time of the embedded clause (i.e. in (39a), 'she will make a call if it is ready'). These interpretations are also available in the StD analogue of (39a). In the WF V3 pattern in which a central adverbial clause combines with a subject-initial V2 clause (39b), the embedded construal is unavailable: the adverbial clause can only be interpreted as modifying the matrix time.[17]

(39) a. *Oa-t gereed was, zei ze da ze ging bellen.*
        if-it ready was said she that she would call
        'She said that she would call if it was ready.'

     b. *Oa-t gereed was, ze zei da ze ging bellen.*
        if-it ready was she said that she would call

---

17 In this respect, the pattern differs from so-called *hanging-topic left dislocation* (HTLD) which allows construal in embedded domains. This suggests that an analysis adopting a null resumptive (e.g. *dan* 'then') is not adequate. Thanks to Hubert Truckenbrodt (p.c.) for bringing up this point.

These data confirm that the status of the initial adjunct in a V3 configuration differs from that in the V2 configuration and they are in line with Broekhuis and Corver's (2016) proposal that V3 patterns arise due to the presence of main clause external constituents.

6   Summary

This chapter focuses on the availability of central adverbial clauses as initial constituents in V2 transgressions, i.e. patterns in V2 languages in which the finite verb is preceded by two constituents, thus leading to a V3 pattern. If the initial constituents in these V3 configurations are analyzed as main clause external constituents (Broekhuis & Corver, 2016), the prediction would be that central adverbial clauses should be excluded from this position. At first sight, the prediction seems correct: the judgement in (40) is for StD. In this example, a central adverbial clause is merged with a fully-fledged V2 root clause and the central adverbial clause would have to be taken to occupy the main clause external slot. Its clause external position entails that the adverbial clause will not be (sufficiently) syntactically integrated to provide the temporal or modal values for the associated proposition.

(40) *[Als mijn tekst morgen   klaar is,] [ik] zal je   hem opsturen.
       if   my   text tomorrow ready is,   I   will you him send
     'If my text is ready tomorrow, I will send it to you.'

However, one problem for the prediction is that in WF, itself a *bona fide* V2 language, the analogue of (40) is acceptable. In addition, even in StD the prediction is not fully borne out. In several V3 contexts, one of which is illustrated in (41), the initial central adverbial clause modifies the temporal or modal values of the associated clause, but despite this, it appears in what seems to be a main clause external position (in the sense of Broekhuis & Corver, 2016):

(41) [Als mijn tekst klaar is,] [aan wie] moet   ik hem opsturen?
       if   my   text ready is   to whom should I him send
     'If my text is ready, to whom shall I send it?'

I have argued that the crucial distinction between (40) and (41) is that the root clause in (40) is a subject-initial V2 clause, while that in (41) is non subject-initial V2. These data thus suggest that in StD the internal syntax of the V2 clause determines the possible syntactic integration of the central adverbial clause in the main clause external position. Or, to put it differently, that properties of narrow syntax are relevant at the level of discourse interpretation.

Acknowledgements

This research was conducted as joint work with Ciro Greco and presented at *DGfS* 2017, in the workshop AG2 *Information Structuring in Discourse*, at the Universität des Saarlandes, Saarbrücken, as well as in the workshop *Subordinate Clauses in Generative Linguistics*, at University College London, May 2017.

I thank the audiences for their comments. Special thanks go to Werner Frey, Terje Lohndal, Andrew Radford, and Sten Vikner, for comments on various versions of this work.

The research was funded by FWO project 2009-Odysseus-Haegeman-G091409.

References

Astruc-Aguilera, Lluisa. (2005). The form and function of extra-sentential elements. *Cambridge Occasional Papers in Linguistics, 2*, 1–25.
Auer, Peter. (1996). The pre-front field in spoken German and its relevance as a grammaticalization position. *Pragmatics, 6*, 295–322.
Austin, John L. (1956). Ifs and cans. In *Proceedings of the British Academy* (Vol. 42, pp. 109–132).
van der Auwera, Johan. (1986). Conditionals and speech acts. In E.C. Traugott, A. ter Meulen, J. Snitzer Reilly and C.A. Ferguson (Eds.), *On Conditionals* (pp. 197–214). Cambridge: Cambridge University Press.
Banfield, Ann. (1982). *Unspeakable Sentences*. London: Routledge.
Bhatt, Rajesh, & Roumyana Panchev. (2006). Conditionals. In M. Everaert, & H. van Riemsdijk (Eds.), *The Blackwell Companion to Syntax* (Vol. 1, pp. 638–687). Hoboken, NJ: Wiley-Blackwell.
Biberauer Theresa, & Ian Roberts. (2014). Rethinking formal hierarchies: A proposed unification. *Cambridge Occasional Papers in Linguistics, 7*, 1–35.
Boogaert, Ronny. (2007). Conditionele constructies met *moest(en)* en *mocht(en)* in Belgisch-Nederlands en Nederlands Nederlands. *Neerlandistiek.Nl, 7*(05).
Broekhuis, Hans, & Norbert Corver. (2016). Main clause external elements. In H. Broekhuis, & N. Corver, *Dutch Syntax. Verbs and Verb Phrases*. (Vol. 3, Ch. 14). Amsterdam: Amsterdam University Press.

Catasso, Nicholas. (2015). On Postinitial *Aber* and other syntactic transgressions: Some considerations on the nature of V2 in German. *Journal of Germanic Linguistics, 27*, 317–365.

Chomsky, Noam. (2008). On phases. In R. Freidin, C.P. Otero, & M.L. Zubizarreta (Eds.), *Foundational Issues in Linguistic Theory: Essays in Honor of Jean-Roger Vergnaud*. Cambridge, MA: MIT Press.

Cinque, Gulgielmo. (1999). *Adverbs and Functional Heads*. Oxford: Oxford University Press.

Cinque, Guglielmo. (2008). Two types of non-restrictive relatives. In O. Bonami, & P.C. Hofherr (Eds.), *Empirical Issues in Syntax and Semantics 7* (pp. 99–137). Paris: CNRS.

Comrie, Bernard. (1986). Conditionals: A typology. In E.C. Traugott, A. ter Meulen, J.S. Reilly, & C.A. Ferguson (Eds.), *On Conditionals* (pp. 77–102). Cambridge: Cambridge University Press.

Craenenbroeck, Jeroen van, & Liliane Haegeman. (2007). The Derivation of subject-initial V2. *Linguistic Inquiry, 38*, 167–178.

D'Avis, Franz Josef. (2004). In front of the prefield—inside or outside the clause? In H. Lohnstein, & S. Trissler (Eds.), *The Syntax and Semantics of the Left Periphery* (pp. 139–177). Berlin: De Gruyter.

Debrabandere, Frans. (1976). De SVf-volgorde in zinnen met een aanloop. *Handelingen van de Koninklijke Commissie voor Toponymie en Dialectologie, 50*, 87–97.

Demirdache, Hamida, & Myriam Uribe-Etxebarria. (2004). The syntax of time adverbs. In J. Guéron, & J. Lecarme (Eds.), *The Syntax of Time* (pp. 143–180). Cambridge, MA: MIT Press.

Demske, Ulrike. (2015, May 29–31). *Adverbials and the left periphery: Syntax and Information Structure in the History of German*. [Conference presentation abstract], Diachronic Generative Syntax Conference. Reykjavik, Iceland.

Devos, Magda, & Reinhilde Vandekerckhove. (2005). *Westvlaams*. Tielt: Lannoo.

Donaldson, Bryan. (2012). Initial subordinate clauses in Old French: Syntactic variation and the clausal left periphery. *Lingua, 122*, 1021–1046.

Ducrot, Oswald. (1983). *Le Sens Commun. Le Dire et le Dit*. Paris: les Editions de Minuit.

Elhadad, Michael, & Kathleen R. McKeown. (1990). Generating connectives. In *Proceedings of the 13th International Conference on Computational Linguistics (COLING)* (Vol. 3, pp. 97–101). Helsinki, Finland.

Emonds, Joe. (2004). Unspecified categories as the key to root constructions. In D. Adger, C. DeCat, & G. Tsoulas (Eds.), *Peripheries* (pp. 75–121). Dordrecht: Kluwer.

Endo, Yoshio, & Liliane Haegeman. (2014). Adverbial concord: merging adverbial clauses. In S. Kawahara, & M. Igarashi (Eds.), *MIT Working papers in Linguistics* (Vol. 73, pp. 25–44). Cambridge, UK: Cambridge University Press.

Frascarelli, Mara. (2016). *Dislocations and framings*. [Unpublished Manuscript, Università Roma Tre].

Frey, Werner. (2012). Peripheral adverbial clauses, their licensing and the prefield in German. In E. Breindl, G. Ferraresi, & A. Volodina (Eds.), *Satzverknüpfung—Zur Interaktion von Form, Bedeutung und Diskursfunktion* (pp. 41–77). Berlin: De Gruyter.

Frey, Werner, & Liliane Haegeman (forthcoming). *Adverbial clauses*. [Unpublished Manuscript, Leibniz-ZAS and University of Ghent].

Giorgi, Alessandra. (2014). Prosodic signals as syntactic formatives in the left periphery. In A. Cardinaletti, G. Cinque and Y. Endo (Eds.), *On Peripheries, Exploring Clause initial and Clause final Positions* (pp. 161–188). Tokyo: Hituzi Syobe Publishing.

Greco, Ciro, & Liliane Haegeman. (2016). *Frame setters and the macro variation of subject-initial V2*. lingbuzz/003226

Greco, Ciro, Liliane Haegeman, & Trang Phan. (2017). Expletives and Speaker-related Meaning. In M. Sheehan and L. Bailey (Eds.), *Order and Structure in Syntax II: Subjecthood and Argument Structure* (pp. 69–93). Berlin: Language Science Press.

Griffiths, James, & Mark de Vries. (2013). The syntactic integration of appositives: Evidence from fragments and ellipsis. *Linguistic Inquiry, 44*, 332–344.

Haegeman, Liliane. (1991). Parenthetical adverbials: the radical orphanage approach. In S. Chiba (Ed.), *Aspects of Modern Linguistics* (pp. 232–254). Tokyo: Kaitakushi Press.

Haegeman, Liliane. (1996). Verb second, the split CP and null subjects in early Dutch finite clauses. *GenGenP*. http://ling.auf.net/lingBuzz/001059

Haegeman, Liliane. (2002). Anchoring to the speaker, adverbial clauses and the structure of CP. In S. Mauck, & J. Mittelstaedt (Eds.), *Georgetown University Working Papers in Theoretical Linguistics* (Vol. 2, pp. 117–180). Washington DC: Georgetown University.

Haegeman, Liliane. (2003). Conditional Clauses: External and Internal Syntax. *Mind & Language, 18*, 317–339.

Haegeman, Liliane. (2004). The syntax of adverbial clauses and its consequences for topicalisation. *Antwerp Papers in Linguistics*. 107. *Current Studies in Comparative Romance Linguistics*, 61–90.

Haegeman, Liliane. (2006). Conditionals, factives and the left periphery. *Lingua, 116*, 1651–1669.

Haegeman, Liliane. (2009). Parenthetical adverbials: The radical orphanage approach. In B. Shaer, P. Cook, W. Frey, & C. Maienborn (Eds.), *Dislocated Elements in Discourse: Syntactic, Semantic and Pragmatic Perspectives* (pp. 331–347). London: Routledge. Reprinted from Haegeman (1991).

Haegeman, Liliane. (2012). *Adverbial Clauses, Main Clause Phenomena and the Composition of the Left Periphery*. Oxford: Oxford University Press.

Haegeman, Liliane, & Yoshido Endo. (2017). *Adverbial clauses and adverbial concord*. [Unpublished Manuscript, Ghent University].

Haegeman, Liliane, & Ciro Greco. (2018). West Flemish V3 and the interaction of syntax and discourse. *Journal of Comparative Germanic Linguistics, 21*, 1–56.

Haegeman, Liliane, Benjamin Shaer, & Werner Frey. (2009). Postscript: Problems and solutions for orphan analyses. In B. Shaer, P. Cook, W. Frey, & C. Maienborn (Eds.), *Dislocated Elements in Discourse: Syntactic, Semantic and Pragmatic Perspectives* (pp. 348–365). London: Routledge.

Haspelmath, Martin, & Ekkehard König. (1998). Concessive Conditionals in the languages of Europe. In J. van der Auwera (Ed.), *Adverbial Constructions in the Languages of Europe* in collaboration with D.P.O. Baoill (pp. 563–640). Berlin: De Gruyter.

Holmberg, Anders. (2015). Verb second. In T. Kiss, & A. Alexiadou (Eds.), *Syntax. An International Handbook of Contemporary Syntactic Research* (2nd. ed., pp. 343–384). HSK Series. Berlin: De Gruyter.

Hornstein, Norbert. (1993). *As Time Goes By: Tense and Universal Grammar*. Cambridge, Mass: MIT Press.

Huddleston, Rodney. (1984). *Introduction to the Grammar of English*. Cambridge: Cambridge University Press.

Iatridou, Sabine. (1994). On the contribution of conditional *then*. *Natural Language Semantics*, 171–199.

Kearns, John. (2006). Conditional assertion, denial, and supposition as illocutionary acts. *Linguistics and Philosophy, 29*, 455–485.

König, Ekkehard, & Johan van de Auwera. (1988). Clause integration in German and Dutch. In J. Haiman, & S. Thomson (Eds.), *Clause Combining in Grammar and Discourse* (pp. 101–133). Amsterdam/Philadelphia: John Benjamins.

Koster, Jan. (2000). *Extraposition as parallel construal*. [Unpublished Manuscript, University of Groningen].

Lybaert, Chloé, Bernard De Clerck, Jorien Saelens, & Ludovic Decuypere. (2019). A corpus-based analysis of V2 variation in West Flemish and French Flemish dialects. *Journal of Germanic Linguistics, 31*(1), 43–100.

Mikkelsen, Line. (2015). VP anaphora and verb-second order in Danish. *Journal of Linguistics, 51*, 595–643.

Postma, Gertjan. (2011, June 23–24). *Modifying the hearer. The nature of the left periphery of main clauses in Frisian and Dutch*. [Conference presentation], Comparative Germanic Syntax Workshop 26, Meertens Institute Amsterdam, The Netherlands.

Quirk, Randolph, Sidney Greenbaum, Geoffrey Leech, & Jan Svartvik. (1985). *A Comprehensive Grammar of the English Language*. London: Longman.

Reichenbach, Hans. (1947). *Symbolic Logic*. Berkeley: University of California Press.

Reis, Marga. (1997). Zum syntaktischen Status unselbständiger Verbzweit-Sätze. In C. Dürscheid, K.-H. Ramers, & M. Schwarz (Eds.), *Sprache im Fokus. Festschrift für Heinz Vater zum 65. Geburtstag* (pp. 121–144). Tübingen: Niemeyer.

Rizzi, Luigi. (1997). The fine structure of the left periphery. In L. Haegeman (Ed.), *Elements of Grammar* (pp. 281–337). Dordrecht: Springer.

Saelens, Jorien. (2014). *Topicalisering zonder inversie: een ingveonisme* [Master thesis, Ghent University].

Salvesen, Christina. (2017). *Resumptive particles and V2*. [Unpublished Manuscript, University of Oslo].

Schwartz Bonnie, & Sten Vikner. (1996). The verb always leaves IP in V2 clauses. In A. Belletti, & L. Rizzi (Eds.), *Parameters and Functional Heads* (pp. 11–62). Oxford: Oxford University Press.

Sigurdsson, Halldor. (2016). The Split T analysis. In K. Eide (Ed.), *Finiteness Matters: on Finiteness related Phenomena in Natural Languages* (pp. 79–92). Amsterdam/Philadelphia: John Benjamins.

Skårup, Povl. (1975). Les premières zones de la proposition en ancient français: essai de syntaxe de position. *Revue Romane*, Special Issue 6. Akademisk Forlag: Kopenhagen.

Travis, Lisa. (1984). *Parameters and effects of word order variation*. [Doctoral dissertation, Massachusetts Institute of Technology].

Vanacker, Valère F. (1977). Syntactische overeenkomsten tusen Frans-Vlaamse en Westvlaamse dialekten. *De Franse Nederlanden. Les Pays-Bas Francais. Jaarboek* Rekkem: Ons Erfdeel, 206–216.

Vercouillie, Jozef. (1885). Spraakleer van het Westvlaamsch Dialect. *Onze Volkstaal*, 2, 3–47.

Vries, Mark de. (2009). The left and right periphery in Dutch. *The Linguistic Review*, 26, 291–327.

Williams, Edwin. (1977). Discourse and Logical Form. *Linguistic Inquiry*, 8, 101–139.

Wolfe, Sam. (2016). On the left periphery of V2 languages. *Selected Papers from the 41st Incontro di Grammatica Generativa. Rivista di Grammatica Generativa* (Vol. 38, pp. 287–310).

Zwart, Jan-Wouter. (1997a). The Germanic SOV languages and the universal base hypothesis. In L. Haegeman (Ed.), *The New Comparative Syntax* (pp. 246–264). New York: Addison-Wesley.

Zwart, Jan-Wouter. (1997b). *Morphosyntax of Verb Movement: A Minimalist Approach to the Syntax of Dutch*. Dordrecht: Kluwer.

Zwart, Jan-Wouter. (2005). Verb second as a function of Merge. In M. den Dikken, & C.M. Tortora (Eds.), *The Function of Function Words and Functional Categories* (pp. 11–40). Amsterdam/Philadelphia: John Benjamins.

CHAPTER 8

Discourse Conditions on Relative Clauses: A Crosslinguistic and Diachronic Study on the Interaction between Mood, Verb Position and Information Structure

Marco Coniglio and Roland Hinterhölzl

1 Verb Placement and Discourse Relations in Relative Clauses

It is standardly assumed that, in restrictive relative clauses, the relative clause specifies a property that restricts the reference of the head noun, as in the German example in (1).

(1) *Das Blatt hat eine Seite, die ganz schwarz ist*
    the sheet has a side that completely black is
    'The sheet has a side that is completely black' (Gärtner, 2001, p. 98)

In German relative clauses, the finite verb is typically in final position. However, Gärtner's groundbreaking works (2001, 2002) prove the existence of a special class of (restrictive) relative clauses that exhibit Verb Second order (V2 relatives). Gärtner argues that V2 relatives have a discourse structure that is quite different from the one of verb-final relative clauses (verb-final relatives). In particular, he surmises that, in V2 relatives, the main clause establishes a topic that is elaborated on by the comment represented by the relative clause, as in (2) (cf. Bourgonje & Stede, this volume, for a definition of the notions of topic and comment).

(2) [_Topic_ *Das Blatt hat eine Seite,*] [_Comment_ *die ist wohl ganz schwarz*] (cf. Ebert, Endriss & Gärtner, 2007)

In this paper, we discuss the properties of verb placement in Modern German relative clauses and link it synchronically to mood alternations as can be observed in the Romance languages, in particular to Italian. Then, starting from the observation that Old High German (OHG) also exhibits mood alternations—like Italian—and alternations in verb placement—like Modern

German—, we will provide a diachronic account for the development of the language from a system similar to that displayed by the Romance languages to the one displayed by Modern German.

The paper is organized in the following way. Section 2 briefly summarizes the most important properties of V2 relatives. Section 3 presents the standard account of V2 relatives by Gärtner. Section 4 presents data that strongly indicate that the distinction between V2 relatives and verb-final relatives is synchronically paralleled by mood alternation in relative clauses in Italian. Section 5 discusses mood alternations in relative clauses from the perspective of Information Structure, while Section 6 accounts for their syntactic properties. From the diachronic perspective, Section 7 and 8 present a corpus-based investigation and discussion of the different properties of mood and verb placement in OHG relative clauses. In Section 9, a scenario accounting for the diachronic development is sketched.

2 Properties of V2 Relative Clauses

This section is entirely based on Gärtner and colleagues' seminal work on V2 relatives (cf. Gärtner 2001, 2002; Ebert, Endriss & Gärtner, 2007) and serves as the background for the discussion of the properties of relative clauses in Italian (see the discussion in Catasso & Hinterhölzl, 2016, pp. 99 ff.) and in OHG. The first property concerns the fact that the content of the relative clause is asserted licensing the occurrence of modal particles (cf. Coniglio, 2011), as has been illustrated in (2) above. Second, a V2 relative is subject to obligatory extraposition, as is illustrated in (3) (cf. Holler, 2005; Jasinskaja & Poschmann, this volume, for the interaction between discourse relations and the attachment of appositive relative clauses).

(3) a. *Hans hat eine Frau,   die   {*hat} blaue Augen {hat}, getroffen*
       Hans has a   woman that has blue eyes   has met
       'Hans met a woman that has blue eyes.'

   b. Hans hat eine Frau getroffen, die {hat} blaue Augen {hat}

The third property concerns the fact that the head noun cannot be in the scope of a negative, interrogative or conditional operator, as is illustrated in (4).

(4) a. *Kein Professor mag eine Studentin,   die {*zitiert} ihn nicht*
no   professor likes a   student.FEM who   cites   him NEG
{*zitiert*}.
cites
'No professor likes a student who doesn't cite him.' (cf. Gärtner, 2002, p. 107)

b. *Mag Professor Müller eine Studentin,   die {*zitiert} ihn nicht*
likes professor Müller a   student.FEM who   cites   him NEG
{*zitiert*}?
cites
'Does Professor Müller like a student who doesn't cite him?' (Catasso & Hinterhölzl, 2016, p. 102)

The fourth property concerns a restriction on the determiner of the head noun. The latter must be an indefinite or weak DP, as is illustrated in (5) and (6) below (data from Catasso & Hinterhölzl, 2016).

(5) a. *Das ist ein Buch, das   hat keinen Punkt   und kein Komma.*
this is a   book that.NOM has no   full-stop and no   comma
'This is a book that has no full stops and no commas.' (DLF, Sept. 9th, 2010)

b. *Es gibt (viele) Leute, die   haben tolle Ideen–*
EXIST many people that.NOM have great ideas
nur es   passiert relativ wenig.
only EXPL happens quite little
'There are (many) people who have great ideas—however, very little is going on.' (tlz, Jul. 6th, 2014)

(6) a. *Ich kenne einen, dem   hat ein Zugunglück   das Leben*
I   know one   that.DAT has a   train-accident the life
gerettet.
saved
'I know a man whose life was saved by a train accident.' (character's direct speech from Eckhard Bahr, 2007, p. 111)

b. *Es gibt auch einige, die   würde man gerne aus der*
   EXIST also   some   that.ACC would one   gladly out the
   Geschichte schubsen.
   story   nudge
   'There are some [passages] that one would just love to strike out.'
   (amazon.de, online user's comment, Jun. 30th, 2012)

The fifth property concerns a restriction on the relative pronoun. The latter must be a *d*-pronoun, as is illustrated in (7).

(7) a. *Es gibt Probleme, die   /*welche   sind nicht lösbar.*
       EXIST problems that.NOM   which.NOM are not solvable

   b. *Es gibt Probleme, die   /welche   nicht lösbar sind.*
      EXIST problems that.NOM   which.NOM not solvable are
      'There are problems that are not solvable.' (Wiener Zeitung, Mar. 28th, 2013)

3 The Standard Analysis

Gärtner (2001, 2002) posits an analysis of V2 relatives that accounts for all these properties in a very elegant way. In particular, he surmises that in V2 relatives two (main) clauses are coordinated, accounting for the presence of V2 in the relative clause and relating it to the proto-assertional force of the relative, as is illustrated in (8).

(8) [$_{\pi P}$ [$_{CP1}$ Das Blatt hat eine Seite [$_{\pi°}$ REL [$_{CP2}$ die ist ganz schwarz]]]
    'The sheet has one side that is all black.' (cf. Gärtner, 2001, p. 105)

The strength of Gärtner's original analysis of V2 relatives is that he convincingly argues that the contexts in which V2 relatives are excluded are those that fail to set up a discourse referent for the interpretation of the weak demonstrative element introducing V2 relatives, thereby connecting the properties 1–3 to property 4: V2 relatives must be headed by a discourse-anaphoric *d*-pronoun that is only licensed if—after processing the main clause (hence the obligatory extraposition of the relative clause)—a discourse referent has been established in the semantic representation, excluding definite head nouns and indefinite head nouns in the scope of a negative, interrogative or conditional operator.

The problem with this approach is that this syntactic analysis renders the semantic interpretation of V2 relatives a rather complex issue (cf. Catasso & Hinterhölzl, 2016, pp. 99 ff.), since the content of the relative clause must be integrated into the interpretation of the DP heading it during the computation of the matrix clause to derive the correct restrictive interpretation, as is illustrated by the difference in interpretation between (9a) and (9b). While (9a) states that many of the houses in Apfeldorf are empty, but does not state that Apfeldorf has many houses, (9b) asserts that Apfeldorf has many houses and that all of them are empty.

(9) a. Apfeldorf hat viele Häuser, die stehen leer.
'Apfeldorf has many houses that are empty.'

b. Apfeldorf hat viele Häuser. Diese stehen leer.
'Apfeldorf has many houses. These are empty.'

This means that in the course of the derivation the *d*-pronoun must be reinterpreted as a relative pronoun, implying that the relative pronoun in a V2 relative must have the presupposition of a *d*-pronoun, but the denotation of a regular relative operator. In the following section, we will show that the distributional differences of V2 relatives and verb-final relatives in German are paralleled by relative clauses marked with the indicative and the subjunctive mood in Italian.

We will show that these correspondences are not accidental and argue that while German V2 indicates that the embedded proposition is epistemically anchored to the speaker, the alternation between the indicative and the subjunctive in Italian has essentially the same function, indicating whether the embedded proposition is anchored to the utterance event or to the event denoted by the matrix verb.

4 Indicative versus Subjunctive and V2

To start out with, we illustrate an interpretational effect of German V2 relatives that Gärtner (2001, 2002) detected, but has not been discussed in the previous section (see also the discussion in Catasso & Hinterhölzl, 2016, pp. 99 ff.). While a verb-final relative is compatible with a *de re* and a *de dicto* interpretation of the head noun, a V2 relative only permits its interpretation as *de re*, as is illustrated in (10).

(10) a. *Hans sucht   eine Frau,   die   blaue Augen hat.* (*de re, de dicto*)
    Hans looks.for a   woman who blue   eyes   has

   b. *Hans sucht   eine Frau   die   hat blaue*
    Hans looks.for a   woman who has blue
    Augen. (*de re, *de dicto*)
    eyes
    'John is looking for a woman who has blue eyes.'

The verb-final relative clause in (10a) is compatible with the interpretation that Hans has a specific person in mind (*de re*) or that he does not have a specific person in mind but only cares about the fact that the relevant woman, whoever she may be, has blue eyes (*de dicto*). In contrast, the V2 relative in (10b) is only compatible with the interpretation that Hans has a specific person in mind (*de re*).

As for Italian, (11a) shows that a relative clause marked with the subjunctive mood permits a *de dicto* (i.e. non-specific) interpretation of its head noun, while the relative clause marked with the indicative mood in (11b) is only compatible with its *de re* interpretation, requiring a specific interpretation of the head noun, at least in written Standard Italian (data from Catasso & Hinterhölzl, 2016, p. 109; cf. Farkas, 1992; Quer, 1998; Giannakidou, 2009, 2013).

(11) a. *Gianni cerca   una donna   che   abbia   gli occhi*
    John looks.for a   woman who has.SUB the eyes
    blu. (*de dicto*)
    blue

   b. *Gianni cerca   una donna   che   ha   gli occhi blu.* (*de re*)
    John looks.for a   woman who has.IND the eyes blue
    'John is looking for a woman who has blue eyes.'

These facts raise the question whether this parallelism is accidental. The following data however indicate that the parallelism between V2 relatives and verb-final relatives in German and the mood alternations in Italian relatives is quite systematic, calling for a unified account.

First, Catasso and Hinterhölzl (2016) note that contexts that require the subjunctive mood in Italian, namely relative clauses with a final or a consecutive interpretation, exclude V2 order in German (cf. Meinunger, 2004, 2006), as is illustrated in (12) and (13), taken from Catasso and Hinterhölzl (2016, p. 110).

(12) a. *Prendo un autobus che mi porti in centro.*
    [I] take a bus that me take.SUB to center

   b. *Ich nehme einen Bus, der mich ins Zentrum bringt.*
    I take a bus that me to-the center takes

   c. **Ich nehme einen Bus, der bringt mich ins Zentrum.*
    I take a bus that takes me to-the centre
    'I take a bus that takes me downtown.'

(13) a. *È difficile trovare un vestito che lei non possa indossare.*
    is difficult find a dress that she NEG can.SUB wear

   b. *Es ist schwierig, ein Kleid zu finden, das ihr nicht steht.*
    it is difficult a dress to find that her NEG suits

   c. **Es ist schwierig, ein Kleid zu finden, das steht ihr nicht.*
    it is difficult a dress to find that suits her NEG
    'It is difficult to find a dress that doesn't suit her.'

Second, they note that the contexts that we discussed in the previous section which exclude V2 in German require the subjunctive in Italian, as is illustrated for head nouns in the scope of a negative or interrogative operator in (14) and (15) respectively (cf. Catasso & Hinterhölzl, 2016, p. 111).

(14) a. *Non c'è nessuno che sia meglio di te.*
    NEG EXIST nobody who is.SUB better than you

   b. *Es gibt niemanden, der besser ist als du.*
    EXIST nobody who better is than you

   c. **Es gibt niemanden, der ist besser als du.*
    EXIST nobody who is better than you
    'There is nobody who is better than you.'

(15) a. *Esiste un vestito che ti piaccia veramente?*
    exists a dress that you.DAT pleases.SUB really

   b. *Gibt es überhaupt ein Kleid, das dir gefällt?*
    EXIST MOD.PRT a dress that you.DAT pleases

c. *Gibt es überhaupt ein Kleid, das gefällt dir?
   EXIST MOD.PRT a   dress that pleases you.DAT
   'Is there a dress that you like anyway?'

To sum up, we have seen that the overlap in interpretative and distributional effects between mood alternations in Italian relatives and the positional alternation of the finite verb in German relatives is significant, calling for a unified account. This parallelism is complemented by information-structural considerations, as is briefly discussed in the following section.

5 Indicative versus Subjunctive and Information Structure

Catasso and Hinterhölzl (2016, p. 113) show that, as is illustrated in (16), the content of the relative clause is mapped into the restriction of the quantifier in subjunctive-marked clauses, as the paraphrase in (17a) indicates, while the content of the relative clause can be mapped into the nuclear scope of the quantifier in indicative-marked clauses, as the paraphrase in (17b) indicates. In particular, the latter mapping is obligatory, if the relative clause contains a focused element, as is indicated by capital letters in (16b) (data from Catasso & Hinterhölzl, 2016, p. 113).

(16) a. *In quel periodo ho   incontrato poche persone che fossero*
       in that period I.have met   few   persons who were.SUB
       ricche.
       rich

   b. *In quel periodo ho   incontrato poche persone che ERANO*
      in that period I.have met   few   persons who were.IND
      ricche.
      rich
      'At that time, I met few people that were rich.'

(17) a. for few people that were rich, it holds that I have met them
    b. for few people that I encountered, it holds that they were rich

In other words, we are dealing with an effect of quantificational variability induced by focus (cf. among many others Herburger, 2000). Herburger (2000) argues that the quantificational NP undergoes quantifier raising (henceforth: QR) to IP (following May, 1977). In this process, focused material is interpreted in the VP and is thus mapped onto the nuclear scope, as is illustrated in (18) (Catasso & Hinterhölzl, 2016, p. 113).

(18) a. We hired few incompetent cooks
(= for few incompetent cooks, it holds that we hired them)
b. We hired few INCOMPETENT cooks.
(= for few cooks we hired, it holds that they were incompetent)

The content of a restrictive relative clause is typically presupposed, or at least taken to be not at issue, in order to guarantee its function to narrow down the reference of the head noun successfully. As is illustrated in (19), the content of the relative clause cannot be directly refuted, but is subject to rejection of a presupposition.

(19) A: The woman that moved in downstairs is a lawyer.
B: That is not true. She is a secretary.
B: % That is not true. Nobody moved in downstairs
B: Wait a minute! Who moved in downstairs?

Along this line, we account for the above effect in our approach by surmising that the subjunctive in the relative clause indicates that its content (which has the function of characterizing an individual) is not at issue and is mapped into the restriction of the determiner. This implies that the relative clause marked with the subjunctive is obligatorily pied-piped by QR of the quantifier in the head noun, while the indicative indicates that the relative clause is mapped into the nuclear scope of the determiner and is asserted. This could be achieved by assuming that a relative clause marked with the indicative mood must be obligatorily extraposed (but see also the discussion in the following section). We conclude that also this interpretative effect of indicative-marked relative clauses in Italian parallels the interpretative effect of V2 in German relative clauses, since we noted in Section 2 above, that the content of V2 relatives is generally taken to be asserted (cf. Catasso & Hinterhölzl, 2016, p. 113).

Now let us address the question of what could be the reason for these parallel effects between verb position in German and mood alternation in Italian. In Hinterhölzl (2020), it is shown that adverbial clauses in German and complementizer-introduced complement clauses with V2 (V2C) in North-Germanic (cf. Vikner, 1995), Frisian (cf. de Haan & Weerman, 1986) and German (cf. Freywald, 2008) share the distributional properties (1–3) discussed in Section 2 above with V2 relatives, calling for a uniform analysis. In Gärtner (2001, 2002), the distributional properties of V2 relatives are derived from the requirements imposed by the *d*-pronoun. A unified analysis of these cases, however, calls for an alternative explanation that derives these distributional properties from the impact of V2 that these constructions share.

V2Cs also show that the position targeted by the finite verb in these cases of embedded V2 is lower than the position targeted by the finite verb in matrix clauses. It is thus plausible that this lower position is to be identified with a Mood projection between ForceP and FinP in the system of Rizzi (1997). Consequently, Hinterhölzl (2020) argues that V2 relatives—like V2 adverbials and V2Cs—are regular embedded clauses and that embedded V2 indicates the assertive potential of the embedded clause. In particular, Hinterhölzl (2020) proposes that V2 indicates that the speaker (alone) has evidence for the embedded proposition. This needs to be licensed by a real speech act—in this case by an assertive operator—by entering into a local relation with the Force head in the matrix clause, triggering extraposition of the V2-clause to a position in the local C-domain of the matrix clause (cf. Hinterhölzl, 2020).

Assuming that the alternation between the indicative and the subjunctive in Italian indicates that the embedded proposition is anchored with respect to the utterance situation, to its participants—in particular to the speaker—, and to the event denoted by the matrix verb—in particular to its subject—, the indicative mood in embedded clauses in Italian and embedded V2 in German share the property of being linked to the utterance situation and the speaker.

If this approach is on the right track, then an alternative account of V2 relatives in German is in order that explains a) the restriction to indefinite and weak determiners in the head noun, b) the restriction of the relative pronoun to *d*-pronouns in the relative clause and c) the parallel impact of mood alternation on the *de re* and *de dicto* interpretation of the head noun in Italian. Such an alternative account is sketched in following section.

6   A Matching Analysis of Restrictive Relative Clauses

On the basis of the data discussed in Section 4 and 5 above, the question arises as to how mood distinctions can become relevant for the interpretation of the head noun. A possible account has been developed in Catasso and Hinterhölzl (2016), the most important tenets of which we will sketch below. The interested reader is referred to this paper for a full account.

The answer to the questions raised at the end of the last section involves the assumption of a matching analysis of relative clauses plus the notion of individual concepts, i.e. the assumption that a nominal is individuated with respect to a situation (cf. Carnap, 1928; Elbourne, 2005), as is illustrated in (20).

In this approach, a relative clause specifies the situation with respect to which the head noun is evaluated in the main clause, as is illustrated in (21b) for the clause in (21a).

(20) the book(x, s) denotes the unique individual x such that x is a book in s

(21) a. John read the book that Mary recommended.
b. in s_1 John read the unique book x in s_2 such that Mary recommended x in s_2

The determiner restriction in V2 relatives follows from a matching analysis à la Cinque and the conditions on phonological deletion, as is illustrated in (22). In a matching analysis, the external head must be matched by a relative-clause-internal copy of its NP part, where the lower copy is subject to phonological deletion under semantic identity (cf. Hulsey & Sauerland, 2006).

(22) [$_{DP}$ the [$_{NP}$ book] [$_{CP}$ [$_{NP}$ ~~book~~] [$_{C'}$ that John read t]]] (Hulsey & Sauerland, 2006)

This partial matching requirement follows from Cinque's (2013) comparative investigation of relative clauses in the languages of the world. In particular, Cinque argues that finite restrictive relative clauses (and amount relatives) are merged above weak determiners, in Milsark's (1974) sense. That is, relative clauses are merged above multal and paucal quantifiers, cardinals, the indefinite determiner and adjectives, and below strong determiners (definite articles, demonstratives, universal quantifiers, etc.). The structure that Cinque thereby assumes is a single double-headed structure, as is illustrated in (23). This structure is assumed to underlie the different types of relative clauses—head-internal and head-external ones—that are attested cross-linguistically. This explains the determiner restriction in V2 relatives in a syntactic manner and, as we will see, in a more accurate way than Gärtner's original account.

(23) John read [the [CP book$_1$ that Mary recommended t$_1$] book]

In our approach using individual concepts, phonological deletion under semantic identity is guaranteed if the external and internal head are interpreted with respect to the same situation. There are basically two possibilities to achieve this: a) via a relative operator in a verb-final relative and b) via coreference in the case of V2 relatives.

1) In the first case, a restrictive relative clause specifies via a relative operator the situation with respect to which the head noun in the main clause is interpreted. The relative operator that should not be identified with the relative pronoun binds the event argument of the verb that has been anchored via Tense and Mood, accounting for the relevance of the mood distinction: the situation will be either a situation introduced by the matrix verb, hence a situation in an alternative world (subjunctive) or the utterance situation, hence a situation in the actual world (indicative).

Catasso and Hinterhölzl (2016, p. 116) identify the relative operator with a relative head in C that is realized as *wo* in various German dialects, like Bavarian and Hessian, but is silent in Standard German and blocks V2 (cf. (24), adapted from Bayer, 1984, p. 216). Bavarian shows that the relative pronoun is semantically empty and only functions as host of the phi-features of the deleted internal NP that are not recoverable from the context. In the case of a verb-final relative, the determiner/quantifier of the head noun is interpreted in the matrix clause.

(24) a. *I sog's dem Mõ (der) wo im Gartn arwat*
      I say-it to.the man.DAT who.NOM wo in.the garden works

   b. *Der Mantl *(den) wo i kaffd hob wor z'rissn*
      The coat.NOM which.AKK wo I bought have was torn

   c. *Die Lampn (die) wo i geseng hob wor greißlich*
      The lamp.NOM which.AKK wo I seen have was ugly

In the case in (25), which reproduces a typical example in Gärtner (2001, 2002), this means that the relative clause denotes the set of objects x and the set of situations s such that x is a house in s and s is a situation in the actual world and x is empty in s (cf. (25b)). When the relative clause is combined with the head noun, predicate modification ensures that the individual variable and the situation variable of the external head are identified with the set of objects and the set of situations denoted by the relative clause, allowing for phonological deletion of the lower NP under semantic identity. The rest of the main clause in (25) then specifies that many of these houses x that are empty in s belong to Apfeldorf.

(25) a. *Apfeldorf hat viele Häuser, die (wo) leer stehen.*
      Apfeldorf has many houses which wo empty are
      'Apfeldorf has many houses that are empty.'

b. λs λx house (x, s) & s in w_a & empty(x, s) (meaning of the relative clause)

2) In the V2 case, illustrated in (26), identity under coreference is achieved if the embedded NP (deleted under semantic identity) is discourse-anaphoric and the matrix clause establishes a discourse referent—a set of houses in a given situation—that is taken up by the head noun in the relative clause.

(26) *Apfeldorf hat viele Häuser, die stehen leer.*
Apfeldorf has many houses which are empty
'Apfeldorf has many houses that are empty.'

In this case, the embedded NP enters an Agree relation with a context operator that is valued with the most salient discourse referent that matches its phi-features (cf. Hinterhölzl, 2019). We leave it open at this point whether the *d*-pronoun is a spell-out of this topic head binding the discourse-anaphoric NP (cf. Portele & Bader, this volume) or serves as a host for the phi-features within the embedded NP. For the sake of simplicity, we assume that the *d*-pronoun is spelled out in the head position of φP of the embedded head noun in (27) below. Most importantly, there is no relative operator blocking verb movement into the C-domain in the embedded clause. It is the configuration of matching NPs that ensures that coreference with a discourse antecedent, which otherwise is an optional phenomenon, leads to the parallel evaluation of the arguments of the external and internal NP.

As argued above, extraposition of the relative clause is taken to be triggered by V2. For the illocutionary interpretation as an asserted clause, it is sufficient that extraposition of the relative clause takes place at LF. In the case at hand, however, extraposition of the relative clause already occurs in overt syntax such that the entire matrix clause has been processed and the relevant discourse referent been established, when the extraposed relative clause is processed.

Due to extraposition, the quantifier/determiner of the head noun must be interpreted in the relative clause, as is illustrated in (27c). (27a) displays the basic matching structure at the beginning of the derivation: the relative clause is a sub-constituent of the external head in the matrix clause. (27b) displays the structure at PF, after phonological deletion of the internal matching head. (27c) displays the relevant structure at LF, after the relative clause has been extraposed to a high position in the matrix clause. (27d) specifies the LF after the quantifier has undergone QR in the relative clause, accounting for its strong proportional reading as is discussed below.

In this structure, the quantifier cannot be interpreted in the main clause, since it would leave us with unbound traces in the relative clause and is thus interpreted in the embedded clause (Fig. 8.1). In this clause, the constituent *viele Häuser* is discourse-anaphoric yielding the strong reading: many of the houses in *s*—where *s* is the situation containing the houses in Apfeldorf—are empty. In this case, the phi-features cannot be deleted since they indicate the presupposition of the internal head noun that a discourse referent with the corresponding phi-features has been established.

(27) Apfeldorf hat viele Häuser, die stehen leer.
   a. [$_{CP}$ Apeldorf hat [$_{DP}$ [$_{CP}$ [$_{\varphi P}$ [$_{CardP}$ viele Häuser]] [$_{C}$ stehen [$_{IP}$ leer]]] [$_{CardP}$ viele Häuser]]]
   b. [$_{CP}$ [$_{CP}$ Apfeldorf hat [$_{DP}$ t$_i$ [$_{CardP}$ viele Häuser]]] [$_{CP}$ [$_{\varphi P}$ die [$_{CardP}$ viele Häuser]] [$_{C}$ stehen [$_{IP}$ leer]]]$_i$]
   c. [$_{CP}$ [$_{CP}$ Apfeldorf hat [$_{DP}$ t$_i$ [$_{CardP}$ viele Häuser]]] [$_{CP}$ [$_{\varphi P}$ [$_{CardP}$ viele Häuser]] [$_{C}$ stehen [$_{IP}$ leer]]]$_i$]
   d. [$_{CP}$ [$_{CP}$ Apfeldorf hat [$_{DP}$ t$_i$ [$_{CardP}$ viele Häuser]]] [$_{CP}$ viele [$_{\varphi P}$ die [$_{CardP}$ viele Häuser]] [$_{C}$ stehen [$_{IP}$ leer]]]$_i$]

This account is superior to Gärtner's original proposal since the determiner *viele* in (27) has a strong interpretation, requiring that the set of houses is given in (27). This observation weakens Gärtner's solution for the exclusion of definite determiners in V2 relatives: he proposes that only indefinite and weak determiners can introduce the discourse referent that serves as antecedent for the *d*-pronoun in the relative clause. Note that besides this, it is also completely unclear why this *d*-pronoun cannot have an antecedent in the matrix clause, let's say, a definite DP whose referent was introduced in a previous clause in the discourse. In our syntactic account of the determiner restriction in V2 relatives, this question does not even arise. Moreover, the present account can also explain why downward entailing weak determiners like *wenige* 'few' are excluded from V2 relatives:

(28) *Apfeldorf hat wenige Häuser, die stehen leer.
   'Apfeldorf has few houses that are empty.'

This follows from the condition of deletion of the determiner in the higher copy in (29), since the proposition *Apfeldorf hat viele Häuser* 'Apfeldorf has many houses' entails the proposition *Apfeldorf hat Häuser* 'Apfeldorf has houses', quantifier deletion in the main clause is possible in (27).

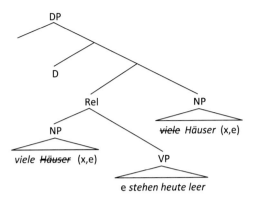
FIGURE 8.1 Analysis of V2 relatives

(29) *Condition on the deletion of the higher copy of the quantifier:*
The higher copy of the quantifier can be deleted if the proposition with QNP in the main clause entails the proposition with NP in the main clause.

Deletion of the higher copy, however, is excluded in (28), since the proposition that Apfeldorf has few houses does not entail the proposition that Apfeldorf has a plurality of houses, that is, at least two houses, since the former proposition is compatible with a situation in which Apfeldorf has only one or no houses.[1,2] Gärtner (2002) accounts for this property of V2 relatives by assuming that the nominal description in the matrix clause must constitute a topical phrase, raising the question why definite head nouns are excluded in V2 relatives, in addition to the question of how the topic status of the determiner

---

[1] The difference to (16b) above follows from the contribution of V2 in V2 relative clauses. Given that QR adjoins a quantifier phrase to TP (cf. May, 1977) and that V2 requires the relative clause to adjoin to a functional category—in all likelihood to MoodP, in the C-domain—, the content of the relative clauses cannot be mapped into the nuclear scope of the quantifier if the quantifier is interpreted in the matrix clause, leaving as the only option its interpretation in the embedded clause, embodying the additional restriction on the deletion of the quantifier in (29).

[2] The difference between (28) and (16b) then indicates that V2 in embedded clauses in German is not completely equivalent to the indicative mood in these clauses in Italian. One way to account for this difference would be to assume that the indicative mood (due to the opposition with the subjunctive mood) is interpretable and together with focus licenses a local assertion operator in the embedded clause and hence does not trigger obligatory extraposition onto a category in the C-domain of the matrix clause as arguably embedded V2 does. We will leave this issue for further research.

viele 'many' differs from the topic status of the determiner *wenige* 'few', since both of them require a given discourse antecedent and can thus be said to be topical.

To conclude, the puzzle consists in the fact that the determiners are required to be indefinite or weak ones in V2 relatives, but receive a strong or a specific interpretation (in case of an indefinite). In the present approach this complex property is explained by the syntactic account of the determiner restriction and a treatment as an effect of quantification variability—(27) is interpreted as many of the houses of Apfeldorf are empty—that is only possible with proportional readings that open up a flexible domain of quantifier restriction and nuclear scope determined by other grammatical factors. Embedded V2 like indicative plus focus thereby indicates that the relative clause is mapped into the nuclear scope of the quantifier, while the subjunctive indicates that the relative clause is mapped into its restrictor.

Having sketched an account that explains why mood alternations in Italian have the same function as word order alternations in modern German, we will now turn to OHG and to the diachronic scenario. Since this stage of the German language displayed both mood alternations and the alternation between V2 and verb-final orders in relative clauses, the obvious question arises whether OHG behaved like Italian (and the Romance languages) or like Modern German. In the following section, we address this question.

7 The Situation in Old High German

As is well-known, Modern German has almost completely lost mood distinctions in relative clauses in the course of its history. In contrast, OHG relative clauses allowed for both V2/verb-final orders like Modern German, on the one hand, and mood distinctions like the Romance languages, on the other (cf. Erdmann, 1886, p. 164; Behaghel, 1928, pp. 618 ff.; Ebert, Reichmann & Solms, 1993, p. 450; Paul, 2007, p. 435; Axel-Tober, 2012). The contrast between (30a) and (30b) exemplifies possible alternations in the position of the finite verb, while (30c) shows that mood alternations are also attested.[3]

(30) a. [...] *osee propheta, dher **quhad** heilegu gheistu:*
Hosea prophet who said.IND Holy.INSTR Ghost.INSTR
'[...] Prophet Hosea, who said inspired by the Holy Spirit:' (I DF, 8, 3)

---

3 The following data are taken from the *Referenzkorpus Altdeutsch*, presented in 7.1.

b. [...] *so ih fona dhemu nam, dher ær   fora   dhir **uuas**.*
   as I from that   took who before before you was.IND
   '[...] as I took it away from the one who came before you.' (I DF, 9, 2)

c. *Huuer ist dher dhiz al ni   **chisehe***
   who   is who this all NEG sees.SUB
   in im   selbem nu   uuesan arfullit?
   in him himself now be   fulfilled
   'Who is that does not see all this now fulfilled in his person?' (I DF, 8, 3)

Given that both types of alternations are attested in OHG, the following questions arise:

a. How is mood alternation in OHG relative clauses to be interpreted as set against the facts in the Romance languages?
b. How are OHG V2 relatives to be interpreted as set against the Modern German facts?
c. How was it possible for German to develop from the situation attested in OHG to the one attested at the present day?

These and other issues will be tackled in the following sections, based on a corpus study of some OHG texts (cf. Coniglio, 2017).

7.1   *Corpus-Based Investigation*

This pilot study is based on the following early OHG texts from the 8th and 9th century (i.e. on the major texts of the reference corpus that were available at the time the research was conducted):

a. Isidor (2nd half of the 8th c.)
b. Benediktinerregel (ca. 800)
c. Monseer Fragmente (2nd half of the 8th c.)
d. Tatian (ca. 830)
e. Otfrids Evangelienbuch (2nd half of the 9th c.)

All the texts considered were already linguistically annotated in the *Referenzkorpus Altdeutsch*, which is available online[4] and searchable via ANNIS (Krause & Zeldes, 2016).[5]

---

4 Donhauser, Karin, Gippert, J., & Lühr, R.; ddd-ad (Version 1.0), Humboldt-Universität zu Berlin. http://www.deutschdiachrondigital.de/. http://hdl.handle.net/11022/0000-0003-37E5-D.
5 http://corpus-tools.org/annis/.

For reasons of comparability, we randomly selected the same number of relative clauses, namely 50, with a total of 250 tokens. Since the corpus is not annotated with respect to verb placement and to the specificity (*de re* vs. *de dicto* interpretation) of the referent, the 227 indicative and 23 subjunctive clauses were further enriched with annotation of relevant syntactic and semantic information.[6] The following sections will present some results of this survey (originally presented in Coniglio, 2017).

7.2 Mood Alternation and Specificity

A first question arises as to whether the (non-)specific (*de dicto* vs. *de re*) reading of the head noun of OHG relative clauses is expressed by means of verbal mood or by verb placement (or by both). Let us consider the first hypothesis. If this interpretative effect of the head noun can be explained in terms of verbal mood as in the Romance languages, then we would expect that the indicative mood correlates with the specificity (*de re* interpretation) of the head noun (31) and that the subjunctive mood appears when the head noun has a non-specific (*de dicto*) interpretation (32), as is exemplified by the following examples from the corpus.

(31) [...] *drúhtin got* [...], *ther únsih irlósta*
 Lord god who us redeemed.IND
 'God, our Lord, [...] who redeemed us' (O I 10, 3 f.)

(32) [...] *er* [...] *then lésan iz gilústi*
 he whom read it pleased.SUBJ
 'he who felt/should feel like reading.' (O I 1, 10)

The distribution of mood alternations in the presence of specific or non-specific referents is shown in Table 8.1 (cf. Coniglio, 2017, p. 254).[7] While it is clear that the indicative is the preferred mood in the case of both specific and non-specific referents, the subjunctive tends to be preferably used in cases in which the referent is non-specific, i.e. the distribution indicates that the subjunctive mood is more frequently used in relative clauses referring to non-specific entities than in relative clauses with specific referents. This is the same situation that we observed in modern Italian.

---

6 We would like to thank Gohar Schnelle and Marten Santjer for helping us with the annotation of the data.
7 The na-cases are cases for which no clear interpretation could be provided.

TABLE 8.1   Specificity of the referent and mood in the relative clause

	Indicative	Subjunctive	na
specific	105	4	2
non-specific	84	18	0
na	33	2	2

Fisher Exact *p* = .0012; φ: 0.23

TABLE 8.2   Specificity of the referents of all subjunctive relative clauses in the *Referenzkorpus Altdeutsch*

	Subjunctive
specific	21
non-specific	340
na	61

Not surprisingly, the four exceptional cases with the subjunctive in a relative clause with specific referents can be explained on different grounds. They are all cases in which rhyme plays a role and/or in which a modalizing element occurs, as is the case in (33). Furthermore, the Latin original could also have influenced the mood alternations.

(33) [...] *thio brústi,   thio Kríst   io   gikústi*
          the breasts that Christ ever kissed.SUBJ
     'the breasts that Christ ever kissed' (O I 11,39)

The exceptionality of such cases is confirmed by an ongoing investigation of all OHG relative clauses in the *Referenzkorpus Altdeutsch*, for which only the results referring to the subjunctive relative clauses are available at the present time (n = 422). The distribution of specific and non-specific referents is represented in Table 8.2.

If we exclude the ambiguous cases, about 94% of subjunctive relative clauses are associated with a non-specific referent. This result is even clearer than in the pilot study above and conclusively indicates a strong interaction between the (non-)specific (i.e. *de re* vs. *de dicto*) interpretation of the referent and mood in OHG relative clauses, exactly as observed in the modern Romance languages.

7.3 Verb Position and Specificity

The second hypothesis we would like to explore is whether verb placement in OHG relative clauses is linked to the (non-)specific interpretation of the head noun, as is the case in Modern German. As we have seen in the previous sections, a large amount of literature describes the properties of V2 relatives in Modern German (cf. Gärtner, 2001, 2002). Interestingly, Axel-Tober (2012, pp. 207 ff.) shows that this special type of clause already existed in OHG and was particularly frequent in Middle High German (MHG). In particular, she argues that the properties of older V2 relatives are exactly the same as in Modern German. Thus, the question is whether a correlation between the type of head noun and the position of the verb can be empirically shown based on the reference corpus (cf. Coniglio, 2017, p. 255).

In general, we must be careful when analyzing the verb position in the OHG texts considered here because these texts are mostly translations from Latin sources or poetic texts. Nonetheless, we found some clear cases that are reminiscent of the V2 relatives discussed by Gärtner (2001, 2002, etc.) for Modern German and by Axel-Tober (2012) for historical German, as in the following example:

(34) [...] *chuninge · der **frumita** bruthlauft* sinemo sune [...]
      king.DAT that made wedding.feast his.DAT son.DAT
'[...] to a king that prepared a wedding feast for his son [...]' (MF XV, 5 f.)

In this case, we have a specific indefinite antecedent for the relative clause and at the same time a V2 order. Much more frequent is the case of other types of antecedents, as in the following example, in which a non-specific indefinite antecedent is associated with a verb-final (or at least verb-late)[8] order in the relative clause:

---

8 In a verb-late order (not to be confused with V3 orders, see Haegeman, this volume), the finite verb is neither in the second, nor in the final position of the clause. This order is typical of subordinate clauses in which for example one or more constituents have been extraposed to the right of the verb for information-structural reasons (Hinterhölzl & Petrova, 2009), thus giving the impression that the verb has moved to their left, as for example in (30c) above. These cases have been analyzed on a par with verb-final orders since they do not feature V-to-C movement as V2 orders do. Also cf. the discussion about (36) below.

TABLE 8.3 Specificity of the referent and verb position in the relative clause

	V2	Verb-late/final	na
specific indefinite	3	2	0
other type	33	104	5
na	20	73	10

Fisher Exact p = .10; φ: 0.15

(35) *neouueht* [...], *daz fer sii,*
    nothing   that far is.SUBJ
    'nothing [...] that is far away/abstracted' (Ben.Reg. 2)

Table 8.3 summarizes the distribution of verb ordering with respect to the different types of antecedent (cf. Coniglio, 2017, p. 255). In the table, we decided to clearly distinguish between specific indefinite antecedents and other types of antecedents because their *de re* or specific interpretations alone are not sufficient for them to qualify as antecedents of V2 relative clauses. According to Gärtner (2001, 2002, etc.), they must be specific and indefinite at the same time, as we have seen in Sections 2–4.

The distribution is not statistically significant, so we could conclude that specific indefinite antecedent are not more often associated with a V2 order in the relative clauses than other types of antecedents (cf. Coniglio, 2017, p. 255). This would mean that the situation in OHG is different from the one in Modern German. However, unfortunately, only five relative clauses with a specific indefinite antecedent could be found in the small group of clauses considered. Thus, the observed distribution could be just due to chance (3 V2 vs. 2 non-V2 cases). Much more interesting is the fact that we have a clear preference for verb-late/final orders with other types of antecedents (104 vs. 33).

7.4   *Mood Alternation and Verb Position*

Let us now turn to one last question, i.e. whether a direct correlation between mood and verb position can be observed in OHG (cf. Coniglio, 2017, p. 256). Given the parallel facts observed in the previous sections for Modern German and Italian, the subjunctive should be typically found in OHG verb-late/final clauses, while V2 relatives should only display the indicative. This would be a logic expectation in a language like OHG, which displays both mood and verb placement alternations.

TABLE 8.4 Verb position in the relative clause and mood alternation

	Indicative	Subjunctive	na
V2	51	5	0
verb-late/final	162	17	1
na	9	2	3

Fisher Exact p = 1; φ: 0.01

In order to investigate the interaction between the two variables, Table 8.4 was generated. As can be observed, there does not seem to be a clear difference between V2 and verb-late/final relative clauses with respect to the realization of mood. In both cases, the indicative is preferred and the ratio of indicative and subjunctive cases is about 10:1. The Fisher Exact test indicates that V2 relatives do not exhibit the indicative more often than verb-late/final relative clauses (cf. Coniglio, 2017, p. 256). This seems to confirm that, in OHG, verb placement does not interact with mood in determining the interpretation of the head noun of relative clauses (as is the case in Modern German).

8 Discussion of the Data

The discussion above pointed out that the situation in OHG is very different from the one in Modern German, but pretty much similar to the one observed for Italian. While, in Modern German, we can postulate a correlation between the specificity (*de re* vs. *de dicto* interpretation) of the referent and position of the finite verb based on modern theoretical approaches (cf. Gärtner, 2001, 2002, etc.), such correlation could not be empirically demonstrated for OHG. For this stage of the language, the specificity of the referent correlates with the verbal mood as in Italian (and in some other modern Romance languages). The initial and the final situations are represented in Fig. 8.2, where we see the correlation observable or postulated for OHG and Modern German, respectively.

For OHG, there is no empirical evidence in the corpus for a correlation between the verb position and either specificity of the referent or mood. One could conclude that this is a typical scenario of diachronic change: the language starts from a situation in which mood correlates with the specificity of

FIGURE 8.2 Correlations in OHG and Modern German (respectively)

the referent of a relative clause and changes to a system in which the position of the verb depends on the properties of the referent.

Note, however, that the empirical facts are based on a theory-neutral annotation of the examples in our dataset, but some theoretical considerations are necessary at this point. As discussed in Coniglio (2017, pp. 256 ff.), all the variables considered display stronger correlations if we resort to recent theoretical explanations. In fact, many examples that seem to exhibit V2 patterns at the surface—and that have been annotated as such—should better be analyzed as a different type of word order (cf. Kroch & Santorini, 1991; Pintzuk, 1991; Tomaselli, 1995; Hinterhölzl, 2004; Schlachter, 2004, 2012; Axel, 2007; Petrova & Hinterhölzl, 2010; Weiß, forthcoming, etc.). As illustrated in example (36), the VO order must not be necessarily a V2 order in OHG—i.e. the verb can be in a late/final position and still be followed by its object(s) (cf. Coniglio, 2017, p. 257).

(36) *Daz ist daz hêreste guot,   daz der   uore   gegariwet ist*
     that is the greatest wealth that PART.REL before afforded is
     gotes trûtfriunden
     God's intimate.friends.DAT
     'This is the greatest wealth which is provided to God's intimate friends before' (HiH 153, 36)

Basically, two main types of explanations have been proposed for similar examples, and both rely on information-structural factors that are responsible for triggering the "final" VO order. One possible interpretation is that—as illustrated in (37)—in such cases, the basic word order is OV, exactly as in most Modern German subordinate clauses, but that the object is moved to the right of the verb for information-structural reasons (cf. Axel, 2007, p. 80).

(37) [$_{VP}$ t$_i$ V] O$_i$

Another interpretation to be found in the literature is that the verb is base-generated in a position preceding the object or as having moved to that position for information-structural reasons (cf. Tomaselli, 1995; Schlachter, 2004, 2012;

Hinterhölzl, 2009; Petrova & Hinterhölzl, 2010; Coniglio, Linde & Ruette, 2017; Weiß, forthcoming, but also Petrova & Speyer, 2011, for Old English, etc.):

(38) [$_{VP}$ V O]   or   V$_i$ [$_{VP}$ O t$_i$]

Independently of the analysis adopted, there seems to be consensus in the literature as to the reasons for this marked order in subordinate clauses. Recent works have proven that the main factor triggering these deviations is information-structural in nature, being related to the focus-background-structure of the utterance (cf. Schlachter, 2004, 2012; Hinterhölzl, 2009; Petrova & Hinterhölzl, 2010). Hinterhölzl (2009, p. 48) illustrates this by means of the following examples. In (39), the discourse-given DP "thin ouga" precedes the finite verb in the conditional clause, but the focussed predicative "luttar" follows it. The predicative "p[et]rus" is postponed in (40) since it represents new information focus. In the relative clause in (41), the direct object "diuual" is focused and placed to the right of the finite verb.[9]

(39) *liohtfaz thes   lihhamen ist ouga / oba thin ouga **uuirdit** luttar/*
     light   of.the body   is eye   if your eye   becomes bright
     thanne ist al thin lihhamo liohter
     then   is all your body   bright
     Lat. *Lucerna corporis. est oculus. / si fuerit oculus tuus simplex. / totum corpus tuum lucidum erit.*
     'The light of the body is the eye. If your eye becomes bright, then all your body is bright.' (T 69, 21ff., adapted from Hinterhölzl, 2009, p. 48)

(40) *ther giheizan **ist** p&rus*
     who named   is Petrus
     Lat. *qui vocatur p&rus*
     'who is named Petrus' (T 54, 15, adapted from Hinterhölzl, 2009, p. 48)

---

9 In a recent paper, Coniglio, Linde and Ruette (2017) test these recent theoretical theories based on a sample of relative clauses in non-translated OHG texts and show that, also in relative clauses, the OV/VO order is determined by information and discourse structure. In particular, narrow focus of the object is associated with a VO order, while contrastive focus and broad focus trigger OV orders. These empirical results are partially similar to the (mostly theoretical) results in Hinterhölzl (2009), Petrova and Hinterhölzl (2010), and Schlachter (2004). Furthermore, it is shown that non-restrictive relative clauses exhibit more often VO orders than restrictive relative clauses. This is expected if one considers that non-restrictive relative clauses have a greater illocutionary potential (cf. Holler, 2005).

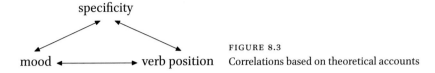

FIGURE 8.3
Correlations based on theoretical accounts

(41) *Inti bráhtun imo / alle ubil habante* / [...] *Inti thie thár*
 and brought him all evil having-NOM.PL and those PRT
 hab&un diuual
 had devil
 Lat. *& obtulerunt ei / omnes male habentes /* [...] *& qui demonia habebant*
 'and they brought him all the sick ones and those that had the devil' (T 59, 1, adapted from Hinterhölzl, 2009, p. 48)

Following such theoretical accounts, many of the orders annotated as V2 orders in our dataset can in fact be interpreted as VO orders (clearly diagnostic cases being very rare in our corpus): they only surface as V2 orders since they display no material in the so called "middle field" (cf. Coniglio, 2017, p. 258). According to this analysis, examples like (42a) could thus be described—despite the surface V2 order—as verb-late orders (as in (42b)) even if the finite verb seems to appear in second position:

(42) a. [...] *dhiu chrumba nadra* [...]
  the crooked viper
  dhea chisaughida gotes uuordes [...]
  that suckled God.GEN word.GEN
  '[...] the crooked viper [...] that suckled God's word [...]' (I IX,10)

 b. [_CP *dhea* ... [_V?P [_V *chisaughida*] [_DP *gotes uuordes*]]]

Our intuition is that, if such apparent V2 cases are excluded, we would probably get neater correlations between the three variables considered (specificity, mood and verb position), as represented in Fig. 8.3.

This would indicate that Old High German has both the possibility to mark specificity by means of mood alternations as Italian and some Romance languages and by means of verb placement as Modern German. The diachronic scenario would be easily explained, since the loss of mood alternations in German subordinate clauses would necessarily leave just one option for marking the (non-)specificity of the referent of the relative clause, i.e. via verb placement. However, since it would not be methodologically correct to present a distribution based on a possible interpretation of the data, we will refrain from doing so.

With respect to this point, we are currently conducting a more complex research on the interaction between mood and verb position in OHG and in Old English (Coniglio, De Bastiani, Hinterhölzl & Weskott, t.a.). This survey confirms the empirical results of this investigation, at least for OHG, while the situation in Old English seems to indicate a possibly more advanced development, with neater correlations between mood alternations and verb placement. This new investigation is based on a seminal work by Gärtner and Eythórsson (2020), which we will briefly present in the next section. Starting from their model, we intend to sketch a diachronic scenario for the development from the Italian-like situation in OHG to the one represented by Modern German.

9 From Morphological Mood to Syntactic Verb Position

This final section sketches a first scenario for the change that we observed from OHG to Modern German. Our investigation has shown that verbal mood requires different interpretations of the referents of relative clauses. For the older Germanic languages, verbal mood is also taken to indicate the (in)dependent status of a sentence (cf. Schrodt, 1983; Petrova, 2008, for OHG; Mitchell, 1985; Vezzosi, 1998, for OE, etc.), as is often claimed for the Romance languages (Farkas 1985; Giorgi & Pianesi, 1997; Quer, 1998, etc.). This is possibly related to the fact that, as discussed in the previous sections, at least in languages displaying such alternations, the indicative is typically used in assertive contexts, while the subjunctive is used in presupposed, backgrounded or non at-issue contexts.

Furthermore, verb placement in OHG has also been shown to mark the clausal status (for example by Axel, 2007). Nonetheless, as we have seen, the position of the verb is often claimed to be the reflex of Information Structure, especially of the focus/background structure (cf. Hinterhölzl & Petrova, 2009; Petrova, 2009, 2011; Hinterhölzl, 2015; Coniglio, Linde & Ruette, 2017).

The situation in the modern Germanic languages is different. In general, mood is no longer used to indicate the (in)dependent status of the clause. In contrast to the Romance languages, its usage contexts are mostly restricted to reported speech, counterfactuality, etc. As we have seen for Modern German in the previous sections, the modern Germanic languages mostly use verb placement for marking clausal (in)dependency.[10]

---

10 According to several studies, the Romance languages use mood alternations also to indicate (in)dependency (Meinunger, 2004, 2006), but see Poletto (2000) and Ledgeway (2012), etc. arguing that verb placement also plays a role.

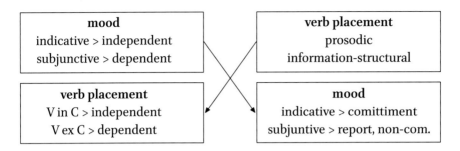

FIGURE 8.4 Clausal (In)dependency Marking
ADAPTED FROM GÄRTNER & EYTHÓRSSON, 2020

Based on data from Icelandic (and German), Gärtner and Eythórsson (2020) argue that a diachronic scenario can be reconstructed for all the Germanic languages. In their view, older Germanic recruits mood for marking clause (in)dependency, while verb placement (verb fronting vs. verb in situ) is just a reflex of prosody and Information Structure (see the upper part of Fig. 8.4). In later stages, most of the Germanic languages use verb placement for clausal marking, while mood acquires different semanto-pragmatic functions (bottom part of Fig. 8.4).

Elaborating on Gärtner and Eythórsson's proposal, we posit a first stage (stage A) representing the initial situation in which the subjunctive mood expresses clausal dependency independently of finite verb position. In this stage the position of the finite verb is determined by information-structural factors, as is typical of OHG, where backgrounded material precedes the finite verb, while focused material follows the verb (cf. Hinterhölzl, 2004; Petrova & Hinterhölzl, 2010). We thus expect that the default position of the finite verb in clauses marked with the subjunctive mood is final, since the content of these clauses is presupposed or at least not at issue, as we have seen in Section 5. On the other hand, the indicative mood expresses clausal independency irrespective of the position of the finite verb at this stage. In clauses marked with the indicative mood, the position of the verb is more flexible, since independent clauses have an autonomous focus-background structure, in which the finite verb separates the background from the focused material. Thus, we expect the default position of the finite verb to be medial (verb-late order).

The second stage (stage B)—towards which OHG was probably already moving—can be taken to set in when the subjunctive starts to get lost in certain environments. In this stage, mood alternations will represent a mixed picture. The subjunctive mood—where present—will continue to indicate clausal dependency (43), while the indicative mood becomes ambiguous and indicates clausal dependency in final position (44)—due to the presupposed status of dependent clauses in the unmarked case—and clausal independency and information-structural distinctions in late/medial position (45)—due to the main clause properties of embedded clauses in the marked case. This stage may very well be represented by OHG, as illustrated by the following examples from *Isidor*:

(43) *Huuer ist dher dhiz al ni chisehe in im selbem nu uuesan*
  who is who this all NEG sees.SUB in him himself now be
  arfullit?
  fulfilled
  'Who is that does not see all this now fulfilled in his person?' (I DF, 8, 3)

(44) *[...] so ih fona dhemu nam, dher ær fora dhir **uuas**.*
  as I from that took who before before you was.IND
  '[...] as I took it away from the one who came before you.' (I DF, 9, 2)

(45) *[...] osee propheta, dher **quhad** heilegu gheistu:*
  Hosea prophet who said.IND Holy.INSTR Ghost.INSTR
  '[...] Prophet Hosea, who said inspired by the Holy Spirit:' (I DF, 8, 3)

Especially the contrast between (44) and (45) deserves attention. The final position of the verb "uuas" in (44) is compatible with the presupposed status of the relative clause. Isidor is quoting 1 Chronicles (17, 13): "I will be his father and he will be my son. I will never take away my mercy from him, as I took it away from the one who came before you." The content of the material preceding the indicative verb "uuas" is not focused. While the asserted content is that he will never take away his mercy from him, the adverbial and the relative clause are probably only restating something known to the addressee.

Even more interesting is the case in (45). Here, Isidor is claiming that Hosea cannot be a liar because—as a prophet—he spoke those words inspired by the Holy Spirit. Thus, it is highly plausible that the prominent post-finite position of "heilegu gheistu" is linked to the higher discourse-structural and information-structural potential of the relative clause.

Note that it is difficult to pinpoint the possible causes and grammatical processes leading to this second stage, where the subjunctive is gradually replaced by the indicative also in typical subjunctive domains. Even though this point must be left for further research, Petrova (2008, p. 215), Coniglio (2017, p. 263), and Coniglio, Hinterhölzl and Petrova (2018, p. 31) indicate two main morpho-phonological and syntactic changes progressively affecting the language as a possible explanation for this gradual change, namely 1) the impoverishment of verb morphology (and consequent mood syncretism) and 2) the emergence of analytic constructions using auxiliary and modal verbs in combination with full verbs (instead of the synthetic subjunctive forms of the full verbs). Since these changes can already be observed in OHG, they could explain why the indicative mood was already supplanting the subjunctive during this period.

The third stage of the diachronic scenario (stage C) is reached when the option of having focused material in post-finite position is lost. This stage can be identified with the slow process of reducing post-finite DP-arguments in MHG (and Early New High German, cf. Coniglio & Schlachter, 2015). The cause of this process may be the loss of extraposition of focused material in the standard OV account or the loss of the finite verb movement to a sentence medial position triggered by information-structural properties (illustrated in Section 8). The latter assumption—loss of movement of the finite verb to a sentence medial position—would then yield the rather plausible and natural conclusion that the medial verb position in embedded clauses in this stage is reanalyzed from movement to a medial position for information-structural reasons into movement of the verb to the C-domain (to some high Mood head) for marking clausal dependency. In this scenario, we would expect that real V2 in embedded clauses arises at the end of the MHG period, when VO orders have been (or are) driven out of the language.

Conclusions

We have first shown that alternations in verb order in relative clauses in Modern German has essentially the same function as mood alternations in these clauses in the Romance languages, in particular, in Italian. Second, we have shown that mood alternation in OHG has essentially the same function as mood alternation has in Italian. Then, it was shown that alternations in word order in relative clauses in OHG cannot be related to the specific or non-specific interpretation of the head noun as it can in Modern German, but is triggered mostly by information-structural conditions. We have finally sketched a historical scenario for the relevant change from OHG to Modern German based on the model of Gärtner and Eythórsson (2020) for the entire Germanic language family. This account crucially links the change in the expression of mood and the loss of VO orders—which are a side effect of the information-structural potential of indicative-marked clauses—to a reanalysis of embedded verb-late orders in MHG to embedded V2 orders in modern German.

Acknowledgements

Roland Hinterhölzl takes responsibility for sections 2 to 6, Marco Coniglio for sections 7 to 8. Both take responsibility for sections 1 and 9. We thank the organizers and the audience of the workshop "Information structuring in discourse" (Saarbrücken, Mar. 8th–10th, 2017), as well as the reviewers for their insightful comments.

References

Axel, Katrin. (2007). *Studies on Old High German Syntax. Left sentence periphery, verb placement and verb-second*. Amsterdam/Philadelphia: John Benjamins.

Axel-Tober, Katrin. (2012). *(Nicht-)kanonische Nebensätze im Deutschen. Synchrone und diachrone Aspekte*. Berlin: De Gruyter.

Bayer, Josef. (1984). COMP in Bavarian syntax. *The Linguistic Review, 3*, 209–274.

Behaghel, Otto. (1928). *Deutsche Syntax: Eine geschichtliche Darstellung* (Vol. 3, Die Satzgebilde). Heidelberg: Winter.

Carnap, Rudolph. (1928). *Der logische Aufbau der Welt*. Hamburg: Meiner.

Catasso, Nicholas, & Roland Hinterhölzl. (2016). On the question of subordination or coordination in V2-relatives in German. *Linguistische Berichte, 21*, 99–123.

Cinque, Guglielmo. (2013). *Typological Studies. Word order and relative clause*. New York/London: Routledge.

Coniglio, Marco. (2011). *Die Syntax der deutschen Modalpartikeln: Ihre Distribution und Lizenzierung in Haupt- und Nebensätzen*. Berlin: Akademie-Verlag.

Coniglio, Marco. (2017). Verbal Mood in Early Old High German Relative Clauses. *Annali di Ca' Foscari. Serie occidentale, 51*, 245–269.

Coniglio, Marco, Chiara De Bastiani, Roland Hinterhölzl, & Thomas Weskott. (to appear). The right mood, in the right place: On mood and verb placement in Old Germanic subordinate clauses. In P. Crisma, & G. Longobardi (Eds.), *Special Issue of Journal of Historical Syntax*. Oxford: Oxford University Press.

Coniglio, Marco, Roland Hinterhölzl, & Svetlana Petrova. (2018). Mood alternations in Old High German subordinate clauses. *Annali di Ca' Foscari. Serie occidentale, 52*, 7–37.

Coniglio, Marco, Sonja Linde, & Tom Ruette. (2017). Relative clauses in Old High German. A corpus-based statistical investigation. *Journal of Germanic Linguistics, 29*(2), 101–146.

Coniglio, Marco, & Eva Schlachter. (2015). Das Nachfeld im Deutschen zwischen Syntax, Informations- und Diskursstruktur. Eine diachrone, korpusbasierte Untersuchung. In H. Vinckel-Roisin (Ed.), *Das Nachfeld im Deutschen. Theorie und Empirie*. Berlin: De Gruyter.

Ebert, Christian, Cornelia Endriss, & Hans-Martin Gärtner. (2007). An Information Structural Account of German Integrated Verb Second Clauses. *Research on Language and Computation*, 5(4), 415–434.

Ebert, Robert P., Oskar Reichmann, & Hans-Joachim Solms. (1993). *Frühneuhochdeutsche Grammatik*. Tübingen: Niemeyer.

Elbourne, Paul D. (2005). *Situations and Individuals*. Cambridge, MA: MIT Press.

Erdmann, Oskar. (1886). *Grundzüge der deutschen Syntax nach ihrer geschichtlichen Entwicklung*. Stuttgart: Cotta.

Farkas, Donka. (1985). *Intensional Descriptions and the Romance Subjunctive Mood*. Garland.

Farkas, Donka. (1992). On the Semantics of Subjunctive Complements. In P. Hirschbühler, & E.F.K. Koerner (Eds.), *Romance Languages and Modern Linguistic Theory* (pp. 67–104). Amsterdam/Philadelphia: John Benjamins.

Freywald, Ulrike. (2008). Zur Syntax und Funktion von *dass*-Sätzen mit Verbzweitstellung. *Deutsche Sprache*, 36, 246–285.

Gärtner, Hans-Martin. (2001). Are there V2 relative clauses in German? *Journal of Comparative Linguistics*, 3, 97–141.

Gärtner, Hans-Martin. (2002). On the Force of V2 Declaratives. *Theoretical Linguistics*, 28, 33–42.

Gärtner, Hans-Martin, & Thórhallur Eythórsson. (2020). Varieties of Dependent V2 and Verbal Mood: A View from Icelandic. In R. Woods, & S. Wolfe (Eds.), *Rethinking Verb Second* (pp. 208–239). Oxford: Oxford University Press.

Giannakidou, Anastasia. (2009). The dependency of the subjunctive revisited. Temporal semantics and polarity. *Lingua*, 120, 1883–1908.

Giannakidou, Anastasia. (2013). (Non)veridicality, evaluation, and event actualization. Evidence from the subjunctive in relative clauses. In R. Trnavac, & M. Taboada (Eds.), *Nonveridicality and Evaluation. Theoretical, Computational, and Corpus Approaches* (pp. 17–47). Leiden: Brill.

Giorgi, Alessandra, & Fabio Pianesi. (1997). *Tense and Aspect. From Semantics to Morphosyntax*. Oxford: Oxford University Press.

Herburger, Elena. (2000). *What counts. Focus and quantification*. Cambridge, MA: MIT Press.

Hinterhölzl, Roland. (2004). Language Change versus Grammar Change: What Diachronic Data Reveal About the Distinction Between Core Grammar and Periphery. In E. Fuss, & C. Trips (Eds.), *Diachronic Clues to Synchronic Grammar* (pp. 131–160). Amsterdam/Philadelphia: John Benjamins.

Hinterhölzl, Roland. (2009). The Role of Information Structure in Word Order Variation and Word Order Change. In R. Hinterhölzl, & S. Petrova (Eds.), *Information Structure and Language Change. New Approaches to Word Order Variation in Germanic* (pp. 45–66). Berlin: De Gruyter Mouton.

Hinterhölzl, Roland. (2015). An interface account of word-order variation in Old High German. In T. Biberauer, & G. Walkden (Eds.), *Syntax over Time* (pp. 299–318). Oxford: Oxford University Press.

Hinterhölzl, Roland. (2019). The Role of Topics in Licensing Anaphoric Relations in VP-ellipsis. In V. Molnár, V. Egerland, & S. Winkler (Eds.), *Architecture of Topic* (pp. 67–93). Berlin: De Gruyter.

Hinterhölzl, Roland. (2020). Assertive potential, speaker evidence and embedded V2. In H. Lohnstein, & A. Tsiknakis (Eds.), *Verb Second. Grammar Internal and Grammar External Interfaces* (pp. 147–168). Berlin: De Gruyter.

Hinterhölzl, Roland, & Svetlana Petrova. (2009). *Information structure and language change: New approaches to word order variation in Germanic*. Berlin: De Gruyter Mouton.

Holler, Anke (2005). *Weiterführende Relativsätze. Empirische und theoretische Aspekte*. Berlin: Akademie-Verlag.

Hulsey, Sarah, & Ulrich Sauerland. (2006). Sorting out relative clauses: A reply to Bhatt. *Natural Language Semantics, 14*, 111–137.

Krause, Thomas, & Amir Zeldes. (2016). ANNIS3. A new architecture for generic corpus query and visualization. *Digital Scholarship in the Humanities, 31*(1), 118–139.

Kroch, Anthony S., & Beatrice Santorini. (1991). The Derived Constituent Structure of the West Germanic Verb Raising Construction. In R. Freidin (Ed.), *Principles and Parameters in Comparative Grammar* (pp. 269–338). Cambridge, MA: MIT Press.

Ledgeway, Adam. (2012). Greek Disguised as Romance? The Case of Southern Italy. In M. Janse, B.D. Joseph, A. Ralli, & M. Bagriacik (Eds.), *Proceedings of the 5th International Conference on Greek Dialects and Linguistic Theory* (pp. 184–228). Patras, Greek.

May, Robert. (1977). *The Grammar of Quantification* [Doctoral dissertation, Massachusetts Institute of Technology].

Meinunger, Andre. (2004). Verb Position, Verbal Mood and the Anchoring (potential) of Sentences. In H. Lohnstein, & S. Trissler (Eds.), *Syntax and Semantics of the Left Periphery* (pp. 313–341). Berlin: De Gruyter.

Meinunger, Andre. (2006). On the Discourse Impact of Subordinate Clauses. In V. Molnár, & S. Winkler (Eds.), *The Architecture of Focus* (pp. 459–488). Berlin: De Gruyter.

Milsark, Gary. (1974). *Existential Sentences in English* [Doctoral dissertation, Massachusetts Institute of Technology].

Mitchell, Bruce. (1985). *Old English Syntax* (Vols. 1–2). Oxford: Clarendon.

Paul, Hermann. (2007). *Mittelhochdeutsche Grammatik*. Tübingen: Niemeyer.

Petrova, Svetlana. (2008). *Zur Interaktion von Tempus und Modus. Studien zur Entwicklungsgeschichte des Konjunktivs im Deutschen*. Heidelberg: Winter.

Petrova, Svetlana. (2009). Information structure and word order variation in the OHG Tatian. In R. Hinterhölzl & S. Petrova (Eds.), *Information structure and language change: New approaches to word order variation in Germanic* (pp. 251–279). Berlin: De Gruyter Mouton.

Petrova, Svetlana. (2011). Modeling word order variation in discourse: On the pragmatic properties of vs order in Old High German. In E. Welo (Ed.), *Indo-European Syntax and Pragmatics: Comparative Approaches, Sonderheft von Oslo Studies in Language, 3*(3), 209–228.

Petrova, Svetlana, & Roland Hinterhölzl (2010). Evidence for two types of focus positions in Old High German. In G. Ferraresi, & R. Lühr (Eds.), *Diachronic Studies on Information Structure. Language Acquisition and Change* (pp. 189–217). Berlin: De Gruyter.

Petrova, Svetlana, & Augustin Speyer (2011). Focus movement and focus interpretation in Old English. *Lingua, 121*(11), 1751–1765.

Pintzuk, Susan. (1991). *Phrase Structures in Competition: Variation and Change in Old English Word Order* [Doctoral dissertation, University of Pennsylvania].

Poletto, Cecilia. (2000). *The Higher Functional Field: Evidence from Northern Italian Dialects*. Oxford: Oxford University Press.

Quer, Josep. (1998). *Mood at the interface.* [Doctoral dissertation, Universiteit Utrecht].

Rizzi, Luigi. (1997). The Fine Structure of the Left Periphery. In L. Haegeman (Ed.), *Elements of Grammar. Handbook in Generative Syntax* (pp. 281–337). Dordrecht: Kluwer.

Schlachter, Eva. (2004). Satzstruktur im Althochdeutschen. Eine Skizze zur Position des Verbs im Isidor-Traktat des 8. Jahrhunderts. In K. Pittner, R.J. Pittner, & J.C. Schütte, (Eds.), *Beiträge zu Sprache und Sprachen. 4. Vorträge der Bochumer Linguistik-Tage* (pp. 179–188). München: Lincom.

Schlachter, Eva. (2012). *Syntax und Informationsstruktur im Althochdeutschen. Untersuchungen am Beispiel der Isidor-Gruppe*. Heidelberg: Winter.

Schrodt, Richard. (1983). *System und Norm in der Diachronie des deutschen Konjunktivs. Der Modus in ahd. und mhd. Inhaltssätzen*. Tübingen: Niemeyer.

Tomaselli, Alessandra. (1995). Cases of Verb Third in Old High German. In A. Battye, & I. Roberts (Eds.), *Clause Structure and Language Change* (pp. 345–369). Oxford: Oxford University Press.

Vezzosi, Letizia. (1998). *La sintassi della subordinazione in anglosassone*. Neapel: Edizioni Scientifiche Italiane.

Vikner, Sten. (1995). *Verb movement and expletive subjects in the Germanic languages*. Oxford: Oxford University Press.

Weerman, Fred, & Gerhard de Haan. (1986). Finiteness and verb fronting in Frisian. In H. Haider, & M. Prinzhorn (Eds.), *Verb Second Phenomena in Germanic Languages* (pp. 77–110). Dordrecht: Foris.

Weiß, Helmut. (forthcoming). Die rechte Peripherie im Althochdeutschen. Zur Verbstellung in dass-Sätzen. *Tagungsakten der Arbeitstagung der Indogermanischen Gesellschaft*.

CHAPTER 9

What's in an Act?
Towards a Functional Discourse Grammar of Platonic Dialogue and a Linguistic Commentary on Plato's *Protagoras*

Cassandra Freiberg

1 Introduction

This paper provides a historical perspective on the subject matter of this volume. It is concerned with the Ancient Greek language and in particular with the discourse[1] type of Platonic dialogue. It undertakes a practical study in the relationship between the form of specific linguistic utterances on the one hand, and higher-order discourse structure on the other. It focuses on the interaction of different linguistic levels—traditionally called syntax, semantics, pragmatics, and phonology—in shaping Elementary Discourse Units (EDUs). Methodologically, its two basic components are (A) a systematic grammatical analysis of the particular idiom represented in the discourse type under scrutiny, and (B) a philological-linguistic analysis of a representative stretch of running discourse. Part (B) will be concerned with the beginning of the dialogue *Protagoras*. Most examples in Part (A) will be taken from the same dialogue.

The method and presentation of linguistic analysis synthesizes and thereby further develops approaches already extant in Ancient Greek linguistics, most notably that of Scheppers (2011) and works carried out within the framework of Functional Discourse Grammar (FDG) or its predecessor Functional Grammar (FG).

The present paper goes beyond extant work in Part (A) in that it proposes to use the FDG-framework not for the description of a single linguistic phenomenon only, but also for a re-examination of Ancient Greek grammar in

---

[1] I use the term *discourse* to refer to any instantiation of the process of language-based communication between human individuals, be it factual or fictional. A *text*, by contrast, is the static fixation of such a communication process in written form (cf. Freiberg, 2012, p. 4, fn. 1).—On the specifics of Platonic dialogue as a discourse type cf. Scheppers (2011, p. 314); sect. 2 of the present paper.

general. As a first step towards such a revised grammatical overview, it will concentrate on a description of those features of the language that are most relevant to identifying EDUs and building hierarchical discourse structures in actual running discourse both beyond and below of them. Adopting FDG terminology, it will speak of Discourse Acts (DAs) instead of EDUs. The paper will develop Scheppers' work further in Part (B) by introducing a sub-EDU-level of analysis which can also be targeted by higher-order discourse structure. This level of analysis will be called that of the Subact of Reference/Ascription.

Among the approaches represented in the original workshop, the present one is most akin to the multi-level approach to discourse coherence taken by Manfred Stede and his team (cf. Stede, 2016; Bourgonje & Stede, this volume), in that it strives for a comprehensive, multi-faceted annotation of natural-language text, as well as to the Language into Act Theory (*L-AcT*; cf. Cresti, 2000; Raso, Cavalcante & Mittmann, 2017; Cavalcante, 2020), because it assumes a primacy of prosodic-pragmatic correspondence when it comes to the formal-functional definition of Discourse Acts and Subacts in Ancient Greek.

The remainder of this paper is organized as follows: Section 2 introduces Platonic dialogue in general and Plato's *Protagoras* in particular as the objects of the study. Section 3 first presents the basic notions of FDG and will then provide an overview over the central grammatical features of the Ancient Greek language as used by Plato organized according to the principles of the FDG-framework. This section thus serves to familiarize the reader both with those structures of the language as well as those theoretical concepts that will feature in the analysis of a sample passage of running discourse, which will follow in section 4. The reader, however, may feel free to jump to section 4 directly, experiencing Ancient Greek first in the wild and homing in on the systematic display of its structures in section 3. Both ways of approaching the language complement each other in my view and are thus equally important to my method. Section 5 will evaluate the study and point out directions for further research.

2   Platonic Dialogue

2.1   *Definition*

Platonic dialogues can be characterized as written accounts of fictitious conversations between Plato's (c. 428–348 BC) teacher Socrates and one or more interlocutors which serve the purpose of the pursuit of true knowledge, wisdom, or virtue. Like any dramatic genre, they broach at least two communicative situ-

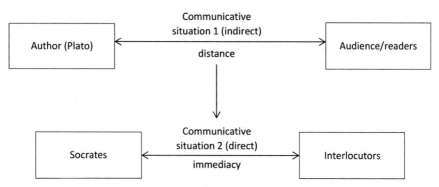

FIGURE 9.1 Communicative situations in Platonic dialogue

ations: (1) an indirect, or dialogue-external, one between the respective author and his audience or readers; (2) a direct, internal one between the characters of the dialogue (fig. 9.1).[2]

36 Platonic dialogues are transmitted to us in 51 Byzantine manuscripts from the 9th century AD or later (Irwin, 2008, pp. 64, 71), supplemented by quotes in other ancient works. While some of these manuscripts do contain punctuation marks, these cannot be taken to go back to ancient tradition, let alone to the author himself. Writing in Plato's time and throughout antiquity was done in capital letters, mostly unspaced, and without punctuation. Punctuation marks in our editions therefore reflect choices of the modern editor.

The absolute and relative chronologies of the dialogues have remained a matter of debate. Mainly on stylometric grounds, two groups are now being distinguished: an early group, and a middle/late one (cf. Söder, 2017, for further details). The earlier dialogues are more vivid; representing seemingly natural scenes of conversation between Athenians of the time. The later dialogues reduce the scenic aspect and focus more strongly on the philosophical contents, at times becoming almost monologues by the main character interspersed with some standard phrases uttered by his interlocutors, encouraging him to go on. In terms of content, the dialogues become more doctrinal.[3]

---

[2] Some dialogues even contain more than one internal level of communication, because the actual philosophical discussion proper is embedded into one or more framing conversations. The *Protagoras* is such a case, cf. sect. 2.3.
[3] For further characterization of this development cf. already Hirzel (1895, vol. 1, pp. 247–259).

2.2 Platonic Dialogue and Discourse Segmentation

Somewhat paradoxically, however, it is the earlier rather than the later Platonic dialogues that posit a specific challenge to the *orality approach*[4] to Ancient Greek discourses, under which both the FDG-approaches as well as Scheppers' work may be subsumed.

In a seminal paper from 1992, Slings proposed a three-fold distinction of Ancient Greek discourses according to whether they display poetic, quasi-spoken or written language. In the poetic as well as the quasi-spoken language, the EDU is not the syntactically-semantically defined clause, but the Discourse Act, a cognitive-pragmatic unit, which finds its linguistic expression in the form of an Intonational Phrase. Rooted in the constraints of online-language production, Discourse Acts are subject to the One New Idea Constraint (Chafe, 1994; cf. Bakker, 1997, for the Homeric poems), i.e. they cannot convey more than one new piece of information at a time.

Although the earlier dialogues should represent a prime example of quasi-spoken Greek, Slings (1992, pp. 104 f. incl. fn. 43) already noted that they did not behave as expected concerning the doubling of the modal particle *án* 'maybe, possibly', a phenomenon which is ultimately connected with the applicability of the One New Idea Constraint. Against this background it is conspicuous that Scheppers (2011) chose four of the middle/late dialogues for his study of discourse segmentation and that his approach worked well. Verano (2015, 2018) concentrated on the *Republic* (late phase) and the *Apology* (early phase, but a speech of self-defense and therefore monological). No study has yet investigated the applicability of the orality approach to the earlier dialogues.

How could this discrepancy be explained? And which hypotheses should guide such a study of the earlier dialogues?—Verano (2015, ch. 3.2.3) already underlined that the communicative situation between the author and his audience/readers is a distanced one in the sense of Koch and Oesterreicher (1985), while the dialogue-internal communicative situation between Socrates and his interlocutor(s) is one of immediacy (cf. again fig. 9.1).[5] As far as discourse segmentation is concerned, the internal communicative situation between the characters thus needs to comply with the One New Idea Constraint to a certain degree in order to be convincing as a representation of actual conversation, while the external communicative situation between the author and his audience/readers avoids fragmentation (Chafe, 1982), i.e. the distribution of information over several Discourse Acts. Accordingly, we should expect

---

4 For the term as well as a critical review cf. Devine & Stephens (2000, pp. 206–209).
5 The same point has been sketched with respect to Ancient Greek drama by van Emde Boas (2017, pp. 4 f.).

both (a) passages which lend themselves to an analysis into Discourse Acts that correlate with Intonational Phrases obeying the One New Idea Constraint and corresponding to simple clauses or noun phrases, and (b) Discourse Acts which correlate with more integrated Intonational Phrases, corresponding to more complex syntactic structures. Approaches which focus on those features of Ancient Greek discourses that can be linked with Chafe's concept of fragmented language or Koch and Oesterreicher's language of immediacy, like Verano's (2015, 2018) own approach or Allan's (2016) to Herodotus, are one-sided and need to be developed further in order to capture the variety of the discourse type. Platonic dialogues imitate actual conversations only to the extent that this is necessary and useful for their respective artistic and philosophical purposes.

Another feature to be captured are subtle ironies, allusions, etc. targeting individual linguistic units that may stem from any of the communicative situations of the dialogues. Firstly, they are signs of careful planning on the part of the author, which is only possible with the aid of writing. As an example cf. (1) where Socrates suggests to his young friend Hippocrates that they should go outside and have a walk in the yard until the break of day instead of going to see the sophist Protagoras straightaway.

(1) *periióntes autoû diatrípsōmen héōs àn **phôs** génētai*[6]
    periióntes   *autoû diatrípsōmen*
    walk.around.PTCP.PRS.M.NOM.PL[7] there spend.time.AOR.SUBJ.1PL
    héōs àn   *phôs*   *génētai*
    until PTCL.ever light.NOM become.AOR.SUBJ.3SG

---

6 The text of the quotes is taken from Burnet's edition.
   The romanization of the Greek quotes follows the American Library Association—Library of Congress standard published at https://www.loc.gov/catdir/cpso/romanization/greek.pdf [last access: 2020-05-25], with the exception of ⟨χ⟩ being represented by ⟨kh⟩. This standard meets the needs of the present paper best because it results in a trans*cription* of the Classical Attic Greek originals rather than a strict trans*literation*; this permits e.g. the representation of ⟨υ⟩ as ⟨y⟩ in monophthongs, but as ⟨u⟩ in diphthongs. The alternative of giving two separate lines for transliteration and transcription would have reduced readability and increased the numbers of pages. Additionally, the acute ⟨´⟩, grave ⟨`⟩, and circumflex ⟨^⟩ accents are retained; vowel length is indicated by a macron ⟨¯⟩ not only for /ē/, /ō/, which are written with different letters from short /ĕ/, /ŏ/ in the Greek script, but for all vowels, giving a more adequate impression of Classical Attic Greek phonology.
7 The glosses largely follow a streamlined version of the Leipzig Glossing Rules as developed by Keydana, Widmer and Hock for the new de Gruyter series *Mouton Handbooks of Indo-European Typology*.—Gender is not indicated with nouns because it is lexically fixed. Number

'let us walk around there and wait until the break of **day** [*phôs*]/the creation of **a man** [*phós*]' (Pl. *Prt.* 311a4f.)⁸

When bearing an acute accent instead of a circumflex the noun *phós* is a poetic synonym for *anér* 'man'.⁹ Socrates' utterance thus may be attributed with four different communicative functions:¹⁰ (a) the immediate suggestion to Hippocrates of waiting until it is getting light; (b) an announcement to Socrates' Friend as well as the external reader of the ensuing examination of Hippocrates in the yard (Pl. *Prt.* 311a8–314b4); (c) an ironical critique on Protagoras, who is said to spend much time inside and thus exhibits unmanly behavior (Pl. *Prt.* 311a5–7, cf. Denyer & Manuwald, ad loc.), which should be understood by the Friend as well as the contemporaneous external reader; (d) a discourse-structural announcement foreshadowing the topic of the myth of Prometheus who brought fire to mankind in the process of its creation, which Protagoras will recount during the Central Discussion (Pl. *Prt.* 320c8–322d5).

Secondly, such linguistic effects can also bear on the size and shape of EDUs, mostly in the form of additional prosodic effects or morphosyntactic cues like particles, but also in distributing the information to be conveyed over fewer or more Discourse Acts. A prime example of this is likewise found in the *Protagoras*, cf. (2) below: Socrates is asked by Protagoras to repeat why he together with Hippocrates came to see Protagoras. Socrates, who is already

---

is not indicated with any type of nominal forms in the singular because this is regarded as the default value. Among the verbal categories, ACT and IND are regarded as default values and hence not indicated. MP or MID are likewise not indicated if they are the default voice of this particular verb in the tense/aspect-stem at hand (e.g. *érkhomai* 'come, go' is always MP in the present tense).

8   Quotes from Ancient Greek texts will be referenced throughout the paper according to the conventions of the reference dictionary by Liddell, Scott & Jones (*LSJ*): The abbreviation of the author's name comes first and in regular typeset, then in italics the abbreviation of the work title, finally again in regular typeset the indication of a section or page/line number. The counting method is author-specific. Quotes from Plato still count according to the so-called Stephanus edition dating from 1578 where pages were subdivided into four lettered sections, which could in turn be counted in lines. Reference to the very first line of the dialogue *Protagoras* e.g. is made by "Pl. *Prt.* 309a1".—The translations are my own unless otherwise indicated.

9   Whether *phôs* 'light' and *phós* 'man' should be etymologically connected, is still a matter of debate, cf. Beekes s.v. *phós*.

10 As far as I can see, the equivocalness arising from the sequence of letters ⟨ΦΩΣ⟩ [*PHŌS*] has gone unnoticed by previous commentators. It is not mentioned in any of the commentaries cited in the bibliography.

annoyed by Protagoras' pathetic behavior and long-windedness, replies in a mocking imitation of Protagoras' style:

(2)   *Hippokrátēs gàr hóde tynkhánei en epithȳmíāi ȏn tês sês synousíās:* hóti
      oûn autôi apobésetai, eán soi synêi, hēdéōs án phēsi pythésthai
      Hippokrátēs   gàr   hóde   tynkhánei   en
      Hippocrates.NOM PTCL.for this.here.M.NOM happen.PRS.3SG in
      epithȳmíāi ȏn   tês   sês
      desire.DAT be.PTCP.PRS.M.NOM ART.F.GEN POSS.2SG.F.GEN
      synousíās   hóti   oûn   autôi
      being.with.GEN INTER.N.NOM PTCL.so he.M.DAT
      apobésetai   e=án   soi   synêi
      step.off.from.FUT.3SG if=PTCL.possibly you.DAT be.with.PRS.SUBJ.3SG
      hēdéōs án   phēsi   pythésthai
      gladly PTCL.possibly say.PRS.3SG learn.AOR.INF
      'My friend Hippocrates finds himself desirous of joining your classes; and therefore he says he would be glad to know what result he will get from joining them.' (Pl. *Prt.* 318a2–4; transl. Lamb)

For the external reader, this statement serves to clearly distance Socrates from Hippocrates' matter and also casts doubt on the seriousness of Hippocrates himself: Literally, Socrates says 'Hippocrates here happens to find himself [...]'—an expression which can also be used as a mitigating politeness formula, but in the present context suggests for the external reader that Hippocrates might not have reflected on this wish too much and might change it after the discussion.[11]—As far as segmentation of the passage is concerned, one would

---

11   That the concrete formulation Socrates chooses might have a sexual overtone, as Denyer (ad loc.) remarks, can of course not be ruled out, cf. the less ambiguous formulation in *Gorg.* 455c6f. *mathētḗs sou boulómenos genésthai* 'willing to become a pupil of yours', which was adduced by Adam and Adam already. Physical and intellectual intercourse are presented as being intrinsically connected in the view of Socrates throughout the dialogues (cf. e.g. his contribution to the *Symposium*). However, in the light of Pl. *Prt.* 317c6–d1, it is surprising that Socrates deliberately chooses for an ambiguous formulation in the direct conversation with Protagoras and it probably is intended as ironic, too. In any case, this point does not affect my argument.

What seems to be more important for the understanding of the passage, and more relevant to the present line of reasoning, is the fact that Socrates' more restricted formulation of Hippocrates' desire to be with Protagoras in 318a2f. replaces his earlier, apodictic formulation in 316c1f. *toûto dè oíetaí hoi málista genésthai ei soì syngénoito* 'he believes he can best gain it [i.e. consideration in the city] by consorting with you'

like to segment the first clause into two Intonational Phrases, namely *Hippokrátēs gàr hóde* and *tynkhánei en epithȳmíāi ȍn tê̂s sê̂s synousíās*; however, this is difficult to motivate in existing approaches. We will return to this point in sect. 3.6.

2.3 *The* Protagoras

For the purposes of the present paper, which is mainly concerned with the chronology of Plato's works presupposed in Slings (1992), the *Protagoras* can be classified as one of the earlier dialogues. For a somewhat more precise location of the Protagoras within the *Corpus Platonicum* cf. Irwin (2008, sect. 7) and the relevant sections in the commentaries.

The *Protagoras* is concerned with the question of whether virtue (*aretḗ*) can be taught and whether the sophists, as represented by the eponymous Protagoras, are suitable teachers of virtue. Protagoras is a historical figure of the 5th century BC; he earned large amounts of money by travelling through Hellas and teaching young men the art of "turning the weaker argument into the stronger one" (Pl. *Ap.* 19b5–c1). This profession, of course, was at odds with the search for wisdom of the historical as well as the fictitious Platonic Socrates. The latter, therefore, is portrayed in the dialogue as engaging in a lengthy discussion with the sophist. This discussion is brought about by the plea of Socrates' younger friend Hippocrates who is eager to become one of Protagoras' pupils and asks Socrates to speak in his favor to the great sophist (Pl. *Prt.* 310e2f.).

The central discussion is embedded into two frames (cf. fig. 9.2): Socrates discussing Hippocrates' plea with him, which amounts to their decision to go and test Protagoras in person (Frame 1), and an introductory frame which sets the scene for the other two encounters, namely an accidental meeting between Socrates and an unnamed Friend on the street (Frame 2).[12]

2.4 *The Passage in Question (Pl.* Prt. *309a1–b9)*

The passage I want to discuss in sect. 4 is the very beginning of the dialogue. It is thus the start of Frame 2 leading up to Socrates' recount of Frame 1 and the Central Discussion:

(transl. Lamb), which would under this reading be perfectly sound as transmitted by the manuscripts rather than requiring emendation (cf. the explanations of Wayte & Manuwald, ad loc.).

12 Interestingly enough, though, the two frames are not resumed again after the discussion. The dialogue ends shortly after the Central Discussion with *taûta eipóntes kaì akoúsantes apêimen*—'This having said and heard we went away' (362a4).

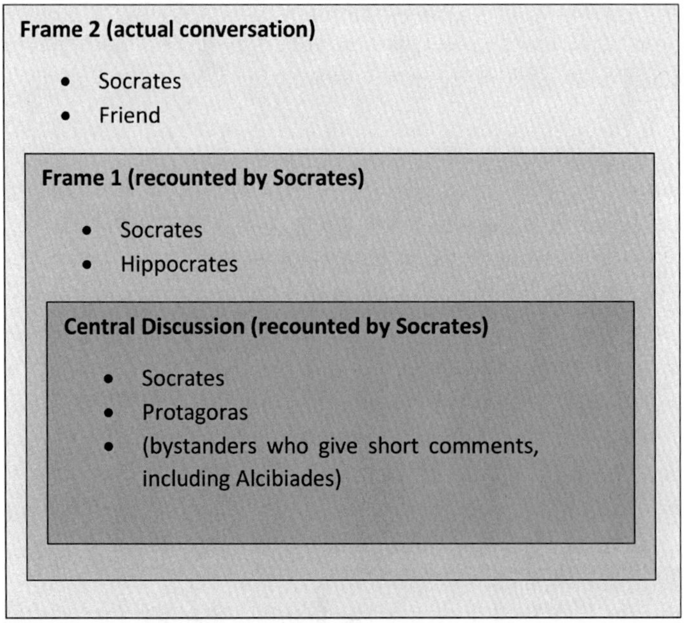

```
┌─────────────────────────────────────────────────┐
│ Frame 2 (actual conversation)                   │
│                                                 │
│   • Socrates                                    │
│   • Friend                                      │
│  ┌───────────────────────────────────────────┐  │
│  │ Frame 1 (recounted by Socrates)           │  │
│  │                                           │  │
│  │   • Socrates                              │  │
│  │   • Hippocrates                           │  │
│  │  ┌─────────────────────────────────────┐  │  │
│  │  │ Central Discussion (recounted by    │  │  │
│  │  │ Socrates)                           │  │  │
│  │  │                                     │  │  │
│  │  │   • Socrates                        │  │  │
│  │  │   • Protagoras                      │  │  │
│  │  │   • (bystanders who give short      │  │  │
│  │  │     comments, including Alcibiades) │  │  │
│  │  │                                     │  │  │
│  │  └─────────────────────────────────────┘  │  │
│  └───────────────────────────────────────────┘  │
└─────────────────────────────────────────────────┘
```

FIGURE 9.2 Communicative situations in the *Protagoras*

(3) Pl. *Prt.* 309a1–b9; transl. Lamb:

Hetaîros	Friend
póthen, ỗ Sṓkrates, phaínēi? ễ[13] *dễla dề hóti apò kynēgesíou toũ perí tền Alkibiádou hṓrān?*	Where have you been now, Socrates? Ah, but of course you have been in chase of Alcibiades and his youthful beauty!
kaì mến moi kaì próiēn idónti kalòs mèn ephaíneto anềr éti, anềr méntoi, ỗ Sṓkrates, hṓs g' en autoîs hēmîn eirễsthai, kaì pṓgōnos ếdē hypopimplámenos.	Well, only the other day, as I looked at him, I thought him still handsome as a man—for a man he is, Socrates, between you and me, and with quite a growth of beard.
Sōkrátēs	Socrates
eîta tí toũto? ou sỳ méntoi Homḗrou epainétēs eî, hòs éphē khariestátēn hḗbēn eînai toũ hypēnḗtou, hền nỹn Alkibiádēs ékhei?	And what of that? Do you mean to say you do not approve of Homer, who said that youth has highest grace in him whose beard is appearing, as now in the case of Alcibiades?

---

13 *Pace* Burnet. Suggestion by Gerard Boter. Cf. also LSJ s.v. ἦ [ễ], Adv., II 1 a and the commentary on DAs 4–6 in sect. 4.2 below.

Hetaîros	**Friend**
tí oûn tà nŷn? ê par' ekeínou phaínēi? kaì pôs prós se ho neānías diákeitai?	Then how is the affair at present? Have you been with him just now? And how is the young man treating you?
Sōkrátēs	**Socrates**
eû, émoige édoxen, oukh hḗkista dè kaì têi nŷn hēmérāi: kaì gàr pollà hypèr emoû eîpe boēthôn emoí, kaì oûn kaì árti ap' ekeínou érkhomai.	Quite well, I considered, and especially so today: for he spoke a good deal on my side, supporting me in a discussion—in fact I have only just left him.
átopon méntoi tí soi ethélō eipeîn: paróntos gàr ekeínou, oúte proseîkhon tòn noûn, epelanthanómēn te autoû thamá.	However, there is a strange thing I have to tell you: although he was present, I not merely paid him no attention, but at times forgot him altogether.

While this introduction indeed "has the air of gossip" (McCabe, 2008, p. 89), it already serves to arouse certain expectations and questions in the recipient: Socrates and an unnamed Friend are portrayed as running into each other on the street. The Friend thus asks Socrates where he is coming from, and offers a suggestion himself—that Socrates surely comes from his young favorite Alcibiades, who is praised for his beauty. The Friend, however, thinks that Alcibiades by now is a grown-up man and thus too old to be Socrates' lover. Socrates cleverly rejects this by an appeal to the great poet Homer, whom the Friend surely admires. The Friend, however, does not give up on his idea and asks again whether Socrates comes from Alcibiades, and about Alcibiades' relationship with him. Socrates briefly replies that it is "good," explaining that Alcibiades supported him in a discussion (i.e. the Central Discussion of the dialogue), and takes this opportunity to shift the topic of the conversation from the young and handsome Alcibiades to the famous sophist Protagoras: While engaging in the discussion with the latter, he barely took notice of the former. A little later (309c9–d2), Socrates will describe Protagoras—of course not without irony—as more beautiful than Alcibiades, due to his great wisdom. The introduction thus builds up some suspense before the introduction of Protagoras as Socrates' proper object of interest. It also serves to make clear that Socrates is not in the first place attracted by beauty of the body, but of the soul in general (cf. Taylor *ad* 309a2), and to distance Socrates from Alcibiades (Ramsey, 2012, pp. 62–64).—Note that his association with Alcibiades and the latter's later shady career were important factors for the accusations brought forward against the historical Socrates (cf. Ramsey, 2012), which led up to his execution in 399 BC.

3 Sketching a Functional Discourse Grammar of Platonic Dialogue

3.1 *Introduction to Functional Discourse Grammar*

FDG is typologically and hence also empirically oriented. Like its predecessor Functional Grammar (FG), its design has partly been inspired by work of classicists such as Caroline Kroon (Kroon, 1995; Hannay & Kroon, 2005). The central publication on FDG is the monograph by Kees Hengeveld and J. Lachlan Mackenzie dating to 2008 which I refer to as "FDG 2008" throughout this paper.

FDG takes an intermediate position between functionalist and formalist approaches to language structure (cf. FDG, 2008, pp. 26f.).[14] It emerged around the year 2000 as the successor of Simon Dik's Functional Grammar (Dik, 1978, 1997a,b) in order to capture phenomena extending beyond the borders of clauses as well as deviations from standard clause form, i.e. ellipses or *holophrases* (cf. Hannay & Kroon, 2005, p. 89; on the motivation of the term holophrase cf. FDG, 2008, pp. 3f.). To this end, it implemented central notions from the Geneva School of Discourse Analysis (Roulet, 1985; Roulet, Filliettaz & Grobet, 2001) and replaced the clause with the Discourse Act as the central unit of linguistic analysis, i.e. the EDU.

The introduction of FDG as a framework for the study of individual Ancient Greek particles and their grammaticalization has already borne fruit, cf. Allan, 2017a,b. The recent handbook *Particles in Ancient Greek Discourse* (Bonifazi, Drummen, & de Kreij, 2016) also adopted, if not a fully-fledged FDG-framework, yet the same discourse analytical notions of Acts and Moves as central units of discourse structure. Crepaldi (2018) made use of both the Geneva Model and an FDG-framework for her analysis of adversative particles in Euripides. Other areas of application are being explored now, as well, cf. e.g. la Roi (2020) on the expression of realizable wishes in Ancient Greek.—Allan (2019) linked the Chafeian concept of Intonation Unit (Chafe, 1994) with the FDG-concept of Discourse Act, showing how a passage from the *Odyssey* may be analyzed in terms of sequences of nuclear and subsidiary Discourse Acts, the latter exerting either Orientation or Elaboration functions.

---

14 For a comparison to other approaches to grammatical structure in general cf. FDG (2008, sect. 1.4.2.)—For a discussion of its position within functionalist theories cf. Butler (2003) and Hengeveld and Mackenzie (2015, sect. 14.3).

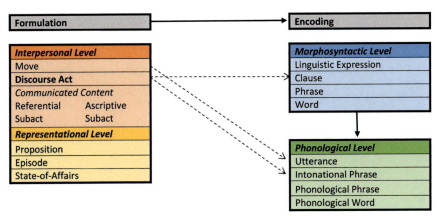

FIGURE 9.3 FDG-architecture

3.2 *FDG Architecture*

Functional Discourse Grammar represents the Grammatical Component of a wider theory of verbal interaction. This Grammatical Component is organized in four levels: The Interpersonal and Representational Level serve to *formulate* the language producer's message, which then gets *encoded* at the Morphosyntactic and Phonological Levels. The Interpersonal Level largely corresponds to what otherwise is called pragmatics, i.e. it "deals with all the formal aspects of a linguistic unit that reflect its role in the interaction between the Speaker and the Addressee" (FDG, 2008, p. 46). The Representational Level, by contrast, is concerned with semantics, in the sense that it captures the way in which simple or complex lexical units relate to the extra-linguistic world they describe (cf. FDG, 2008, pp. 128f.). As is indicated by the thick arrows in fig. 9.3 above, pragmatics and semantics both together govern morphosyntax in FDG, and the three of them govern phonology (top-down approach, cf. FDG, 2008, p. 13). The dotted arrows indicate assumed standard correspondences between Layers of the different Levels.

In the following discussion of FDG-architecture, I will concentrate on those parts which are most relevant to the present study. I will introduce them in a piecemeal fashion, concentrating on those Levels and Layers that are most relevant to the identification of EDUs in Platonic discourse. For a comprehensive overview the reader is referred to FDG (2008) or the articles Hengeveld and Mackenzie (2015) as well as Keizer and Olbertz (2018). A comprehensive FDG-description of modern English grammar is provided by Keizer (2015).

3.3 The Interpersonal Level

On the Interpersonal Level, three different Layers of actions are discerned: (1) the Move, (2) the Discourse Act, (3) the evocation of a Communicated Content consisting of one or more Referential and/or Ascriptive Subacts (FDG, 2008, p. 107).

3.3.1 Move (M)

According to standard FDG-theory, the Move is "the largest unit of interaction relevant to grammatical analysis" (FDG, 2008, p. 50).

(4) MOVE
The higher-rank unit called *move* is defined as the minimal free unit of discourse that is able to enter into an exchange structure. Unlike the act, a move is defined not only in terms of communicative unity, but also in terms of thematic unity. A move usually consists of a central act (which is the most important act in view of the speaker's intentions and goals) and one or more subsidiary acts, which also cohere thematically with the central act. (Kroon, 1995, p. 66)

As Moves according to this definition are to be identified in terms of thematic unity, they cannot be defined autonomously, but only in relation to another Move, so that a thematic break becomes detectable. This holds for subsequent Moves within one turn by the same speaker as well as Moves uttered by different speakers within a conversation. Ideally, a Move should consist of at least two sub-units, but Moves, where one Discourse Act corresponds with a Move are also possible. Whether a certain Discourse Act should also be awarded Move-status can best be measured according to the criterion of communicative autonomy:

(5) Whereas a Discourse Act [...] may provoke a backchannel (i.e. a response that encourages the Speaker to continue), only a Move can provoke a reaction from the interlocutor (an answer to a question, an objection to a point of argument, etc.), and that reaction must itself take the form of a Move. (FDG, 2008, p. 50)

An analysis of the sample passage from the beginning of the *Protagoras* (cf. sect. 2.4) is presented in sect. 4.2, Table 9.1. Cf. Crepaldi (2018, pp. 9–11) for a segmentation of a passage from tragedy (E. *Hipp*. 88–113).

3.3.2　Discourse Act (DA)

The Discourse Act may be defined as proposed by Kroon:

(6) DISCOURSE ACT
Acts can be defined as the smallest identifiable units of communicative behaviour. In contrast to the higher order units called moves they do not necessarily further the communication in terms of approaching a conversational goal. (Kroon, 1995, p. 65)

The Discourse Act represents the central unit of linguistic analysis in FDG. It is not defined by a link to any particular morphosyntactic configuration, as long as it can be said to have sufficient communicative import to the ongoing discourse. In the following Exchange, for example, Socrates' answer to his Friend's question is constituted by a single Noun Phrase functioning as a temporal Modifier on the State-of-Affairs (SoA) evoked by the Friend. Communicatively, this is sufficient in order to answer his question in the affirmative and to assert additional information about the SoA in question.—Such structures are ubiquitous in Ancient Greek texts.

(7)　Friend:　*ô tí légeis? Prōtagórās epidedḗmēken?*
　　　　　　ô　　*tí*　　　*légeis*　　*Prōtagórās*
　　　　　　PTCL.O INTER.N.ACC say.PRS.2SG Protagoras.NOM
　　　　　　epidedḗmēken
　　　　　　come.to.town.PF.3SG
　　　　　　'O, what are you saying? Protagoras is in town?'

　　　Socrates:　*trítēn ge ḗdē hēmérān*
　　　　　　　　trítēn　　*ge*　　　　　*ḗdē*　　*hēmérān*
　　　　　　　　third.F.ACC PTCL.at.least already day.ACC
　　　　　　　　'For the third day already' (Pl. *Prt.* 309d3f.)

According to the canonical version of FDG presented by Hengeveld and Mackenzie in their 2008 monograph, a Discourse Act is in essence characterized by bearing a discrete Illocution (FDG, 2008, p. 63).

The study of illocutionary force has been, in Ancient Greek linguistics, as well as in the FDG tradition, largely tied to clause types.[15] FDG uses the concept of *basic illocution* to connect the two. The set of basic illocutions of a language is

---

15　It hence does not fully align with the classifications of the Austin-Searlean tradition

defined as the set of "different grammatical (including phonological) structures that are in a default relation with specific communicative goals of the speakers using these structures" (Hengeveld et al., 2007, p. 75). For Ancient Greek, the following basic illocutions are commonly[16] recognized: DECLARATIVE, INTERROGATIVE, DIRECTIVE, DESIDERATIVE[17] (i.e. wishes), EXCLAMATIVE.[18]

(8) DECLARATIVE
Prōtagórās, éphē, hḗkei
Prōtagórās   éphē   hḗkei
Protagoras.NOM say.IPF.3SG have.come.PRS.2SG
'**Protagoras**, he said, **has come**' (Pl. *Prt.* 310b7f.)

(Austin, 1962; Searle, 1979), with the exception of Biraud (2010) and van Emde Boas (2017).—For another introduction to the FDG-approach cf. also la Roi (2020).

16 Somewhat surprisingly, literature specifically dealing with illocutions in Ancient Greek is rather sparse. The recent *EAGLL* does not provide any entry on "illocution", "illocutionary force" or "speech act". I hope to provide a more detailed review of the *status quaestionis* elsewhere in the future.—Here I refer to CGCG (2019, §38)as well as Wakker (1994); Revuelta Puigdollers (2005, 2017); Biraud (2010); van Emde Boas (2017). Additionally, an in-depth study of Ancient Greek directives and their subtypes is provided by Denizot (2011).
  On methodological *caveats* in the study of Illocutions in a corpus language cf. van Emde Boas (2017, p. 18, fn. 33); CGCG (2019, §38.1); Revuelta Puigdollers (2017) offers suggestions for overcoming these problems.

17 The term DESIDERATIVE borrowed from Revuelta Puigdollers' Spanish term *desiderativa* matches the general naming format, but is unfortunate from the point of view of historical linguistics, because in Greek, wishes are not formulated using an Indo-European desiderative form of the verb, but the so-called optative mood. Traces of a desiderative can be found in the future stems. Designating the basic illocution as OPTATIVE, on the other hand, is not appropriate, either, because in FDG-terminology the OPTATIVE-illocution only includes positive wishes, while in Greek also negative wishes, or imprecations, may be expressed with the same clause pattern, cf. the examples given by la Roi (2020).—The second point also applies to DIRECTIVES, which should—as a supercategory—include both positive as well as negative directives for which different formations existed in Ancient Greek, cf. Revuelta Puigdollers (2005, 2017); Denizot (2011).

18 The data suggest adoption of an additional category COMMISSIVE (e.g. Pl. *Prt.* 310e1f.), which has only been acknowledged by Wakker (1994), Biraud (2010) and van Emde Boas (2017). Faure (2012) advocates recognizing the deliberative not only as a clause type, but also as a separate illocution. Within the FDG-framework DELIBERATIVES could be said to constitute a questioning counterpart of directives as Telling Behavioural Illocutions (cf. FDG, 2008, p. 75, fig. 7). More research is needed on this theoretical point as well as on Illocutions in Ancient Greek in general.

(9) INTERROGATIVE
lége dḗ, tí hēgêi eînai tòn sophistḗn?
lége   dḗ   tí   hēgêi   eînai
say.PRS.IMP.2SG PTCL.then INTER.N.ACC hold.PRS.2SG be.PRS.INF
tòn   sophistḗn
ART.M.ACC sophist.ACC
'Tell me then, please, **what do you take a sophist to be?**' (Pl. *Prt.* 312c4f.)

(10) DIRECTIVE
Prōtagórān gár toi deómenoi ideîn ḗlthomen. eisángeilon oûn
Prōtagórān   gár   toi   deómenoi
Protagoras.ACC PTCL.for PTCL.mark.you ask.PTCP.PRS.MP.N.PL
ideîn   ḗlthomen   eisángeilon   oûn
see.AOR.INF come.AOR.1PL announce.AOR.IMP.2SG PTCL.then
'I tell you we have come to ask if we may see Protagoras. **So go and announce us!**' (Pl. *Prt.* 314e1f.; transl. Lamb)

(11) DESIDERATIVE
ei gár, ê̂ d' hós, ô̂ Zeû kaì theoí, en toútōi eíē
ei gár   ê̂   d'   hós   ô̂   Zeû   kaì
if PTCL.for say.IPF.3SG PTCL.but he.M.NOM PTCL.O Zeus.VOC and
theoí   en toútōi   eíē
god.VOC.PL in this.N.DAT be.PRS.OPT.3SG
'Would to Zeus and all the gods, he exclaimed, **only that were needed!**'
(Pl. *Prt.* 310d8-e1; transl. Lamb; also cited in Wakker, 1994, p. 384, fn. 43)

(12) EXCLAMATIVE
ô̂ tí légeis? Prōtagórās epidedḗmēken?
'o, what are you saying?! Protagoras is in town?!' (Pl. *Prt.* 309d3; cf. (7) above)

As is indicated in fig. 9.4 by the bracketing of the Addressee and the Communicated Content, FDG also permits to model purely expressive speech acts like *ouch*, *yuck*, or *wow*, which do not transmit any Content. They can be uttered by a Speaker as an expression of his feelings in reaction to a certain event even in absence of any possible Addressee (cf. FDG, 2008, pp. 63f., 76). These may be said to stand in a relationship of gradualness with EXCLAMATIVES, which likewise express spontaneous reactions to an unexpected stimulus, but do contain some Communicated Content, cf. (12) above. Consider e.g. the exclamation of the door-keeper at Socrates' and Hippocrates' arrival:

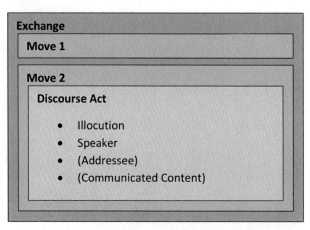

FIGURE 9.4 Basic elements of an Exchange and definitory characteristics of a Discourse Act in FDG

(13) *éā, éphē, sophistaí tines*
     éā   éphē   sophistaí   tines
     PTCL.oho say.IPF.3SG sophist.NOM.PL   INDEF.M.NOM.PL
     'oho!, he said, some sophists' (Pl. *Prt.* 314d3)

3.3.3   Subacts Constituting the Communicative Content

The Communicated Content "corresponds to the choices the Speaker makes in order to evoke a picture of the external world s/he wants to talk about" (FDG, 2008, p. 87). The Layer of the Communicated Content thus serves in order to locate the speaker's "organizing and rhetorical perspective on the ideas conveyed" (Kroon, 1995, p. 61) in the FDG-model of linguistic structure. Communicated Contents are not identical to Propositional Contents, but typically correspond to them.[19] It is thus at the Layer of the Communicated Content that the mapping between the Interpersonal and the Representational Levels takes place (FDG, 2008, p. 87).

Two types of actions regularly carried out by Speakers are located at the level of the Communicated Content (cf. again fig. 9.3 in sect. 3.2): Subacts of Reference and Subacts of Ascription, cf. the definitions in (14) and (15) below. A Communicated Content consists of at least one such Subact (FDG, 2008, p. 88).

---

19   For further details on the distinction between Communicated and Propositional Content cf. FDG (2008, pp. 144 f.).

(14) REFERENTIAL SUBACT
A Subact of Reference (R_1) is an attempt by the Speaker to evoke a referent, i.e. a null, singleton, or multiple set of entities or qualities. (FDG, 2008, p. 88)

(15) ASCRIPTIVE SUBACT
A Subact of Ascription (T_1) is an attempt by the Speaker to evoke a Property. Despite the word 'ascription', it need not be the case that the Speaker is actually ascribing a Property to a referent: in uttering *It is raining*, for example, the Speaker is merely evoking a meteorological Property without evoking any referent; raining is not being 'ascribed to', but simply 'ascribed'.[20] (FDG, 2008, p. 88)

With regard to the Friend's Act uttered in (7) above, we may say that the Communicated Content consists of one Subact of Reference evoking an individual called 'Protagoras' and a Subact of Ascription which evokes the Property of 'being in town':

(16) (*Prōtagóras*)$_\text{REFERENCE}$ (*epidedémēken*)$_\text{ASCRIPTION}$
'Protagoras is in town' (Pl. *Prt.* 309d3; cf. (7) above)

These Subacts, or the Communicated Content as a whole, may carry information-structural Functions. This brings me to another basic feature of FDG-architecture, namely the internal structure of Layers, which I will elaborate on in the following subsection, taking the Communicated Content as an example.

3.3.4   Operators, Modifiers, Functions: The Case of the Communicated Content

FDG holds that the basic import that a given linguistic expression has on a given Layer may be modified, specified or extended by three types of mechanisms (FDG, 2008, p. 14; also cf. Hengeveld, 2017, sect. 2.3): (1) lexical expressions which modify the basic import, and hence are called Modifiers; (2) grammatical strategies which operate on the basic import, and hence are called Operators; (3) grammatical strategies which indicate how the linguistic expression in question relates to one or more other linguistic expressions on this very Layer. These are called Functions.

---

20   Properties in FDG constitute two of the lower Layers within the Representational Level and comprise the predication frames (Configurational Properties) as well as lexemes ((Lexical) Properties) of a given language, cf. FDG (2008, ch. 3.6, 3.7), respectively.

Information structure was expressed in Ancient Greek by means of word order and information-structural particles, presumably hand in hand with prosodic mechanisms.[21] Information-structural properties of a given constituent in a clause may be represented as Functions on the Layer of the Communicated Content. The clause given above in (16) would in principle allow for two readings: one where Protagoras is in Narrow Focus, and a thetic[22] one where both the subject and the predicate are focused. This could be formalized in FDG as follows:

(17) Narrow Focus reading
(Prōtagóras)$_{Foc}$ epidedḗmēken
(C_I: [(T_I: *epidedḗmēken* (T_I)) (R_I: *Prōtagóras* (R_I))$_{Foc}$] (C_I))

(18) Thetic reading
(Prōtagóras *epidedḗmēken*)$_{Foc}$
(C_I: [(T_I: *epidedḗmēken* (T_I)) (R_I: *Prōtagóras* (R_I))]$_{Foc}$ (C_I))

The Communicated Content C_I consists of a Subact of Ascription T_I and a Subact of Reference R_I. They stand in a non-hierarchical relationship, which is indicated by the square brackets. Both, however, are hierarchically subordinate to C_I. They are hence enclosed by the structure (C_I: – (C_I)). In (17), only R_I is under the scope of the Focus Function. In (18), The Focus Function scopes over both T_I and R_I, which is why it is annotated as a subscript to the closing square bracket.

In the present case, actually, both readings seem to be relevant: The Friend is surprised about Socrates' news that the famous Protagoras would be in town (Narrow Focus reading). Socrates downplays the fact that he encountered a celebrity and continues by giving more information about how long Protagoras has already been in Athens (thetic reading).

Socrates' answer contains the particle *ge*. Dik (1995, pp. 43–45) and Bertrand (2010, p. 221) argued that the particle has a delimitative function, exerting "a delimitation in the process of reference of the word to which it is attached"

---

[21] On information structure in Ancient Greek cf. Dik (1995, 2007); Matić (2003); Bertrand (2010); Allan (2014); Lühr (2015); Goldstein (2016) as well as the EAGLL-articles "Information Structure and Greek", "Focus", and "Topic", which provide the Greek in transliteration.—On detecting prosodic marking of information structure in Ancient Greek cf. especially Bertrand (2011).

[22] On the possibility of thetic readings for narrow focus constructions in Ancient Greek cf. Bertrand (2010, sect. 2.2.2.3).

(Bertrand, 2010, p. 212, transl. CF; also cf. Scheppers, 2011, pp. 212f.). In other words, the particle contrasts the referent evoked with the set of all possible referents in the given discourse context and singles it out among them ('this X'), cf. also the account by Goldstein (2019). I thus propose to formalize the description of *ge* as an Operator of Selecting Contrast[23] on Referential Subacts, be they carriers of Topic Function, Focus Function or even none of the two (cf. Dik, 1995, p. 44; Bertrand, 2010, p. 127, fn. 38). Operators are notated in lower case before the variable of the relevant Layer. Applied to Socrates' answer we might thus arrive at the following formalization:

(19) *trítēn ge édē hēmérān*
    $(\text{contr}_{\text{SELECTING}}\ R_I: [trítēn\ hēmérān]\ (R_I))_{\text{Foc}}$

Finally, I would like to illustrate the lexical strategy of Modifiers by a phenomenon which we find very often in Platonic dialogue and which is also located at the Layer of the Communicated Content in FDG, namely attribution of quoted speech by insertions like *éphē* 'he said' in (20) below, formalized in (21) as an internal appendix to the structure (C_I: – (C_I)) separated by a colon. In using the Modifier, the Speaker is specifying that the Communicated Content he transmits is not his. Rather, he is "acting the part[]" of the original Speaker (FDG, 2008, p. 104). Hengeveld and Mackenzie point out that such Modifiers are communicatively weak and hence may diachronically undergo processes of grammaticalization or fossilization, like the relic form *quoth* 'said he' from the Middle English verb *quethan* 'say' which has otherwise got out of use. As example (20) shows, Ancient Greek source Modifiers often enter the syntactic domain constituted by their Heads and take second position therein, which is the standard position for phonologically weakened material, cf. sect.

---

23 *Selecting* in the terminology of Dik (1997a, sect. 13.4.2), where Focus and Contrast are not distinguished as separate information-structural dimensions. The particle is not *restricting* because it suspends implicatures of exhaustivity, cf. Goldstein (2019, p. 281).
    Note that Contrast is addressed as a "function" in FDG (2008, sect. 2.7.2.4), just like Topic and Focus. In the case of Contrast, at least, which Hengeveld and Mackenzie define in the broader sense of "signal[ling] the Speaker's desire to bring out the particular differences between two or more Communicated Contents or between a Communicated Content and contextually available information" (FDG, 2008, p. 96), it is possible to view it partially as an Operator, which pertains to the relationship between the Subact/Communicated Content in question and the extra-linguistic context, as assumed for *ge* above, and partially as a Function, which signals an opposition between two text-internal units as is e.g. the case with Subacts accompanied by *mén ... dé ...* 'X on the one hand ..., Y on the other ...', cf. the general description of Operators vs. Functions in FDG (2008, p. 14).

3.5.1 below. The phrase ê̂ d' hós 'said he', which we encountered in example (11), contains the imperfect form of the otherwise uncommon verb ēmí 'speak' (cf. LSJ and Beekes, s.v.) as well as the nominative singular hós of the Indo-European anaphoric pronoun *só-/tó- which became grammaticalized in post-Homeric Greek as the article, exhibiting the alternative nominative form ho (cf. Schwyzer, 1953, pp. 610f.). hós may thus be regarded as a relic form preserved in this special environment.

(20) [Socrates reports what Hippocrates answered when he asked him whether he knew what a Sophist was:]
oîmaí g', éphē, eidénai
oîmaí   g'   éphē   eidénai
believe.PRS.1SG PTCL.at.least say.IPF.3SG see.PF.INF
'I think I know, **he said**' (Pl. *Prt.* 312c4)

(21) (C_I: [R_J : (([contr$_{SELECTING}$ R_I: [*oîmaí*] (R_I)]$_{Foc}$ *eidénai*) (R_J)] (C_1): ***éphē*** (C_1))[24]

3.4 *The Morphosyntactic Level*

Ancient Greek, like other ancient Indo-European languages, disposes of a very complex morphosyntax, especially in the domain of the verb. I will here limit myself to those aspects that will be most relevant to general issues of discourse segmentation and/or to the discussion of our sample passage from the *Protagoras* in sect. 4. My focus will hence lie on Ancient Greek clause types. Clauses express fully-fledged Propositions and are thus prone to be carriers of an Illocution, i.e. Discourse Acts, too. I will postpone the discussion of Themes, i.e. a special subtype of extra-clausal constituents or fronted elements which has also been awarded DA-status, to sect. 3.6, i.e. after the discussion of the Phonological Level.

3.4.1   Clauses

For Ancient Greek, four types of clauses may be discerned: (1) finite main clauses, (2) finite subclauses, (3) participial clauses, (4) infinitival clauses.

As Bertrand (2010, pp. 312, 320) pointed out, finite main and subclauses are not syntactically distinguished in Ancient Greek except for the latter being introduced by an introductive[25] which indicates their respective status (e.g. a relative pronoun). Differences in verb placement (as e.g. in Modern High

---

24 The Referent that Hippocrates evokes here, is the Proposition that he believes to know what a Sophist is, i.e. a third-order entity, cf. FDG (2008, sect. 3.2.1.2).
25 On the term *introductive* cf. fn. 37 below.

German, which exhibits V2 in main clauses and Vend in subclauses)[26] are not traceable in Ancient Greek. Rather, word order is sensitive to information-structural distinctions. Finite subclauses do show some alternate behavior, however, when it comes to the selection of the mood of their matrix predicate, cf. now CGCG (2019, § 40.5–40.15). To what extent the situation in Ancient Greek is comparable to that in Old High German sketched by Coniglio and Hinterhölzl (this volume), and what the consequences would be for discourse segmentation, must be left for further research.[27] For the time being, I adopt Scheppers' (2011, p. 194) view that finite main and subclauses both qualify to constitute separate Discourse Acts in Ancient Greek.—Finite clauses have incidentally been illustrated in the discussion of Ancient Greek Illocutions (sect. 3.3.2 above).

---

26 The cases of so-called V3 main clauses discussed by Haegeman (this volume) for Dutch do not present straightforward exceptions to the rule stated above for German. From an FDG-view point, they constitute separate Discourse Acts exerting the function of a THEME or SETTING (depending on whether one wishes to acknowledge the SETTING as a separate category or not), cf. Rijksbaron's (1986) FG-analysis of similar cases in both Dutch and Ancient Greek. Adverbial clause and main clause hence constitute independent domains for the computation of constituent order. Word order in the main clause accordingly varies between either V2 or V1, not V3 or V2. Diachronically, these patterns may give rise to new clause structures, of course, but I think we have not yet reached that stage, at least not in standard German. Sentences like *Wenn mein Text fertig ist, an wen soll ich den dann schicken?* 'When my text is ready, to whom shall I send it?' (= equivalent to Haegeman, this volume, ex. (40)) would still be considered syntactically bi-clausal, although they can also be uttered with accelerated speech rate and a single compressed intonational pattern (for example, but not exclusively, in contexts with heightened emotionality like *Wenn's dir nicht passt, dann geh doch!* 'Just go away, if you don't like it!', inspired by Rijksbaron, 1986, p. 4, ex. (7)–(8)). Furthermore, I suppose that the differences between the patterns discerned by Haegeman (this volume) might rather be explained by the relationship between the two clauses, or their import to the overall discourse structure, than by clause-internal traits of the main clause. Observe that non-standard German also allows for this pattern with non-contrastive subjects, e.g. *Wenn du Hilfe brauchst, ich bin da.* 'If you need help, I'm always there/here for you'.

    The same holds *mutatis mutandis* for the V2 relatives discussed by Coniglio and Hinterhölzl (this volume), in which the main clause qualifies as a THEME and the relative, if not as the nuclear, then at least as an equipollent Discourse Act (cf. the introduction to section 4.2 below on the notion of *equipollence* in FDG). V2 in the relative clause is not surprising, given its "assertive potential" (Coniglio & Hinterhölzl, this volume, sect. 5). Again, what seems to be problematic is the exact relationship between the two DAs (cf. Coniglio & Hinterhölzl, this volume, sect. 3), for a THEME should by definition constitute a subsidiary Discourse Act (cf. FDG, 2008, p. 55). A similar problem arises with non-restrictive relative clauses on which cf. FDG (2008, p. 57), with further refs.

27 I thank the third anonymous reviewer for drawing my attention to this intriguing issue through his critique on the present alinea.

Participial clauses formally fall into genitive absolutes, which have a subject referent that is not evoked in their matrix clause and take genitive case for both the participle and its subject expression, and conjunct participles which relate either to the subject or another major constituent of the matrix clause (cf. Buijs, 2005, ch. 5.2). Functionally, they express different kinds of adverbial relations such as temporal succession, cause, goal, or manner, which however, in most cases are not overtly signaled (but cf. Buijs, 2005, pp. 129–134). In the relevant literature, three to four subtypes of participial clauses are discerned according to their relationship with the matrix verb as far as temporal semantics, modality and polarity as well as their information structure/pragmatic function are concerned (cf. Goldstein, 2010, ch. 8, 2016, ch. 7; Bary & Haug, 2011; Scheppers, 2011, pp. 406–408; Pompei, 2012). Among these types, the SETTING has played the most prominent role in literature on information structure as well as discourse segmentation because it intersects with a type of extra-clausal constituent of the same name identified in S. Dik (1997b, pp. 396–398) (cf. Allan, 2006, 2009, 2014, pp. 183–185; H. Dik, 2007, pp. 36f.; Bertrand, 2010, pp. 294–298, 315f.). SETTINGS provide a spatio-temporal background for the matrix event. They hence are very often anaphoric, referring back to some other State-of-Affairs already mentioned in or inferable from the preceding discourse. In (22) below, for example, the participle *aporoûnti*, is formed from the same verbal lexeme[28] *aporéō* lit. 'to have no way out' as the matrix verb in the preceding clause:

(22) [Epimetheus had no gift left to give to mankind as its special strength. He did not know (*ēpórei*) what to do.]
[***aporoûnti dè autôi***]_{SETTING} *érkhetai Promētheùs* [...]
aporoûnti   dè   autôi   érkhetai
be.at.loss.PTCP.PRS.M.DAT PTCL.but he.M.DAT come.PRS.3SG
Promētheùs
Prometheus.NOM
'As he was casting about, Prometheus arrived [...]' (Pl. *Prt.* 321c3; transl. Lamb)

Infinitival clauses, as a rule of thumb, just like participial clauses, constitute separate Discourse Acts in cases where they clearly refer to separate States-of-

---

28   This phenomenon is known as Tail-Head-Linkage, cf. FDG (2008, pp. 158f.), Allan (2016). It is probably employed here by Plato, who has Protagoras recount the myth of the creation of mankind and the theft of fire by Prometheus, in order to create a somewhat solemn or archaic speaking style, appropriate both to the mythical sujet of the narrative and the overall characterization of Protagoras in the dialogue.

Affairs, e.g. after reporting verbs where the SoA of reporting and the reported SoA do not per se coincide, such as in the following example:

(23) *phēsìn gàr Theódōros | ékhein me soì hómoion*
 phēsìn   gàr   Theódōros   ékhein   me   soì
 saith.PRS.3SG PTCL.for Theodoros.NOM have.PRS.INF I.ACC you.DAT
 hómoion
 like.N.ACC
 'for Theodoros says **that I have a similar [face] as you**' (Pl. *Tht.* 144d9-e1; transl. CF; also cited by Scheppers (2011, p. 196, sect. 10.2.1 (3)))

3.4.2 Vocatives

Vocatives are identified as a separate category of syntactic constructions[29] on the basis of their prototypical morphosyntactic shape, namely that of a noun phrase assigned vocative case, optionally introduced by the vocative particle *ô̄* 'o', cf. (24). In the reference grammar by Kühner and Gerth, vocatives are regarded as constituting autonomous clausal domains irrespective of their position (K/G I, 1955, § 357, no. 1). However, Wackernagel (1892, pp. 424f.), Fraenkel (1965), Bertrand (2010, ch. 4.1.2.2) and Scheppers (2011) worked out that they may take a wide variety of positions with respect to the other clause and it can be assumed that their phonological status varies according to their position and additional factors such as overall speech tempo: either they precede or follow another clause, or they are placed within a clause at a boundary between two Intonational Phrases, or they even behave like a clitic and take second position within an Intonational Phrase (cf. Bertrand, 2010, ch. 4.1.2.2, for statistics concerning Homer as well as the major Classical Greek authors).

(24) *orthôs, éphē, promēthêi, ô̄ Sṓkrates, hypèr emoû*
 orthôs éphē   promēthêi   ô̄   Sṓkrates
 right   say.IPF.3SG use.forethought.PRS.2SG PTCL.O Socrates.VOC
 hypèr emoû
 for   I.GEN
 'You do right, **Socrates**, he said, to be so thoughtful on my behalf' (Pl. *Prt.* 316c5; transl. Lamb)

---

29 For the differentiation between vocative-form, vocative-construction and vocative-utterance, i.e. vocative as a speech act, cf. Ctibor (2017, pp. 46f.).

Despite the ground-breaking study by Fraenkel (1965), the functional range of the vocative construction has not fully been explored yet for Classical Greek. Good starting points for a classification of vocative functions are provided by Hock (2007), who treats post-classical Greek, and Ctibor (2017) on Latin vocatives.[30]—Tentatively summarizing the literature so far, one can say that vocatives may firstly constitute fully-blown Discourse Acts, exerting an illocutionary function of (a) calling for the attention of the intended addressee (CALL); (b) "specifying/confirming the addressee as the addressee" (Ctibor, 2017, p. 53; ADDRESS); (c) expressing the unexpectedness of a given situation (EXCLAMATION). Secondly, vocatives may function as illocutionary Modifiers on another Discourse Act by emphasizing the sincerity and/or commitment of the speaker. Thirdly, vocatives may even emphasize (a part of) the Communicated Content of a Discourse Act (Fraenkel, 1965, p. 30). This is what Scheppers (2011, p. 212) assumes in the case of fronted interrogatives followed by a vocative. Lastly, vocative constructions were used by both Greek and Latin authors as structuring devices marking important points or breaks in the discourse structure, cf. Scheppers (2011, ch. 14.5); Ctibor (2017, sect. 4). In this case, it would be most natural to assume a double function of discourse structuring and CALL/ADDRESS.[31]

3.5 The Phonological Level

As has been illustrated in fig. 9.3 in sect. 3.2 above, FDG-layering within the Phonological Level follows the widely acknowledged prosodic hierarchy (Nespor & Vogel, 1986).[32] Note that not every language makes use of all the possible layers (acknowledged by FDG, 2008, pp. 421f., 428). It is thus a separate task for the linguist to establish the actual prosodic hierarchy effective in the language he or she is interested in. Concerning Ancient Greek, the most extensive, yet still somewhat unsatisfying, treatment of this problem is to be found in Devine and Stephens (1994); for a more recent overview of standing questions in the field cf. the EAGLL-articles Goldstein (2014a,b,c).

The reader may wonder how one might possibly establish the prosodic hierarchy of a dead language. As Goldstein's articles show, some cues are transmitted in our texts, as well as in inscriptional material and musical documents.

---

30 Note that Dickey (1996) takes a sociolinguistic and hence different perspective, investigating different Forms of Address. For a discussion of the two approaches with regard to Latin cf. Ctibor (2017, sect. 7).
31 On possible theoretical implications of this claim cf. Scheppers (2011, p. 330).
32 The FDG-model, however, also allows for recursivity (FDG, 2008, pp. 421f., 428).

One of them, and also the most relevant if it comes to discourse segmentation, is the position of clitics or postpositives.[33]

I will follow an approach wherein the placement of postpositives in Ancient Greek is predominantly prosody-induced (cf. also e.g. Bertrand, 2010; Goldstein, 2010; Goldstein & Haug, 2016;),[34] and postpositives may, conversely, serve as a diagnostic for prosodic boundaries in discourse segmentation (Fraenkel, 1933 and later). This has already been practised for Platonic dialogue and Lysias' speeches in an extensive corpus study by Scheppers (2011).—Scheppers, however, assumed that postpositive placement was governed by phonological rules only at the level of the Intonational Phrase, but by morphosyntactic rules below the Intonational Phrase, cf. Scheppers (2011, sect. 7.1–7.2, 8.3).

My discussion will hence focus on the Intonational Phrase and the Phonological Phrase. My presentation will be guided by the hypothesis that postpositives are not only relevant for the identification of Intonational Phrases, as has been assumed by Scheppers (2011), but also for the identification of Phonological Phrases. This claim is already included in Goldstein (2010, 2016, sect. 3.3) and Bertrand (2010, règle 24, sect. 4.4.1.3), but has not yet been fully integrated into Ancient Greek discourse segmentation practice.

---

33   Ancient Greek *clitics* are generally subdivided into two sets, based on the Hellenistic accentuation system (On Ancient Greek accentuation cf. Allen (1973, ch. 15, 1987, ch. 6); Probert (2006, part I)): Firstly, enclitics in the narrower sense, which do not bear a graphical accent, but may have accentuated counterparts such as enclitic forms of personal pronouns. Secondly, postpositives which likewise cannot appear in first position of a prosodic unit, but do bear a graphical accent—this class mostly consists of connective particles and the modal particle *án*. I will here deviate from this convention and use the term *postpositive* as a cover term for both enclitics and postpositives in the narrower sense, following Dover, 1960, p. 12 (also cf. Scheppers, 2011; Bertrand, 2010, pp. 359f.). This is because (i) postpositive elements have to be opposed to prepositive elements like the article and prepositions; (ii) finer-grained distinctions can be made within the continuum, so to say, of enclitics and postpositives, cf. the classes of postpositives distinguished by Scheppers (2011, p. 57, Table 1.1).—For a critique of the traditional subdivision cf. also Goldstein (2016, pp. 49f.).

34   For a comparison of the prosody-dominant approach to more syntax-based ones cf. Goldstein (2010, ch. 4); especially Goldstein (2014d, sect. 5).

As Goldstein argues, there surely is both a syntactic as well as a prosodic aspect to this problem. The aim of my research is only to help us view the prosodic side in its own right alongside the syntactic one, insofar as this is possible in the case of Ancient Greek. I am convinced that this will help us arrive at more profound conclusions in the end, cf. also the argument in Ladd (2008, p. 289), concerning the determination of the prosodic hierarchy of modern languages.

3.5.1 Intonational Phrase (IntPhr)

In Ancient Greek linguistics just like in FDG, a default correlation is assumed between the Discourse Act and the Intonational Phrase.

Caroline Féry defines the Intonational Phrase in her recent monograph on intonation with reference to Pierrehumbert (1980) as follows:

(25) The ι-phrase is the domain of intonation proper, in the sense that the entire tone sequence of this domain must be well formed in a language-dependent way. Every ι-phrase has at least one pitch accent and one boundary tone, taken from an inventory of pitch accents and an inventory of boundary tones [...]. (Féry, 2017, p. 60)

For Ancient Greek, it is generally assumed that the most salient and prosodically prominent element tends towards first position, serving as a prosodic host for postpositives (cf. e.g. already Wackernagel, 1892, with further refs.; Delbrück, 1900, p. 56; agnostic Goldstein, 2010, ch. 3, sect. 1.4). Based on Scheppers' research, the prosodic structure of an Ancient Greek Intonational Phrase could accordingly be schematized as in (26) below: The Intonational Phrase starts with the Nucleus—i.e. Féry's pitch accent in (25) above as the most prominent element in the Phrase—in first position (P1). More strictly speaking, the Nucleus is constituted by the accented syllable of the word in question. The Nucleus may optionally be preceded by less prominent material, functioning as an Upbeat to the Nucleus (labelled P0 here). Postpositives would take second position (P2) after the Nucleus. Other elements follow inasmuch as they are required; the maximum number of positions within the Intonational Phrase is not *a priori* fixed. According to the phonological model adopted here—but not in Scheppers (2011)—, the Intonational Phrase may additionally exhibit a *Head*, which constitutes an element of secondary prominence within the Phrase. It remains to be seen to what extent Heads coalesce with Féry's boundary tones (cf. the discussion in Ladd, 2008, sect. 8.1.2), in case the model stands the test of more extensive research. What I want to point out here is, first of all, that the assumption of a left-aligned nuclear pitch accent is typologically conspicuous (cf. e.g. Ladd, 2008, p. 131; Féry, 2013, p. 702; Peters, 2014, p. 19;). However, it might be comparable to the situation in Hungarian (cf. Féry, 2013, sect. 4.2.1), a language that has already served as inspiration for the development of information-structural templates like the one established for Ancient Greek.[35]

---

[35] This point is in need of further investigation; cf. Féry's (2013, p. 726) remark on a pos-

(26) INTERNAL STRUCTURE OF AN INTONATIONAL PHRASE IN ANCIENT GREEK[36]
([(0–1) introductive] [prosodically prominent element]—[(0-x) postpositives]—other elements)₁

Upbeat	**Nucleus**		Head	*Post-Head*
P0	P1	P2 [...]	Px	Py

Let's try to apply the scheme to a short stretch of running text from the *Protagoras*. The excerpt in (27) represents one phonological Utterance which falls into three clause-shaped Intonational Phrases. In the first one, Upbeat and Nucleus coalesce, because the combination of the introductive[37] *ei* 'if' and the modal particle *án*, which normally is a postpositive, is here merged into one accent-bearing syllable, which receives maximal prominence according to discourse context: *ā̂n* 'if ever' scopes over both the content of IntPhr a and b. This analysis is supported by the postpositive pronoun *autôi* taking P2 directly after it. The Head is constituted by the accented syllable *-gý-* in *argýrion*; *-rion* forms the Post-Head. The second Intonational Phrase starts with the connective particle *kaí* 'and', which as an introductive takes P0. The first syllable of the verb *peítheis* receives nuclear prominence; the accented syllable in *ekeînon* most probably constitutes a Head to this Intonational Phrase, i.e. a second intonationally prominent point.[38] In the last IntPhr, it seems rather straightforward

---

sible mismatch between Hungarian syntax and prosody, with left-alignment in the syntax, but right-alignment made possible in the prosodic structure by generalized post-nuclear deaccentuation.—As prosody is that linguistic means of expression most directly linked to pragmatics, one should ultimately also consider this question in connection with Bertrand's interpretation of the pre-verbal narrow focus position in Ancient Greek, which, according to him, turns the rest of the clause into a presupposed open proposition (Bertrand, 2010, p. 120), i.e. (I add) into material which is prone to undergo processes of phonological reduction; cf. also the general claim in Scheppers (2011, p. 162) that "the prosodic status of a word crucially involves its pragmatic/cognitive status in any particular context".

36   In the second line, I present my own inversion of the standard scheme as established by the British School in phonology (Palmer, 1922; O'Connor & Arnold, 1973), which assembles Pre-Head—Head—Nucleus—Tail, all optional except for the Nucleus. In the Ancient Greek scheme, the Upbeat is a mirror-image of the Tail.

37   *Introductive* is a cover term introduced by Scheppers to designate (i) relative pronouns and other subordinators, (ii) connective particles marking grammatical coordination, (iii) illocutionary markers, including interrogatives and what has traditionally been called interjections (Scheppers, 2011, pp. 72f.). Introductives may either themselves constitute the Nucleus of their Intonational Phrase, or an Upbeat to the Nucleus (Scheppers, 2011, p. 79).

38   Note that a form of *ekeînos* 'that one' was deliberately chosen over a form of *autós* 'he'.—Cobet believed that *kaì peítheis ekeînon* is a later interpolation based on Pl. *Prt.* 311d3f.

to identify *sophón* as the Head. Telling which would be the nuclear syllable, however, is not as easy. It could either be *sè* 'you', or the accented syllable of the verb *poiései* 'he will make'. The first option seems to correspond to a pragmatic reading more along the lines 'if …, he will make YOU wise, too' (narrow focus reading), while the second option would rather convey 'if …, he WILL make you WISE, too' (polarity focus reading). Maybe even the intonational contour is more complex and both readings merge, yielding an interpretation like 'If […], he'll MAKE YOU WISE, too. It's as easy as that'.[39]—Note that the rhythm changes from an iambic to a trochaic one between *kaì* 'also, too' and *sè* 'you'.

(27) [Young Hippocrates complains to Socrates that Protagoras alone was wise, but not willing to share his wisdom with him:][40]

a. (àn *autôi didôis argýrion*)ᵢ
àn   autôi   didôis   argýrion
if.ever he.M.DAT give.PRS.SUBJ.2SG money.ACC

b. (*kaì* **peítheis** *ekeînon*)ᵢ
kaì   peítheis   ekeînon
and persuade.PRS.SUBJ.2SG that.one.M.ACC

c. (*poié?sei kaì sè? sophón*)ᵢ
poiései   kaì   sè   sophón
make.FUT.3SG PTCL.also you.ACC wise.M.ACC
'If you give him a fee and win him over, he'll make you wise too' (Pl. *Prt.* 310d7f.; transl. Lamb)

---

where, however, we find *autón* instead of *ekeînon*—a fact which Cobet did not discuss. The distribution of anaphoric *autós* and deictic *ekeînos* in complex sentences would form an interesting topic for further study of the relationship between discourse structures and their manifestation in individual linguistic utterances.

39 Note that in the autosegmental-metrical approach to phonology as presented in Ladd, 2008, Nuclei which spread over more than one single syllable, are licensed. However, given the state of research on these questions with regard to Ancient Greek, I think it is better to keep the model simple, and hence easier to test, first, starting out with the hypothesis of a one-to-one correspondence.

40 Following Scheppers (2011), I will mark introductives by red text and postpositives by blue text here and in the remainder of this paper. Intonational Phrases are indicated by round brackets indexed with a subscript Iota as $(xyz)_\iota$; Phonological Phrases are indexed in the same way with a Phi as $(xyz)_\varphi$. Super- and subscript question marks $^?$, $_?$ indicate insecurity, either with regard to segmentation or prosodic interpretation.—A combination of bold print and italics here, but not in the rest of the paper, indicates what I take

3.5.2 On the Ambivalent Status of Ancient Greek *kaí*

The little excerpt presented in (27) also brings us to another important point, namely the ambivalent status of the Ancient Greek particle *kaí*. It may either function (a) as a connective particle 'and', linking two conjuncts of various syntactic size, ranging from sub-constituents to whole sentences, or (b) as a contrastive particle 'also, even'[41] attaching to a single constituent or sub-constituent (cf. the latest accounts by Crespo, 2017a,b). In the first case, it introduces the second conjunct. This is what we find in (27b). In the second case, it precedes the element it modifies, and hence may normally be said to be phonologically prepositive as in (27c) (Scheppers, 2011, pp. 79, 189f.).

(28) CONNECTIVE *kaí*
(*taûta*)₁ (*érese toîs paroûsi*)₁ (***kaì** pántes epḗinesan*)₁
taûta   érese   toîs
this.N.NOM.PL please.AOR.3SG ART.M.DAT.PL
paroûsi   kaì pántes   epḗinesan
be.present.PTCP.PRS.M.DAT.PL and all.M.NOM.PL approve.AOR.3PL
'[His proposal] was approved by the company, **and** they all applauded [it]'
(Pl. *Prt.* 338b2; transl. Lamb)

(29) CONTRASTIVE *kaí*
(*êsan dé tines **kaì tôn epikhōríōn** en tôi khorôi*)₁
êsan   dé   tines   kaì   tôn
be.IPF.3PL PTCL.but INDEF.M.PL PTCL.also ART.M.GEN.PL
epikhōríōn   en tôi   khorôi
of.the.country.GEN.PL in ART.M.DAT.SG choir.DAT
'but **some of our own inhabitants** were **also** dancing attendance' (Pl. *Prt.* 315b2; transl. Lamb modified by CF)

Per Scheppers' account, only in the first case does the appearance of *kaí* have any direct bearing on discourse segmentation: If *kaí* is used as a connective, and the two conjuncts are clausal, sentential or otherwise pragmatically salient and/or phonologically heavy enough to constitute separate Intonational Phrases, then an IntPhr-boundary is assumed before the particle (e.g.

---

to be the Nucleus of the Intonational Phrase; bold print alone the Head in accordance with scheme (26) above.

41 In Dik (1997a, sect. 13.4.2), this was called *expanding* contrastive focus and is here classified as a subtype of Contrast, in line with the discussion presented in sect. 3.3.4.

in (28)). If *kaí* is used as a contrastive particle, it behaves like a prepositive and thus—according to Scheppers—is subject to morphonological rules according to which it merges with the word it modifies, as in (29). Under these circumstances, the particle does not indicate an IntPhr-boundary, unless the combination of *kaí* and the modified word is moved into first position within the relevant IntPhr, e.g. because it bears information-structural narrow focus.

We will see in the next section, however, that *kaí* as a contrastive particle may well indicate a prosodic boundary at the level of the Phonological Phrase.

3.5.3 Phonological Phrase (PhPhr)

The Phonological Phrase normally correlates with a Subact on the Interpersonal Level (FDG, 2008, p. 436); it may be said to roughly equal a syntactic phrasal constituent[42] like a DP (Féry, 2017, pp. 37, 59).

Phonological Phrases in Ancient Greek may accordingly be identified by the presence of an information-structural particle which takes second position within that phrase. This is a stronger formulation of Scheppers' claim that what he calls /q/-postpositive particles actually constitute "focus markers"[43] (Scheppers, 2011, p. 174), and show, as far as word order is concerned, a behavior on a par with that of articles and prepositions. Cf. e.g. the following example involving the particle *ge* which we encountered already in sect. 3.3.4:

(30) ((*sophistḕn dḗ toi*)_φ (*onomázousí ge*)_φ)_ι (*ô Sókrates*)_ι (*tòn ándra eînai*_? *éphē*_?)_ι

sophistḕn	dḕ	toi	onomázousí
sophist.ACC	PTCL.of.course	PTCL.as.you.know	call.PRS.3PL

ge	ô	Sókrates	tòn	ándra	eînai
PTCL.at.least	PTCL.O	Socrates.VOC	ART.M.ACC	man.ACC	be.PRS.INF

éphē
say.IPF.3SG

'"A sophist, to be sure, that's what they say he is, Socrates", he replied' (Pl. *Prt.* 311e4f.)

---

42 This comparison is basically intended as an aid for conceptualization. Note that the existence of a syntactic VP in Ancient Greek has been called into question independently and on the basis of different primary data by Bertrand (2010, sect. 4.4.2.2), Goldstein (2016, sect. 2.2) and Keydana (2018).

43 Scheppers' notion of *focus* is broader than the usual information-structural notion, extending it, as it were, also to the discourse level. For details cf. Scheppers (2011, ch. 10.3, 21.4).

The whole phrase may be moved to the left edge of the overarching Intonational Phrase, if it constitutes the most salient element (Scheppers, 2011, p. 174) and thus is subject to the left-alignment constraint outlined in the preceding section:

(31) (nề tòn Día)₁, ((eis kairón ge)_φ (paratetýkhēken hēmîn en toîs lógois)_φ (Pródikos hóde)_φ)₁
nề   tòn   Día   eis   kairón   ge
PTCL.by ART.M.ACC Zeus.ACC into right.moment.acc PTCL.indeed
paratetýkhēken   hēmîn   en toîs   lógois
happen.to.be.present.PF.3SG we.DAT in ART.M.DAT.PL debate.DAT.PL
Pródikos   hóde
Prodikos.NOM this.here.M.NOM
'Upon my word, how opportunely it has happened that Prodicus is here to join in our discussion' (Pl. *Prt.* 340e8f.; transl. Lamb)

The same basically applies to *kaí* if it functions as a contrastive particle, cf. the following analysis of (29) above:

(32) ((êsan dé tines)_φ (kaì tôn epikhōríōn)_φ (en tôi khorôi)_φ)₁ (Pl. *Prt.* 315b2; = (29) above)

3.6 On the Status of Themes

Having discussed the Interpersonal, the Morphosyntactic and the Phonological Level, we may proceed to those linguistic structures which represent points of tension between the three Levels.

Notorious are extra-clausal constituents (Dik, 1997b, ch. 17) such as Themes. Themes are left-dislocated constituents exerting an information-structural Topic-function for the remainder of the clause. Within the present approach, Themes are conceptualized as constituents exerting the function of a Subact of Reference which have been promoted from the status of a Phonological Phrase to that of an Intonational Phrase (cf. Bertrand, 2010, règle 15).[44]

---

[44] The same reasoning basically applies to Tails, i.e. right-dislocated constituents which are topical with respect to the clause proper. The concrete functional description of Tails as Corrections (FDG, 2008, pp. 55f.) has, however, been challenged by Bertrand (2010, pp. 289–291), and they should be discussed in connection with the functions of subsidiary Discourse Acts in general. I leave this to future work.

(33) [*kaì egṑ*]_THEME [*gignṓskōn autoû tḕn andreíān kaì tḕn ptoíēsin*]_SETTING, *tí oûn soi, ên d' egṓ, toûto? môn tí se adikeî Prōtagórās?*

kaì	egṑ	gignṓskōn		autoû	tḕn	andreíān
and	I.NOM	know.PTCP.PRS.M.NOM		he.M.GEN	ART.F.ACC	bravery.ACC

kaì	tḕn	ptoíēsin	tí		oûn	soi
and	ART.F.ACC	excitement.ACC	INTER.N.NOM		PTCL.so	you.DAT

ên	d'	egṓ	toûto	m=ôn		tí
say.IPF.1SG	PTCL.but	I.NOM	this.N.NOM	NEG=PTCL.then		INTER.N.ACC

se	adikeî	Prōtagórās
you.ACC	do.wrong.PRS.3SG	Protagoras.NOM

'And I, noticing his bravery and his excitement, I said: "Well, what is that to you? Protagoras did not do any harm to you, did he?"' (Pl. *Prt.* 310d2–4)

Bertrand (2010, pp. 277–281) did not identify any significant difference between the information-structural function of Themes and clause-initial Topics. Theme-constructions, however, provide a clearer division between the Reference and the ensuing Ascription of a Property to the evoked referent (Principle of Separation of Reference and Role [Lambrecht, 1994, sect. 4.5.1]; for Greek cf. Bertrand, 2010, pp. 280f., 258; Allan, 2014, p. 189). The data presented in Allan (2014, p. 187, Table 1) suggest that there might be a difference between the two categories concerning the degree of referent accessibility and topic persistence. A more detailed study of this question is still lacking because it would necessitate not only an examination of information structure, but also of discourse structure.[45]—For example, in the passage quoted under (33) above, Socrates for the first time takes charge of the course of the conversation with Hippocrates, who has just recounted in a little monologue how he came to call on Socrates so early in the morning because Protagoras is in town. This shift in perspective is indicated through a Theme-Setting-sequence.

In practice, Themes can best be identified either through intervening participial clauses, which separate them from the matrix clause, like in the previous example, or through ensuing correlative discourse structures, as in the following:

---

[45] Interestingly enough, analyses of co-reference structures in texts as implemented in the Potsdam Commentary Corpus (Stede, 2016), have not been conducted for Ancient Greek. The potential of the annotations provided in the ISAIS-corpus has to my knowledge not yet been fully explored in this regard, either.—This may be due to the fact that the language makes extensive use of subject and hence topic coding via verbal morphology only (subject-/topic drop; cf. the data presented in Lühr, 2015, pp. 212f., Table 3).

(34) [Hippocrates asks Socrates to put in a good word for him with Protagoras:]
 egṑ gàr   **as far as I am concerned myself**
  háma *mèn* *kaì neṓterós eimi,*   for one thing I am too young
  háma *dè*   for another
   oudè heṓrāka Prōtagórān pṓpote I've never yet seen Protagoras
   oud' akḗkoa oudén   nor heard him speak a word

egṑ gàr háma mèn   kaì
I.NOM PTCL.for partly PTCL.on.the.one.hand PTCL.just
neṓterós eimi háma dè   oudè
younger.M.NOM be.PRS.1SG partly PTCL.on.the.other.hand not.only
heṓrāka Prōtagórān pṓpote oud' akḗkoa oudén
see.PF.1SG Protagoras.ACC ever.yet nor hear.PF.1SG nothing.N.ACC
(Pl. *Prt.* 310e3f.; transl. Lamb modified by CF)

As Bertrand (2010, pp. 382f.) already pointed out with regard to example (35) below from Herodotus, we might not always be confronted with a fully-fledged Theme in cases where the expression of the Referential Subact as a separate Intonational Phrase is warranted only by the presence of a postpositive in the clausal remainder. Here, we may well be dealing with what Hannay and Kroon (2005, sect. 6.2.2) called *launching*. They define launching as the "[i]ntonational separation of syntactically integrated elements" (Hannay & Kroon, 2005, p. 110). Recall that, in the present account what is warranted by the position of postpositive *min* in (35), is first of all a prosodic boundary and not necessarily a syntactic one. According to Goldstein's analysis of Herodotean Greek, topicalized phrases generally adjoin to S (Goldstein, 2016, p. 172), i.e. they do not create a new syntactic layer above S different from it. Goldstein (2016, sect. 5.4) suggested that in cases like (35) they serve to license new subjects. They are thus still integrated into the syntactic structure of the matrix clause, while being realized in a separate Intonational Phrase prosodically.[46]

(35) (*kaì hē gynḕ*)₁ (*eporâi min exiónta*)₁
 kaì hē   gynḕ   eporâi   min
 and ART.F.NOM woman.NOM catch.sight.PRS.3SG he.ACC
 exiónta
 go.out.PTCP.PRS.M.ACC
 'and the woman catches sight of him as he is leaving' (Hdt. 1.10.2; text Wilson)

---

46 Note that *kaí* here is generally interpreted as the connective 'and.' For a further discussion of this instance cf. Freiberg (2017[2018], sect. 3.4).

While the whole complex should be investigated more thoroughly, for the time being the concept of launching to my mind helps us get a grasp on instances in Plato, such as (2) presented in sect. 2.2 above. In that case the launching can be put down to the overall more copious speaking style that Socrates adopts as well as the circumstance that he is in fact presenting Hippocrates to the bystanders who newly joined their conversation with Protagoras. We would thus arrive at the segmentation presented in (36). The two Intonational Phrases seem to be linked by a roughly anapaestic distribution of lexical accents. Due to the use of the periphrastic construction with *tynkhánei*, the lexically more important elements *epithȳmíāi* and *synousíās* are both moved towards the right edge of the second Intonational Phrase while the finite verb itself takes first position.[47]

(36) (*Hippokrátēs gàr hóde*)₁ (*tynkhánei en epithȳmíāi ȍn*? *tês sês synousíās*)₁ (*hóti oûn autôi apobḗsetai*)₁ (*eán soi*? *synêi*)₁ (*hēdéōs án phēsi*? *pythésthai*)₁ (Pl. *Prt.* 318a2–4; = (2) above)

4 Analyzing Pl. *Prt.* 309a1–b9

While the previous section provided a systematic overview over the relevant features of Platonic grammar within an FDG-framework, we will now embark on the analysis of the sample passage from the beginning of the *Protagoras* presented in sect. 2.4. Our main focus in sect. 4.2 will lie on the identification of Discourse Acts and on the analysis of their internal structure. Table 9.1 will provide a visualization of the discourse structures that arise from these Discourse Acts in our short excerpt. An exhaustive discussion of these structures would require a separate paper. The annotations presented there thus rather serve as an aid to orientation and test for conclusiveness of the segmentation undertaken in sect. 4.2.

4.1 *Methodological Considerations*

Discourse Acts, as pragmatic units, should first of all be identified on the basis of their communicative import within the relevant discourse context. This is of course an interpretative and hence to a certain extent subjective task.[48] However, it can be guided by formal cues, cf. Scheppers (2011, ch. 10).

---

47 Such examples should thus be taken into account for a further investigation into Ancient Greek alignment constraints as mentioned in sect. 3.5.1 incl. fn. 35.
48 As Stede (2018, p. 186) points out, subjective choices in the interpretation of the status of a certain segment is not problematic, as long as it be principled.

On the Morphosyntactic Level, a Discourse Act very often corresponds to some form of clause. The appearance of a clausal unit in discourse may hence be seen as an indicator of the DA-status of the relevant stretch of discourse. As we saw in sect. 3.4.1, Ancient Greek disposes of finite main and subclauses as well as participial and infinitival clauses. Vocatives (sect. 3.4.2), like other types of parenthetical structures, potentially constitute separate DAs, too. Sect. 3.6 discussed extra-clausal constituents such as Themes and touched upon the fact that correlative discourse structures (parallelisms, contrasts, etc.) likewise suggest DA-boundaries (cf. ex. (34)). In the latter case, clause syntax shades into discourse syntax, as it were.—On the Phonological Level, Discourse Acts find their expression in Intonational Phrases, which in modern languages can be identified on the basis of their bearing a discrete intonational contour, consisting of a nuclear pitch accent and a boundary tone or a Head, i.e. a secondary pitch accent. In Ancient Greek, such intonational contours can be traced indirectly, because nuclear pitch accents, which lie on the most salient element within the Intonational Phrase, tend to align with the left edge of the Phrase, cf. sect. 3.5.1. As was argued in sect. 3.5, Ancient Greek function words show either introductive, prepositive or postpositive behavior, and accordingly as a rule appear in P0, P1, or P2 of an Intonational Phrase or—*pace* Scheppers (2011)—a Phonological Phrase. They thus not only help us identify Discourse Acts, but also Subacts of Reference or Ascription. In FDG terminology, they correspond to Operators or Functions on these Subacts or DAs and thus bring to the fore their particular role within local or global discourse context.

Segmentation of the discourse will be exhaustive, i.e. no stretch of discourse will be left out, and I will start from a strict *maximal segmentation principle*,[49] counting any vocatives or parenthetical structures as separate DAs. As Scheppers (2011, p. 228) notes, the resulting segmentation can be compared "to a rather slow and very deliberate performance" of the passage in question.

4.2 Segmentation and Commentary

The segmentations will be discussed in smaller pieces which correspond to the eight principal Moves discernible in the passage, cf. Table 9.1. Moves there are assigned functions in accordance with the principles of Discourse and Conversation Analysis (Roulet et al., 2001; Schegloff, 2007). Discourse Acts will be abbreviated A. Nuclear (n) and equipollent (e) Discourse Acts are annotated for their Illocutions, while subsidiary (s) Discourse Acts are annotated for their import on the nuclear Discourse Act. Two Discourse Acts are characterized as

---

[49] Scheppers (2011) already used the term, but regularly assumed a merger of vocatives with the Intonational Phrases preceding them.

equipollent, if they are symmetric as to their import to the higher-order discourse structure (cf. FDG, 2008, pp. 52f.). Subscript _d marks discontinuous units. Structure build-up is recursive, i.e. the embedding of e.g. one Move into another is licensed.

M1: request for information by the Friend

> *póthen   ô̂   Sṓkrates   phaínēi*
> whence PTCL.O Socrates.VOC appear.PRS.2SG
> 'Whence, o Socrates, do you come?'

> *ê̂   dêla dè̂   hóti apò kynēgesíou*
> PTCL.is.it clear PTCL.of.course that from hunt.GEN
> 'Surely you come from a hunt'

> *toû   perì   tḕn   Alkibiádou   hṓrān*
> ART.N.GEN about ART.F.ACC Alcibiades.M.GEN prime.F.ACC
> 'that [i.e. the hunt] for Alcibiades' prime'

	Discourse Act + translation	Prosodic criteria	Syntactic criteria
1	*póthen* whence	interrogative in P1	[DA 1+3:] finite main clause
2	*ô̂ Sṓkrates* o Socrates	*ô̂* in P1	vocative
3	*phaínēi* do you come		[cf. DA 1]
4	*ê̂ dêla dè̂* isn't it plain	*ê̂* in P0 *dè̂* in P2	
5	*hóti apò kynēgesíou* that [you come] from a hunt	*hóti* in P0	ellipsis equivalent to a finite subclause
6	*toû perì tḕn Alkibiádou hṓrān* [the hunt] after Alcibiades' prime		apposition

1–3. At the very beginning of the dialogue the Friend asks Socrates where he is coming from. A vocative is inserted into the question. The interrogative *póthen* 'whence' is not only a marker of illocutionary force, but also constitutes that content-element which is focused within the overall clause *póthen* [...] *phaínei*. The vocative thus here exerts the third, emphasizing function mentioned in sect. 3.4.2. The strict maximal segmentation principle suggests treating *ô Sṓkrates* as a separate Discourse Act. Actually, speech rate at the beginning of the *Protagoras* does seem to be rather low, compare e.g. the beginning of the Menexenus, which starts with a call to Menexenus in the nominative instead of the vocative case (cf. K/G I, 1955, § 357, no. 2 incl. fn. 1), and where the verb form *phaínei* is completely omitted:

(37) Pl. *Menex.* 234a1–3; transl. Lamb:

Sōkrátēs	Socrates
ex agorâs ḕ póthen Menéxenos?	From the agora, Menexenus, or where from?
Menéxenos	Menexenus
ex agorâs, ô Sṓkrates, kaì apò toû bouleutēríou.	From the agora, o Socrates, and the Council Chamber.

ex   agorâs   ḕ   póthen   Menéxenos
out.of agora.GEN or   whence   Menexenos.NOM

ex   agorâs   ô   Sṓkrates   kaì   apò   toû
out.of agora.GEN PTCL.O Socrates.VOC and   from   ART.N.GEN
bouleutēríou
council.chamber.GEN

4–6. DA 4 constitutes an epistemic marker on the ensuing DAs 5–6, which may be said to syntactically depend from it. Development of such short phrases as *ê dêla dḗ* 'of course it is clear' into a single Modifier, which would not receive DA-status anymore, is likely, and the medieval manuscripts often do not separate *dêla* and *dḗ* but write *dēladḗ*. Note, however, that *ê dêla dḗ* here exploits the basic objective epistemic meaning of simple *dêla dḗ*, which also exists in Plato (cf. e.g. Pl. *Prt.* 311c8), for rhetorical purposes: The mode of reasoning here is not deduction, but abduction (cf. also Pl. *Menex.* 234a4). The meaning of *ê dêla dḗ* is thus still compositional. The particle *ē* should be accented with a circumflex here, because it rather indicates polarity focus[50] than expressing disjunction

---

50   Polarity focus is a subtype of contrastive focus targeting the truth value of the whole proposition (cf. Stommel, 2012, p. 27). For a treatment of polarity focus in Ancient Greek cf. Bertrand (2010, pp. 150–153) and Goldstein (2013).

('or') as in the above example from the *Menexenus*. The two meanings are traditionally assigned to two different lexical entries, distinguished by accentuation, although realization of the accent might not perfectly correlate with semantics, being influenced by additional prosodic factors. My interpretation thus necessitates a change in the text, as Gerard Boter (p.c.) pointed out to me, cf. fn. 13 in sect. 2.4.

Based on the findings by Bakker (2009) concerning articulation of noun phrases in Herodotus, it seems likely that *toû perì tḕn Alkibiádou hṓrān* is an apposition expressed in a separate Discourse Act, rather than a modifier within a complex prepositional phrase **apò kynēgesíou toû perì tḕn Alkibiádou hṓrān*. The main reason for this is that *apò kynēgesíou* is not referential, but ascriptive (cf. Devine & Stephens, 2000, pp. 250–258; Bakker, 2009, pp. 189 ff.). If we wanted to fully spell out the syntax of the elliptic DA 5, we would arrive at a structure **hóti phaínēi apò kynēgesíou* 'that you are coming from a hunt' = 'that you have been hunting'. For a similar type of structure compare German *Er kommt von Arbeit* as a reduced form of *Er kommt von der Arbeit*, where *Arbeit* is not referential, either, and English *I went to work by bus*, where neither *work* nor *bus* are referential (cf. FDG, 2008, p. 114, ex. (293)–(295)).—This analysis is also supported by the status of both terms within the local and global discourse structure: *apò kynēgesíou* 'Surely, you're coming from a hunt …' on the one hand functions as a presentative construction leading up to the introduction of Alcibiades, about whom the Friend wants to talk to Socrates. On the most local level of the discourse, DA 5 is pragmatically subordinate to DA 6. On the other hand, Socrates will refute at the end of our excerpt (DAs 29–31) that he has been chasing after Alcibiades, quite to the contrary: He did not pay him any attention at all, which suggests that DA 5 might be more important to the overall structure than DA 6.[51] Assuming an equiordination of the two Discourse Acts thus balances these two possible interpretations which are not mutually exclusive, but come to play only at different hierarchical levels of the discourse structure.

M2: appeal by the Friend

kaì   mḗn   moi   kaì   próiēn
PTCL.also PTCL.verily I.DAT PTCL.just the.other.day
idónti
see.PTCP.AOR.M.DAT
'to me as well, when I saw him just the other day'

---

[51] Note that in the *Sophista*, the hunting style of a lover (here attributed to Socrates) and that of a sophist turn out to be quite the opposite (Pl. *Soph.* 222d3–223a11).

kalòs   mèn   ephaíneto   anḕr
beautiful.M.NOM PTCL.on.the.one.hand seem.IMPF.3SG man.NOM
éti
ADV.still
'he seemed still beautiful as a man'

anḕr   méntoi   ô̂   Sṓkrates
man.NOM PTCL.yet PTCL.o Socrates.VOC
'but yet [he seemed] a man'

hṓs ge   en autoîs   hēmîn   eirêsthai
how PTCL.at.least in self.M.DAT.PL we.DAT say.INF.PF.MP
'so to say between us'

kaì   pṓgōnos   ḗdē   hypopimplámenos
PTCL.also beard.GEN already begin.to.have.PTCP.PRS.MP.NOM
'also growing a beard already'

	Discourse Act + translation	Prosodic criteria	Syntactic criteria
7	*kaì mḗn moi* and yet, to me	*mḗn moi* in P2	Theme
8	*kaì próiēn idónti* seeing [him] just the other day		participial clause Setting
9	*kalòs mèn ephaíneto anḕr éti* he seemed still beautiful as a man	focal *kalós* left-aligned *mén* in P2	finite main clause
10	*anḕr méntoi* but yet a man	*méntoi* in P2	holophrastic main clause
11	*ô̂ Sṓkrates* o Socrates	*ô̂* in P1	vocative
12	*hṓs g' en autoîs hēmîn eirêsthai* as to say between us	*hṓs* in P1	infinitival clause Parenthesis
13	*kaì pṓgōnos ḗdē hypopimplámenos* with a beard already growing, too		participial clause Afterthought

7–9. DAS 7–9 instantiate the pattern [Theme]—[participial Setting][52]—[main clause]. They may thus be discerned from each other on syntactic-pragmatic grounds. Additionally, we encounter the postpositive particles *mén* in DA 7 and *mén* in DA 9 as indicators of prosodic boundaries. *kaí* functions as a contrastive particle in both DAs 7 and 8, and thus does not indicate IntPhr-level segmentation. However, it might signal that DA 8 is constituted by two Phonological Phrases: ((*kaì próiēn*)_φ (*idónti*)_φ)_ι.

DA 9 shows an interesting internal make-up: The focal element *kalós* is placed at the left edge of the Intonational Phrase and bears nuclear stress. Its head noun *anḗr* only appears after the verb because, as a Subact of Reference, it pertains to Alcibiades who has already been activated in the previous discourse. We are thus dealing with a split-NP or *hyperbaton* (on the exact type cf. Bertrand, 2010, pp. 392–394). Yet the construction in this particular case is also reminiscent of an *antitopic* in the sense of Lambrecht (1994, pp. 202–205), as is evidenced by Bekker's conjecture *hanḕr* 'the man'.[53] Plato certainly plays on this particular presuppositional structure, since the reference to Alcibiades as a 'man' will become the central claim of the Friend in the ensuing discourse units. One might, therefore, be tempted to posit another prosodic boundary before *anḗr*, at least at the level of a Phonological Phrase, instead of merging it with the verb *ephaíneto*, as would normally be predicted from Bertrand's (2010, pp. 379f.) and Goldstein's (2016, ch. 6) accounts.

(38) ((*kalòs mèn*)_φ (*ephaíneto*)_φ (*anḕr éti*)_φ/ι)_ι
 Split-NP reading: Beautiful he still seemed as a man
 Antitopic reading: Beautiful he seemed, as a/the man still

10–13. The left boundary of DA 10 is secured by the appearance of *méntoi* in second position. *méntoi* here correlates with *mén*, indicating the contrast between the two DAs (cf. Crepaldi, 2018, pp. 105f.). To the vocative in DA 11, the maximal

---

52   Note that the participle in this case cannot anaphorically refer to any SoA mentioned in the previous discourse. The Setting SoA of seeing Alcibiades is therefore somewhat atypically expressed by an aorist participle which can serve to set a definite point in the past as the new reference time for the next SoA, cf. Bary & Haug (2011); Scheppers (2011, p. 406 incl. fn. 383); Allan (2014, p. 184 incl. fn. 5), with further refs.

53   For antitopics in Homeric Greek cf. Bertrand (2010, ch. 3.4.2).
    As far as our passage at hand is concerned, note that Athenaeus' version, were we find *ho anḕr* 'the man' is not a word by word quote from Plato, but a mere paraphrase and thus cannot be taken to support Bekker's conjecture.—In order to find a principled solution to this problem, comparable but distinct cases like Pl. *Prt*. 315e7f. and Pl. *Phd*. 58e3 should be taken into account.

segmentation principle applies again. This vocative functions as an illocutionary Modifier on the preceding DA (cf. sect. 3.3.4, 3.4.2 above). DA 12 has a parenthetical flavor (cf. the common formula *hṓs épos eipeîn* 'as it were, so to say'). It is constituted by an infinitival clause introduced by the conjunction *hṓs* in P1. DA 13 is a participial subclause which presents an argument in favor of the claim put forward by the Friend in DA 10. Following Scheppers (2011, p. 407) I refer to such instances as Afterthoughts. The particle *kaì* again is an Operator of Contrast, but seems to scope over the whole participial clause.

M3: Socrates' non-compliance

> *eîta   tí   toûto*
> then   INTER.N.NOM   this.N.NOM
> 'now, what's that?'
>
> *ou   sỳ   méntoi   Homḗrou   epainétēs   eî*
> NEG   you.NOM PTCL.why? Homer.GEN   praiser.NOM   be.PRS.2SG
> 'aren't you a supporter of Homer?'
>
> *hòs   éphē*
> REL.M.NOM   say.IMPF.3SG
> 'who [i.e. Homer] said'
>
> *khariestátēn   hḗbēn   eînai   toû*
> most.charming.F.ACC   youthful.prime.ACC be.PRS.INF ART.M.GEN
> *hypēnḗtou*
> youth.with.first.beard.GEN
> 'that the most charming prime is that of a youth just getting a beard'
>
> *hḕn   nŷn Alkibiádēs   ékhei*
> REL.F.ACC now Alcibiades.NOM   have.PRS.3SG
> 'which [i.e. prime] now Alcibiades is in'

Discourse Act + translation	Prosodic criteria	Syntactic criteria
14 *eîta tí toûto* now, what's that	*eîta tí* in P1	holophrastic main clause

(*cont.*)

Discourse Act + translation	Prosodic criteria	Syntactic criteria
15 *ou sỳ méntoi Homérou epainétēs eî* aren't you a supporter of Homer	*ou* in P0/P1 *méntoi* in P2	finite main clause
16 *hòs éphē* who said	*hós* in P1	relative clause
17 *khariestátēn hḗbēn eînai toû hypēnḗtou* [that] the most charming prime was that of the first beard	*khariestátēn* left-aligned	infinitival complement clause
18 *hèn nŷn Alkibiádēs ékhei* which Alcibiades now possesses	*hḗn* in P1	relative clause

14–18. The leftward prosodic boundary of DA 14 is indicated by the two introductives *eîta* and *tí*, the latter functioning as an interrogative. The rightward boundary is evidenced by the presence of the negation *ou* in P0/P1 of the next DA as well as *méntoi* in P2.

DA 14 bears EXCLAMATIVE Illocution. As was stated in sect. 3.3.2, EXCLAMATIVES are interactional Discourse Acts which either do not contain any Communicated and Propositional Content at all, or otherwise only presuppose it as known to the Addressee (cf. FDG, 2008, pp. 73, 77f., who speak of MIRATIVES). In our case, however, Socrates assumes that the Friend does not share his presupposition and thus spells it out in DAs 15–18. This is why the exclamative Discourse Act 14 may also be interpreted as an Illocutionary Modifier on the ensuing DA 15. For an example of a solitary exclamative cf. Men. *Sam.* 589–596; for a more detailed treatment of Ancient Greek exclamatives cf. Biraud and Faure (2015).

DA 15 actually might very well represent a case of launching (cf. sect. 3.6 above). Whether forms of the copula are to be regarded as postpositive or not, is still a matter of debate. Scheppers' data did not yield any greater P2-tendency for *eimí* 'to be' than for other Ancient Greek verbs (cf. Scheppers, 2011, sect. 5.2.1). However, the distribution of this DA over two Intonational Phrases as presented in (39) below might be licensed by the local discourse structure: DA 16–18 depend on the Subact of Reference evoking Homer in DA 15. Additionally, information structure here is reversed: In a declarative clause, *sý* would constitute the Topic. However, in the interrogative, it is in Focus. What Socrates wants to know is whether his Friend is an admirer of Homer or not; *méntoi* indicates that he expected him to be one. *Homérou epainétēs eî* is presupposed as an open proposition by *ou sỳ méntoi* and serves as its indirect Topic (Bertrand, 2010, p. 342). A similar case can be found in the *Hippias Minor*, cf. (40).[54]

(39) (*ou sỳ méntoi*)₁ (*Homérou epainétēs eî*)₁

(40) *lége dé moi, ô Hippíā, ou sỳ méntoi émpeiros eî logismôn kaì logistikês*
       lége   dé   moi ô   Hippíā   ou   sỳ
       tell.PRS.IMP.2SG PTCL.then I.DAT PTCL.O Hippias.VOC NEG you.NOM
       méntoi   émpeiros   eî   logismôn   kaì
       PTCL.surely practised.NOM   be.PRS.2SG calculation.GEN.PL and
       logistikês
       arithmetic.GEN
       'Tell me, then, Hippias, **are you not** skillful in arithmetical calculations?'
       (Pl. *Hp. mi.* 366c5f.; transl. Lamb)

DAS 16 and 18 constitute non-restrictive relative clauses (NRRCS), with *hòs éphē khariestátēn hḗbēn eînai toû hypēnḗtou* consisting of a matrix verb of saying/reporting and a dependent AcI-construction. Appended NRRCS are regarded as autonomous EDUs cross-linguistically (cf. e.g. Stede, 2018, p. 152).[55] DA 17 basically represents a copular clause which is dependent on DA 16 in terms of morphosyntax. Its information structure, however, is complex because a predicational reading ('The prime of the first beard is THE MOST CHARMING ONE.') and a specificational reading ('The most charming prime is THE ONE OF THE FIRST BEARD.') overlap (cf. Declerck, 1988). *khariestátēn* as the Focus of the predicational reading is moved to the left edge of the corresponding Intonational Phrase; *toû hypēnḗtou* as the Focus of the specificational reading to the right. *hḗbēn eînai* is presupposed in both readings and thus takes the pragmatically and prosodically weaker position in between the two. The internal structure of the corresponding Intonational Phrase might thus be schematized as follows:

---

54 Note that according to a TLG-search *ou sỳ méntoi* represents a rather infrequent pattern *ou ... méntoi*. Much more often we encounter structures of the type *ou méntoi ... ge*, where *méntoi* operates on the DA- or Illocutionary Layer, while *ge* operates on the Subact of Reference (cf. Allan, 2017a, p. 290, ex. (8), (9a,b)). The exact functional distribution of the two patterns is in need of further exploration.

55 Note that DAS 15–18 are annotated as equipollent in Table 9.1, while general FDG-theory assumes a relationship of "dependence between two Nuclear Discourse Acts" (FDG, 2008, p. 57) between NRRCS and the main clause they are attached to. For a differentiated view cf. Jasinskaja and Poschmann, this volume.

(41) ((*khariestátēn*)₍φ₎ (*hḗbēn eînai*)₍φ₎ (*toû hypēnḗtou*)₍φ₎)₍ι₎

As far as the progression of the discussion is concerned, note that Socrates actually does not take a stance on whether Alcibiades is already a man or still a youth, because Hom. *Od.* 10.278 f., to which he seems to be most directly alluding, uses both terms and says that Hermes was arriving *neēníēi andrì eoikṓs*, i.e. 'like a young man', also cf. Pl. *Prt.* 316a4f., where Socrates says that he only acknowledges Alcibiades' beauty because he follows the judgement of his Friend.

M4 + M5: Return to his original request and additional request by the Friend

tí	*oûn*	*tà*	*nŷn*	*ề*	*par'*
INTER.N.NOM	PTCL.therefore	ART.N.ACC.PL[56]	now	PART.is.it	from

ekeínou   phaínēi
that.one.M.GEN appear.PRS.2SG
'So what now? Do you come from him [i.e. Alcibiades]?'

kaì	*pỗs*	*prós*	*se*	*ho*	*neāníās*
and	INTER.how	towards	you.ACC	ART.M.NOM	youth.NOM

diákeitai
to.be.disposed.PRS.3SG
'and how is the young man disposed towards you?'

	Discourse Act + translation	Prosodic criteria	Syntactic criteria
19	*tí oûn tà nŷn* so what now	*tí* in P1 *oûn* in P2	elliptic main clause
20	*ề par' ekeínou phaínēi* do you come from him	*ề* in P1	finite main clause
21	*kaì pỗs prós se ho neāníās diákeitai* and how is the young man disposed towards you	connective *kaí* in P0 *pỗs* in P1	finite main clause

---

56 In Ancient Greek, it was possible to combine any kind of lexeme with a neuter article in order to create a noun from it.

19–21. The prosodic boundary between DAs 18 and 19 is warranted by the presence of the interrogative *tí* in P1, and of *oûn* in P2. Note that from a syntactic point of view, DA 19 represents an elliptic main clause. Its pragmatic functions nevertheless are clearly discernible within the discourse context as marking the Friend's indignance about Socrates' objection and his wish to take up again a thread of discourse started earlier. As it also constitutes an EXCLAMATIVE, the same reasoning as to its DA-status applies as with DA 14.

DA 20 is an interrogative clause headed by the particle *ê* in first position, which, like in DA 4, indicates polarity focus. DA 21 constitutes an interrogative clause with connective *kaí* in P0, preceding the interrogative *pôs* 'how' in P1. Prosodically, *kaí* thus constitutes the Upbeat of the Intonational Phrase, and *pôs* its Nucleus. *pôs* is the pragmatically most salient element; it combines the indication of the Illocution with information-structural Focus Function. According to Bertrand (2010, ch. 4.3) interrogative foci precede the clause proper and may constitute their own Intonational Phrase. As no further segmentation cues are available here, I posit one complex Intonational Phrase which subdivides into three Phonological Phrases:

(42) ((*kaì pôs prós se*)_φ (*ho neāníās*)_φ (*diákeitai*)_φ)_ι

prós se constitutes a Topic and is the pragmatically weakest element in the DA. It is thus prone to merge with the much more prominent *pôs*. *ho neāníās* seems to combine Topic and Focus function. The Friend here not just continues referring to Alcibiades from the preceding DA, but uses the subject switch to replace his earlier Ascription *anḗr* 'man' (DA 10) by the new Ascription *neāníās* 'youth'. He thereby complies with Socrates' objection that young men who grow their first beard are the most beautiful and closes the embedded exchange started with his appeal in M2, cf. Goldstein's (2010, pp. 159f.) account of presupposition cancelling with fronted interrogatives. Whether this indicates a contemptuous overtone for this Intonational Phrase is, however, not clear.

M6 + M7: Socrates' replies to M4 + M5

eû   émoi=ge   édoxen
well I.DAT=PTCL.at.least seem.AOR.3SG
'[He is] well [disposed towards me], it seemed to me at least'

oukh hḗkista dè   kaì   têi   nŷn hēmérāi
NEG least   PTCL.but[57] PTCL.also ART.F.DAT now day.DAT
'not least also today'

kaì   gàr   pollà hypèr emoû eîpe
PTCL.also PTCL.for much over I.GEN say.AOR.3SG
boēthôn   emoí
help.PTCP.PRS.NOM I.DAT
'for he also said much in my favor, helping me [in a discussion]'

kaì oûn   kaì   árti   ap' ekeínou   érkhomai
and PTCL.so PTCL.also just.now from that.one.M.GEN come.PRS1SG
'and indeed, I have only just left him'

	Discourse Act + translation	Prosodic criteria	Syntactic criteria
22	*eû* well		elliptic main clause
23	*émoige édoxen* it seemed to me at least		finite main clause Parenthesis
24	*oukh hḗkista dè kaì têi nŷn hēmérāi* not least also today	*oukh* in P0 *dé* in P2	elliptic main clause
25	*kaì gàr pollà hypèr emoû eîpe* for he also said much in my favour	*gár* in P2	finite main clause
26	*boēthôn emoí* supporting me		participial clause
27	*kaì oûn kaì árti ap' ekeínou érkhomai* and indeed, I have only just left him	connective *kaí* in P1 *oûn* in P2	finite main clause

22–27. DA 22 is a holophrastic expression which exactly provides the amount of information asked for in the preceding DA 21 = M 5. *émoige édoxen* is a typical (*quasi-*)*parenthetical expression* in the sense of Scheppers (2011). According to

---

57   *dé* in such instances marks the transition to the next topic or thought, cf. Bakker (1993).

the maximal segmentation principle, we treat it as a separate Discourse Act. The combination of the particle *ge*, which was discussed in sect. 3.3.4 above, and the emphatic dative personal pronoun *emoí* is generally taken to be lexicalized, cf. the retraction of the accent: *emoí ge* vs. *émoige*.

DA 24 is another ellipsis elaborating on DA 22. It displays the alternative form *oukh* of the negation *ou*, as an assimilation to the following aspirated *hḗkista*, in first position, and the particle *dé* in second position. *kaì têi nŷn hēmérāi* does not constitute a separate Discourse Act; *kaí* here only is introducing a second Subact within DA 24. The internal prosodic structure of DA 24 may thus be schematized as in (43) below.

(43) ((*oukh hḗkista dè*)_φ (*kaì têi nŷn hēmérāi*)_φ)_ι

In DA 25, *kaí* likewise functions as an Operator of Contrast. However, the postpositive particle *gár* secures an IntPhr-boundary before it. DA 26 is a participial clause which elaborates on the exact way in which Alcibiades spoke in favor of Socrates: *boēthôn emoí* 'supporting me in a discussion'. Formally, the presence of the additional personal pronoun *emoí*, which is triggered by the fact that the participial verb requires a different case-assignment than the matrix verb, makes it clear that we have a second anaphoric reference to the person of Socrates. This seems to be an additional criterion in favor of positing an EDU-boundary before the participle here. Note that we find the emphatic form in both cases (*emoû* vs. clitic *mou; emoí* vs. clitic *moi*).

In DA 27 we encounter connective *kaí* in P1 preceding *oûn* in P2. The following *kaí* is again an instance of the contrastive particle which operates at the level of a Phonological Phrase and might suggest the following subdivision of the overall Intonational Phrase:

(44) ((*kaì oûn*)_φ (*kaì árti*)_φ (*ap' ekeínou*)_φ (*érkhomai*)_φ)_ι

M8: Socrates' objection against M1 and topic shift

> *átopon   méntoi   tí   soi   ethélō*
> out.of.place.N.ACC PTCL.yet INDEF.N.ACC you.DAT want.PRS.1SG
> *eipeîn*
> say.AOR.INF
> 'yet I want to tell you something strange/different'

paróntos gàr ekeínou
be.present.PTCP.PRS.M.GEN PTCL.for that.one.M.GEN
'for although he was present'

oúte proseîkhon tòn noûn
neither hold.to.IMPF.1SG ART.M.ACC mind.ACC.SG
'not only did I pay no attention to him'

epelanthanómēn te autoû thamá
forget.IMPF.1SG and he.M.GEN often
'but often I forgot about him altogether'

	Discourse Act + translation	Prosodic criteria	Syntactic criteria
28	*átopon méntoi tí soi ethélō eipeîn* yet I want to tell you something strange	*méntoi, ti,* and *soi* in P2	finite main clause
29	*paróntos gàr ekeínou* although he was present	*gár* in P2	participial clause
30	*oúte proseîkhon tòn noûn* not only did I pay no attention to him	*oúte* in P1	finite main clause
31	*epelanthanómēn te autoû thamá* but I often forgot about him altogether	*te* and *autoû* in P2	finite main clause

28–31. In DA 28 we find with *méntoi tí soi* three postpositives forming a chain in P2. *méntoi* here indicates the Topic-shift that takes place between DAS 27 and 28. *ti* syntactically constitutes the head of a noun phrase *átopón ti* 'something strange/different'. Given examples such as (46) below, where the appearance of the modal particle *án* indicates an IntPhr-boundary before *hēdéōs*, we may extrapolate a prosodic boundary also in cases like DA 28. However, I believe that there is a slight difference between the two because in DA 28, *átopon méntoi tí* would already have been completely sufficient in order to express Socrates' communicative intention. *soi ethélō eipeîn* thus seems to be presupposed rather than constituting a fully-fledged separate Intonational Phrase, cf. (45) below.— Note that *hē̂mîn* in (46) is a non-argument dative pronoun, which can easily be said to merge with the core NP into a larger one, while *soi* in DA 28 represented in (45) is an argument dative pronoun 'I want to tell you [...]'. The direction of clisis for *soi* is not entirely clear.⁵⁸

(45) ((*átopon méntoi tí*)_φ (*soi ethélō eipeîn*)_φ)_ι

(46) (*toû méntoi xénou hēmîn*)_ι (*hēdéōs àn pynthanoímēn*)_ι
    toû   méntoi   xénou   hēmîn   hēdéōs àn
    ART.M.GEN PTCL.however stranger.GEN we.DAT gladly PTCL.possibly
    pynthanoímēn
    learn.PRS.OPT.1SG
    'but from our stranger here, I would like to find out [...]' (Pl. *Sph.* 216d2f.; segmentation and transl. Scheppers, 2011, p. 374)

DA 28 functions as a metadiscoursive Marker scoping over the next three Discourse Acts. These display one of the very pervasive patterns of Ancient Greek discourse structure: A genitive absolute representing a Setting (DA 29) precedes two DAs verbalizing two coordinated Events. The appearance of the particle *te* in both DAs 30 and 31 as well as the presence of a negation in P1 of DA 30 further vouch for the segmentation proposed here. Last but not least consider as a segmentation criterion enclitic *autoû* following *te* in DA 31.⁵⁹ Correlative units introduced by *oúte ... te ...* 'not only ..., ... even ...' express a climax, cf. Denyer ad loc.

With M8, Socrates finally rejects the implicature that the Friend made in M1, namely that Socrates was particularly interested in Alcibiades, and prepares for the topic shift in the conversation from his alleged relationship with Alcibiades to his encounter with Protagoras.

---

58 On the possibility of proclitic pronouns in Classical Attic Greek cf. Pardal Padín (2015, 2017, part IV).

59 A point which might deserve further investigation is that we find an anaphoric pronoun *autoû* in DA 31, but not in DA 30. This suggests that for DA 30, the reference to Alcibiades performed in DA 29 by means of the genitive of the demonstrative pronoun *ekeînos* 'that one' is still operative. This, however, would run counter to the discourse structure as expressed by verbal morphosyntax, i.e. the genitive absolute (DA 29) as a Setting scoping over the two finite main clauses in DAs 30 and 31. From a morphosyntactic point of view, it is interesting to note that *prosékhō tòn noûn* requires a dative object or a prepositional object of the form *prós* + Acc/Dat (LSJ s.v. *prosékhō* no. 3). This means that the elliptical expression in DA 30 actually requires an underlying case assignment which differs from that of the genitive *ekeínou* in DA 29, while *autoû* in DA 31 performs another overt case shift, returning to the genitive.

TABLE 9.1   Discourse structure of Pl. *Prt.* 309a1–b9

				Hetaîros
1	M1: request for information	Mn: question	An_d: INTER-CONTENT_d	*póthen,*
2			As: interactional marker	*ô Sṓkrates,*
3			An_d: INTER-CONTENT_d	*phaínēi?*
4		Mn: reply	As: epistemic marker	*ê dêla dè*
5			Ae: DECL	*hóti apò kynēgesíou*
6			Ae: DECL	*toû perì tḕn Alkibiádou hṓrān*
7		M2: appeal	As: Theme	*kaì mḗn moi*
8			As: Setting	*kaì próiēn idónti*
9			Ae: DECL/contrastive	*kalòs mèn ephaíneto anḕr éti,*
10			Ae: DECL/contrastive	*anḕr méntoi,*
11			As: interactional marker	*ô Sṓkrates,*
12			As: mitigation	*hṓs g' en autoîs hēmîn eirêsthai,*
13			As: argument	*kaì pṓgōnos ḗdē hypopimplámenos.*
				Sōkrátēs
14		M3: non-compliance	As: exclamation	*eîta tí toûto?*
15			Ae: INTER-POLAR	*ou sỳ méntoi Homḗrou epainétēs eî,*
16				*hòs éphē*
17			Ae: DECL	*khariestátēn hḗbēn eînai toû hypēnḗtou,*
18			Ae: DECL	*hḕn nŷn Alkibiádēs ékhei?*
				Hetaîros
19	M4: repetition M1 = request for information	M4: counter-question	As: exclamation	*tí oûn tà nŷn?*
20			An: INTER-POLAR	*ê par' ekeínou phaínēi?*
21	M5: additional request for information	M5: compliance	An: INTER-CONTENT	*kaì pôs prós se ho neānías diákeitai?*
				Sōkrátēs
22	M6: reply to M5	An: DECL	An: DECL	*eû,*
23			As: epistemic marker	*émoige édoxen,*
24			An: DECL	*oukh hḗkista dè kaì têi nŷn hēmérāi:*
25		Ms: statement	As: evidence	An: assertion	*kaì gàr pollà hypèr emoû eîpe*
26				As: elaboration	*boēthôn emoí,*
27	M7: reply to M4	An: DECL		*kaì oûn kaì árti ap' ekeínou érkhomai.*
28	M8: objection against the implicature formulated in M1	As: structural marker		*átopon méntoi tí soi ethélō eipeîn:*
29		Mn: statement	As: Setting	*paróntos gàr ekeínou,*
30			Ae: DECL	*oúte proseîkhon tòn noûn,*
31			Ae: DECL	*epelanthanómēn te autoû thamá.*

5 Conclusion

This study is concerned with Platonic dialogue, a particularly complex and intriguing discourse type which has been influencing Western European thinkers and writers ever since. In particular, it focuses on the *Protagoras*, one of the earlier dialogues.

It has been conceived above all as a practical contribution to discourse segmentation in Ancient Greek as well as to the systematic study of the relationship between the form of concrete linguistic utterances and the discourse structures they are embedded in. Its guiding principle has been the titular question: *What's in an Act?*. It may be spelled out in three sub-questions: (i) How can we define an Elementary Discourse Unit (EDU) in Platonic dialogue? (ii) Which linguistic shapes can this EDU take? (iii) Which theoretical equipment do we need in order to reflect in our analyses how different levels of language—pragmatics, (semantics,) syntax, and phonology—contribute to shaping EDUs in discourse?

Methodologically, the study proceeded in two ways: First of all by a systematic review of Ancient Greek grammar as represented in the Platonic dialogues and especially the *Protagoras* (sect. 3). Inspired by earlier work in Ancient Greek linguistics, the framework for this review was provided by Functional Discourse Grammar (FDG). In this framework, the EDU is conceptualized primarily as a Discourse Act, i.e. the smallest step a language producer takes in order to achieve his communicative goal (cf. Kroon, 1995, p. 65), which is standardly expressed by a clause on the Morphosyntactic Level, and by an Intonational Phrase on the Phonological Level. Within the FDG-framework, a further correspondence between Subacts of Reference or Ascription and Phonological Phrases could be motivated for Ancient Greek *pace* Scheppers, 2011. Sect. 3.6 introduced the concept of launching (Hannay & Kroon, 2005) as a form of pragmatics-syntax-phonology mismatch, where one Discourse Act corresponds to one clausal unit in the syntax, but two Intonational Phrases in phonology.—Due to the fresh typological perspective on Ancient Greek grammar, a surprising research gap could be identified as concerns Illocutions in sect. 3.3.2, although these did not represent the main focus of the study.

The grammatical review prepared for a detailed study of Discourse Acts in Pl. *Prt.* 309a1–b9, resulting in a linguistic commentary on that passage (sect. 4). Prosodic segmentation at the Layer of the Phonological Phrase could be motivated for DA 17 *khariestátēn hḗbēn eînai toû hypēnḗtou*, DA 24 *oukh hḗkista dè kaì têi nŷn hēmérāi*, DA 27 *kaì oûn kaì árti ap᾽ ekeínou érkhomai* as well as DA 28 *átopon méntoi tí soi ethélō eipeîn*, and seems likely regarding DA 21 *kaì pỗs prós se ho neānías diákeitai* and DA 9 *kalòs mèn ephaíneto anḕr éti*. A case of launching was identified in DA 15 *ou sỳ méntoi Homérou epainétēs eî.*—Regarding the phrase ê̓ dêla dè (DA 4) in this and similar passages, it was proposed to read epexegetic ἦ [ê̓] (LSJ s.v. ἦ, Adv. II 1 a) instead of disjunctive ἤ [é̓] (LSJ s.v. ἤ (A)). The question of accentuation of the particle, however, needs to be investigated separately.

On the whole, the study thus represents a first step towards continuing and refining Scheppers' research on discourse segmentation and coherence in Platonic dialogue by laying more emphasis on the investigation of the repercussions of discourse structure on the linguistic features of individual Discourse Acts, a research avenue explicitly pointed out by Scheppers himself (Scheppers, 2011, p. 401). By showing that the beginning of the *Protagoras* as an earlier Platonic dialogue also lends itself to an analysis into Discourse Acts that correspond to Intonational Phrases, the paper in the end also is an important contribution to the orality approach towards Ancient Greek discourses in general (cf. Slings, 1992; Bakker, 1997) and complements recent work by Verano (2018) on the *Apology*, which also is classified as one of the early dialogues, but actually represents a fictitious defense speech and not a dialogue proper. Methodologically, it paves the way for a balanced study of both the oral as well as the literate features of Platonic dialogue (cf. sect. 2.2) and thus for a more thorough linguistic understanding and appreciation of this unique discourse type.

Acknowledgements

My warmest thanks go to Barbara Hemforth, Anke Holler, Katja Suckow, and Israel de la Fuente for organizing the workshop "Information Structuring in Discourse" and to the latter three for editing these proceedings, as well as Martin Kümmel for originally drawing my attention to the workshop. I also want to express my gratitude to Rutger Allan and Gerard Boter for their intensive and well-informed support in preparing the original talk during a research stay at VU Amsterdam funded by the *Deutsche Akademische Austauschdienst (DAAD)*. A first written version of this paper profited in various respects from the feedback of Marco Coniglio and Clara Crepaldi. The second version was much influenced by the pertinent remarks of Gohar Schnelle and two anonymous reviewers. Special thanks are due to them for fighting their way through a not very readable draft. Richard Faure, Camille Denizot and Ezra la Roi provided expert advice on questions of illocutionary forces in Ancient Greek and/or the reading of Pl. *Prt.* 309a6. The completion of the second version would not have been possible without the trust and support of my boss Wolfgang Hock. As my PhD supervisor, he also provided thorough remarks on it, which have partly been integrated during the final revision process of the paper, partly still await realization in future research. The same goes for the pertinent observations by a third anonymous reviewer, to whom I feel very much obliged. Last but not least, I am grateful to Lukas Kahl, who proofread the second as well as the final version and likewise provided valuable comments, and Henrik Hornecker, who assisted me in checking the transliterations and glosses.

References

Dictionaries and Encyclopediae

Beekes   Beekes, Robert. (2010). *Etymological Dictionary of Greek*. Leiden: Brill.
EAGLL   Giannakis, Georgios K. (2014). *Encyclopedia of Ancient Greek Language and Linguistics* (Vols. 1–3). Leiden: Brill.
LSJ   Liddell, Henry G., & Robert Scott. (1940). *A Greek-English Lexicon. revised and augmented throughout by Sir Henry Stuart Jones with the assistance of Roderick McKenzie and with the cooperation of many scholars* (9th ed.) [with a supplement from 1968]. Oxford: Clarendon.

Grammars

CGCG   van Emde Boas, Evert, Albert Rijksbaron, Luuk Huitink, & Mathieu de Bakker. (2019). *Cambridge Grammar of Classical Greek*. Cambridge: Cambridge University Press.
K/G   Kühner, Raphael, & Bernhard Gerth. (1955[1898–1904]). *Ausführliche Grammatik der griechischen Sprache. Satzlehre*. 2 parts. 4th ed. = Reprint of the 3rd ed. Darmstadt: Wissenschaftliche Buchgesellschaft.
Schwyzer, Eduard (1953): *Griechische Grammatik. Auf der Grundlage von Karl Brugmanns griechischer Grammatik. Erster Band: Allgemeiner Teil. Lautlehre. Wortbildung. Flexion*. München: C.H. Beck.

Corpora

ISAIS   Informationsstruktur in älteren indogermanischen Sprachen. https://korpling.org/annis3/#_c=SVNBSVNfMS4w [last access: 2020-05-25]
TLG   Thesaurus Linguae Graecae. http://stephanus.tlg.uci.edu/ [last access: 2020-05-25]

Editions of and Commentaries on the Protagoras

Bekker   *Platonis dialogi graece et latine ex recensione Immanuelis Bekkeri. Partis primae volumen prius*. Berlin 1816.
Burnet   *Platonis opera recognovit brevique adnotatione critica instruxit Ioannes Burnet [...]. Tomus III: Tetralogias V–VII continens*. Oxford 1903.

Adam & Adam	*Platonis Protagoras with Introduction, Notes, and Appendices by J. Adam and A.M. Adam.* Cambridge 1893.
Denyer	*Plato. Protagoras.* Edited by Nicholas Denyer. Cambridge 2008.
Cobet	Cobet, C.G. (1880). Ad Platonis Protagoram. *Mnemosyne* 8(3), 328–344.
Lamb	*Plato in Twelve Volumes II. Laches · Protagoras · Meno · Euthydemus with an English Translation by W.R.M. Lamb.* Cambridge, MA/London 1924.
Manuwald	*Platon. Protagoras. Übersetzung und Kommentar von Bernd Manuwald.* Göttingen 1999.
Taylor	*Plato. Protagoras. Translated with Notes by C.C.W. Taylor.* Revised Edition. Oxford 1991.
Wayte	*Platonis Protagoras. The Protagoras of Plato. The Greek text revised with an analysis and english notes by William Wayte, M.A.* […]. 6th edition. Cambridge/London 1890.

Secondary Literature

Allan, Rutger J. (2006). Herodotus' historiën als sprekend leesboek: Herodotus tussen oraliteit en geletterdheid. *Lampas, 39*, 19–32.

Allan, Rutger J. (2009). Orale elementen in de Homerische grammatica. Intonatie-eenheid en enjambement. *Lampas, 42*, 136–151.

Allan, Rutger J. (2014). Changing the Topic. Topic Position in Ancient Greek Word Order. *Mnemosyne, 67*(2), 181–213.

Allan, Rutger J. (2016, May 18–20). *Herodotus' style als 'Sprache der Nähe'* [Conference presentation]. Language in Style, Oxford, United Kingdom.

Allan, Rutger J. (2017a). Ancient Greek adversative particles in contrast. In C. Denizot, & O. Spevak (Eds.), *Pragmatic Approaches to Latin and Ancient Greek* (pp. 273–301). Amsterdam/Philadelphia: John Benjamins.

Allan, Rutger J. (2017b). The grammaticalization of Greek particles. A Functional Discourse Grammar approach. F. Logozzo, & P. Poccetti (Eds.), *Ancient Greek linguistics: New perspectives, insights and approaches* (pp. 103–118), Berlin/Boston: De Gruyter.

Allan, Rutger J. (2019). Construal and Immersion: A Cognitive Linguistic Approach to Homeric Immersivity. In P. Meineck, W.M. Short, & J. Devereaux (Eds.), *The Routledge Handbook of Classics and Cognitive Theory* (pp. 59–78). London/New York: Routledge.

Allen, W. Sidney. (1973). *Accent and Rhythm. Prosodic features of Latin and Greek: A Study in Theory and Reconstruction.* Cambridge: Cambridge University Press.

Allen, W. Sidney. (1987). *Vox Graeca. A Guide to the Pronounciation of Classical Greek* (3rd ed.). Cambridge: Cambridge University Press.

Austin, John L. (1962). *How to do things with words.* Oxford: Clarendon.

Bakker, Egbert J. (1993). Boundaries, Topics, and the Structure of Discourse. An Investigation of the Ancient Greek Particle DÉ. *Studies in Language, 17*(2), 275–311.

Bakker, Egbert J. (1997). *Poetry in Speech. Orality and Homeric Discourse.* Ithaca/London: Cornell University Press.

Bakker, Stéphanie J. (2009). *The Noun Phrase in Ancient Greek. A Functional Analysis of the Order and Articulation of NP Constituents in Herodotus.* Leiden: Brill.

Bary, Corien & Dag T.T. Haug. (2011). Inter- and Intrasentential Anaphora: The Case of the Ancient Greek Participle. In N. Ashton, A. Chereches, & D. Lutz (Eds.), *Proceedings of SALT 21* (pp. 373–392). New Brunswick, Canada.

Bertrand, Nicolas. (2010). *L'ordre des mots chez Homère. Structure informationelle, localisation et progression du récit* [Doctoral dissertation, Université de Paris-Sorbonne].

Bertrand, Nicolas. (2011, January 6–9). *Prosody and Information Structure in Homeric Greek* [Conference presentation]. APA/AIA Annual Joint Meeting, San Antonio, TX, United States. https://www.academia.edu/1719147/Prosody_and_information_structure_in_Homeric_Greek [last access: 2020–05–22].

Biraud, Michèle. (2010). *Les interjections du théâtre grec antique. Étude sémantique et pragmatique.* Louvain-la-Neuve: Peeters.

Biraud, Michèle, & Richard Faure. (2015, December 3–4). *La coopération expressive: étude de l'exclamation en grec classique* [Conference presentation]. Exclamation et Intersubjectivité, Nice, France.

Bonifazi, Anna, Annemieke Drummen, & Mark de Kreij. (2016). *Particles in Ancient Greek Discourse. Five Volumes Exploring Particle Use Across Genres.* Washington DC: Center for Hellenic Studies. https://chs.harvard.edu/CHS/article/display/6220 [last access: 2020-05-25].

Buijs, Michel. (2005). *Clause Combining in Ancient Greek Narrative Discourse. The Distribution of Subclauses and Participial Clauses in Xenophon's* Hellenica *and* Anabasis. Leiden/Boston: Brill.

Butler, Christopher S. (2003). *Structure and Function. A Guide to Three Major Structural-Functional Theories* (Vols. 1–2). Amsterdam/Philadelphia: John Benjamins.

Cavalcante, Frederico A. (2020). *The Information Unit of Topic: a cross-linguistic, statistical study based on spontaneous speech corpora* [Doctoral dissertation, Universidade Federal de Minas Gerais].

Chafe, Wallace L. (1994). *Discourse, Consciousness, and Time. The Flow and Displacement of Conscious Experience in Speaking and Writing.* Chicago: University of Chicago Press.

Crepaldi, Clara L. (2018). *Partículas Adversativas do Grego Antigo: ἀλλά, ἀτάρ, μέντοι e καίτοι em Eurípides* [Doctoral dissertation, Universidade de São Paulo].

Crespo, Emilio. (2017a). A unitary account of the meaning of *καί*. In C. Denizot, &

O. Spevak (Eds.), *Pragmatic Approaches to Latin and Ancient Greek* (pp. 257–272). Amsterdam/Philadelphia: John Benjamins.

Crespo, Emilio. (2017b). Focus adverbs in Classical Greek. In F. Logozzo, & P. Poccetti (Eds.), *Ancient Greek linguistics: New perspectives, insights and approaches* (pp. 133–154). Berlin: De Gruyter.

Cresti, Emanuela. (2000). *Corpus di italiano parlato* (Vols. 1–2). Firenze: Accademia della Crusca.

Ctibor, Michal. (2017). Pragmatic functions of the Latin vocative. In C. Denizot, & O. Spevak (Eds.), *Pragmatic Approaches to Latin and Ancient Greek* (pp. 45–62). Amsterdam/Philadelphia: John Benjamins.

Declerck, Renaat. (1988). *Studies on Copular Sentences, Clefts, and Pseudo-Clefts*. Leuven: Leuven University Press.

Delbrück, Berthold. (1900). *Vergleichende Syntax der indogermanischen Sprachen* (Vol. 3). Strassburg: Trübner.

Denizot, Camille. (2011). *Donner des orders en grec ancien. Étude linguistique des formes de l'injonction*. Mont-Saint-Aignan Cedex: Publications des universités de Rouen et du Havre.

Devine, Andrew M. & Laurence D. Stephens. (1994). *The Prosody of Greek Speech*. New York/Oxford: Oxford University Press.

Devine, Andrew M. & Laurence D. Stephens. (2000). *Discontinuous Syntax. Hyperbaton in Greek*. New York/Oxford: Oxford University Press.

Dickey, Eleanor. (1996). *Greek Forms of Address. From Herodotus to Lucian*. Oxford: Clarendon.

Dik, Helma. (1995). *Word Order in Ancient Greek. A Pragmatic Account of Word Order Variation in Herodotus*. Amsterdam: Gieben.

Dik, Helma. (2007). *Word Order in Greek Tragic Dialogue*. Oxford: Oxford University Press.

Dik, Simon C. (1978). *Functional Grammar*. Amsterdam: North-Holland.

Dik, Simon C. (1997a). *The Theory of Functional Grammar. Part 1: The Structure of the Clause* (2nd, rev. ed. by Kees Hengeveld). Berlin/New York: De Gruyter Mouton.

Dik, Simon C. (1997b). *The Theory of Functional Grammar. Part 2: Complex and Derived Constructions* (ed. by Kees Hengeveld). Berlin/New York: De Gruyter Mouton.

Dover, Kenneth J. (1960). *Greek Word Order*. Cambridge: Cambridge University Press.

van Emde Boas, Evert. (2017). *Language and Character in Euripides' Electra*. Oxford: Oxford University Press.

Faure, Richard. (2012). La délibération et le subjonctif délibératif dans la prose grecque classique. *Syntaktika, 43*, 5–62.

Féry, Caroline. (2013). Focus as Prosodic Alignment. *Natural Language Linguistic Theory, 31*, 683–734.

Féry, Caroline. (2017). *Intonation and Prosodic Structure*. Cambridge: Cambridge University Press.

Fraenkel, Eduard. (1933). Kolon und Satz. Beobachtungen zur Gliederung des antiken Satzes II. *Nachrichten von der Gesellschaft der Wissenschaften zu Göttingen. Philosophisch-historische Klasse*, 1933(3), 319–354.

Fraenkel, Eduard. (1965). *Noch einmal Kolon und Satz* (= Sitzungsberichte der Bayerischen Akademie der Wissenschaften. Philosophisch-historische Klasse 1965, 2). München: Verlag der Bayerischen Akademie der Wissenschaften.

Freiberg, Cassandra. (2012). *Zu einer Modifikation der Rhetorical Structure Theory und deren Anwendung auf Ciceros vierte Philippische Rede* [Unpublished manuscript, University of Jena].

Freiberg, Cassandra. (2017[2018]). Between Prosody and Pragmatics. Discourse Segmentation in Ancient Greek and Its Application to Hdt. 1.8.1 and 1.10.2. *Historische Sprachforschung, 130*, 193–235.

Goldstein, David M. (2010). *Wackernagel's Law in Fifth Century Greek* [Doctoral dissertation, University of California].

Goldstein, David M. (2013). Iterated Modal Marking and Polarity Focus in Ancient Greek. *Transactions of the Philological Society, 111*(3), 354–378.

Goldstein, David M. (2014a). Intonational Phrase. In *EAGLL* (Vol. 2, pp. 253–256).

Goldstein, David M. (2014b). Phonological Phrase. In *EAGLL* (Vol. 3, pp. 87–89).

Goldstein, David M. (2014c). Utterance. In *EAGLL* (Vol. 3, pp. 454–455).

Goldstein, David M. (2014d). Wackernagel's Law I. In *EAGLL* (Vol. 3, pp. 508–513).

Goldstein, David M. (2016). *Classical Greek Syntax. Wackernagel's Law in Herodotus*. Leiden: Brill.

Goldstein, David M. (2019). Discourse Particles in LSJ. A Fresh Look at γε. In C. Stray, M. Clarke, & J.T. Katz (Eds.), *Liddell and Scott. The History, Methodology, and Languages of the World's Leading Lexicon of Ancient Greek* (pp. 268–287). Oxford: Oxford University Press.

Goldstein, David M., & Dag T.T. Haug. (2016). Second-Position Clitics and the Syntax-Phonology Interface: The Case of Ancient Greek. In D. Arnold, M. Butt, B. Crysmann, T. Holloway King, & S. Müller (Eds.), *Proceedings of the Joint 2016 Conference on Head-Driven Phrase Structure Grammar and Lexical Functional Grammar, Polish Academy of Sciences, Warsaw, Poland* (pp. 297–317). Stanford, CA: CSLI Publications.

Hannay, Mike, & Caroline Kroon. (2005). Acts and the relationship between discourse and grammar. *Functions of Language, 12*(1), 87–124.

Hengeveld, Kees. (2017). A hierarchical approach to grammaticalization. In K. Hengeveld, H. Narrog, & H. Olbertz (Eds.), *The Grammaticalization of Tense, Aspect, Modality, and Evidentiality from a Functional Perspective* (pp. 13–37). Berlin: De Gruyter.

Hengeveld, Kees, & J. Lachlan Mackenzie. (2008). *Functional Discourse Grammar. A Typologically-Based Theory of Language Structure*. Oxford: Oxford University Press.

Hengeveld, Kees, & J. Lachlan Mackenzie. (2015). Functional Discourse Grammar. In B. Heine, & H. Narrog (Eds.), *The Oxford Handbook of Linguistic Analysis* (2nd ed., pp. 311–344). Oxford: Oxford University Press.

Hengeveld, Kees, Eli Nazareth Bechara, Roberto Gomes Camacho, Alessandra Regina Guerra, Taísa Peres de Oliveira, Eduardo Penhavel, Erotilde Goreti Pezatti, Liliane Santana, Edson Rosa Francisco de Souza, & Maria Luiza de Sousa Teixeira. (2007). Basic illocution in the native languages of Brazil. *Alfa: revista de lingüística, 51*(2), 73–90.

Hirzel, Rudolf. (1895). *Der Dialog. Ein literarhistorischer Versuch* (Vols. 1–2) Leipzig: S. Hirzel.

Hock, Wolfgang. (2007). Das große *O!* Omega bei Anruf, Anrede und Ausruf im nachklassischen Griechisch und im Kirchenslavischen. In W. Hock, & M. Meier-Brügger (Eds.), *DARЪ SLOVESЬNY. Festschrift für Christoph Koch zum 65. Geburtstag* (pp. 135–153). München: Sagner.

Irwin, Terence H. (2008). The Platonic Corpus. In G. Fine (Ed.), *The Oxford Handbook of Plato* (pp. 63–87) Oxford: Oxford University Press.

Keizer, Evelien. (2015). *A Functional Discourse Grammar for English*. Oxford: Oxford University Press.

Keizer, Evelien, & Hella Olbertz. (2018). Functional Discourse Grammar: A brief outline. In E. Keizer, & H. Olbertz (Eds.), *Recent Developments in Functional Discourse Grammar* (pp. 1–15). Amsterdam/Philadelphia: John Benjamins.

Keydana, Götz. (2018, September 13–14). *Constituent structure in non-informant languages: Evidence from inscriptions* [Conference presentation]. Schriftkonventionen in pragmatischer Perspektive. Arbeitstagung der Indogermanischen Gesellschaft, Brussels, Belgium.

Koch, Peter, & Wulf Oesterreicher. (1985). Sprache der Nähe—Sprache der Distanz. Mündlichkeit und Schriftlichkeit im Spannungsfeld zwischen Sprachtheorie und Sprachgeschichte. *Romanistisches Jahrbuch, 36*, 15–43.

Kroon, Caroline. (1995). *Discourse Particles in Latin. A study of* nam, enim, autem, vero *and* at. Amsterdam: Gieben.

Ladd, D. Robert. (2008). *Intonational Phonology* (2nd ed.). Cambridge: Cambridge University Press.

Lambrecht, Knud. (1994). *Information structure and sentence form. Topic, focus, and the mental representations of discourse referents*. Cambridge: Cambridge University Press.

la Roi, Ezra. (2020). The Variation of Classical Greek Wishes. A Functional Discourse Grammar and Common Ground Approach. *Glotta, 96*(1), 213–245.

Lühr, Rosemarie. (2015). Traces of discourse configurationality in older Indo-European languages? In C. Viti (Ed.), *Perspectives on Historical Syntax* (pp. 203–232). Amsterdam/Philadelphia: John Benjamins.

Matić, Dejan. (2003). Topic, focus, and discourse structure. Ancient Greek word order. *Studies in Language*, 27(3), 573–633.

McCabe, Mary M. (2008). Plato's Ways of Writing. In G. Fine (Ed.), *The Oxford Handbook of Plato* (pp. 88–113). Oxford: Oxford University Press.

Nespor, Marina, & Irene Vogel. (1986). *Prosodic Phonology*. Dordrecht: Foris.

O'Connor, Joseph D., & Gordon F. Arnold. (1973). *Intonation of Colloquial English* (2nd rev. ed.). London: Longman.

Palmer, Harold E. (1922). *English Intonation With Systematic Exercises*. Cambridge: Heffer & Sons.

Pardal Padín, Alberto. (2015). La proclisis de los pronombres personales átonos en el drama ático clásico. *Ianua Classicorum. Temas y formas del Mundo Clásico*, 1, 589–598.

Pardal Padín, Alberto. (2017). *La interacción entre fonología y syntaxis en griego antiguo* [Doctoral dissertation, Universidad Autónoma, Madrid].

Peters, Jörg. (2014). *Intonation*. Heidelberg: Winter.

Pierrehumbert, Janet B. (1980). *The phonology and phonetics of English intonation* [Doctoral dissertation, Massachusetts Institute of Technology].

Pompei, Anna. (2012). Participio Greco e Converbi. *Archivio Glottologico Italiano*, 97(2), 160–204.

Probert, Philomen. (2006). *Ancient Greek Accentuation. Synchronic Patterns, Frequency Effects, and Prehistory*. Oxford: Oxford University Press.

Ramsey, Reuben. (2012). Plato's Oblique Response to Issues of Socrates' Influence on Alcibiades: An Examination of the *Protagoras* and the *Gorgias*. In M. Johnson, & H. Tarrant, (Eds.), *ALCIBIADES and the Socratic Lover-Educator* (pp. 61–76). London: Bloomsbury.

Raso, Tommaso, Frederico A. Cavalcante, & Maryualê M. Mittmann. (2017). Prosodic forms of the Topic information unit in a cross-linguistic perspective. A first survey. In A. de Meo, & F.M. Dovetto (Eds.), *La comunicazione parlata / Spoken Communication* (pp. 473–498). Canterano: Aracne.

Revuelta Puigdollers, Antonio. (2005). Modo y modalidad en griego antiguo. La negación. In D. Jiménez López (Ed.), *Syntaxis griega*. https://www.academia.edu/2018711/_2005_13._Modo_y_modalidad._La_negaci%C3%B3n [last access: 2020–05–25].

Revuelta Puigdollers, Antonio. (2017). Illocutionary force and modality. How to tackle the issue in Ancient Greek. In C. Denizot, & O. Spevak (Eds.), *Pragmatic Approaches to Latin and Ancient Greek* (pp. 17–43). Amsterdam/Philadelphia: John Benjamins.

Rijksbaron, Albert. (1986). *The pragmatics and semantics of conditional and temporal clauses. Some evidence from Dutch and Ancient Greek* (= working papers in functional grammar, 13). Amsterdam: University of Amsterdam.

Roulet, Eddy. (1985). *L'Articulation du discours en français contemporain*. Bern: Lang.

Roulet, Eddy, Laurent Filliettaz, & Anne Grobet. (2001). *Un modèle et un instrument d'analyse de l'organisation du discours*. Bern: Lang.

Schegloff, Emanuel A. (2007). *Sequence Organization in Interaction. A Primer in Conversation Analysis* (Vol. 1). Cambridge: Cambridge University Press.

Scheppers, Frank. (2011). *The Colon Hypothesis. Word Order, Discourse Segmentation and Discourse Coherence in Ancient Greek*. Brussels: VUBPRESS.

Searle, John R. (1979). *Expression and meaning. Studies in the Theory of Speech Acts*. Cambridge: Cambridge University Press.

Slings, Siem R. (1992). Written and Spoken Language: An Exercise in the Pragmatics of the Greek Sentence. *Classical Philology*, 87, 95–109.

Söder, Joachim. (2017). Absolute und relative Chronologie. Fragen der Periodisierung. In C. Horn, J. Müller, & J. Söder (Eds.), *Platon-Handbuch. Leben—Werk—Wirkung* (pp. 23–27). Stuttgart: Metzler.

Stede, Manfred (Ed.). (2016). *Handbuch Textannotation—Das Potsdamer Kommentarkorpus 2.0*. Potsdam: Universitätsverlag Potsdam. https://publishup.uni-potsdam.de/frontdoor/index/index/docId/8276 [last access: 2020-05-25].

Stede, Manfred. (2018). *Korpusgestützte Textanalyse. Grundzüge der Ebenen-orientierten Textlinguistik* (2nd, rev. ed.). Tübingen: Narr Francke Attempto.

Stommel, Hildegard. (2012). Verum-Fokus als Kontrast-Fokus. In H. Lohnstein, & H. Blühdorn (Eds.), *Wahrheit—Fokus—Negation* (pp. 15–29). Hamburg: Buske.

Verano, Rodrigo. (2015). *La reformulación discursiva en griego antiguo. Un estudio sobre La República de Platón* [Doctoral dissertation, Universidad de Sevilla].

Verano, Rodrigo. (2018). The Truth Alone Will Suffice: Traces of Spoken Language in Plato's *Apology of Socrates*. *Scripta Classica Israelica*, XXXVII, 25–43.

Wackernagel, Jacob. (1892). Über ein Gesetz der indogermanischen Wortstellung. *Indogermanische Forschungen*, 1, 333–436.

Wakker, Gerry. (1994). *Conditions and Conditionals. An Investigation of Ancient Greek*. Amsterdam: Gieben.

Printed in the United States
By Bookmasters